Essentials

P9-DTS-127

of PSYCHOLOGICAL ASSESSMENT *Series*

Everything you need to know to administer, interpret, and score the major psychological tests.

I'd like to order the following
ESSENTIALS OF PSYCHOLOGICAL ASSESSMENT:

- ❏ WAIS-III Assessment / 28295-2 / $34.95
- ❏ CAS Assessment / 29015-7 / $34.95
- ❏ Millon Inventories Assessment / 29798-4 / $34.95
- ❏ Forensic Psychological Assessment / 33186-4 / $34.95
- ❏ Bayley Scales of Infant Development-II Assessment / 32651-8 / $34.95
- ❏ Myers-Briggs Type Indicator® Assessment / 33239-9 / $34.95
- ❏ WISC-III and WPPSI-R Assessment / 34501-6 / $34.95
- ❏ Career Interest Assessment / 35365-5 / $34.95
- ❏ Rorschach® Assessment / 33146-5 / $34.95
- ❏ Cognitive Assessment with KAIT and Other Kaufman Measures 38317-1 / $34.95
- ❏ MMPI-2 Assessment / 34533-4 / $34.95
- ❏ Nonverbal Assessment / 38318-X / $34.95
- ❏ Cross-Battery Assessment / 38264-7 / $34.95
- ❏ NEPSY® Assessment / 32690-9 / $34.95
- ❏ Individual Achievement Assessment / 32432-9/$34.95
- ❏ TAT and Other Storytelling Techniques Assessment / 39469-6 / $34.95

Please send this order form with your payment (credit card or check) to:
**JOHN WILEY & SONS, INC., Attn: J. Knott, 10th Floor
605 Third Avenue, New York, N.Y. 10158-0012**

Name _____

Affiliation _____

Address _____

City/State/Zip _____

Phone _____ E-mail _____

❏ Would you like to be added to our e-mailing list?

Credit Card: ❏ MasterCard   ❏ Visa   ❏ American Express
(All orders subject to credit approval)

Card Number _____

Exp. Date _____ Signature _____

TO ORDER BY PHONE, CALL 1-800-225-5945
Refer to promo code #1-4081

To order online: www.wiley.com/essentials   ⓦWILEY

Essentials of Psychological Assessment Series

Series Editors, Alan S. Kaufman and Nadeen L. Kaufman

Essentials

of TAT and Other Storytelling Techniques Assessment

Hedwig Teglasi

John Wiley & Sons, Inc.

NEW YORK · CHICHESTER · WEINHEIM · BRISBANE · SINGAPORE · TORONTO

Copyright © 2001 by John Wiley & Sons, Inc. All rights reserved.
Published simultaneously in Canada.

No part of this publication may be reproduced, stored in a retrieval system or transmitted in any form or by any means, electronic, mechanical, photocopying, recording, scanning or otherwise, except as permitted under Sections 107 or 108 of the 1976 United States Copyright Act, without either the prior written permission of the Publisher, or authorization through payment of the appropriate per-copy fee to the Copyright Clearance Center, 222 Rosewood Drive, Danvers, MA 01923, (978) 750-8400, fax (978) 750-4744. Requests to the Publisher for permission should be addressed to the Permissions Department, John Wiley & Sons, Inc., 605 Third Avenue, New York, NY 10158-0012, (212) 850-6011, fax (212) 850-6008, E-Mail: PERMREQ@WILEY.COM.

This publication is designed to provide accurate and authoritative information in regard to the subject matter covered. It is sold with the understanding that the publisher is not engaged in rendering professional services. If legal, accounting, medical, psychological or any other expert assistance is required, the services of a competent professional person should be sought.

Designations used by companies to distinguish their products are often claimed as trademarks. In all instances where John Wiley & Sons, Inc. is aware of a claim, the product names appear in initial capital or all capital letters. Readers, however, should contact the appropriate companies for more complete information regarding trademarks and registration.

Library of Congress Cataloging-in-Publication Data:
Teglasi, Hedwig.
    Essentials of TAT and other storytelling techniques assessment / Hedwig Teglasi.
        p. cm. — (Essentials of psychological assessment series)
    Includes bibliographical references and index.
    ISBN 0-471-39469-6 (paper : alk. paper)
        1. Thematic Apperception Test.   2. Personality assessment of children.   I. Title.
    II. Series

    RC473.T48 T44 2001
    155.4'182844—dc21

                                                                                2001024343

Printed in the United States of America.

10   9   8   7   6   5   4   3

Library
University of Texas
at San Antonio

CONTENTS

SERIES PREFACE

n the *Essentials of Psychological Assessment* series, we have attempted to provide the reader with books that will deliver key practical information in the most efficient and accessible style. The series features instruments in a variety of domains, such as cognition, personality, education, and neuropsychology. For the experienced clinician, books in the series will offer a concise yet thorough way to master utilization of the continuously evolving supply of new and revised instruments as well as a convenient method for keeping up to date on the tried-and-true measures. The novice will find here a prioritized assembly of all the information and techniques that must be at one's fingertips to begin the complicated process of individual psychological diagnosis.

Wherever feasible, visual shortcuts to highlight key points are utilized alongside systematic, step-by-step guidelines. Chapters are focused and succinct. Topics are targeted for an easy understanding of the essentials of administration, scoring, interpretation, and clinical application. Theory and research are continually woven into the fabric of each book, but always to enhance clinical inference, never to sidetrack or overwhelm. We have long been advocates of "intelligent" testing—the notion that a profile of test scores is meaningless unless it is brought to life by the clinical observations and astute detective work of knowledgeable examiners. Test profiles must be used to make a difference in the child's or adult's life, or why bother to test? We want this series to help our readers become the best intelligent testers they can be.

In *Essentials of TAT and Other Storytelling Techniques Assessment,* Dr. Hedwig Teglasi links the projective hypothesis, which is the theoretical foundation of all thematic apperceptive techniques, with current constructs in the study of personality. Emphasizing the Thematic Apperception Test (TAT), the book also covers the Children's Apperception Test, the Tell-Me-A-Story Test (TEMAS), and the Roberts Apperception Test for Children (RATC). The interpretive procedures highlight narrative structure and storytelling process. Specific guidelines, including worksheets and illustrative examples, are provided in each of four areas: cognitive, emotional, interpersonal, and motivational/self-regulatory processes.

Alan S. Kaufman, PhD, and Nadeen L. Kaufman, EdD, Series Editors
Yale University School of Medicine

One

OVERVIEW

Methods for eliciting and interpreting stories told about pictured scenes are known generically as *thematic apperceptive techniques* and are classified as projective instruments. In essence, they are performance measures of personality with the instructions and the stimuli presenting standard elements that set the task demands (Teglasi, 1998). Stories are evaluated by qualified professionals in accord with their theoretical framework and training as well as preference for a particular scoring scheme. The most popular set of pictures designed to elicit stories is the one introduced by Morgan and Murray (1935) as the Thematic Apperception Test (TAT). However, the use of these pictures did not remain wedded to Murray's interpretive system, and a plethora of interpretive approaches was subsequently developed. Additionally, a variety of different picture stimuli and accompanying interpretive procedures were introduced as variations of the TAT.

HISTORY OF THEMATIC APPERCEPTION TECHNIQUES

The introduction of the TAT stimuli (Morgan & Murray, 1935; Murray, 1938, 1943) popularized the idea that telling a story to pictured scenes depicting complex social situations would reveal important aspects of personality. The use of pictures to elicit stories had been reported prior to the introduction of the TAT but only in four obscure studies (cited in Tomkins, 1947). Following the introduction of the TAT stimuli and the need-press system of interpretation, numerous other storytelling techniques were developed. However, surveys of clinicians indicate that the TAT remains the most popular, ranking among the top 10 most frequently used assessment tools (Archer, Marnish, Imhof, & Piotrowski, 1991; Watkins, Campbell, & McGregor, 1988; Watkins, Campbell, Nieberding, & Hallmark, 1995).

At the time that the TAT was being developed, the Rorschach technique, emphasizing *perception* was gaining popularity. For Murray (1938), the TAT offered the advantage of assessing *apperception*. He defined perception as recognition of an object based on sensory impression and apperception as the addition of meaning to what is perceived. Accordingly, telling stories about pictured scenes was an apperceptive task requiring the interpretation of the pictured cues to discern characters' motives, intentions, and expectations. Although Murray introduced a specific, theoretically based system for interpreting the stories told to TAT pictures, the appeal and the flexibility of the storytelling technique led to the introduction of many different sets of picture stimuli and many interpretive approaches for the TAT pictures (see Rapid Reference 1.1).

Historically, interpretive procedures for the TAT and its derivatives have been developed either for the study of personality or for clinical use. Personality researchers adhered to strict psychometric standards devising well-defined and reliably coded criteria to assess specific personality constructs (see Smith, 1992). In contrast, clinicians did not find such narrowly defined constructs to be useful because the constructs did not, nor were they intended to, assess the functioning of the "whole" person. Many insisted that the TAT be *interpreted* and not *scored* (see edited volume by Gieser & Stein, 1999). Generally, clinicians preferred to use the technique as a flexible tool for eliciting information that they would then interpret in light of their professional training and expertise. Such an approach is exemplified by Bellak's (1975, 1993) application of psychoanalytic theory to the interpretation of TAT stories. Despite the popularity of the TAT among clinicians, there is no consensus on a particular scoring system nor a comprehensive set of norms for clinical use. Nevertheless, specific coding procedures have been developed for clinical purposes that are reliably scored and correlate with adjustment (see McGrew & Teglasi, 1990). The psychoanalytic perspective has dominated the clinical use of the TAT by clinicians, but more recently, other perspectives have been applied to the interpretation of stories such as schema theory (Cramer, 1996; Teglasi, 1993, 1998) and social cognition (Westen, Klepser, Ruffins, Silverman, Lifton, & Boekamp, 1991).

THEORETICAL FOUNDATIONS

Subsequent to the formulation of the projective hypothesis (Frank, 1939), the TAT and other measures permitting open-ended responses were designated as

≡ *Rapid Reference 1.1*

Storytelling Assessment Instruments

Thematic Apperception Test

Harvard University Press
79 Gardner Street
Cambridge, MA 02138

Materials: set of cards, manual

Cost for set of cards: $54.00, cost for manual: $10.00

User qualifications: certified professional

Robert's Apperception Test for Children

Western Psychological Services
12031 Wilshire Blvd.
Los Angeles, CA 90025-1251

Time: 20–30 minutes

Materials: complete kit contains one set of test pictures, record booklets (25), manual

Cost for complete kit: $120.00

Also available: test pictures for Black children, cost $59.50

Tell-Me-A-Story

Western Psychological Services
12031 Wilshire Blvd.
Los Angeles, CA 90025-1251

Time: 45–60 minutes (short version), 120 minutes (long version)

Materials: complete kit contains one set of stimulus cards, one set of stimulus cards–minority version, record booklets (25), administration instruction card, and manual

Cost for complete kit: $260.00

Children's Apperception Test

CPS Inc.
PO Box 83
Larchmont, NY 10538

Materials: complete kit contains CAT, CAT-S, and CAT-H Picture Cards and Manuals, 25 Bellak Short Form Blanks (TAT, CAT, SAT, revised 1992), and 30 Haworth Schedules of Adaptive Mechanisms

Cost for complete kit: $119.00

<table>
<tr><td>

DON'T FORGET

....

Attributes of Projective Techniques (including TAT)

- Stimuli are sufficiently ambiguous to preclude a ready response, thereby requiring individual interpretation.
- There are many "correct" ways to approach the task.
- The response is open-ended and maximizes the imprint of organization.

</td></tr>
</table>

projective techniques. A fundamental assumption of all projective methods, including thematic apperceptive techniques, is the "projective hypothesis," which posits that stimuli from the environment are perceived and organized by the individual's specific needs, motives, feelings, perceptual sets, and cognitive structures, and that in large part this process occurs automatically and outside of awareness (Frank, 1948). What all projective techniques have in common is that they set a task that allows the expression of individuality in perceiving the task demand and in organizing the response.

Thematic Apperception, the Projective Hypothesis, and Schema Theory

The projective hypothesis and schema theory are similar in their central tenets. Both point to the role of previously organized mental "sets" in the interpretation of current stimuli, and both emphasize that the influence of these mental structures often occurs outside of conscious awareness. In essence, schema theory and research may be viewed as elaborating the workings of the projective hypothesis and as supporting performance measures of personality such as the TAT. Moreover, increasing appreciation of narrative as a mode of thought bolsters the use of storytelling as a tool for assessing personality. *Schemas* are defined as mental structures constituting internal representations of past experiences that guide the interpretation of new experiences. These mental structures allow the individual to compare current information with what is already known, thereby influencing the interpretations of subsequent encounters with the world (Cantor, 1984; Taylor & Crocker, 1981). In line with the projective hypothesis, the development of schemas and their retrieval from memory represent an unconscious process through which past perceptions influence the interpretation of current situations (Fiske, Haslam, & Fiske, 1991;

Ingram & Kendall, 1986; Wyer & Srull, 1994). The following vignette shows the crucial roles of schemas in a relatively straightforward exchange: George, an 11-year-old receiving special educational services, was shopping at the local supermarket with his mother and happened to see his former summer camp counselor. After greeting her enthusiastically and exchanging hugs, he said to her, "Thank you so much for visiting me. I hope you come again soon." An important function of schemas is to provide a template for understanding how various stimuli "go together." Though George clearly expressed his positive emotions, his schema for understanding this encounter was not adapted to fit the context.

A fuller appreciation of the relationship between schema theory and the projective hypothesis necessitates a distinction between two types of knowledge structures that organize experience: One is independent of the knower, and the other is unique to the knower (Mandler, 1982; Wozniak, 1985). The formula for calculating the circumference of a circle exemplifies schemas that organize knowledge independently of the knower's personal experiences and are open to public verification. Also independent of the knower are knowledge structures (called social schemas or scripts) that are widely shared within a culture. Such social schemas refer to general expectations about commonly occurring situations, such as visiting a dentist or ordering a meal in a restaurant. Behavior in such situations is "scripted" according to clear expectations (Abelson, 1981; Schank & Abelson, 1977). Social schemas, however, do not account for individual differences in schemas that are products of personal experiences and the processes contributing to the organization of those experiences. Each individual develops unique patterns of assumptions about the self, the world, and relationships, arriving at a particular stance toward life through the complex interplay of maturation, temperament, cognitive development, and socialization (Stark, Rouse, & Livingston, 1991). Personal schemas are representations that are idiosyncratic to the knower because their development is influenced by individual differences shaping the transaction with the environment as well as the interpretation of those transactions (see Teglasi & Epstein, 1998). Individuals' strategies for synthesizing cues provided in the scenes portrayed in TAT pictures and for organizing the response are analogous to the manner in which they apply previously acquired knowledge for adaptive use in novel, stressful, or ambiguous situations. Likewise, schema the-

> # DON'T FORGET
>
> Projective techniques are concerned primarily with the application of knowledge structures that are unique to the knower to organize responses to ambiguous stimuli.

ory assumes that successful adaptation to unfamiliar situations requires the coordination of what one "perceives" in the present with what one "knows" from previous experience.

The construct of the personal schema brings together models of perception, cognition, memory, affect, action, and feedback, thereby incorporating the various perspectives for understanding personality (Horowitz, 1991; Stein & Young, 1992; Tomkins, 1962, 1987). The schema construct bridges the study of normal personality processes with the study of psychopathology because schema-driven information processing allows previously organized knowledge to influence perception of ongoing experiences in adaptive or maladaptive ways. Knowledge structures that accurately represent reality increase efficiency in identifying perceptions, organizing them into meaningful units, filling in missing information, and devising a strategy for seeking new information as needed. However, maladaptive schemas bias attention and information processing to conform to an initial misconception and resist change despite contradictory evidence (see Beck & Clark, 1997; Horowitz, 1991).

Scripts or schemas may be further organized into *metascripts* (Singer & Salovey, 1991) that reflect the individual's style of dealing with scripts. These superordinate schemas may explain resilience because they influence how individuals reshape their schemas when confronted with daily stress, unforeseen failure, or unexpected upheaval. Those with more complex schemas may be more prepared to replay negative information to explore a variety of alternative conceptualizations. Consequently, it is important to assess the style of synthesizing experience through the organization and re-organization of schemas. When the individual is actively contemplating an interpersonal situation or task, such as telling stories about pictorial stimuli, he or she constructs a working model that combines internal and external sources of information (see

> # CAUTION
>
> Personal schemas are resistant to change because the processes that led to their development may still be operating and because schemas tend to organize and modify new experiences to fit the preexisting structures.

≋Rapid Reference 1.2

Enduring Schemas versus Working Models

Understanding the role of schemas in adapting to new circumstances requires a distinction between *enduring schemas* and *working models* (see Horowitz, 1991).

- *Enduring schemas*—intrapsychic meaning structures containing generalized formats of knowledge that can be activated by other mental activities related to that knowledge (Fiske & Taylor, 1991).
- *Working models*—stimuli from a current situation (or task) integrated with past knowledge through triggering of an associative network of enduring personal schemas. The working model may incorporate elements from different enduring schemas in the individual's repertoire.

The wider the repertoire of enduring personal schemas, the more flexibility there is in constructing working models of current interpersonal or other problem-solving situations. Discrepancies between working models and active, enduring schemas may contribute to upsetting emotional experiences (i.e., disappointment, anger). Working models may not match the actual qualities of current social situations (i.e., false beliefs) leading to errors in judgment and behavior and to subsequent negative emotions.

Rapid Reference 1.2). Stories evoked by pictures permit the evaluation of personal schemas that contribute to an individual's distress or counterproductive behavior and the identification of distortions and deficits in processing information.

Stories derived from TAT pictures are expected to be organized productions rather than fantasies or random associations (Holt, 1961). Just as the identification of blot contours in the Rorschach technique is expected to be guided by the reality constraints of the stimuli, the TAT stories must be compatible with the scenes depicted. A scene that can be explained easily in terms of a routine, overlearned situation requires the application of intact schemas representing familiar, scripted knowledge, whereas an unusual or complex scene calls for more flexible use of inner structures to explain the scene and comply with instructions. The stories reveal the narrator's use of schemas to interpret the pictured scene and organize ideas as analogs to his or her performance in similarly unstructured life situations (Bellak, 1975, 1993). In ambiguous situations, the schemas associated with potent emotions may come to the surface. Thus, one of the advantages of presenting stimuli with many possible responses (such as the TAT) is to allow the emergence of the most salient schemas. While permitting a wide range of responses, TAT stimuli are sufficiently structured to detect problems with interpreting the scenes, permitting the separate evaluation of the structural organization and content of the story.

Storytelling and Dual Theories of Information Processing

Dual theories of information processing account for the development of the two categories of mental structures described earlier as social and personal schemas. Piagetian operations of conservation of physical relations including number, weight, and volume exemplify schemas that are absolute and not relative to the individual's personal experience and are, therefore, amenable to logic and concrete external proof. In contrast, schemas about the self and others have no physical existence, and because these knowledge structures are shaped by emotions as well as by the individual's attentional and cognitive styles, they are not as neatly amenable to validation by objective data or by logical analysis. Rather, they are bolstered by consensus among like-minded individuals.

As individuals interact with their social and physical worlds, they develop theories of reality through two independent but interactive modes of processing information, sometimes referred to as *rational* and *experiential* systems of thought (see Epstein, 1994; Epstein & Pacini, 1999). The rational system processes information dispassionately using deliberate, effortful, analytic strategies, whereas the experiential system, driven by emotion, processes information automatically and outside of awareness. Conflict between the two systems has been described as a discrepancy between the "heart" and the "head." The "heart" tends to harbor convictions that do not require new evidence because they are ingrained and because its connection to emotion gives it credibility. The "head" responds to logic, and rational ideas may change more easily with new evidence. Of course, there are points in between the extremes reflecting compromises between the two thought systems. Both social or scientific (rational) and personal (experiential) schemas function as resources for organizing information, often operating without awareness or deliberate effort, such as when constructing grammatically correct sentences without actively thinking about the rules of grammar (see Rapid Reference

≣Rapid Reference 1.3

Rational and Experiential Thought Processing

The rational and experiential systems operate by different rules, but the two modes of information processing normally inform one another. Nevertheless, under the influence of intense emotion, thinking is transformed to conform to the mode of the experiential system and becomes increasingly divorced from the rational mode. Emotion-driven thinking is characterized as rapid, holistic, associative, categorical, personal, concrete, unreflective, action oriented, resistant to change, and self-evidently valid ("seeing is believing"). Rational thinking is characterized as slow, analytical, logical, abstract, more highly differentiated, integrated (cross-context processing), and may change rapidly in line with logical proof (Epstein, 1994).

1.3). The automaticity of schemas is advantageous because they free up resources for other priorities (Muraven, Tice, & Baumeister, 1998), but the same automaticity and speed also make schemas difficult to control when they are maladaptive.

Dualities in the processing of information correspond to a basic dichotomy between the "experiencing self," driven by emotion that imparts a sense of genuineness, and the "verbally defined self," guided by more dispassionate processing of verbal information (James, 1890). Dualities are evident in self-definition, self-efficacy, and response-outcome expectancies (see Rapid Reference 1.4).

A duality in the motivational system, described as a contrast between *implicit* and *self-attributed* motives (McClelland, Koestner, & Weinberger, 1989), maps onto the dichotomy between experiential versus rational systems and between the authentically experienced versus verbally defined self. Implicit motives are dispositional preferences for particular qualities of affective experiences, grounded in personally significant experiences and spurring spontaneous reactions. In contrast, self-attributed motives are conceptualizations about the self that may be more rooted in logical, cultural, and social bases for a desired self-description rather than personal inclination. Self-attributed motives forecast responses to situations that provide incentives for expressing socially promoted values or for presenting the self in a particular light but are not necessarily linked to the individual's affective preferences. Implicit motives

Rapid Reference 1.4

Dual Theories of Information Processing: Self-Definition and Self-Efficacy

• *Self-definition.* The subjectively sensed duality in the self has been affirmed through descriptions of discrepancies between the real and ideal self (Markus & Nurius, 1986; Rogers, 1951), between the authentic and inauthentic self (Broughton, 1981; Harter & Monsour, 1992; Horney, 1950), between the actual self and the ideal self, or the "ought" self (Higgins, 1987, 1991), and in differentiating between the functions of the id and ego, contrasting the emotional and motivational forces of the id with the regulatory roles served by the ego and superego (Freud, 1923, 1961). The contrast between the experiencing self as faithful to inner feelings and thoughts and the verbally defined self as presenting a front to the outside world is paralleled by discrepancies in responses to self-report and storytelling measures (Spangler, 1992).

• *Self-efficacy and response-outcome expectancy.* Intellectually and emotionally based versions of self-efficacy and response-outcome expectancy (Sappington, Russell, Triplett, & Goodwin, 1981) correspond to rational and experiential modes of processing information. Bandura (1977) defined *response-outcome expectations* as beliefs about the general likelihood of certain behaviors to produce outcomes and *self-efficacy expectations* as beliefs about one's ability to perform the behaviors to bring about the desired outcomes.

Expectancies that are intellectually derived from experience by anticipating regularities and discerning logical patterns may be altered by emotional reactions such as feelings of discouragement accompanying experiences that are also represented in memory (e.g., "feel as if I were helpless when my father criticizes me"). Intellectually and emotionally based expectancies change differently in response to intervention. Intellectually based expectancies change when new information is provided, whereas emotionally based expectancies change in response to variation in the emotional context in which the information is presented. The important point with respect to assessment is that undifferentiated measures of constructs such as *self-efficacy* and *response-outcome* contingency confound conceptually important distinctions.

develop through intrinsic enjoyment generated when doing tasks or experiencing activities or situations and, therefore, predict self-selected, goal-related activities (Biernat, 1989; Koestner, Weinberger, & McClelland, 1991; McClelland et al., 1989).

Stories, such as those told in response to TAT stimuli, assess implicit motives, whereas self-report techniques that generally elicit well-articulated and cognitively elaborated social values or representations of the self measure self-attributed motives. The absence of correlations between implicit and self-attributed measures of the achievement motive is consistent with the view that each taps different dimensions of the motivation construct. A meta-analytic comparison of the TAT-based measure of achievement motivation and questionnaire methods provides compelling evidence that the two types of measures predict different outcomes in line with expectations about the two types of motives (Spangler, 1992). The TAT-assessed implicit motives predicted long-term behavioral trends, whereas questionnaire measures of self-attributed motives predicted short-term choice behaviors. Thus, implicit and self-attributed personality variables develop through different pathways, have different patterns of relationships with other variables, and require different assessment procedures.

The dichotomy between the rational and experiential systems of information processing has implications for the use of storytelling as a tool to assess the schemas that represent these two modes of thought. Bruner's (1986) distinction between propositional and narrative thought parallels the processes of the rational and experiential systems. *Propositional thought* is public, logical, formal, theoretical, general, and abstract. *Narrative thought* is story-like, concrete, specific, personally convincing, imagistic, interpersonal, and includes characters, settings, intentions, emotions, actions, and outcomes. Increased interest in the contribution of affect to the development of cognitive structures (Bower, 1981, 1991; Bower & Cohen, 1982; Singer & Salovey, 1988) is compatible with a greater appreciation for narrative and contextual modes of cognition. The acceptance of affect as a filtering mechanism that influences day to day experience, together with the understanding that experiences are represented in memory as stories (i.e., sequences of events that take place in a particular time and place and are accompanied by thoughts and feelings) point to the importance of narrative modes of cognition for the study of personality (e.g., Howard, 1991; McAdams, 1993; Tomkins, 1962).

The basic contrast between narrative and propositional thought is not between thinking and feeling but between ways of knowing. One way of knowing is associated with feelings and experience that cannot be publicly validated or directly taught whereas the other is associated with knowledge structures that can be verified independently of the knower and conveyed through explicit instruction. These two modes of cognitive functioning provide distinct ways of ordering experience. Propositional or paradigmatic thought employs operations by which one establishes categorization or conceptualizations (Bruner, 1986; Hermans, Kempen, & Van Loon, 1992; Vitz, 1990) and encompasses logical or scientific universals that transcend personal experience and specific context. In contrast, narrative thought is invested with emotion and contextualized in relation to specific persons, times, and places. Logical thought aims to establish truth, whereas the narrative mode convinces by its meaningfulness (Parry & Doan, 1994). However, logical and deliberate thought may be used to organize experiences according to temporal and causal sequences of events including cause-effect and means-ends connections. Stories carry the implicit structures that organize the links among intentions, actions, and anticipated outcomes in given circumstances (Oatley, 1992). Thus, the organization of these narrative elements is an expression of the principles by which individuals order their experiences (see Rapid Reference 1.5).

TAT Stories, Real-Life Experiences, and Information Processing

As the language of experience, the story is the primary means by which episodes in everyday life are represented in memory (Schank, 1990). Yet, the "story" is not objective but rather filtered through the person's understanding of the causes of the event or its importance to the individual's current or future goals (e.g., Singer & Salovey, 1993; Woike, 1995). Self-relevant narratives such as the "life story" (McAdams, 1993) or experiences described by clients to their therapists do not correspond to historical facts but constitute "story lines" that have been transformed by psychological processes (Schafer, 1992). Similarly, the details of stories told to TAT stimuli are not assumed to represent actual life experiences, but, like other sources of narrative (the interview, autobiographic stories, specific recollections, diaries), TAT stories are amenable to analysis in terms of the principles that organize experience such as means-ends sets (e.g., Alexander, 1988; Arnold, 1962; Schank, 1990). The pictures provide the "givens" to be explained, and the story is the superimposition of narrative patterns that constitute internal representations of prior

≡ Rapid Reference 1.5

Empirical and Conceptual Support for the Assessment of Schemas with Storytelling

1. A growing body of literature urges researchers to focus on stories as the natural mode through which individuals make sense of their experiences (e.g., Bruner, 1990; McAdams, Diamond, de St. Aubin, & Mansfield, 1997). The ability to construct stories with a sensible sequence of events, reasonable causal relationships, and cohesive emotional experiences is an important developmental task of childhood, with implications for mental health (Mancuso & Sarbin, 1998). Storytelling is closely linked to listening and to reading comprehension (Blankman, Teglasi, & Lawser, 2000).

2. The principles that organize experience are evident through various narrative procedures including early memories, autobiographical recollections, and stories told to picture stimuli (Demorest & Alexander, 1992).

3. Socially competent behavior involves complex skills starting with accurate encoding and interpretation of relevant cues from external and internal sources, formulating intentions, maintaining goals, generating appropriate responses, and using strategies to enact and evaluate the chosen response (Dodge & Price, 1994; Elias & Tobias, 1996). Although these components of social problem solving may be conceptually separated, they are linked together in the story form as a framework for thinking about social situations (e.g., Teglasi & Rothman, 2001).

4. Schemas that represent relationships maladaptively are functionally related to psychopathology (e.g., Downey, Lebolt, Rincon, & Freitas, 1998; Oppenheim, Emde, & Warren, 1997). Schematic processing problems that reduce flexibility in processing information promote vicious cycles where ineffective schemas are preserved, thereby maintaining dysfunctional emotions, attitudes, and behaviors (Greenberg, Rice, & Elliott, 1993).

experience serving as the schemas for ordering the individual's ongoing encounters with the world (see Rapid Reference 1.6).

Systematic ordering of current experiences depends on the activation of schemas representing previously organized knowledge and on the availability of cognitive, attentional, and emotional resources to process information in the surroundings. Individuals vary in the accuracy and complexity of their schemas. For some, the internal representation of experience is coherently organized, presenting a detailed, balanced, and flexible panorama of feelings and

≡ *Rapid Reference 1.6*

The Relationship of TAT Stories to Life Experiences

1. Individuals learn "lessons" from the regularities of day to day experiences. When a lesson repeatedly occurs, it may become a type of structure (like grammar) that exists apart from the specific incidents (sentences) from which the lesson arose (Schank, 1990;Tomkins, 1987). Because abstracted schemas are based on numerous experiences (real or vicarious), they are readily activated (Murray, 1938), particularly in ambiguous situations or by tasks such as the TAT.

2. Individual differences in the synthesis of experiences applied to daily life are paralleled by variations in the construction of TAT stories as (a) piecemeal associations, (b) a direct replay of actual experiences selected from memory, (c) imposition of narrative patterns borrowed from books, other media, or stereotypes, or (d) application of convictions or lessons "abstracted" from experience (Teglasi, 1993) to meet task demands.

3. The inner logic and cohesiveness of the stories together with their content represent how individuals learn from day to day experiences and how they apply their knowledge to meet the task demand (e.g., accurately interpreting the stimuli and following instructions).

4. Content that is repeated provides clues about the narrator's concerns or preoccupations (Henry, 1956). However, addressing both the structure and content overcomes the pitfall of attributing too much weight to content (that may be pulled by the stimuli or recent experiences) but not meaningfully incorporated into structures that guide the synthesis of experience (Teglasi, 1998).

intentions that provides an accurate and nuanced map of reality. For others, the inner world is organized according to gross categories or polarized dichotomies that simplify perceptions of the environment. For still others, the inner world is comprised of piecemeal ideas rather than cohesive patterns of thought. Schema development, however, is the product of the individual's synthesis of prior experience. Hence, the accuracy and completeness of schemas may be constrained if information processing is chronically disrupted by problems with the regulation of attention, cognition, or emotion, or by a poor fit between the individual's temperamental tendencies and environmental expectations or by adverse social-environmental conditions. Temporary difficulties of "on-line" information processing caused by intense emotion or other factors may limit the adaptive use of previously well-organized schemas. Emotional, cognitive, attentional, and motivational variables that influence the synthesis of information vary according to functional demands of and previous experiences with various activities and situations. Therefore, dysfunctional schemas are often situation-specific. Individuality and situation-specificity of schemas contribute to the heterogeneity of schematic processing difficulties within disorders such as anxiety and depression (Foa & Kozak, 1991; Greenberg, Elliott, & Foerster, 1991; Safran & Greenberg, 1988) that may be targeted for intervention (Goldfried, Greenberg, & Marmar, 1990; Shirk, 1998; Shirk & Russell, 1996).

Understanding the influence of schemas on current adjustment requires knowledge of situation- or task-specific processes (cognitive, emotional, attentional) that are "on-line" along with previously organized schemas that are activated in the situation. In reference to a given situation, it is important to consider the individual's momentary awareness of self and the world, the schema-driven explanation of what is observed, and the interplay between immediate awareness and explanation (Guidano, 1995) as follows:

1. *Awareness of moment to moment experience.* The feeling and subjective experience, such as the sense of anxiety or dread, characterizing the individual's engagement in a particular situation constitute an irrefutable "fact" of experience (subjective reality). Subjective states influence not only what is considered relevant in the surroundings but also what is prominent in memory. For instance, anxiety leads to heightened awareness of cues signaling threat (Barlow, 1988) and triggers recollections of other situations associated with anxiety.

2. *Reasons or explanations accounting for the moment to moment "facts."* The "facts" of experience in the current circumstance and as drawn from memory are explained according to the individual's developing "theories" about the self, others, and the world. These conceptions (schemas) allow individuals to understand social interactions and to reason about their own and others' beliefs, desires, or intentions. Schemas, like all good theories, organize information by pointing to what is relevant, thereby promoting selective processing of information such that some observations are highlighted and others discounted. Thus, moment to moment "facts" are woven into schemas

that "explain" them. For example, the ebb and flow of experiences associated with chronic anxiety might lead to a dichotomous construing of the world as being benign or threatening, of outcomes as being predictable or unpredictable, and of the self as controlling or as being controlled by unpleasant affective experiences. Intense feelings of anxiety may lead the individual to avoid encounters he or she fears and may result in understandings about self and others that are heavily influenced by anxiety and based on limited experience. Cultural factors such as acceptability of certain feelings in a given context or strictness of gender roles or class distinctions as well as other environmental influences mediate how the social "facts" pertain to the self. When individuals attend to social cues, they must distinguish between relevant and irrelevant signals and differentiate between social cues that are prompted by their own actions and those that are prompted by the biases of others. Thus, the appraisal of social cues is complicated by the possibility that others' reactions are tainted by prejudices regarding attributes such as physical disabilities, race, ethnic group, gender, or sexual orientation. This extra layer becomes incorporated into schemas acting as an internal context against which subsequent experiences are evaluated.

3. *Dynamic interplay between the schemas and the content of immediate awareness.* The interplay between facts and explanations influences how individuals adapt existing schemas ("theories") to new circumstances, how new data modifies schemas, or, conversely, how individuals maintain schemas in light of contradictory information that may be misperceived or ignored. This interplay, often targeted for therapeutic intervention, constitutes the patterns by which the individual derives lessons from ongoing experiences and applies schemas to new encounters.

How individuals mediate between the "facts" and schema-driven explanations (e.g., distinguish their emotional reaction from the "objective" characteristics of the situation) depends on the organization and complexity of their schemas. Intense negative affect, difficulty with selective attention, or difficulty with symbolizing and organizing experiences disrupt schema development because they alter the "facts" of experience and complicate the task of making logical connections among ideas to derive meaningful lessons from daily encounters. Moreover, any severe and recurring emotional experience such as trauma, stress, or abuse can adversely affect the individual's sense of self in the world. Finally, previously organized schemas may be temporarily disrupted for various reasons such as extreme anxiety, stress, or trauma. The assessment of schemas with thematic apperception techniques is possible because constructing a "story" to standard stimuli reveals *what* ideas come to awareness and *how* they "go together" (see Rapid Reference 1.7).

≡Rapid Reference 1.7

Social Problem Solving and Standard Questions for Eliciting TAT Stories

What is happening in the picture? Before a concern or problem is resolved, it must first be identified. The individual's storehouse of memories and schemas for understanding social situations is the source for generating ideas about the tensions depicted in the scene and for organizing these ideas. Describing isolated stimulus features does not satisfy the demands of the instructions.

What happened before? The sequence of unfolding events including those prior to the scene depicted reveals the narrator's schemas about social causality (e.g., cause-effect reasoning) and time perspective. The narrator's style of processing social information is seen not only in the interpretation of the immediate circumstances presented in the stimuli but in placing events in a historical context by postulating sequences of events leading up to the scene.

What is the person (or people) thinking and how is that person (or people) feeling? These questions evoke the narrator's understanding of the inner world and capacity to coordinate the inner life and external circumstances of the various characters portrayed in the scene or introduced into the story. Reasoning about intentions, values, and goals is a key component of social information processing. A cohesive story requires the narrator to incorporate the characters' thoughts, feelings, or intentions in ways that coordinate with each other and with sequences of events or circumstances, actions, and outcomes.

How does the story end? In a well-constructed story, the details cohere around the ending. Although TAT instructions do not specifically ask for actions or plans to resolve the dilemmas set before the characters, the means to resolving tensions or accomplishing goals are implicit in the storytelling task. The perceived means-ends connections are crucial aspects of schemas and of narratives and are therefore considered the basis for understanding the lesson, moral, or import of the story (Alexander, 1988; Arnold, 1962; Schank, 1990). The narrator's resources for problem solving are indicated not only by the manner in which the characters resolve the dilemmas introduced into the story but also by the manner in which the narrator meets the problem-solving demands of the storytelling task.

EMPIRICAL FOUNDATIONS OF STORYTELLING TECHNIQUES

Reliability and validity are not established generically for the storytelling technique and must be demonstrated separately for each set of pictures, administrative procedure, and interpretive method. Therefore, evidence supporting or disconfirming a specific approach to narrative assessment is the property of that particular method and is limited in generalizability. Psychometric standards apply with equal rigor to "objective" (questionnaire) and "projective" (performance) measures such as thematic apperceptive techniques. However, in their application, psychometric principles must be suited to the nature of the technique. Users of projective techniques rely on the establishment of relevant and reliable criteria for interpretation just as users of questionnaire techniques count on previously developed items and scales as relevant and reliable units of measurement (see Cramer, 1996; Teglasi, 1993; Teglasi, 1998).

Reliability

The general concept of *reliability* in psychological assessment refers to the attribute of consistency in measurement.

Rater Reliability

The product of storytelling is an open-ended response that requires interpretive judgment and documentation of the reliability of the judgment. Interrater reliability addresses the question of whether the interpretive procedure applied by different raters to identical responses yields the same result. Interrater reliability for thematic techniques tends to be high when interpretive criteria are clearly designated and interpreters are well trained in the rating procedure (Karon, 1981). Under such conditions, agreement calculated between two (or more) raters or a rater and a set of practice materials scored by an expert often exceeds the .80 to .85 range, which is generally considered adequate (Lundy, 1985). Clear criteria and ad-

> # DON'T FORGET
> ....
> **Types of Reliability:**
> 1. *Rater reliability or decisional reliability*—agreement among various raters as to the meaning of the same data
> 2. *Test-retest*—the consistency of the data obtained over time
> 3. *Internal consistency*—the consistency of items within a test

equate training reduce the bias by differential experience of the interpreter and by variation in values or assumptions about what responses reflect. Though not generally reported in the literature, in clinical use it may be important to establish the reliability of a single rater over time.

Decisional Reliability

Another way of evaluating the reliability across raters is to examine the agreement in global judgments or decisions derived from the protocol rather than focusing on specific units. This form of reliability more accurately reflects the clinical use of the TAT where clinicians apply their knowledge of research and theory to draw conclusions. One problem is that professionals with different theoretical foci tend to emphasize different aspects of the protocol. However, Shneidman (1951) demonstrated that 16 clinicians using their own methods came to similar conclusions. An important influence on reliability of decisions relates to the number of performance samples or cards administered. For a reliable assessment with the TAT, it has been recommended that clinicians obtain at least six stories from each respondent (Lundy, 1985; Smith, 1992).

Test-retest Reliability

Two important considerations in documenting reliability upon retesting are (a) whether the focus is on similarity of story content or similarity of the clinician's judgment (Karon, 1981), and (b) whether the personality construct under consideration is relatively stable or fluctuating (Cramer, 1996). The reliability of the specific content is less relevant than consistency of the interpretive meaning of the response with the passage of time. Moreover, given that personality may be subject to change, the time interval between testing and retesting is crucial, and the degree of consistency must be viewed in light of data and theory about expected change in the particular unit on which reliability is sought. Structural characteristics of TAT stories tend to remain stable (at least in the short term) as shown by test-retest correlations (Locraft & Teglasi, 1997).

Internal Consistency

Items of a test measuring a specific construct are expected to correlate with each other. The higher the correlation among the items, the more consistently each item measures the overall purpose of the scale; hence the higher the internal consistency as measured by coefficient alpha. When this principle is applied to the TAT, each picture is considered as one item. *Split-half reliability* (in which scores on one half of the test such as odd and even items are correlated with the other) is another way of estimating the internal consistency of the TAT. This method is not usually appropriate with the TAT because the number of stories told is often not sufficient for this purpose. A more general problem concerns all approaches to internal consistency. Given that the pictures are designed to elicit different themes (Morgan & Murray, 1935), it would be inappropriate to rely on story content to establish internal consistency (Lundy, 1985). Indeed, with respect to thematic content, the TAT does not meet the tenets of classical psychometric theory because test-retest reliabilities have been higher than measures of internal consistency (alpha coefficients), a pattern that is contrary to traditional psychometric assumptions (Lundy, 1985). However, consistency of other variables not influenced directly by the picture is conceptually defensible. Stylistic units that are unrelated to the stimulus, such as the number of words per story, have been much higher than internal consistency in the more content-related variable of need for achievement (Atkinson, Bengort, & Price, 1977). Internal consistency appears to be high with structural or formal qualities of the story, such as the accuracy of the match between the story and the stimulus or the degree of cohesiveness among story details (Blankman, Teglasi, & Lawser, 2000).

Validity

Validity refers to how well an instrument measures what it purports to assess.

Face Validity

The concept of *face validity* refers to whether the "appearance" of a test is consistent with what it is designed to measure. Because the test taker does not know how the stories are to be interpreted, face validity is a matter of acceptability of the storytelling procedure on its "face." Telling stories about social scenes that depict tension does appear to be a "face valid" measure of social informa-

> **DON'T FORGET**
> ....
> **Types of validity:**
> 1. face validity
> 2. content validity
> 3. criterion or incremental validity
> 4. construct validity

tion processing. Face validity, according to the Standards for Educational and Psychological Testing, is not an acceptable basis for drawing conclusions from a test.

Construct Validity

Construct validity is "an integration of any evidence that bears on the interpretation or meaning of test scores" (Messick, 1989, p. 17) including all forms of reliability and other indicators of validity. Validation of the TAT for clinical use starts with the translation of narrative elements into meaningful psychological constructs. For example, frequency counts of aggressive content, even if reliable across raters, are of limited value without construct validation linking a network of interpretive units and supporting data to clinically relevant psychological constructs (see Teglasi, 1993, 1998). Indeed, aggressive themes in TAT stories are meaningful only in reference to evoking circumstances, intentions, outcomes, and a relationship to the stimulus. Developing and validating units for interpreting TAT stories also require careful attention to measurement issues such as the possible confounding influence of story length in some interpretive systems (e.g., Veroff, Atkinson, Feld, & Gurin, 1960). Two proposals to resolve this problem are the use of a correction factor for story length (e.g., Cramer, 1987; Murray, 1943; Winter, 1982) and the use of interpretive units such as the story import (e.g., Arnold, 1962) that are not referenced directly to the words in the story. According to Messick (1989) "Validity is an integrated evaluative judgment of the degree to which empirical evidence and theoretical rationales support the *adequacy* and *appropriateness* of *inferences* and *actions* based on test scores or other modes of assessment" (p. 13).

Criterion Validity

A measure is considered valid if it correlates with other measures designated as criteria. However, it seems logical that both the predictor (TAT responses) and criterion variables (real life responses) would be subject to construct validation (Messick, 1989) because both the predictor and criterion must relate to the construct or constructs under consideration. Accordingly, a given performance measure would be understood in terms of its functional demands, and responses would be expected to generalize to other tasks and life situations only if they make similar functional demands (i.e., measure the same dimension of the construct). This emphasis on construct validity places equal value on prediction and explanation as fundamental to validation efforts. The need to distinguish between prediction and explanation is demonstrated by findings that TAT and self-report measures of achievement motivation both correlate with external criteria, but the patterns of correlations are different (see Spangler, 1992 for a review). These differences support the conclusion that self-report and storytelling measure different achievement-related constructs, and they cannot be used interchangeably.

Incremental Validity

An instrument may be considered useful if it adds information to other measures in the battery by raising the overall correlation with the criterion (Mischel, 1968). The more multiply determined and complex a criterion, the more important it is to account for the role of multiple variables. An example of incremental validity is the prediction of grade point average (GPA) from a combination of IQ and TAT scores, noting the contribution that each adds to the other.

CAUTION

The terms "objective" and "projective" imply that the former is less subjective. However, as George Kelly (1958) points out, both objective and projective methods have subjective elements, though they occur in different parts of the assessment process: Reliability of items on a rating scale is essentially a matter of consistency in the respondents' interpretation of questions, whereas reliability of inferences based on thematic apperceptive methods rests on a combination of the stimulus, the response, the method of interpretation, and the skill of the interpreter.

Content Validity

The *content validity* of thematic apperception techniques may refer to picture stimuli, to the interpretive units, or both. Regarding picture stimuli, clinicians should be concerned with sufficiency of sampling thematic content (e.g., types of relationships, emotions, or situations), whereas the adequacy of the units to measure the phenomenon under consideration (e.g., object relations) is a concern with interpretive strategy.

🖎 TEST YOURSELF 🖎

1. **The Rorschach is primarily a test of** *perception*, **whereas the TAT is a test of** *apperception*. True or False?

2. **Historically, criteria for coding stories have been most clinically useful if**

   (a) they were narrowly specified and psychometrically validated.

   (b) they provided broad interpretive guidelines.

   (c) both "a" and "b."

   (d) neither "a" nor "b."

3. **Schema theory supports the following assumptions that are central to the "projective hypothesis":**

   (a) importance of previously organized "sets" for the interpretation of current experience.

   (b) importance of mental processes that operate outside of awareness.

   (c) both "a" and "b."

   (d) neither "a" nor "b."

4. **Knowledge structures or schemas organize information that is**

   (a) independent of the knower and amenable to public verification.

   (b) limited to the knower and not amenable to validation by logical analysis.

   (c) both "a" and "b."

   (d) neither "a" nor "b."

5. **TAT stories may constitute**

   (a) a replay of actual experiences.

   (b) ideas borrowed from the media.

   (c) abstractions synthesized from life experiences.

   (d) all of the above.

6. **Storytelling is useful to assess schemas and social problem-solving strategies in**

   (a) highly familiar scripted situations.

   (b) novel, stressful, complex, or emotionally charged situations.

   (c) both "a" and "b."

   (d) neither "a" nor "b."

(continued)

7. Dual theories of information processing contrast

(a) the "experiencing" self, influenced by emotion and the verbally defined self.

(b) emotion-driven thinking and rational analytic mode of thinking.

(c) narrative thought and propositional thought.

(d) all of the above.

8. Individual differences in emotional, cognitive, and attentional processes influence the development of schemas. True or False?

9. All reliability and validity evidence may be subsumed under the rubric of construct validation. True or False?

10. Storytelling and self-report measures may be used interchangeably. True or False?

11. Documenting the psychometric qualities of the TAT is complicated by

(a) the need to establish validity and reliability for each interpretive method.

(b) the need to demonstrate reliability for each rater.

(c) both "a" and "b."

(d) neither "a" nor "b."

Answers: 1. True; 2. b; 3. c; 4. c; 5. d; 6. b; 7. d; 8. True; 9. True; 10. False; 11. c.

Two

ESSENTIALS OF STORYTELLING ADMINISTRATION

Thematic apperceptive techniques have been described as performance measures of personality with the pictured stimuli and the instructions constituting standard elements of the storytelling task (Teglasi, 1998). If thematic apperceptive techniques are to reveal competencies such as sizing up social cues and reasoning about social situations, then the pictured stimuli along with the instructions must impose those demands.

STIMULI

The name Thematic Apperception Test (TAT) refers to the specific stimuli and instructions introduced by Murray (1943). However, the term *thematic apperception* has been used in a generic sense and not restricted to one set of picture cards (Keiser & Prather, 1990). Subsequent to the introduction of the TAT, various sets of stimuli have been developed to elicit themes according to a given theoretical orientation (Blacky Test, Blum, 1950; Tasks of Emotional Development, Cohen & Weil, 1975) or to sample attitudes in a specific situation (School Apperception Method, Solomon & Starr, 1968; Education Apperception Test, Thompson & Sones, 1973). Pictures were also introduced for use with specific populations such as children (Children's Apperception Test, Bellak & Bellak, 1949; Roberts Apperception Test for Children, McArthur & Roberts, 1982; Children's Apperceptive Storytelling Test, Schneider, 1989); adolescents (Symonds Picture Story Test for Adolescents, Symonds, 1939, 1943); senior adults (Senior Apperception Test, Bellak & Bellak, 1973; Gerontological Apperception Test, Wolk & Wolk, 1971); and specific ethnic groups (Tell-Me-A-Story), Constantino, Malgady, & Rogler 1988; Thompson, 1949). Sets of stimuli have also been introduced in response to criticisms that the TAT pictures are achromatic, negative in emotional tone, and lacking in racial diversity (e.g., Holmstrom, Silber, & Karp, 1990; McArthur & Roberts, 1982; Schneider, 1989; Thompson & Sones, 1973). The TAT pictures also have been criticized for featuring people wearing dated clothing and hair styles (Henry, 1956; Murstein, 1968) and for their predominantly negative tone (Ritzler, Sharkey, & Chudy, 1980). Despite these criticisms, the TAT stimuli remain the most popular (see Teglasi, 1998). The introduction of different stimuli because they are colorful or because they are more modern has not led to the abandonment of the original set because the new pictures did not incorporate the strengths of the original TAT stimuli. A better understanding of the stimulus qualities may lead to more effective use of thematic apperceptive techniques (Murstein, 1965; Zubin, Eron, & Schumer, 1965).

Stimuli play an important role in shaping the stories, and the value of the pictures resides in their ability to elicit responses with interpretive meaning for important areas of functioning. However, desired stimulus variables differ according to what is being assessed. To date, the introduction of new stimuli has not brought us closer to a theoretical understanding of the role of various properties of pictured stimuli nor to an agreed upon scoring system. Broad conclusions about the advantages of various characteristics of stimuli, such as their ambiguity (the number of cues guiding the response and the definitiveness of the cues), cannot be drawn without reference to the scoring system, the nature of the population, or intended use. When studying hostility, researchers have argued that pictures with low relevance for unacceptable behavior measure drive toward its expression, whereas pictures with high relevance measure inhibition or guilt about its expression (Salz & Epstein, 1963). Low ambiguity may be preferable in the assessment of a single motive (Singer, 1981) but higher ambiguity may be advantageous in the relative assessment of two motives (Atkinson, 1992). Richness of personality content varied as a function of three levels of ambiguity (high, medium, low) within the TAT set, with cards of medium ambiguity yielding stories with the most personality information (Kenny & Bijou, 1953). However, studies of ambiguity are inconclusive because investigators compare various degrees of ambiguity that are not standard in regard to an underlying dimension of ambiguity.

Although the development of sets of thematic apperceptive stimuli have focused on their relevance to thematic content (e.g., a particular motive), it is likely that the structural features of stimuli contribute to their usefulness in clarifying psychological functioning apart from their content (Teglasi, 1993,

1998). These structural elements of stimuli include degree of complexity, ambiguity, emotional tone, number of distinguishing details, or disparate cues to be reconciled. These aspects of stimuli could be systematically varied, along with important elements of content (e.g., age, gender, racial features, type of interaction), to permit conclusions about the respondent's performance in varying degrees of structure and about the schemas pertaining to specific types of interactions. Sets of stimuli with graded levels of ambiguity permit the evaluation of the response along a continuum of structure.

The TAT set (Morgan & Murray, 1935; Murray, 1938) is comprised of 30 pictures and one blank card. These cards are organized into four parallel sets of 20 pictures tailored to the age and gender of the respondent. Accordingly, the cards are numbered from 1 to 20, with some containing letter suffixes to designate them as suitable for boys (B), girls (G), males over 14 (M), females over 14 (F), or combinations of those groups (MF, BG, BM, GF). Cards that have no letters following their numbers are considered suitable for both genders and for any age, 4 or above (for a review of the history of the images depicted in TAT pictures, see Morgan, 1995).

Characteristics of the Respondent in Relationship to the Stimulus

The assumption that the storytellers become more invested in the task, telling longer and richer stories if they identify with the characters, provided the rationale for designating "male" and "female" TAT cards. Clinicians thought that the respondents' identification would be enhanced if respondents perceived themselves as being similar to the character or characters depicted in the stimulus. However, college students did not identify more with pictured characters of their own gender (Katz, Russ, & Overholser, 1993). The data showed no gender-based differences in story length, amount of fantasy, or nature of the affect. Furthermore, it is not possible to ascertain on the basis of stimulus similarity that the storyteller does or does not identify with the character. For example, regardless of their gender, most children telling stories about Card 2 of the TAT focus on the young woman in the foreground, although there is a male in the background. Thus, the centrality of the figure seems to be the basis for its prominence in the stories. Currently, TAT cards are not administered according to their original designation as appropriate for adult males and females or boys and girls (e.g., B = boy; M = man; G = girl; F = woman). Thus

Card 3BM, which is designated as appropriate for a boy or a man, is just as often used for a girl or a woman.

In general, adaptations of stimuli for specialized populations do not elicit richer, more productive stories than do the traditional TAT figures (Bailey & Green, 1977; Weisskopf-Joelson, Zimmerman, & McDaniel, 1970). The Gerontological Apperception Test (GAT) introduced for use with aged patients (Wolk & Wolk, 1971) was based on the assumption that many individuals at an advanced age would find it difficult to identify with the situations and characters depicted in the TAT. The GAT depicted "problems specific to the aged such as loss of sexuality, loss of attractiveness, physical limitations, and family difficulties [that] are not usually elicited" (p. 3). However, a comparison of the GAT with the TAT showed no advantage to the GAT (Fitzgerald, Pasewark, & Fleisher, 1974; Pasewark, Fitzgerald, Dexter, & Cangemi, 1976). Similar reasoning was applied to the development of the Senior Apperception Test (Bellak, 1975) which, likewise, did not fare better than the TAT. The essential issue may not be one of similarity, but the capacity of the narrator to grasp the meaning of the experience portrayed.

The original set of TAT cards depicted White characters, and questions have been raised regarding their applicability to other populations. Bailey and Green (1977) modified Murray's TAT cards to provide a more realistic depiction of African American characters than the previous attempt by Thompson (1949), which superimposed dark skin on white features. They compared stories told to the newly developed stimuli, the original TAT cards, and the Thompson modification. While African American respondents (ages 25 to 45) rated both sets of modified cards as facilitating their production, the response content was not affected. Moreover, there were no differences across the three sets of stimuli on ratings of respondents' ability to relate personal feelings. Indeed, perceived similarity of the narrator and pictured character corresponded more to the affective tone of the relationship depicted in the TAT card than to the content of the themes that are frequently elicited (Alvarado, 1994). The concern regarding the issue of similarity between stimulus figures and storyteller may have more to do with sensitivity to the feelings of the respondent than with the utility of the information derived from the assessment.

As stimuli are shaped to incorporate the diversity of the population, it is important for professionals not to abandon other theoretical and empirical considerations. One example is the introduction of the TEMAS ("themes" in

Spanish), an acronym for a projective storytelling technique called *Tell-Me-A-Story* by Constantino, Malgady, and Rogler (1988). The TEMAS stimuli are not equivalent to the TAT pictures, differing in at least two important respects: structure and the number of characters portrayed. The TEMAS stimuli are structured by presenting two sides of a dilemma as alternatives to be reconciled, thereby providing more clues to guide the narrative than the TAT cards. Second, the busier stimuli and greater number of characters in the TEMAS encourage longer stories, particularly if the narrator takes a descriptive approach. Constantino and Malgady (1983) administered two versions of the TEMAS, minority and nonminority, along with the standard TAT pictures to three groups of children: Hispanic, African American, and White. Minority children told longer stories to both versions of the TEMAS than to the standard TAT cards. However, minority students' story length did not differ across the two versions of the TEMAS, suggesting that other aspects of the stimulus besides the social/ethnic features of the characters accounted for the difference. The White children showed equal verbal productivity regardless of stimuli. Moreover, African American and White children demonstrated equal verbal productivity on the TAT. The point here is not to denigrate the TEMAS nor tout the superiority of the TAT but to emphasize the conceptual distinctions and similarities among various methods of assessment rather than to assume them automatically based on superficial resemblance or differences.

Qualities of the Pictured Stimulus

The task of telling a story about a pictured scene implicitly calls for a story that "explains" the stimulus and develops a "context" for the interpretation through an appropriate network of events, thoughts, feelings, intentions, actions, and outcomes. For the assessment of personal schemas, it is most useful to present stimuli depicting scenes that are difficult to explain in terms of the common cultural stereotypes or canned stories. One of the advantages of the TAT set is that the pictures portray situations conveying unfinished business that do not fit the stereotypic mold (Henry, 1956). For instance, Card 4 of the TAT calls for the narrator to reconcile the discrepancy between the close physical proximity of the man and woman portrayed and the contrast between the angry expression on the man's face and the conciliatory expression of the woman.

There are two basic ways to evaluate stimulus pull: (a) types of themes frequently elicited, and (b) qualities of the pictured scene (Peterson & Schilling, 1983). Descriptions of typical themes elicited by various TAT cards are available (Bellak, 1975; Bellak & Abrams, 1997; Henry, 1956; Holt, 1978; Murstein, 1968; Stein, 1955). The thematic pull of the cards has been important to clinicians who are interested in exploring an individual's style of response to identified areas of psychological functioning. However, some cards elicit a wider range of themes than others (e.g., Cooper, 1981; Newmark & Flouranzano, 1973). Perhaps such cards are more useful because they provide greater leeway for the respondent to express psychologically meaningful content. Indeed, Haynes and Peltier (1985) found that nine of the cards that were identified by Newmark and Flouranzano as eliciting a wide range of themes were rated by clinicians as most frequently used.

Attitudes revealed in any particular story may be specific to the interaction of the characters portrayed in the picture presented. Relationships among peers, adults, and children, or between males and females, may engender different schemas. Therefore, an adequate sampling of pictures depicting individuals of various ages, genders, and types of interactions is useful. In addition, the structural qualities of the stimulus influences the ease or difficulty in finding an appropriate explanation for the scene. Stimulus details that are not usually mentioned often influence the story implicitly. Flowers or books in Card 5 are not prominently featured (hence, they are details), but may suggest something about the room. Likewise, the jacket and tie worn by the young man in the foreground in Card 8BM is a detail that may provide cues that shape the story (e.g., "on his wedding day"). Other stimulus details are irrelevant (an "eyebrow" in Card 1 or "the man's underwear" in Card 2). The demands of the task vary according to the qualities of the picture stimuli, and clinicians must evaluate performance in the context of these demands (see Rapid Reference 2.1).

Content and Structure of the Pictured Stimulus

Characteristics of Picture Content

1. *Characteristics of the people.* Who the characters are—in terms of gender or general appearance, feelings, and activities—is central to the

narrative. A thematic apperceptive set should sample different types of relationships to elicit a range of schemas from the respondent. The set should also include pictures that vary in the number of persons portrayed.

2. *Characteristics of the background scene or objects.* The type of setting, such as a rural background, or props, such as a gun, are pertinent to the story content but are not as central as the basic emotions or relationships.

3. *Psychological issue.* The underlying psychological dilemma conveyed by the stimulus configuration (nature of the background, objects, facial expressions, and postures of the characters) constitutes the emotional issue raised or latent meaning of the stimulus (Henry, 1956). For example, Card 1, depicting a boy and a violin, raises the possible conflict between personal inclination and demands of outside agents. Furthermore, perceptions of family relationships may come to the forefront because the violin implies a task that is not required by the educational system but is typically promoted by the family.

4. *Similarity to the respondent.* The match between the age, gender, race, or ethnic background of the respondent and those of characters portrayed in the stimuli has been considered a possible factor influencing the response. Physical similarities (such as age, gender, race) have not been well-researched but may not be critical (Murstein, 1963). What may be paramount is how meaningful the psychological issues portrayed are to the respondent.

≡ *Rapid Reference 2.1*

Components of Stimuli in the TAT Set

1. *Element*—a character, including posture, facial expression, apparent attitude or activity

2. *Feature*—a relatively central object such as violin or book

3. *Detail*—an aspect of the stimulus that can blend into the scene (e.g., the gun in Card 3BM) or an aspect of the scene that is incidental and typically remains implicit (e.g., the boy in Card 1 touching his head to suggest a certain mood or clothing to set a context)

4. *Configuration*—the relationship among the elements, features, and details comprising the scene

Characteristics of Picture Structure

1. *Ambiguity.* Murstein (1963, 1965) distinguished between structure and ambiguity of the TAT pictures. Structure is the property of the stimulus (e.g., clarity about who and what is depicted; provision of cues or props), whereas ambiguity is a function of variation in themes elicited by the card (Newmark & Fluoranzano, 1973). Pictures of moderate ambiguity permit variability in response but provide anchors to guide the professional's interpretation (Lindzey, 1952; Murstein, 1965). In contrast, stimuli that present a clear depiction of what might be happening in the picture reduce the variability in responses. For example, one of the cards in the Tasks of Emotional Development (TED) portrays a middle-aged woman pointing to a child's possessions on the floor while the child looks on. This scene constrains the response more than TAT Card 5, which depicts an older woman looking into a room (various objects in the room, such as books or flowers, are present but are not central). The TED stimulus defines the characters and the conflict by pulling for a story about a parent chastising a child about a specific transgression. The TAT picture does not preclude this theme but permits the selection of numerous others. A quality of the stimulus related to ambiguity is its *stereotypicality,* or the extent to which the stimulus configuration is amenable to a conventional or "scripted" explanation. A stimulus may contain many cues constraining the narrative, and these cues may be more or less in line with the cultural stereotypes. Stimuli that are explained easily by a stereotypic story downplay the demand on the narrator to marshal internally organized resources.

2. *Emotional tone.* Theoretically, the general mood of pictures used in thematic apperceptive techniques may be positive, negative, or neutral. The TAT cards have been criticized for their predominantly negative tone (Ritzler, Sharkey, & Chudy, 1980). However, the negative tone may be advantageous because it presents unfinished business or a dilemma to be resolved, providing the opportunity to observe how the respondent appraises and deals with the tensions depicted in the picture. Essentially, the negative scenes

make it possible to observe how the narrator moves from the sadness or conflict to an adaptive resolution. The Apperceptive Personality Test (APT) was designed to avoid the negative tone of the TAT stimuli (Holmstrom, Silber, & Karp, 1990). Nevertheless, judges rated outcomes of the TAT stories as more favorable than those of the APT stories (subjects did not differ in their ratings of the story outcomes). This finding suggests that the affective tone of the story outcome is a function of the *narrator* rather than the stimulus.

3. *Complexity.* Degree of stimulus complexity varies according to the number and type of discrepant elements that need to be synthesized into a cohesive story (e.g., foreground and background, facial expressions and posture). Unusual details (gun in a surgery scene) call for ingenuity to develop a story that is in tune with the stimuli because they cannot be readily explained.

4. *Intensity.* A dramatic portrayal of the conflict or of the emotion as evident in the TAT stimuli is likely to give the impression of unfinished business and, thereby, draw in the respondent (Henry, 1956). Other stimuli that utilize line drawings (McArthur & Roberts, 1982) or colorful pictures (TEMAS) fall short of the life-like rendering of the people portrayed in the achromatic TAT set.

5. *Universality.* The generality of the emotions or experiences depicted may overcome the necessity of creating separate sets of stimuli that portray different ages, genders, and racial or ethnic groups. It has been suggested that pictures representing relatively universal social situations that most people encounter are suitable across various age and subcultural groups (Veroff, 1992).

ADMINISTRATION

Any unstructured task is sensitive to cues and instructional sets that may guide the response (Dana, 1982). Therefore, it is necessary to establish standard administrative procedures for structuring the task, for providing encouragement, and for prompting responses. It is also important to represent faithfully the narrator's performance of the task. With younger children, issues of sepa-

> ## CAUTION
>
> ....
>
> It is best to administer thematic apperceptive tasks toward the end of a comprehensive battery after rapport has been established because (a) the respondent will feel more comfortable with the examiner as a result of earlier interactions; (b) the respondent's general concerns about the testing can be clarified prior to administering a task that is anxiety-provoking for both adults and children due to its ambiguity (Newmark, Hetzel, & Frerking, 1974; Newmark, Wheeler, Newmark, & Stabler, 1975); and (c) any resistance or anxiety generated will not interfere with performance of subsequent tasks.

ration from parents should be resolved prior to starting the storytelling procedures. When children are reluctant to leave their parents, they are usually persuaded to come with the examiner if parents are permitted to sit outside the testing room where they may be immediately available to their children.

The sequence of cards has an inherent logic, and, generally, they should be administered in numerical order (Arnold, 1962; Bellak, 1986; Karon, 1981). For instance, the first two cards (1 and 2) are relatively benign, whereas cards 3BM and 4 depict more intense emotions. However, as described in the next section, each card has unique qualities, and the professional may use judgment in determining the sequence.

Instructions

The instructions for the TAT ask respondents to construct a complete story that includes the following components (Murray, 1943): What is happening in the picture? What happened before? How are people (persons) in the picture feeling? What are they thinking? How does everything turn out at the end? Each of these task components has been discussed in the previous chapter. Similar instructions apply to other thematic apperception techniques developed after the TAT, including those described in Chapter 8. As long as directions to include specific components of stories are clearly communicated, the exact wording is not crucial. The professional should use language that is appropriate to the narrator's level of understanding.

Instructions for adults are (Murray, 1943):

> I am going to show you some pictures, one at a time, and your task will be to make up a story for each card. In your story, be sure to tell what has

led up to the event shown in the picture, describe what is happening at the moment, what the characters are feeling and thinking, and then give the outcome. Tell a complete story with a beginning, middle, and end. Do you understand? I will write your stories verbatim as you tell them. Here's the first card. (The examiner hands the picture to the client.)

The following modification of the general instructions for younger children is given by Murray (1943):

I am going to show you some pictures, and I would like you to tell me a story for each one. In your story, please tell: What is happening in the picture? What happened before? What are people thinking and how are they feeling? How does it all turn out in the end? So, I'd like you to tell a whole story with a beginning, middle, and ending. You can make up any story you want about the picture. Do you understand? I'll write down your story. Here's the first card. (The examiner hands the picture to the client.)

If the examiner is also audiotaping, he or she may say: "I will write down your stories as you tell them, but I am also tape-recording them in case I miss some of what you say."

Instructions for telling TAT stories do not provide new information but simply reiterate the elements of the familiar story form. Even young children are aware of the basic story structure (Applebee, 1978) and, at least theoretically, it would be sufficient to ask the respondent to tell a whole story with a beginning, middle, and end. However, giving systematic instructions, as proposed by Murray, is advantageous because they set standards for the narrative product and provide a vehicle for standard queries by the examiner. Prompts, especially with children, are frequently necessary, to obtain sufficient material for interpretation. Professionals have proposed departures from the generally accepted procedure to administer the test to clients who have mild or moderate mental disabilities (see Rapid Reference 2.2). Peterson (1990) suggests this variation of the instructions, which gives as few cues as possible: "Tell me a story about what might be happening in this picture" (p. 194). A modification of Murray's instruction, substituting "what is the problem" for "what is happening" in the picture (Ronan, Colavito, & Hammontree, 1993; Ronan, Date, & Weisbrod, 1995), was intended to facilitate scoring according to a problem-solving conceptualization.

≡Rapid Reference 2.2

TAT Administration Guidelines for Clients with Mental Retardation (Hurley & Sovner, 1985)

1. The examiner should use concrete vocabulary when giving directions.

2. The examiner may demonstrate by making up a story to a sample card.

3. Beyond prompting as needed for each component of the directions, the examiner may ask clarifying questions as needed without being "suggestive."

Settings and Materials

The testing room should be comfortable and free of distracting sounds and objects (toys, clutter). Some examiners avoid a direct face-to-face position to minimize the possibility of giving inadvertent cues to the client. However, there is no compelling reason to change seating position or other routines established earlier in the administration. The examiner needs the selected picture cards, tools for writing, and tape recorder.

Encouragement

Although the TAT is considered suitable for children as young as age 4, even older children and adults sometimes have difficulty developing a story that includes all of the elements requested in the directions. It is suggested that examiners follow a standard procedure for prompting at all ages. If the individual has difficulty getting started and instructions have been repeated and clarified, the examiner might say something like, "Start by saying what is happening in the picture." If the respondent starts the story but hesitates, the examiner should nod encouragingly or prompt the storyteller to "go on" in preference to specific questions. Such general prompts are meant to convey the expectation that the storytelling process is not a series of questions and answers (though on some occasions, this is unavoidable). If the narrator seems "stuck" needs more guidance, the next prompt might be, "What happened before?" Next, the examiner should inquire about characters' feelings and thoughts as needed. Finally, if the storyteller does not provide an ending, the examiner should ask, "How does everything turn out at the end?" The examiner may query as needed to clarify ambiguities such as a vague pronoun reference (e.g.,

"Who is she?"). To produce a faithful record, the examiner notes all
queries as well as the respondent's
nonverbal behaviors or pauses in
storytelling or remarks. If the narrator does not respond to encourage-

DON'T FORGET

The examiner may prompt each of
the instructional elements only once
per story.

ment or specific queries, the examiner may suggest coming back to the card
later.

Recording Responses

A tape recorder may be used to back up the examiner's written notes. There are
several advantages to this two-pronged procedure. First, the examiner's hand-
writing retains the interpersonal component of the interaction, calling on the
respondent to pace the story to the requirements of the writer. However, if the
respondent speaks too quickly and the examiner cannot keep up, the tape
recorder becomes essential. Second, even if the examiner is able to keep up
with the respondent's pace, the use of the tape recorder relieves the pressure
to write down every utterance because missing words or sentences or paren-
thetical comments can be filled in later. Third, despite every effort to assure
that the tape recorder works properly, the written protocol provides a back up.

Selecting Cards to be Administered

The TAT *Manual* (Murray, 1943) instructs that 20 cards be administered from
the TAT set, which includes 30 pictures and one blank card. Eleven of the
cards are designated for all respondents, and nine are selected according to age
and gender. It is not required, nor even preferable, that all 20 TAT cards be administered to examinees. A survey of clinicians in juvenile and forensic settings
indicated that the mean number of cards used was 10.25 (Haynes & Peltier,
1985). Generally clinicians administer from 8 to 12 cards. The cards are not selected in accord with their original designations as appropriate for specific ages
and gender but according to clinician's judgment regarding their usefulness to
elicit psychologically meaningful material.

Clinicians choose cards based on the "pull" for certain themes or psychological processes under consideration. Peterson and Schilling (1983) offer a

theoretical discussion of stimuli. Description of themes most frequently elicited by each TAT card (e.g., Bellak, 1975; Henry, 1956; Holt, 1978; Stein, 1955) and a review of perceived usefulness of various cards (Teglasi, 1993) are also available. The first 10 cards of the TAT set depict basic interpersonal relationships that are more likely to elicit emotionally relevant material and are more likely to be used by clinicians than the second set (Cooper, 1981; Ehrenreich, 1990; Worchel, Aaron, & Yates, 1990).

Suggestions for picture selection within the TAT set (Bellak, 1975; Henry, 1956; Teglasi, 1993) indicate that many of the male cards are preferable for both genders because they elicit richer and more complex themes (see Rapid Reference 2.3). In agreement with others, Bellak and Abrams (1997) have proposed a standard set of 8 to 10 cards for use with adults that can be supplemented as needed: 1, 2, 3BM, 4, 6BM, 7GF, 8BM, 9GF, 10, and 13MF. With one exception (13MF), the productive cards seem to work equally well across ages and genders. Cards that do not depict emotions or relationships very clearly or that portray a person immersed in thought with no additional cues (3GF) are not as useful as those that do.

Murray's (1943) description of important stimulus properties and elaboration based on Henry's (1956) review and the author's experience are summarized below for each of the most frequently used TAT cards.

≡Rapid Reference 2.3

TAT Card Selection

There is considerable agreement among clinicians regarding preferences for specific TAT cards. Arnold's (1962) preferred cards (1, 2, 3BM, 4, 6BM, 7BM, 8BM, 10, 11, 13MF, 14, 16, and 20) include all but one (12M) of Bellak's (1986) essential and male cards (1, 2, 3BM, 4, 6BM, 7BM, 11, 12M, and 13MF). Preferences indicated by Rabin and Haworth (1960) for children between the ages of 7 and 11 (1, 3BM, 7GF, 8BM, 12M, 13B, 14, and 17BM) and for adolescents (1, 2, 5, 7GF, 12F, 12M, 15, 17BM, and 18GF) include many of the cards favored by Arnold and Bellak. Hartman's (1970) survey of preferred cards with children under the age of 17 in rank order are 1, 3BM, 6BM, 7BM, 13MF, 7GF, 8BM, 4, 10, 12M, 16 (blank), and 18GF. Teglasi (1993) indicated the following cards as most useful for children and adolescents of both genders: 1, 2, 3BM, 4, 5, 6BM, 7GF, and 8BM but also noted that others have been useful depending on age and referral issues (7BM, 10, 12M, 13B, 13MF, 14, and 17BM).

ILLUSTRATIVE EXAMPLES

The manner in which the narrator or examinee explains the stimulus configuration (elaborated in Chapter 4) is an important aspect of accomplishing the TAT's problem-solving task. Consider two respondents' varying approaches to the first two picture stimuli. Aaron, age 8-3 and a student in a special education program for children diagnosed with emotional disorder, tends to describe irrelevant stimulus details without explaining the gestalt. Subject #14, age 9-7 and a non-diagnosed participant in a study, provides stories based on a meaningful interpretation of the scene. Both students' IQ scores were above average.

Aaron

Card 1. The guy that is, the kid that wanted to draw a picture with stuff that he didn't have. [Examiner (E): What happened before?] He needed some ink and a pencil, but there was a crack in the paper and he didn't have any tape. [E: So what was he thinking?] He's thinking of drawing. [E: And how is he feeling?] Umm, urnm, concerned because he thinks he'll mess up on the picture and everyone will laugh at him [E: And how does it turn out in the end?] He got the tape and finished his picture.

Aaron's story does not deal with the violin but focuses on the minute details of the paper on which the violin is resting ("there was a crack"). Aaron also shows a similar difficulty with maintaining a consistent level of conceptualization in the stark contrast between the character's concerns about being laughed at by "everyone" and the quest for supplies to finish the drawing. The story is not an accurate fit with the contextual cues provided in the picture. The accounting of the boy's facial expression, though not entirely off base, is disorganized.

#14

Card 1. What's that thing right there? Hmmm. Ah, this boy wants to take an instrument lesson. He wants to take piano, and his mom wants him to take violin. So she signed him up for violin lessons. So he's looking at the violin feeling sad. [E: Turns out?] Then on his first violin lesson it turned out that he liked it.

The story precisely captures the relationship between the boy and the violin as depicted in the picture without dwelling on minor or irrelevant details.

Aaron

Card 2. The old barn that had a big plowing field. [short pause] The, the farm didn't have any money, so they couldn't buy any tools but they did have a plow and a horse too. The man who had a horse, the horse was fifty years old and the girl, she always carries a book in her hand and she wraps her hand around it and she always wears her same clothes every day and she wears her hair down really great and she likes plowing the field and she lives in the field farm with all the hay and animals and she lived happily ever after. [E: Tell me what they are thinking.] They are thinking and having a great time with lots of money and they can buy anything they want. [E: Feeling?] They feel, well, they got some money and they feel very, very happy.

Aaron describes irrelevant details (the horse was 50 years old, girl wraps her hand around books) of the card without relating the details to more general concepts other than a recognition of a "farm." Essentially, the details of the picture are not tied to general concepts that relate the characters to each other in the context of the background scene.

#14

Card 2. Ok. A long time ago there was a teenager that lived on a farm with her father, brother, and mother. She liked reading books, but there weren't many books, and they were very expensive. So she would walk a long way just to get books from her neighbors, like Abe Lincoln.

Without dwelling on the details, the narrator has accounted precisely for the stimulus configuration.

✍ TEST YOURSELF ✍

1. **Clinicians select TAT stimuli on the basis of**

    (a)   their original designation of being appropriate for children or adults and for males or females.

    (b)   "pull" for specific thematic content.

    (c)   both "a" and "b."

    (d)   neither "a" nor "b."

2. **Stimuli play an important role in thematic apperception techniques because**

    (a)   they present the emotional, social, and contextual cues to be addressed.

    (b)   they vary in the richness and clinical utility of responses they elicit.

    (c)   they set the problem-solving demand of the task.

    (d)   all of the above.

3. **Individuals tell more clinically useful stories if they are similar in age, gender, or race to the characters depicted.** True or False?

4. **When administering the TAT, the standard instructions simply reiterate what one would typically include in a complete story.** True or False?

5. **Professionals should provide the narrator with as much encouragement as possible to assure the "best" story possible.** True or False?

Answers: 1. d; 2. d; 3. False; 4. True; 5. False

Three

ESSENTIALS OF STORYTELLING INTERPRETATION

The aim of story interpretation is to evaluate the schematic structures and processes that organize otherwise ambiguous or confusing situations. It may be said that schemas enable "intelligent" decisions, particularly in circumstances that require complex judgment. As tools for thinking about experiences, schemas are useful if they are sufficiently accurate and complex to meet the information processing requirements of the situation or task. Consider the following scenario: Alison, an 8-year-old, enthusiastically told her teacher about her weekend. The teacher responded playfully by saying, "Get out of here!" Without hesitation, Alison walked out of the classroom. Although Alison's IQ score was well above average, her schemas for interpreting this interaction did not provide a sufficiently nuanced representation of reality to allow her to coordinate the emotional cues implicit in the teacher's tone of voice and facial expression with the literal meaning of the words and with the situational context.

The TAT was originally designed for ages 4 and up (Murray, 1935). In her review of studies using the TAT, Cramer (1996) concluded that "the same interpretive perspectives that have been found to be useful in the interpretation of adult TAT stories have been found to be equally informative when used with stories of children" (p. 209). Bellak's interpretive systems for adults (TAT) and for children (CAT) are virtually identical (Bellak & Abrams, 1997).

NARRATIVE FORM, PROCESS, AND CONTENT

Patterns in "how" a narrator tells a story and "what" he or she tells elucidate the narrator's schemas. *Form* and *content* in the TAT have been distinguished (Henry, 1956; Holt, 1958; Rappaport, 1947) as products of the storytelling *pro-*

cess (Teglasi, 1993). Because formal qualities of the story and the narrative process provide information about the cohesiveness and reality base of the narrator's schemas, they should be evident across cards within a protocol. In contrast, content is expected to vary with specific stimuli that have been designed to elicit particular themes (Murray, 1935).

Story Form

Given that much of the story content is set by the stimulus, a key to story interpretation is to analyze the structure of the content (McGrew & Teglasi, 1990; Teglasi, 1993) by abstracting a higher-order principle for its organization rather than specific thematic interpretation (Holt, 1958). Three types of formal or structural qualities of stories are distinguished: The first is *import,* which is a generalized property of content constituting the underlying message or "moral" of the story (elaborated later in this chapter); the second is *abstracted content,* or any higher-order designation of content such as time perspective, social appropriateness, or internal or external sources of affect. Abstracted properties of content reflect psychological processes. For example, inappropriate content (regardless of the specifics) is expected to be screened out, and its inclusion suggests impaired functioning. The third type is *structural organization,* in which the organization of the narrator's thought processes and the cohesiveness of his or her schemas are revealed by structural properties such as internal logic, compliance with instructions, or accuracy of stimulus interpretation.

Process of Story Development

The process of constructing and organizing the narrative translates into the story structure. Accordingly, the juxtaposition of ideas as driven by disconnected associations or by a logical synthesis of ideas is evident in the structural organization of the story. The narrative process includes (a) the sequence in which ideas are introduced and elaborated (e.g., reaction to stimulus, examiner's inquiries, previous story elements), (b) apparent planfulness in developing the story, (c) the monitoring of the unfolding details, and (d) flexibility in responses to examiner queries.

CAUTION

In the interpretation of thematic content, the examiner should consider

1. the relationship of content to the stimulus configuration.
2. the formal characteristics of the narrative (logic, coherence) and process of story construction.
3. the import or message expressed by the story as a whole.

Story Content

Content analysis identifies the specific concerns and themes that are salient for the narrator. For example, a recurring description of characters as "tired" or as feeling burdened may have relevance to the experience of the narrator and should be investigated. However, content interpretation is a complex endeavor. Specific content may not express relatively enduring concerns but may be cued by the picture stimuli or constitute fleeting associations of the storyteller. Therefore, simple frequency counts that isolate content from the pull of the stimulus or other aspects of the story are misleading. Despite similar content, a story that evolves through a patchwork of memories or loosely connected associations reveals different psychological processes than a narrative that is constructed through a creative reorganization of ideas represented in memory and in keeping with the stimulus. Thus, aggressive content that is congruent with the stimulus or serves a constructive purpose has different implications than aggression introduced spontaneously with antisocial or unclear intent. The nature of the individual's experiences and concerns (content) is influenced by how those experiences and concerns are organized (form).

Import of the Story

A popular interpretive strategy is to recast the details of a TAT story into more abstract themes that constitute its import, or "moral" (e.g., Arnold, 1962; Bellak, 1975; Teglasi, 1993). The import encapsulates all of the content and structural details to convey the convictions or principles (or lack thereof) guiding the story production. The organizing principles extracted from TAT stories are similar to those derived from stories about actual experiences such as descriptions of important life events (Alexander, 1988; Demorest & Alexander, 1992). These principles or convictions constitute a set of rules governing the relationships among intentions (wishes, emotions, strivings), means, and expected outcomes for self and others in specific contexts. However, if these narrative elements are disorganized, they do not constitute "convictions" in the usual sense of guiding thoughts, feelings, and actions in a systematic way. Thus, the narrative process and structure are critical in determining the "import" of the story. In condensing TAT stories and life narratives into their "import," the emphasis has been on the connections between means and ends because these links constitute the "lessons" learned from life experiences (Arnold, 1962; Bruhn, 1992; Schank, 1990).

On the basis of daily encounters, individuals discern patterns that connect intentions, plans, actions, and outcomes in particular circumstances to form expectations about how their own or others' actions produce positive emotions, ameliorate tensions, or create meaningful outcomes. These patterns, including complexities such as internal or external barriers that hinder the pursuit or attainment of desired outcomes, are filed in memory and subsequently retrieved as lessons based on the individuals' ideas about how intentions, means, and outcomes "go together" (Schank, 1990). The central role of intentions, means, and ends in extracting the message of the story parallels the importance accorded to these variables in developmental research (see Rapid Reference 3.1). A child's ability to verbalize an understanding of the connections among intentions, means, and ends lags behind his or her implicit comprehension, just as a 4-year-old's ability to discuss the rules of grammar lags behind his or her use of language. Despite difficulty verbalizing emotions such as anger or hurt, young children manage to act constructively on their own and others' emotions (Dunn, 1991). Thus, young children differ from adults not in the basic processes of social interaction but in the size of the gap between their implicit and explicit knowledge bases (Premack, 1992). Judging from their daily interactions, children implicitly understand social causality and act on these understandings well before they can grapple with these concepts verbally. The story import reveals implicit understandings rather than verbally organized knowledge of inner states or of social causality.

Instructions for TAT stories require the narrator to coordinate the inner world of intentions, thoughts, and feelings with outward actions and sequences of events. Regardless of thematic content, the coordination among intentions, actions, and outcomes constitutes a basic structure for organizing information about self, others, and the world (e.g., Schank, 1990) and, there-

≡ Rapid Reference 3.1

Intentions, Means, and Ends in Developmental Research

1. An understanding of intentions is a prerequisite for developing a "theory of mind," which is defined as the recognition that individuals have mental states such as motives, beliefs, or goals (Premack & Woodruff, 1978). In turn, this theory of mind makes it possible to predict others' actions (Astington, 1991; Flavell, 1988) by differentiating between what is objective (outer world of events and actions) and subjective (the inner world of thoughts, beliefs, and intentions).

2. Children begin to act intentionally during infancy, and these actions are based on their identification of means and ends (i.e., doing one thing to achieve something else). After becoming aware of means-ends connections (e.g., crying brings parent, pushing an object moves it), the child learns to act intentionally and to assume that others are also acting intentionally (Frye, 1991). For example, after learning to use a gesture intentionally to elicit a response from someone, an infant may recognize the same gesture by someone else as an intentional act and not a mechanical movement.

3. Piaget points to areas such as logico-mathematical thinking as showing the greatest discrepancy between children and adults. However, those who study the theory of mind point to the ways in which adults think remarkably like their 5-year-old selves (e.g., Gardner, 1991).

4. A well-developed theory of mind is a social tool, and problems with the development of a narrative theory of mind (inability to form intentions or generate cohesive ideas) are empirically associated with childhood pathology (Baron-Cohen, 1991).

fore, conveys the moral or import of the story. However, the narrative process must be factored into the import, particularly if story content is disjointed, insubstantial, or based on an inaccurate reading of the stimulus.

DON'T FORGET

The convictions and organizing principles captured by the imports generally operate outside of the narrator's awareness.

The next section describes two types of imports: *content* import (Arnold, 1962), which expresses the subtext of the narrative content, and *process* import, which is based on the narrative process and structural properties of the story (Teglasi, 1993).

Process Import

When content is limited to what is pulled by the stimulus or represents fleeting associations rather than meaningful synthesis of prior experience, the content is relatively unimportant in understanding the narrator's conviction. In these instances, the story structure or the manner in which the story is developed (or the task is avoided) is the template for the ongoing organization and reorganization of experience, thereby constituting the import. The following story told by Ken, a boy aged 8 and one-half (of average intelligence) and diagnosed with ADHD, is best understood in terms of the storytelling process rather than its content.

Card 8BM. They're chopping him, Fred, open and the spirit came out. [E: Before?] Don't know. [E: Thinking?] Get the knife off me.

The content is an idiosyncratic association to the stimulus. The narrator begins with a violent description that is a literal translation of one part of the scene (the background, "they're chopping him") without considering the prominent figure in the front. Moreover, he does not develop a context (e.g., prior events, intentions) for the situation described. Because of the inaccurate interpretation of the scene and meagerness of the narrative, the content of the story is less useful in formulating the import than the style of the response. The following import captures the narrator's approach to the task: "You are very reactive to initial impressions of the immediate circumstances without considering all of the relevant information." This import can be restated as follows: "When a child is presented with complex or threatening stimuli, he overreacts on the basis of appearance without carefully processing the information." Such variations in the wording should not alter the score (as described in Chapter 7).

Content Import

The import distills the story content and storytelling process in relation to the five structural pillars of the narrative: circumstance, intention, complication, means, and outcome. The initial premises of the story, including the nature of the problem, provide the backdrop for evaluating the appropriateness of the connections of intentions to actions and of means to ends. The range of possible or appropriate actions depends on both the dilemma facing the character and the character's inner world. The import captures the logic of the unfolding events and cohesiveness of inner states with circumstances and actions. If one aspect of experience (such as actions or feelings) is overemphasized relative to others, the import likewise reflects that emphasis. However, in formulating the import, most weight is given to how the initial premises and subsequent events relate to the outcome. The reason the outcome of the story is pivotal in determining the import is that a satisfactory ending ties up all the loose ends, thereby imparting coherence to the details. Thus, a story about a bank robbery carries a different message according to whether the robber ends up living happily ever after ("crime pays") or winds up in prison ("crime doesn't pay"). Finally, logical inconsistencies as well as gaps in information processing limit the narrator's understanding of social causality and of the connections between means and ends. Therefore, the interpreter considers not only the story details that are included but also what is missing.

The message or import of the story may be *general*, going beyond the specifics of a given plot, or *situation-specific*, applicable only to the context or circumstances described. A conditional or situation-specific import is worded in an "if . . . then" format. Special circumstances in the story or an unusual state of the character (e.g., during war, when drunk or confused) constitute the "if." Additionally, the interpreter should be alert to systematic variations in the imports describing specific relationships (peer, parent, child) or involving different ages or genders. Variation in responses according to structural qualities of the stimulus (complexity, background) or emotional reaction of the narrator (frightened by the scene) may limit generalization. An import may be written in the first, second, or third person. It may be a simple statement or it may express a complex set of premises. Although a

---

CAUTION

When interpreting imports, keep in mind that

1. negative content may be activated by the picture and may not correspond to the narrator's characteristic affect (e.g., anxiety, depression).
2. the details of the narrative may correspond more to stereotypes or well-known scripts (e.g., story, movie) evoked by the scene portrayed in the picture than to lived experience.
3. the story may detail a specific experience or fleeting association rather than actual convictions.

content import is generally written from the perspective of the character who is described in greatest detail (as the following examples show) the basic conviction representing the narrator's schema should be similar regardless of perspective. A story about a bully implies a victim and vice versa, just as a general conviction such as "might makes right" applies to both the strong and the weak.

In sum, the import is an abstraction that conveys the subtext of the story from the viewpoint of the narrator rather than from the character's vantage point. This basic unit of inference emphasizes the nature of the outcome in relation to the problem set, the goals, or intentions and the connection between means and ends. Content imports not only capture the structure of the content but also incorporate the narrative process. At times, the import is constructed entirely on the basis of the storytelling process.

Examples of Imports

As a first step toward formulating the import, it may be helpful to diagram the underlying structure of the story content according to its key elements: the *problem, dilemma,* or *circumstance* (what is happening in the picture; what happened before), characters' *intentions* (motives, goals, thoughts, feelings), any *complicating factors* (anticipated or unexpected turn of events, internal barriers), *means* (such as actions or other coping strategies), and *outcomes* (how things turn out). After diagramming a story into its structural underpinnings, the clinician derives the import by abstracting the relationships among the structural elements. In doing so, the focus is on the cohesiveness among the external circumstance (dilemma, situation, demands), the characters' inner worlds (thoughts, feelings, intentions, goals), and the characters' plans or actions in relation to the outcome.

Several stories told by Zelda, age 8-10, WISC-III, IQ 113, illustrate how stories are diagrammed and how imports are abstracted. Additionally, for each story, a brief explanation is given for how the content and structure as well as narrative process relate to the import. The evaluation was prompted by parental concerns about poor school performance (grades of C and lower) and teachers' complaints about her slow pace of work and disorganization. Parents indicated concern about her frequent daydreaming but also described her as relaxed, good-natured, and adept interpersonally.

Card 1. The boy . . . is getting ready for a violin lesson but he . . . doesn't know what to . . . where the bow is. So he doesn't know what to do. And his violin lesson is in ten minutes. And this is his first lesson, and he doesn't want to miss it. And . . . and he had been already looking around the whole house for his . . . bow. And now his lesson was only in five minutes. Finally he found his bow and went to violin lessons.

Dilemma or Circumstance	Intention	Complication	Means	Outcome
10 minutes before violin lesson, bow is missing.	Go to lesson.	Bow is still missing; after initial search, no idea what to do.	Use same search strategy again.	Boy fortuitously finds bow in nick of time and goes to lesson.

Import: If a boy has not planned ahead and doesn't know what to do, last minute actions can work out.

Content emphasizing last minute pressure is consistent with qualities of the storytelling process indicating imprecision and difficulty with anticipating and planning ahead. First, the facial expression of the boy shown in the picture as contemplating a violin is not a precise fit with someone agitated about a misplaced bow. Moreover, the entire story takes place in the span of 10 minutes (no indication of a broader context or goal) suggesting that a focus on the immediate situation may interfere with setting priorities and following through on long-term intentions.

The next story further shows that Zelda has difficulty acting on her intentions.

Card 2. The lady . . . she's walking by a place where there are . . . where they are trying to teach horses to do certain things. And she like . . . but she doesn't really understand what they're doing. And she has to go somewhere. But she wants to know what the people are doing with the horses. So she decides to ask the man, even though she doesn't want to. And then she decides not to ask the man because she's too shy and she's got to get somewhere. And then she goes.

In diagramming the story, the content that is pulled by the stimulus is not repeated. The import or moral of the story hinges on the connections among the diagrammed elements.

Dilemma or Circumstance	Intention	Complication	Means	Outcome
Happens to see something that sparks curiosity.	Wants to understand what's happening and decides to ask the man.	Too shy to ask.	Just goes "somewhere."	Seeming acceptance of status quo.

Import: If a lady is curious but finds it difficult to ask a question (feeling shy), she forgets about it and simply goes on with her (vague) activity.

The import suggests an inactive stance toward the process of learning from her environment as an initial intention (to understand) is abandoned. The "lady" has no strategy to find another way to answer her question and loses interest as she shifts her attention to her vague destination ("somewhere"). Generally, intentions are more difficult to sustain when they are vague than when they are well-defined. The next story is about a girl who ignores the external world and remains in her daydreams, but only as long as they are pleasant.

Card 7GE. [E: What is happening in the picture?] There is . . . a mother and a daughter, and the daughter is holding her little sister or brother. Well, her mother is trying to tell her something, but the girl is daydreaming . . . and the girl's not [there] because she's just daydreaming . . . and what the mom wants to tell her is important. And . . . the girl . . . she's dreaming nice thoughts so she doesn't really want to answer her mother. And all of a sudden, the girl . . . she dreamed bad thoughts so she answered her mother finally.

This story is diagrammed twice, once from the perspective of the child and again from the vantage point of the mother. Typically, when a story is examined from the perspectives of different characters, both versions yield a similar import or belief because the interactions are reciprocal (e.g., a story about a child ignoring her mother implies a mother being ignored).

Daughter

Dilemma or Circumstance	Intention	Complication	Means	Outcome
Mother trying to tell daughter something important.	Daughter is daydreaming and doesn't want to answer.	None.	Daughter answers mom when her daydream turns bad.	Status quo is maintained.

Mother

Dilemma or Circumstance	Intention	Complication	Means	Outcome
Same as above.	Wants to inform daughter.	No response from daughter.	None. (passage of time)	Receives answer when daughter feels like giving it.

Import from the child's perspective: When a child is engrossed in her daydreams, she tunes out her parent (mother), even when the parent is saying something important, and the child pays attention only when she feels like doing so.

Import from the mother's perspective: When a mother disturbs her daughter's daydreams, even if what she has to say is important, the mother tolerates being ignored until the daydream passes.

What is common to both perspectives is the lack of connections between external circumstances, intentions, actions, and outcomes. The daughter does not respond to her mother until her daydream turns bad, and the mother simply waits. Despite a seeming recognition that the mother may have something "important" to say, the lure of the inner world prevails. These imports (last minute effort pays off; if something is hard, don't do it; don't leave a pleasant activity to respond to mother) are consistent with the presenting concerns of Zelda's parents and teacher. In addition, Zelda conveys a vague quality by not specifying what the mother is trying to say (other than its being important) nor what the daughter replies. This vagueness (consistent across cards) suggests that Zelda does not actively process the details of her surroundings.

The next story is based on a complex stimulus to which Zelda responds with vague and avoidant content.

Card 8BM. I can't think of anything. [E: What is happening in the picture?] There is a lady standing up and there is a man. There are two men, and they're trying to do something to another man. [E: What might the people be thinking and feeling?] The man . . . the woman . . . the man that's not doing anything. I think he's feeling good and the other man . . . feeling ok, but the other lady isn't feeling as good either. [E: How does it end?] I can't think of anything for that.

Dilemma or Circumstance	Intention	Complication	Means	Outcome
Vague.	Trying to do something (vague) to a man.	Vague.	None.	Some people feel good; others do not.

Import: When a situation is uncomfortable, you just don't deal with it, but you notice how people feel in the moment.

The content per se is not substantial enough to abstract a conviction. Therefore, the above import is derived largely from the narrative process. However, as is often the case, the story line and the storytelling process are parallel. Zelda does not deal with the details of the scene but refers to the people apart from the context that needs to be explained. Her vague treatment of the stimulus corresponds to her description of characters who formulate only vague intentions, who display feelings that are not tied to meaningful experience, and who do not act in a purposeful manner. Her relatively greater difficulty responding to this card (more complex than others) suggests that she may be experiencing more problems with complex and undefined situations.

Card 13B. There's a boy, and he's thinking about what he's going to do during the day 'cause he's bored. He doesn't know what to do. Finally he . . . decides to . . . play with some of his friends but that wouldn't take the whole day because one of his friends is going out before the day is over. So he's trying to think of something to do at the afternoon and then he remembers that not one of his friends are going out in the afternoon. He decides to play with a different friend in the morning and a different friend in the afternoon.

Dilemma or Circumstance	Intention	Complication	Means	Outcome
Boy is bored and seeks to play with friends for the whole day.	Figure out what to do.	A friend needs to leave early.	Decides to play with different friends when they're available.	Problem is presumably solved.

Import: If a boy is bored and wants to play all day, he can decide to play with different friends when they are available.

In this story, Zelda uses problem-solving strategies: The character sets a goal (play with friends to counteract boredom) and makes an appropriate decision. However, her vague style is evident as neither the activity nor the specific friend is pertinent.

Card 4. [E: What is happening in the picture?] A man . . . he's trying to look at something else, while the woman is trying to look at the man. And the man is feeling that he doesn't love the woman but the woman is feeling that he does . . . that she does love him and he loves her. And then she's got a feeling that he doesn't love her that much because he won't stay with her. But the man had done so much for her and been a nice friend so she didn't think that he didn't like her. And she was troubled. So finally she decides that the man likes her but that he also likes some other people too. And she decides that he can go and be with his other friends and it's okay. She can't make him think differently.

This story typically would be diagrammed from the woman's perspective because her viewpoint is emphasized. However, both are given below to illustrate again the applicability of the "message" to both characters.

Woman

Dilemma or Circumstance	Intention	Complication	Means	Outcome
Woman loves man but thinks he doesn't love her.	To make the best of the relationship because he has been a good friend.	None.	Figures out that the man likes her but doesn't love her and decides not to make demands he won't meet.	Man remains her friend but has other friends too.

Man

Dilemma or Circumstance	Intention	Complication	Means	Outcome
Man doesn't love woman who loves him.	Man wants to get away from woman's embrace.	Man likes her as friend.	Won't stay with her.	Woman decides he doesn't have to love her; they can remain friends.

Import: Relationships remain intact if people don't make excessive demands and keep expectations within boundaries that respect their own feelings, and those of others.

The woman reflects on the entire relationship and accepts the man's right to his feelings. Despite a "vague" quality to the narrative, the reasoning about relationships is sophisticated.

Card 6BM. A lady has a visitor, and the visitor knows the lady's a maid, but he doesn't remember his name . . . her name, and he's troubled . . . because he knows that the maid's someone important that he knows, and the maid feels the same way about the man. And . . . the man wants to say hello to the maid, and the maid wants to say hello to the man but neither of them can remember each other's name and who each other are and how they know each other. So they just keep on thinking until finally the man remembers but the maid doesn't. So the man says hello to the maid and then the man remembers . . . and then the maid remembers the man by his voice and how he looks and they both start talking to each other.

Dilemma or Circumstance	Intention	Complication	Means	Outcome
The man who is visiting doesn't recall maid's name and vice versa.	Each wants to say hello to the other.	None.	They keep thinking until man remembers and says hello, thus jogging the maid's memory.	They talk to each other.

Import: It's hard to remember people's names, but if a man and woman think hard, one can suddenly remember and then they can talk to each other.

There is a clear desire by the characters to be respectful to each other, but difficulties such as recalling each other's names (or in Card 7GF, problems disconnecting from a pleasant daydream) complicate their carrying out the intended social behaviors. The explanation for the scene does not fit precisely with the stimulus, and difficulty attuning responses to the nuances of the situation may hinder the pursuit of social goals.

Analysis of Imports

As stated earlier, the import of each story is formulated as a general or situation-specific "moral." Subsequently, the examination of the entire set of imports permits further refinement in the distinction between conclusions that are general or specific. The repetition of similar patterns across cards suggests a characteristic style of responding in less structured circumstances or tasks (Henry, 1956), whereas systematic variation suggests situation-specific responses. For instance, negative expectations may apply only in specific instances (such as when a single character is portrayed) or there may be a general pessimism. Interpersonal relationships may vary according to characters' ages, genders, or roles suggesting similar patterns with peers, parents, or authorities. Variations in narrative process and structural aspects of stories also may be noted across picture stimuli that differ in complexity or present potentially distracting cues such as books, flowers, or a gun. Certain patterns may be observed in abstracted characteristics in the content of stories across cards. Thus, characters' goals may be considered in terms of what is emphasized, such as getting the task done, meeting social expectations, or satisfying an immediate need. Likewise, characteristics of actions, such as being reactive or proactive, may be noted. The sequence of imports may also be analyzed (Arnold, 1962).

This set of stories told by Zelda captures her difficulty planning ahead and her tendency to avoid frustrating activities. Awkward circumstances arise because of forgetfulness or lack of planning. Goal-directed activities are limited in that the desired goal, such as the resumption of the moment by moment give-and-take of social interaction (answering mother or remembering a name to say hello), is often very immediate. Moreover, positive outcomes are often anticipated in the absence of sufficient effort, planning, or strategic action (e.g., finding the bow at the last second). Together, these patterns suggest that the connections between means and ends are not sufficiently well-developed to motivate self-directed effort toward long-term goals. Problems with attention, organization, planning, and with attuning responses to subtle cues in the surroundings may interfere with sustaining independent effort on academic tasks. Zelda experiences more difficulty when faced with complex and undefined situations than when expectations are clear. She displays interpersonal strengths, including adaptive problem-solving strategies in peer situations (between two adults and among children) and willingness to compromise. In close relationships, Zelda considers the needs and perspectives of others and takes a long-term view rather than overreacting to isolated encounters.

Explanatory Hypotheses for Imports

The import of each story is eventually understood in light of other stories and other sources of information. However, initially the interpreter seeks possible explanations for the import by carefully examining the clues within the story itself. As described earlier, sometimes the content of a story is too confusing or limited to permit the examiner to discover the narrator's conviction. In such instances, the import is formulated on the basis of the narrative structure and storytelling process. These types of imports, described earlier as process imports, reveal the storyteller's style of approaching the task (interpreting the stimulus and developing the story) rather than the conviction typically derived from the content imports. However, all stories, including those with adequate content, are amenable to analysis in terms of the storytelling process and structural organization of the narrative. Indeed, as shown earlier, formal and stylistic aspects of the story tend to parallel the content and suggest possible explanations for the conviction expressed. For instance, in Zelda's stories, the failure of characters to plan ahead and to pursue durable goals is consistent with her preoccupation with relatively immediate concerns. Stylistic factors, such as Zelda's imprecision in accounting for the stimulus configurations and vague processing of information, may play a role in her difficulty with setting and pursuing long-term goals. The aims of the interpreter are to discover the guiding rules (scripts or schemas) for organizing life experiences encapsulated by the "import" as well as to identify the relevant psychological processes and specific concerns of the narrator that may explain the import and are relevant to the purpose of the assessment. Thus, the interpreter may explore several possible explanations for the narrator's schema as captured by the import. First, as already noted, the interpreter examines each import in relation to the narrative process and story structure. Second, the interpreter reviews the other stories in the protocol for corroborating information. Finally, at a later stage, the interpreter examines other pertinent information, such as other tests, behavioral observations, school or job performance, social-emotional history, and life circumstances of the narrator. Thus, Zelda's distractibility and inattention reported by her parents and teachers are consistent with the content imports and with narrative process and structure. In following this interpretive procedure, initial emphasis on the individual's style of processing information is subsequently integrated with the social context to answer the referral questions.

Regardless of the story content, the stylistic and organizational features remain relatively constant within a protocol, with some variation attributable to the nature of the stimulus or to individualistic reactions to specific scenes. Such stylistic features focus on patterns of information processing that unify many different domains of functioning, link performance of the storytelling task with other measures in an assessment battery, and explain variation in adjustment across different life situations. Subsequent chapters of the current volume provide guidelines for coding specific cognitive, attentional, and emotional processes that are useful on their own but also contribute to understanding the story imports. Corroboration for conclusions is found in consistency of content, structure, and narrative process across several stories in the protocol as well as in the patterns of responses to other measures in the assessment battery. The combination of performance data elucidates situation- and task-related variability in functioning that corresponds to adjustment in various life domains. Throughout the evaluation, the interpreter takes a scientific hypothesis-testing stance, systematically relating patterns in the data (within and across measures) to relevant psychological constructs.

TEST YOURSELF

1. **Which statement concerning the story import is false?**
   (a) It is formulated by the interpreter.
   (b) It captures the main concerns of the central character.
   (c) It encapsulates the convictions of the narrator.
   (d) It delineates the principles that organize the narrative.
2. **Briefly define the narrative form, process, and content.**
3. **How does the interpreter distinguish between a general and situation-specific import?**
4. **The story structure and narrative process are relevant if**
   (a) content is not amenable to interpretation.
   (b) content is amenable to interpretation.
   (c) both "a" and "b."
   (d) neither "a" nor "b."

5. Explanatory hypotheses for imports are found in all but

(a) story details, structure, and narrative process.

(b) examinee's explanation.

(c) performance on other tests.

(d) background information and current circumstances.

6. Young children's TAT stories reveal their tacit understanding of social causality

(a) better than they can verbalize this knowledge.

(b) as well as they can verbalize this knowledge.

(c) worse than they can verbalize this knowledge.

(d) understanding varies from child to child.

Answers: 1. b; 2. *Form:* generalized property of content based on its organizational or structural characteristics. Form includes (a) the import, (b) any abstracted quality of content (e.g., higher-order designation such as time perspective), and (c) structural organization (e.g., logic or consistency with the stimulus). *Process:* manner of sequencing, planning, and monitoring the flow of ideas. *Content:* specific themes or concerns; 3. The examiner seeks consistency and variation in the narrator's expression of how key elements of the import "go together." These elements include dilemma or circumstance (the problem), intention (inner world of thoughts, feelings, motives, goals), complications, means (actions or decisions), and outcomes; 4. c; 5. b; 6. a.

Four

ESSENTIALS OF TAT ASSESSMENT OF COGNITION

Storytelling is a performance task that reveals aspects of thinking and problem solving in relatively unstructured situations, and its use in the assessment of cognitive processes is not meant to replace or validate the more structured tests of cognition or achievement. Problems in reasoning evident in narratives, though related to adjustment, are not necessarily corroborated by Full Scale IQ scores (e.g., Caplan, Guthrie, Fish, Tanguay, & David-Lando 1990). Cognitive strategies applied to storytelling may be compared with cognitions on various tasks that range on a continuum of structure, novelty, or complexity (Teglasi, 1998) to help explain variation in functioning across tasks and situations requiring different competencies. This chapter describes procedures for evaluating three broad dimensions of cognitions from stories told to picture stimuli: perceptual integration, concrete and abstract thinking, and information processing that includes various aspects of attention and reasoning.

PERCEPTUAL INTEGRATION

In assessing perceptual integration, the primary focus is the accuracy and precision in "explaining" the pictured scenes (Teglasi, 1993). The narrator's approach to interpreting the scene ("what is happening") provides information about the coordination of the perceptual (details of the scene) and conceptual (meaning of the scene) processes. A conceptual process or system applied to the interpretation of perceived information dictates that specific stimuli derive meaning from the relationship among the various perceptual elements (a knife in the kitchen is a tool, but in the classroom it is a weapon). An accurate and integrated accounting of the stimulus would include a conceptual relationship among the perceptual elements of the stimulus rather than a focus on various components (features or details) in isolation. Thus, a high level of perceptual integration requires organization of the emotional and interpersonal cues (facial expression, posture) and the features of the stimulus that set the context (objects, background, clothing). Conceptual structures (sets, expectations, or schemas) organize perceptual inputs into meaningful information. Object permanence and the various conservations are common examples of such structures (Flavell, 1963; Piaget, 1954). Piaget reasons that *centration* (a focus on a narrow aspect of an object) in perceptual processes leads the perceiver to distort the object by formulating partial impressions, apart from the context. Centration is not a purely developmental phenomenon because it can occur at any age due to cognitive or attentional limitations as well as emotional duress. A smoothly operating conceptual framework applied to the TAT task would guide attention to the most relevant stimulus elements and enable the narrator to grasp accurately the "gist" of the stimulus configuration.

Professionals have described the social scenes depicted in the TAT set of stimuli as ambiguous because they are amenable to diverse interpretations. Yet the identity of the characters and the nature of their feelings are clearly discernible on many of the cards (Murstein, 1965). Therefore, clinicians may evaluate how the narrator interprets the stimulus apart from the quality of the story. The posture and facial expression suggest some conflict or negative feeling to be identified more specifically by the narrator. Distortion of basic emotions of TAT stimuli must be examined closely (Rappaport, Gill, & Schafer, 1975; Teglasi, 1993; Tomkins, 1947) because they suggest problems with calibrating responses to situations due either to intense preoccupation or faulty information processing. Omitting or misidentifying minor stimulus features (e.g., gun in Card 3BM) or even major features (e.g., violin in Card 1) is less problematic than misperceiving characters' emotions or relationships to one another (McGrew & Teglasi, 1990) as conveyed through their posture or facial expression (e.g., people hugging in Card 4). With training and practice, interrater reliability in each of the coding parameters described in this chapter is .80 or higher (Blankman, Teglasi, & Lawser, 2000).

PERCEPTUAL INTEGRATION INDICATORS

1. Degree of Congruence with the Stimulus

- *Disregard or misperception of basic emotions or relationships depicted.* Failing to register emotions or inaccurately reading nonverbal expressions while trying to interpret emotions or relationships among characters is far more significant than leaving out or misidentifying objects or other stimulus features. Examples are telling a story about one character when two or more are pictured or failing to acknowledge a tension portrayed.

- *Disregard or misperception of characters' ages.* The thoughts and activities of the characters are not compatible with their ages as portrayed in the picture.

- *Focus on irrelevant stimulus details.* Stimulus components are viewed as irrelevant if they do not contribute to the interpretive meaning of the scene (e.g., Card 1, "he has his hands up to his ears" or Card 2, "man's underwear is showing").

- *Emphasis on perceptual features rather than conceptual meaning.* Narrators rely on what is "seen" in the picture rather than on what is "known": Content is comprised of simplistic associations to the scene or based on isolated parts of the stimulus (e.g., only attending to one component of the stimulus or telling separate vignettes about various components without tying them together). Thus, each character may be described accurately but without an inner psychological process, without a relationship to other characters portrayed, or without a grounding in relevant prior context. Perceptual emphasis is not coded if the narrator's initial strategy is modified.

- *Unresolved vacillation or indecision.* This variable refers to an inability to decide how to interpret the scene, as opposed to an inability to discern an object ("I can't tell, he may be sleeping or he may be crying"). Thus, the narrator provides various alternative explanations for what might be happening in the picture without selecting a particular one.

- *Limited interpretation of emotions and relationships because they are significantly at odds with contextual cues in the stimulus or because of the absence of clear connections to story events.* Despite accurately identifying basic emotions and relationships portrayed in the scene, the narrator's story is not in accord with contextual cues (e.g., clothing or other stimulus features) or with the story events. The narrator may disregard or misperceive a major stimulus feature (an object, such as the violin in Card 1, that provides important contextual cues) but still interpret adequately the emotions and relationships in the picture (e.g., Card 1, "the boy is lonely because he has no one to play with"). A minor stimulus feature refers to an object that is not central (such as the gun in Card 3BM) and could blend into the background scene without close inspection.

- *Adequate relationships among pictured elements but imprecise fit between story details and the stimulus configuration.* The narrator depicts relationships and affects that are consistent with the stimulus but he or she does not fully capture subtleties of affect (its intensity) or the sequence of events does not fit "precisely" with the scene. The description of the scene may be vague, the context (e.g., preceding events) not well-developed, or logic slightly amiss (e.g., naive reasoning).
- *Meaningful and realistic relationships among relevant stimulus features that precisely capture the "gist" of the scene.* The narrative depicts a realistic set of events explaining the scene with appropriate understanding of social causality. Narratives that convey an understanding of psychological processes and portray a sequence of events that are precisely in tune with the stimulus configuration suggest efficient organization of perceptual patterns with conceptual meaning.

Note: The last two categories require more "precise" attunement between the stimulus and the unfolding story. The others focus more on the explanation for "what is happening" in the picture.

2. Levels of Perceptual Integration

In assigning the levels, the interpreter should give most weight to how well the story explains "what is happening in the picture" as conveyed by the emotions and relationships. The interpreter should accord less weight to omission, over-inclusion, or misperception of stimulus features such as objects. The following section describes each of four levels and illustrates them with examples of stories told to TAT Cards 4 and 8BM (see Chapter 2 for description of cards).

1. Discrepant

The premise of the narrator's story is not appropriate to the overall stimulus configuration, as indicated by significantly misperceiving the emotions and relationships depicted or by misreading or failing to recognize tensions in the stimulus. Basically, the following problems suggest that the narrator lacks the inner framework to size up the pictured cues shown: (a) The narrator ignores or misreads important aspects of the scene such as posture, facial expressions, or ages of the person or people (e.g., adults playing childish games); (b) the problem set in the story is out of tune with the stimulus configuration or is related tangentially to the stimulus; (c) the narrator omits a major character from the story; (d) the narrator emphasizes minute details (e.g., eyebrow) without perceiving the gestalt (e.g., emotion); (e) the narrator does not recognize an obvious tension state so that characters looking in different directions or having different facial expressions (such as in Card 4 or 7GF of the TAT) are identified as doing or feeling the same thing.

Two stories told by Aaron, age 8-3, illustrate this level. Aaron has a WISC-III, Full Scale IQ score of 119 (Verbal [VIQ] = 102; Performance [PIQ] = 133) and is receiving special educational services in a self-contained classroom as treatment for an emotional disability. He also receives services for speech and language as well as specific learning disabilities.

Card 4. The man with the big frowny face. There was a man who had a, who always wore a frowny face and he was wearing it for years and year. He done it in his bed, he done it all night, he did it all day, I don't know why he does that frowny face but he does it away. And he blinks one second before and he doesn't have any money. He likes being kissed in the big, big, neck and he likes, always gets a sloppy kiss and he always likes frowning all the time. One day he smiled and they lived happily ever after. The end. [E: Tell me what he was thinking.] He was thinking he'd get a big sad face on his face and he wondered if he will just blink minute after minute. Then he will be a regular guy.

The title Aaron gave the story and the narrative in general centers on one of the persons portrayed, the man with the "frowny face." The woman is vaguely acknowledged in the phrase "they lived happily ever after." The emotion described and the relationship between the two people portrayed are not appropriate matches with the stimulus configuration.

Card 8BM. The man who always had to go to the doctors. And has to look at his mom there. There was a little kid who always hears his mom get little cuts on her. And she wanted to do something else and he was, is doing, not doing nothing, but watching his mother. Then he was trying to get out but he couldn't. One day he ran away, far away. And he had, and then he forgot all about his mother. And then he wandered back home and he was thinking about doing something else but this boring thing and he lived happily ever after. The end. [E: Feeling?] He was feeling a little bored.

Aaron identified the picture as a scene having something to do with a man who "always had to go to the doctors." Presumably while at the doctor's office, the child "hears his Mom get little cuts on her." The narrator does not accurately identify the components of the scene (e.g., person being cut appears to be a man), nor does he meaningfully relate the clues to each other (e.g., does not make an appropriate inference unifying the scene).

2. Literal

The primary misperception is in the failure to grasp the *implicit* meaning of the stimulus. The narrator identifies emotions and ages of characters but does not grasp the psychological processes that connect events, feelings, intentions, and actions. The narrative may be grounded in the "moment" that describes the scene and may not have implied causal connections among past, present, or future events. The narrator may tell separate vignettes to various elements of the stimulus without incorporating them into a common context (e.g., the narrator may acknowledge foreground and background but not relate them meaningfully). Relationships or emotions are not grossly incompatible with the stimulus nor are prominent characters omitted. Rather, emotions and actions may be simplistic, vague, scripted, stereotypic, or comprised of associations to the scene as a whole, rather than a specific accounting of the cues (subtleties of context, facial expressions, or posture) presented. Generally, the narrator emphasizes the "perceptual" rather than the "conceptual." Often there is a superficial, concrete, descriptive use of the stimulus and difficulty cohesively relating the major elements.

Kip, age 9, WISC-III Full Scale IQ score of 98

Card 4. He looks like he's mad, like she did something to him, and she's trying to apologize for what she's done and he's not going to forgive her. [E: Feeling?] Sad, like he's going to cry. [E: Ending?] He ain't going to forgive her and they are going to separate.

The narrator accurately labels feelings, but the story does not convey the psychological processes behind the feelings or actions, nor does it provide sufficient context to explain the feelings and relationships portrayed.

Card 8. The little boy is [laughs] confused. Looks like he doesn't care, his dad is lying on the table, getting operated on. The doctor is scared for the guy's life and looks like the little boy couldn't care less and he's walking out. [E: Ending?] The father is going to live.

Again, the narrator identifies the elements of the picture, but he attributes feelings to what characters seem to be doing in the picture (walking out) rather than inferring about their psychological world, interpersonal relationship, or sequence of events. In these two stories, the narrator is "stuck" by the characters' portrayal in the scene; the literal interpretation seems to mirror a serious inflexibility in functioning.

3. Imprecise

The narrator recognizes the tension state and the story generally captures the implications of the stimulus vis-à-vis emotions and relationships. However, the fit is not precise, as the story may not match with subtle contextual cues or may convey cause-effect understanding that is slightly amiss or vague. Another index of imprecision is the narrator's ignoring or misperceiving a major object.

Josh, age 12-1, WISC-III Full Scale IQ score of 99

Card 4. This one's about a man and a woman who don't get along, but then after a little while of living together, they start to like each other a lot, and then they get married, and they stay married for the next fifty years. [E: Feeling?] Happy.

The story provides a vague explanation for the conflict portrayed in the scene ("they don't get along") without delving into the discrepant emotional states of the two individuals. Such an unclear definition of the conflict (typically) leads to a vague (Pollyanna) resolution.

Card 8BM. This is about a kid who is really bad, and he shoots this person, and the man has to be rushed to the doctor's office, and they perform surgery on him, and then he's better, and the doctors are happy, and they arrested the boy for shooting him.

Again, there is a "kid who is really bad," a vague explanation for the shooting, rather than a specific intention. Moreover, the relationship of the boy to the surgical scene and to the victim is unclear.

4. Accurate

The narrator accounts for all cues and subtleties in the interpretation of feelings and relationships (despite possible omissions or misidentification of minor details). There is a meaningful interpretation of the stimulus configuration that accurately and specifically captures the "gist" of the pictured scene.

Benjie, age 9-11, WISC-III Full Scale IQ score of 139

Card 4. Well, there's a man that looks very mad at someone who annoyed or offended him, and his wife is trying to stop him from doing anything he'll regret such as attacking the person who was offending him. At the end, she'll restrain him and he'll stop and get over his anger.

Here, the narrator precisely articulates the nature of the relationship between the man and woman as well as the nature of the conflict between them.

Card 8BM. A boy, yeah a boy, more like an adolescent has to have surgery and he's dreaming about how it's going to be and he's a little scared so he's thinking how it's going to be. So he sees what's going to happen to him, and it makes him even more scared. I don't know why there's something that looks like a rifle there. [E: End?] He goes through it, and he realizes he was worried about nothing because he didn't even feel it.

The narrator clearly relates foreground and background ("dreaming"), and the story is congruent with the emotions portrayed and the major contextual cues. The narrator notices the rifle but does not work it into the story. Given that the story described a "dream," this omission is not significant.

CONCRETE AND ABSTRACT THINKING

A key component of cognition is the balance between abstract and concrete thought. Concrete thinking is constrained by immediate cues or specific personal experiences (Johnston & Holzman, 1979). Thought processes that are bound by the immediate context (a focus on the stimuli that are externally available versus internally represented) lend themselves to literal interpretation of the information. Abstraction, on the other hand, is defined by the degree to which the internal representation of perceived objects (schemas) are detached from their concrete form. Thus abstract thinking involves relative freedom from the immediate context in favor of the accumulated "lesson" derived from experiences. Behaviorally, abstractness is manifested by using an inner framework to initiate and sustain independent action rather than being compelled by the situation.

Because concrete thinking is tied to the immediate circumstance and does not incorporate long-term time perspective, it fails to integrate past experience and future considerations. If a behavior has relevance only for the present, there is little incentive to tolerate frustration, and external sources of motivation are needed. Moreover, when experience has little to do with what preceded it and with what is expected to follow, the individual is unprepared to apply lessons from the past to the present and to the anticipated future. Without an abstract inner framework to interpret situations and guide behaviors, the individual is likely to engage in trial and error problem solving rather than use cause-effect analysis to plan actions or anticipate outcomes or reactions of others. Furthermore, the individual is unlikely to look inward to reflect on intentions, goals, motives, or actions (see Rapid Reference 4.1).

Difficulty with abstracting and symbolizing affective experiences does

≡ Rapid Reference 4.1

Development of Schemas

Schemas providing rules that govern standards of conduct and expectations of others range from the concrete and simplistic to the abstract and nuanced (e.g., Abelson, 1976; Bretherton, 1990; Teasdale, Taylor, Cooper, Hayhurst, & Paykel, 1995). Developmentally, schemas begin as representations of specific interactions and become more abstract, coming to represent the lessons learned through the regularities in the patterns of experiences (Baldwin, 1992). At a rudimentary level, schemas are compilations of representations of single concrete examples that are used to make snap judgments about seemingly similar instances. At a higher level of abstraction, stereotypic schemas encompass the most representative features of events, persons, or groups. Still more abstract schemas recognize complexities as well as inconsistencies between external reality and the internal representation. At the highest levels of abstraction, schemas include conditional and inferential concepts and higher order rules, along with affective information. An example of the latter would be "If I am nervous, I am very subdued, and others think I am a bore."

not necessarily suggest a similar problem in the impersonal domain. Children with autism exhibit a deficiency in understanding the social world even when their comprehension of the physical world remains intact (Baron-Cohen, Leslie, & Frith, 1986). To study young children's understanding of causal relations, Baron-Cohen and her colleagues used a previously developed picture-sequencing task followed by a request to narrate a story. They presented three types of story sequences: (a) *mechanical,* depicting physical-causal relations; (b) *behavioral,* depicting sequences of overt behavior without requiring reference to mental states; and (c) *intentional,* requiring an intuitive and immediate understanding of a mental state (false belief) to explain the sequence of behaviors. The first two types of sequences were relatively well understood by autistic children with high ability levels, but the intentional stories were poorly understood by autistic children relative to the comparison groups. Compared to children without cognitive impairments and children with Down's Syndrome, the autistic children rarely used mental state expressions (e.g., desire, knowledge, emotion, or action implying an inner state). Given the pattern of findings, the authors concluded that the problem was not the inability of the autistic children to make an inference about "behind the scenes" causes but a specific deficit in conceiving of mental states.

The TAT stories reveal abstract and concrete thinking both through the perception of stimuli and through the content and structure of the unfolding story:

1. *Stimulus.* An abstract interpretation of the picture assigns meaning on the basis of the "gestalt" (coordinating various stimulus elements into a common context) of the scene, transcending the details rather than focusing piecemeal on the components. For example, describing the boy in Card 13B as "he has no shoes," "he's poor," or "he's an orphan" entails increasing distance from the perceptual features of the stimulus and reliance on internally organized schema. Likewise, feelings that emanate from the depiction of a character in the stimulus (e.g., "he looks unhappy") rather than from an attribution to a character's inner state ("he's upset because he can't play the violin") signal concreteness in the interpretation of the stimulus. When responses are closely bound to the stimulus or instructions of the storytelling

> ### CAUTION
>
> An individual who tends to be anxious or is threatened momentarily by the stimulus or the task or who is perhaps adverse to risk may be reluctant to depart from the concrete cues in the TAT picture despite being able to do so in less ambiguous or emotionally charged situations. Thus, emotions generated by the task may restrict flexibility and promote concrete strategies for responding.

task, the narrator is looking to explicit clues from the environment for structure and may perform better in a rehearsed or routine situation and well-learned task.

2. *Story Content.* A narrative indicates concrete thinking if the content focuses on the here-and-now or borrows heavily from fictional plots or stereotypes in an attempt to match a "ready-made" template to the current task.

3. *Narrative Process and Structure.* Difficulties with any of the following organizational components of the narrative suggest concrete thinking: (a) transitional events, in which the narrator has problems with invoking reasonable causes to explain a change in feeling or has problems describing realistic sequences of events in relation to outcomes (e.g., magical or arbitrary turnabout rather than realistic transitional events); (b) context for events, in which the narrator has difficulty providing a reasonable history to events pictured in the stimulus; and (c) coordination of inner life with external circumstances, in which the narrator has limitations coordinating external events with characters' ideas or feelings (e.g., interrelating actions, intentions, thoughts, feelings, and outcomes).

CONCRETE THINKING INDICATORS

1. Formal Elements of Story Structure and Narrative Process

- *The narrator interprets the picture literally.* Events do not depart from the stimulus or from the immediate time frame (no past, no future—even with examiner prompting), and there is minimal expression of thoughts, intentions, feelings, or conflicts. Feelings are tied to the stimulus rather than to characters' thoughts or story events explaining the picture. Emotions, when mentioned, are not explained (e.g., feeling state refers back to the picture rather than to story events).

- *The narrator takes the instructions literally.* The task becomes one of addressing each component of the directions rather than telling a story (with or without examiner prompting).

- *The narrator does not understand that he or she generates the story rather than the story being inherent in the picture.* The narrator has difficulty understanding the storytelling task (e.g., stating that "the picture doesn't tell me a story" or describing elements of the picture without extracting the "meaning").

- *The circumstance does not change and the character does not gain insight or there is an absence of transitional events.* The narrator describes the scene without external change or inner process reframing the scene (insight). The narrator does not adequately explain any change in feeling or circumstance. The context (what happened before, state of the characters, purpose) may be insufficient to understand actions or outcomes (e.g., arbitrary or fortuitous turn of events produces the outcome, feeling turns into its opposite). Change is not restricted to the external circumstance but may occur in feeling or thought. For instance, in a story told to Card 13B, a boy who remains bored after realizing that it is up to him to think of something to do has undergone an internal change.

2. Formal Elements of Story Content

- *Concerns are extremely trivial.* The content emphasizes daily routines typically taken for granted (e.g., eating, sleeping, showering). This category is not coded if such concerns are incidental to larger issues (e.g., involving a relationship).

- *Inner states are stimulus-bound or simplistically associated to events.* Inner states, intentions, or motives are descriptive of the stimuli, vague, or simplistically tied to actions or events (unclear purposes, causes, or antecedents). They appear to be superficial (or stereotypic) reactions rather than internally organized emotions for which the character assumes responsibility.

3. Level of Abstraction in Explaining the Stimulus

Regardless of whether the narrator develops a story beyond explaining "what is happening" in the picture, level of abstraction may be classified as enumerative (naming of objects), descriptive (referring to qualities of objective stimulus features), or apperceptive (interpreting beyond the objective features of the picture) (Byrd & Witherspoon, 1954). Expectations about degree of abstraction in children vary from a predominance of apperceptive responses by kindergarten (Lehman, 1959) or by age seven (Schwartz & Eagle, 1986) or eight (Byrd & Witherspoon, 1954). Others report that descriptive stories are common in third grade (Gardner & Holmes, 1990).

Enumerative Description

Content is limited to the naming of isolated or irrelevant details of the picture without relating various components to each other or to a common theme (e.g., "boy has an eyebrow"). Content may be tied directly to various parts of the picture in succession without capturing the gestalt of the card (e.g., "the girl is carrying books, the lady is leaning against the tree, and the man is working with the horse"). Feelings are tied to the stimulus rather than to story events. This level, suggestive of deficits in abstract thinking, is often tied to low IQ scores.

Tonya, age 16-5, Stanford-Binet IQ score of 42

Card 1. I can't tell if he's asleep or looking down. What is this? . . . [E: Whatever you see.] He's sitting at the table sleeping with his elbows on the table . . . This is hard . . . Can't tell . . . It's the only thing I can think of in this picture. [E: Before?] I don't know. [E: Turns out?] That's hard. [E: Thinking?] Another hard one. [E: Feeling?] He's sad. [E: Why?] I don't know, I can't tell.

Anna, age 7-3; WISC-III Full Scale IQ score of 86 (VIQ = 91; PIQ = 82)

Card 1. I think this boy is fixing something. And, um, he has his hands up into his ears. And, um, he has kind of blondish hair, a white table, and the back is black paper. [E: What is he thinking and feeling?] He's thinking that his thing will work and he's feeling his head.

Both narrators focus on irrelevant, concrete details without providing a meaningful explanation of what might be happening in the picture.

Concrete Description

There is an emphasis on the perceptual features of the picture, but the stimulus elements described are meaningfully related in terms of the connections between emotions and external events. However, the story does not incorporate the psychological world (enduring inner purpose or motives) of characters depicted. Attributing an emotion to a single event without a cohesive tie to the inner world or to a broader set of circumstances is not sufficient to demonstrate an understanding of intentions or the role of emotions in experience.

Jim, age 16, WISC-R Full Scale IQ score of 96, diagnosed with conduct disorder and living in a residential setting

Card 1. He's looking at a violin. Probably bored—doesn't want to do. Somebody put it in front of him. Feeling angry and mad 'cause somebody asking him to do it. So he doesn't do it.

The interpretation of the stimulus is more closely tied to the perceptual features of the stimulus than to inner psychological processes. The boy "is looking," "probably bored," and "somebody put it in front of him." The absence of context (preceding event, purpose, outcome) for interpreting the pictured scene creates the impression of an individual who is reactive to his angry feelings and is bereft of inner resources to represent experience beyond the moment. Likewise, there is no consideration of the person's identity or intentions of the person who put the violin "in front of him."

Amy, age 14-10, WISC-III Full Scale IQ score of 70, provisionally diagnosed with Asperger's Syndrome

Card 1. He looks kinda, um, looks kinda down because it looks like his guitar broke. He looks depressed. [E: Before?] I think he was probably happy. [E: Ending?] I think he, um, just accidentally broke his guitar.

This story offers a perceptual rather than a conceptual emphasis. The "boy" looks down because it "looks like his guitar broke." Such a one-to-one connection between a feeling and relatively minor event does not adequately explain the emotion. If the "guitar" had broken moments before an important solo performance, the implicit meaning of the situation in terms of its emotional impact would have been sufficiently explained.

Aspects of this story point to problems with abstraction, with cause-effect reasoning, and with understanding intentions. For instance, when asked what happened before, Amy was unable to provide a context, simply stating that the boy was "probably happy." Her response to the question, "what happened at the end?" suggests that she may not fully understand the concept of an "ending" to the story.

Interpretive Explanation

An inference is made that "explains" the scene depicted in terms of inner attributes and external events or outward appearance. Such explanations express a relationship among ideas that are abstracted from the stimulus configuration rather than directly tied to the cues. These include motives, reasons, causes, or antecedent events that constitute an appropriate interpretation of the stimulus. Thus, psychological processes and events are distinct, yet cohesive. This level can be attained even at a young age and can be coded even if the story is not developed beyond an explanation of the scene.

Benjie, age 5-0, Stanford-Binet score of 140

Card 1. This boy is sad because he can't play the violin.

The content is an interpretive explanation of the scene because the character's appearance in the picture is coordinated with an appropriate internal reason. In contrast to Amy's and Jim's stories, the feeling is internally organized rather than triggered by an immediate external provocation. The sad feeling stems from the boy's implicit understanding that he is either expected to or wants to play the violin (but can't).

CAUTION

Concrete thinking (bound by the stimulus, instructions, or specific personal experience) is common to individuals with very low IQ scores but occurs independently of IQ scores at higher levels.

INFORMATION PROCESSING

If information is to be remembered and organized, it must first enter awareness. Selective attention or the ability to attend to some things while tuning out others keeps an individual from being bombarded with information that is not relevant to current activity. On the other hand, focusing very narrowly may preclude processing of the complexities needed to make adequate decisions or perform some tasks. Optimal regulation of attentional processes permits the attunement of attention to the information processing demand of the task or circumstance. Attention is a multi-

> **CAUTION**
>
> Phrases that suggest insight (e.g., "will work harder" or "talk about the problem") may reflect "words" that the narrator has heard or read but has not integrated in ways that are useful. Examiners should note the fit between specific content and overall framework of the story (coherence, logic, appropriate linkages among intentions or wishes, actions, and outcomes).

faceted construct involving a complex interplay of interrelated elements that have been linked to neuropsychological models of brain function (Denckla, 1994; Mirsky, Anthony, Duncan, Ahearn, & Kellam, 1991) and clinical disorders (Barkley, 1997; Levine, 1987), as well as meta-cognitive and organizational styles (Torgesen, 1994) in developmental psychology. Attention influences learning or information processing, peer relationships, and, more generally, personality development.

Attention regulation and reasoning are necessary for the organized and systematic processing of information, which in turn permits the individual to discern regular patterns and rules inferred through experience. The stories reveal the narrator's style of processing information through the interpretation of stimuli, planning and monitoring the story progression, logical reasoning to discern cause-effect relationships, time perspective, and relating the inner (thoughts, feelings, intentions, goals) and outer (actions, events, stimuli) worlds as well as coordinating perspectives of different individuals.

INTERPRETING STIMULI

The usefulness of stimuli to assess attentional components of information processing varies according to their complexity and inclusion of potentially diverting elements. Complex stimuli make it possible to note whether the narrator attends to various elements in isolation or unifies the clues in the scene by inferring meaningful relations among the relevant stimulus components. As discussed previously, flexible and sophisticated conceptual schemas promote the imposition of a meaningful interpretation based on accurate perceptions. Stereotypic schemas are templates for organizing perceptions of stimuli according to features most salient in the culture. Concrete, rudimentary, or disorganized schemas foster responses that are immediate, unmodulated, and not mediated by a conceptual process (see also the section on Perceptual Integration).

The following story told by a 21-year-old woman with below average intelligence, incarcerated for drug possession and prostitution, illustrates stimulus interpretation that is not guided by a conceptual process:

Card 8BM. They cutting the man open. They cutting a man, and they in the hospital, and that's a gun. Ain't that a gun? They cutting a man open, and it looks like they gonna kill him. [E: End?] I don't know. Tragedy. [E: Feeling?] I can't see. I don't know how they feel. He looks like he is a lawyer or something.

Rather than imposing an interpretation that explains the discrepant elements, the narrator responds directly to parts of the picture. For instance, "cutting the man open" is a literal translation of part of the scene. After noting the presence of the gun, the narrator assumes that the intention is to kill the man. Finally, the figure in the foreground is described as a lawyer (he's wearing a tie and jacket) without relating him to the rest of the scene.

PLANNING AND MONITORING

The narrator's modulation of behavior during testing, organization of the story, and planfulness of the characters described expresses the degree of planning and monitoring. The manner of administering thematic apperceptive techniques precludes advanced planning by the narrator. The storytelling task involves on-the-spot decisions to choose a general story line, weigh alternative details, or modify the initial approach according to nuances of stimulus cues, insight, or examiner's queries. The operation of schemas guides the introduction and juxtaposition of ideas just as the rules of grammar lend structure to sentences and paragraphs. The schema-guided progression of ideas typically occurs outside of awareness, but the narrator may exert planful and strategic effort to monitor the inclusion and exclusion of detail for cohesiveness and logic while complying with the instructions. As the narrator improvises, he or she has to formulate a dilemma that fits the stimulus configuration and a resolution that addresses the central tensions rather than simply ending the story. Difficulty maintaining attentional focus interferes with planning and monitoring the progression of the story, as well as the activation of organized schemas (due to disruptions in prior learning). When asked to retell a complex and unfamiliar story, the narratives of boys diagnosed with ADHD were more poorly organized, less cohesive, and contained more inaccuracies than those of the control group boys (Tannock, Purvis, & Schachar, 1993). Differences in narrative production were explained as a function of difficulties with organization and monitoring of information relating to problems with executive control. Without well-organized schemas to guide the development of the story, the narrator may react to the stimulus, get lost in the detail or in personal thoughts, and manifest difficulty balancing possibility (wishes) with probability (reality).

The content, in terms of planfulness of the characters, often mirrors the story structure. Narrators who take an unplanned trial-and-error approach to the storytelling task also describe characters who do not set goals, plan ahead, or anticipate consequences. Instead, characters may react to unexpected events or immediate provocation. Thus, planning and monitoring on the part of the narrator is reflected in the construction of the story as well as in the actions or reactions of the story characters. Likewise, the narrator's understanding of cause-effect connections is indicated by the sequence of events (e.g.,

DON'T FORGET

The coherence of the narrative is a reflection of the organization of the schemas guiding their construction. Breakdowns can occur at the following junctures:

- *Attention.* The narrator may find it difficult to focus attention due to problems engaging or sustaining attention, shifting flexibly, or disengaging.
- *Conceptualization.* The narrator may experience difficulty with making inferences to "explain" the central conflict or dilemma implicit in the pictured scene, as well as with generating a plan for constructing the story.
- *Strategic application of knowledge.* If the narrator has learned rote response patterns (i.e., without discerning general principles, patterns, rules, or implications), he or she may be unable to generalize the knowledge to a new situation.

probable versus highly unlikely set of circumstances) and by the tie between characters' effort and outcomes. Individuals plan and monitor their actions in accord with their understanding of social causality. If representations of the world (schemas) lack appropriate cause-effect connections to anticipate future events and likely consequences, the individual will need external structures (e.g., clear and reasonable expectations along with consequences) and cues to guide behavior. The next section describes story characteristics that indicate problems with planning and monitoring.

1. Formal Elements of Storytelling Process and Story Structure (more than one may apply)

- The narrator gives irrelevant responses, silly content, and extraneous chatting while receiving instructions or narrating the story.
- The narrator complains about being bored, wants to stop, or keeps asking how many more.
- The narrator offers first person stories or personalizations that suggest an inability to distance the self from objective demands of the task (e.g., "this reminds me of my grandmother . . .").
- The narrator loses the "set" for telling the story. He or she is drawn away from the initial focus by personal associations or by the examiner's inquiry (i.e., the story veers from initial direction and does not return).
- The narrator displays arbitrary shifts in perspective, inconsistencies in language (pronouns, tenses), or contradictory details in the story.
- The narrator displays poor understanding of causes for events or motives. He or she has substantial difficulty understanding social causality and motives or intentions. Either the concepts are not buttressed by details that are sufficient to convey understanding (e.g., they are vague or stereotyped), or content that is typically left implicit is explicitly stated (e.g., child thanks mother for dinner). Story content may be shallow or superficial (e.g., actions and themes emanate directly from the stimulus rather than from a combination of events and inner states or borrowed from the media or a replay of *specific* encounters), thus failing to convey an understanding of social causality (e.g., "they talk things over and solve their problem" but without a clear understanding of the issues surrounding the conflict or the spe-

cific steps to the resolution). The narrative content does not appear to be based on meaningful synthesis of experience.

- There is no tension or no outcome (if this is checked, the examiner should ignore the two items below).
- Outcome or change occurs without adequate transition or does not follow from previous story events (seems far-fetched, unrealistic, unlikely). For example, actions are insufficient for the outcome.
- Outcome does not adequately address the central conflict, tension, or dilemma as posed by the narrator. The story comes to a conclusion (an ending is provided) without resolving the dilemma posed.

2. Formal Elements of Content (more than one may apply, or, if content is limited, none may apply)

- Story characters don't care, are bored, or engage in wishful thinking or short-term resolutions. This is not coded if the character deals constructively with boredom (e.g., takes responsibility for finding a suitable activity or ultimately becomes interested).
- The story emphasizes immediate gratification or material gain (particularly without adequate effort to earn them).
- Characters act or react without clearly defining the problem or their goal.
- Actions are haphazard and occur without planning or anticipation (e.g., undesired effects, not precisely tied to its purpose). Characters face problems as a result of failure to plan ahead or anticipate likely outcomes of actions.
- Characters jump to inappropriate or premature conclusions; they cannot figure things out, fail to consider reasonable alternatives, or overreact (e.g., "woman is frightened by sounds, but concludes that it was just her dog coming up the stairs." Typically, such familiar sounds would be anticipated).
- Characters either express or act upon a desire to avoid or escape legitimate, age-appropriate restrictions or responsibilities that they consider unfair or incomprehensible.
- Characters continue to behave in ways that contradict how they think they "should" act.

TIME PERSPECTIVE

Time perspective has been defined as "the manner in which individuals and cultures partition the flow of human experience into the distinct temporal categories of past, present and future" (Zimbardo, Keough, & Boyd, 1997, p. 1008). An individual's framework for time is an outgrowth of preferred modes of information processing that become solidified into a functional cognitive style, though it may vary according to the situation. Those who are grounded in the present base decisions on the most salient aspects of the immediate stimulus or setting and are more likely to engage in a broad spectrum of risky behaviors (see Moore & Gullone, 1996; Zaleski, 1994). A teenager who is more concerned about parental punishment than about the long-term consequences of actions such as skipping classes is stuck in an immediate time frame. An individual's concept of time is integral to understanding cause-effect connections, antecedents of current circumstances, or vision of the future. A realistic time perspective permits individuals to anticipate, plan ahead, and subordinate immediate concerns to long-term considerations.

Faulty integration of time perspective occurs in three basic ways. The first is the restriction of the time frames to the immediate, the second is an unrealistic time frame, and the third is a vague sense of time. Intermediate and appropriate time frames reflect higher levels of conceptualizing the time dimension. Coding time frame is pegged to the narrator's conceptualization of time, not necessarily to the events in the story. A checklist of the various time perspectives follows:

- *Immediate time frame.* The storyteller only deals with the present time frame as depicted in the stimulus; the span of the story involves momentary changes in time such as "waiting to see if it stops raining," and the story deals only with immediate concerns, reactions, wishes, or preoccupations. Problem definition or resolution is constrained by the "moment" captured in the scene, such as he was "sad because he was punished," without any indication of reasons or events connected to being punished.
- *Unrealistic time frame.* Implied or explicit time frame does not fit the sequence of events or the problem set. Time is not realistically integrated when sequence of events is dominated by passage of time rather than meaningful experiences or when the jumps are too great

or the intervening events seem to be missing. For some content, immediate time frame is also unrealistic because it is incompatible with the problem set or other aspect of the story.

- *Vague time frame.* It is difficult to infer a clear sense of time from story events.
- *Intermediate time frame.* Narrative goes beyond the moment in its implicit time frame but the story (implicitly or explicitly) introduces long-term issues that remain unsettled.
- *Appropriate time frame.* The unfolding story incorporates a realistic understanding of the passage of time.

PROCESS OF REASONING/COHERENCE OF STORY STRUCTURE

Difficulties in the process of reasoning, mirrored in the narrative progression and resultant story structure, occur along a broad continuum. For instance, difficulty with planning and monitoring (noted earlier) that impedes purposeful and sustained effort or self-monitoring in the absence of structure, though problematic, is not as dysfunctional as a thought disorder that leaves the person with diminished inner resources to make sense of many ordinary life situations. Research on thought disorder has led to the identification of deficits and distortions in thinking (see Rapid Reference 4.2).

Indicators of thought disorder in stories include poor logic; loose associations; distorted grammar; incoherent, incomplete, or fragmented ideas; and descriptions of aspects of the card that are not in the picture (Fish & Ritvo, 1979; Rund, 1986; Shapiro & Huebner, 1976).

The following coding criteria indicate problems with reasoning that disrupt the organizational structure of the stories and impair functioning:

- *Disorganized narrative process or a story discrepant from the stimulus (see Perceptual Integration).* The story may be unrelated to the picture or may center on a wide range of irrelevant stimuli without attending to the most important cues. The narrative may be dominated by meaningless detail or disrupted by the intrusion of personal thoughts, perseverations, or inconsistencies. The narrator may be unable to maintain personal distance from the stimulus, may be overly reactive or fright-

≡ Rapid Reference 4.2

Deficits and Distortions in Thinking

Cognitive impairment is a product of deficits or distortions in thinking (Kendall, 1993). *Distortions* refer to biased, dysfunctional, or disorganized processing of information, such as when thought process is dominated by personalized and tangential associations. Such idiosyncratic thinking translates into stories with content involving significant misperceptions of stimuli or entailing logical flaws, such as sequences of ideas that are contradictory, highly improbable, socially inappropriate, or unrelated to previous ideas (e.g., McGrew & Teglasi, 1990). *Deficits* refer to information processing mediated by schemas that are incomplete or limited, resulting in failure to consider intentions or alternative explanations and in simplified understanding of experiences that impair adjustment (e.g., Crick & Dodge, 1994). Stories told to picture stimuli provide an opportunity to characterize both deficits and distortion in cognition by noting what is incorporated in the thinking process as well as what is missing.

ened by the picture, or may be unable to inhibit associations (e.g., nonsense rhyming, repetition of phrases, introduction of examiner into the story, peculiar or incoherent ideas). The story is made up piecemeal without an organizing schema to focus the progression of ideas (e.g., earlier premises are contradicted by subsequent ideas).

- *Socially unacceptable content or conviction.* The content deviates from the socially accepted norm or is inappropriate to the task. The story portrays a gruesome, hostile, sadistic, or highly unrealistic or unusual sequence of events, leaves the character in an extremely helpless state, or the examinee's behavior during testing is unacceptable or highly unusual (e.g., "If the card falls forward, I'll tell the story. If it falls backwards, I can't."). Story content is a product of cognitive processes brought to bear on the interpretation of experience. Extremely hostile or bizarre content suggests difficulty presenting the self in a socially appropriate manner that may stem from maladaptive thought processes.

- *Incompatible levels of conceptualization.* The clinician should note problems with orderly matching of schemas to the situation at hand such as when the story contains ideas that are conceptually incompatible, when relatively concrete and abstract concerns are seemingly interchangeable (e.g., needing drawing materials and thinking that everyone will laugh at the picture) or when abstract problems have concrete solutions (e.g., a candy bar takes care of homelessness or nightmares).

- *Faulty logic, major contradiction, magical thinking, confusion, or fragments of ideas left incomplete.* Impaired reasoning is suggested by problems adhering to conceptual boundaries in thinking and serious misunderstanding of social causality. Thus, idiosyncratic reasoning or highly unrealistic cause-effect relationships may be evident in story content, story structure, or narrative process. For example, the outcome is jarringly out of line with actions, thoughts, or feelings of characters; a character is left, baffled or immobilized, to wallow helplessly in dire circumstances; the situation deteriorates, and the character is devoid of coping mechanisms to understand or react; or the narrative task is misunderstood (e.g., "can't tell stories because cards are black and white and not colored"). Sequences of events are not only unlikely (improbable) but virtually impossible (implausible). Thus, story content has significant gaps in logic and may include major contradiction in the story line (versus contradictory detail due to lack of precision in monitoring the narrative progression). Stories may include overspecific, overgeneralized, or personalized statements or lack transitions, and content may appear confused, contradictory, or illogical (incompatible details, unrealistic ideas, or fragments of thoughts that remain incomplete).

The term *Communication Deviance (CD)* was introduced based on the observation that when telling stories, certain individuals fail to establish or maintain a shared focus of attention with the listener and manifest problems with the organization and logic of the ideas (Singer & Wynne, 1966). There are three elements of CD:

1. *Closure,* or failing to develop a complete story with a begin-

---

CAUTION

To prevent overdiagnosis or underdiagnosis of thought disorder in children with immature conversational skills, professionals must rely on their own sense of norms of children's speech to detect formal thought disorder and to distinguish between normal speech in young children and imprecision in the expression of ideas. In children without thought disorder, the frequency of illogical thinking and loose associations decreases sharply after about the ages of 6 to 7 (Caplan, 1994).

ning, middle, and end; inclusion of passages with incomplete thoughts, unintelligible sequences, and inconsistent or contradictory details; omission or confusion about central aspects of the picture

2. *Disruption,* or interrupting the examiner while receiving instructions, abandoning the story line to express a tangential thought, or losing the storytelling set

3. *Peculiar verbalizations and misperceptions,* or significantly misperceiving the pictured cues, assigning idiosyncratic meaning to details in the picture, peculiar reasoning, and repeating words, phrases, or ideas unnecessarily. It has been noted that CD appears not to be a culture-bound phenomenon but is relevant across cultures (Doane, Miklowitz, Oranchak, & Flores de Apodaca, 1989).

COORDINATION OF INNER AND OUTER ELEMENTS OF EXPERIENCE

Much of psychopathology may be understood in terms of the failure of cognitive controls to integrate information between the inner and outer environments (Santostefano, 1991). The process of distinguishing between stimuli originating in the outer versus the inner world permits the individual to judge the realities of the environment apart from personal preoccupations. Thus, reality testing requires the individual to coordinate information that is internally represented (i.e., schemas) with external cues. The narrator demonstrates poor reality testing when he or she does not inhibit responses that are socially unacceptable or at odds with the picture presented (both in the Rorschach and the TAT) as well as when stories include logically incompatible details or implausible sequences of events (see previous section on process of reasoning).

Inner representations such as strivings, goals, or a sense of conviction or commitment give meaning and coherence to external reality, allowing individuals to reflect on past experiences, to deliberate before acting, and, ultimately, to act purposefully. Stories that progress through a series of external events or actions with no link to inner states suggest that the narrator is not coordinating the inner and outer dimensions of experience. Similarly, highly trivial or stereotyped (scripted) content suggests that the narrator is not looking beneath the surface. Describing a character as someone who is bored but practices the violin for hours would suggest a disconnection between feelings and actions. The narrator demonstrates coordination of inner and outer perspectives when the characters acknowledge internal and external sources of tension (e.g., remorse, guilt, and shame as well as external punishment following hurtful action) and when characters' outward actions are guided by durable intentions (motives, goals, principles) rather than external provocations. The following indices of problems or strengths with coordinating the inner and outer elements of experience emphasize the connections among circumstances, intentions, means, and outcomes:

- *Impetus for action of characters comes from external demand, greed, or rebellion rather than inner purpose.* An example is fear of punishment without a desire to do what is right.
- *Characters act or react on the basis of vague or undefined emotions, wishful thinking, or previous story event rather than purposeful, realistic attempts at problem resolution.*
- *Characters lack responsibility for actions, outcomes, or welfare of others.* There is an implicit or explicit absence of internally represented moral standards or sense of accountability. For example, there is transgression without internal or external consequence, characters are left in misery by others, serious mistakes are inconsequential, or characters are clearly unresponsive to each other or have no need for closure of obviously "unfinished business."
- *Self-presentation is not congruent with social convention and suggests problems in attunement with the surroundings and with normative expectations.* Problems with socially appropriate self-presentation are reflected in the story content or in the narrator's behavior. Characters are antisocial, morbidly helpless, or significantly at odds with normal interpersonal demands or circumstances. The narrator's demeanor during testing strains acceptable bounds.
- *Wishes and fantasies are distinguished from realistic appraisal.* Inner preoccupations (needs, desires) are separated from reality (external demands). Implications of a situation are sized up by acknowledging inner states as well as external sources of tensions or supports. An accurate reading of the stimulus configuration is necessary.
- *Motives and intentions are linked with appropriate actions and outcomes in ways that are clearly defined rather than vague or stereotyped and keep within a realis-*

tic grasp of social causality. Actions or external occurrences are specifically linked with intentions or emotions; convictions engender constructive actions. Thus, intrapersonal cohesion is evident in congruence among feelings, thoughts, actions, and outcomes (characters' outward actions are coordinated with the inner life of feelings, thoughts, purposes, or motives).

COORDINATION OF PERSPECTIVES OF DIFFERENT INDIVIDUALS

Intrapersonal or self-schemas are structures that connect various components of the inner and outer worlds of one individual, whereas interpersonal schemas pertain to social experiences and expectations across individuals. Both intra- and interpersonal schemas are products of cognitive-emotional processes that are similar in complexity and organization. Therefore, individuals who reason simplistically about their own feelings or motives in various situations apply similar reasoning to understand others. Interpersonal schemas organize perspectives of different individuals by coordinating their inner and outer experiences (intrapersonal schemas). If the intrapersonal schemas are dominated by standards or principles of fair play as opposed to by compliance with social obligations or "duty," then these respective themes will also organize interpersonal encounters. Full coordination of others' intrapersonal schemas would require an implicit understanding that each person brings to the current situation a unique history of experiences and perspectives. TAT cards portraying only one character (1, 3BM) have the potential to reveal coordination of perspectives because intrapersonal schemas include expectations of support or hindrance from others, as well as abstract values or standards (e.g., empathy, courage, commitment) that govern interpersonal relatedness. The following characteristics of TAT stories indicate that the narrator meaningfully coordinates perspectives of different individuals:

- *Views and needs of all characters depicted in the stimulus or story (if characters are added to those pictured) are considered in the resolution rather than centering on only one character.* All characters shown should be included according to their ages and roles as depicted in the card but need not be specifically mentioned. For instance, in Card 2 the characters in the background may be described as the family. If only one character is pictured and none is added, the examiner should consider the implicit connection of this character with others or with societal standards or expectations. This category is not checked if a person portrayed in the stimulus is excluded from the story.

- *Characters are meaningfully related to one another.* Relationships are not one-sided but reciprocal. Characters are responsive to one another rather than entrenched in separate concerns or insights that are not communicated. Multiple perspectives are coordinated so that views and needs of all characters are addressed with appropriate communication among them. This category is not checked if the characters talk past each other or if the relationship has an inferior-superior tone where one individual is successful or heroic while the others suffer, are helpless, or just stand by as foils.

- *Characters retain their individuality (convictions, intentions, outcomes) while interacting in a cooperative or mutually enhancing manner.* Characters who are emotionally engaged with one another maintain appropriate boundaries by allowing independent aims and interests in mutually enhancing interactions. Thus, characters are aware of each other's motives and intentions, share feelings and ideas, or influence or support one another (versus reacting to each others' demands or provocations). Attunement with stimulus configuration has implications for coordinating the inner and outer worlds and for coordinating perspectives of different individuals. Therefore, to code this category, characters' individuality must match their depiction in the stimulus. In other words, different characters' emotions must match pictured cues. For example, characters' posture and facial expressions are congruent with their outer circumstances and with their thoughts and feelings.

- *Details and sequences of events are cohesive.* There are no major gaps and story details are compatible with a unified theme that matches the constructive schemas for intra- and interpersonal problem solving. Relationships of characters to one another are well defined (clear and specific) rather than vague or stereotypic.

COGNITIVE-EXPERIENTIAL INTEGRATION

Thematic apperceptive narratives permit assessment of the complexity of the cognitive-experiential schemas by revealing the extent and clarity of differentiation of dimensions of experience (e.g., in circumstances, thoughts, feelings, actions, intentions, relationships) and the cohesiveness of the integration of the differentiated elements (e.g., causes-effects, means-ends, feelings-thoughts, intentions-actions). What is differentiated is a function of what is salient for the individual, whereas the integration of what is differentiated demonstrates the principles that bring coherence to the narrator's experiences, both moment to moment and in the long term (see Rapid Reference 4.3). In determining the level of cognitive-experiential integration, the specific details of the story are considered in relation to each other, to the overall themes, and to the pictured stimulus (e.g., feelings and intentions tied to each other, to action, and events versus just describing feelings portrayed in the picture). Realistic appraisal of circumstances suffers when the narrator fails to differentiate and coordinate various elements of experience such as the intent and impact of actions or possibility and probability.

Rapid Reference 4.3

Cognitive Complexity

Complexity is a product of differentiation and integration applied to information processing (e.g., Streufert & Nogami, 1989). *Differentiation* is the process of distinguishing different dimensions within a domain or taking different perspectives. This process of differentiation may be qualified according to the clarity or vagueness of the distinctions. *Integration* is the process of relating conceptually the dimensions that are distinguished. Thus, long- and short-term views may be reconciled, and intentions and impact of actions may be clearly differentiated yet coordinated.

Well-developed schemas enhance adjustment because they permit the individual to engage in complex information processing by promoting awareness of intricacies and ambiguities. Individuals who maintain more complex distinctions among various aspects of themselves (self-schema) are better able to cope with stressors (Linville, 1987), presumably because their well-differentiated mental sets enable them to organize external threat and inner states, such as negative emotion. Coming to grips with complicated, ambiguous, or stressful situations (or tasks) requires the individual to draw systematically from schemas, whereas the individual may manage familiar or routine events (or tasks) by applying ready-made or well-learned schemas (e.g., Derry, 1996; Hammer, 1996). It should be noted that the complexity of the thought process may be disrupted during stressful episodes where the individual may function below characteristic levels (see Rapid Reference

> # DON'T FORGET
>
> A narrator's difficulties with flexibly applying schemas to accomplish the storytelling task signal that he or she may have problems dealing with situations making similar demands.

4.4). Stressful events may activate schemas that amplify the feeling of threat and evoke a sense of oneself as vulnerable and unable to cope with the distressing emotion or situation (Shirk, Boergers, Eason, & Van Horn, 1998).

Five Levels of Cognitive-Experiential Integration (choose the level that fits best)

1. Disorganized

The narrator's schemas for understanding experiences are impaired (distorted or simplified) due to limitations in deciphering social cues, grasping implica-

≡Rapid Reference 4.4

Stress and Thought Processes

Certain dimensions of thinking are vulnerable to change during stressful episodes (Pennebaker, 1990):

- *Breadth of perspective.* The focus of attention and thought is narrowed to immediate concerns.

- *Self-reflection.* Individuals are less likely to reflect on the causes and effects of their actions, thoughts, and feelings.

- *Awareness of emotion.* Individuals are less aware of fluctuations in their mood states.

Indeed, high levels of stress result in a general blunting of emotions and failure to examine one's motives. The levels of thought assessed with thematic apperceptive narratives reflect previously organized schemas that are indicative of the individual's characteristic ways of functioning under the relatively unstructured conditions presented by the task. Stress or other unusual circumstances may restrict the thought process.

tions of situations, or distinguishing causes and effects as indicated by any of the following: (a) discrepant level of perceptual integration; (b) problems with reasoning and conceptualization such that ideas that "don't go together" are combined; highly idiosyncratic or illogical assumptions about the self or the world, such as highly implausible or unrealistic events and incompatible or contradictory ideas in the story; (c) inability of the narrator to monitor the flow of ideas (perseveration such as repeated phrases; uncorrected fragments or incomplete ideas; incompatible story components such as jarring contradictions among feelings, thoughts, intentions, or actions); (d) gross departure of content from social expectation (extreme helplessness of any character; bizarre, gruesome, or socially unacceptable story content or inappropriate behavior during test administration); (e) the narrator's inability to understand the task as opposed to finding it difficult; and (f) the narrator's inability to maintain distance from the stimulus by being overly reactive to or frightened by the picture.

Lapses in logical thinking, including marked distortion in understanding of cause-effect relationship or difficulty separating fantasy from reality, may be evident even when content per se is not inappropriate. The stories illustrating this level were told to TAT Card 1 by children who were diagnosed with emotional disorders and were being served in a special education program.

Roger, age 9-8, WISC-III IQ score of 66

Card 1. Are there any colored pictures? [E: No, they're just black and white.] He's like painting. [E: He's painting?] He's thinking of something. I don't know what that is because it's not in color. He's thinking. [E: What's happening?] Nothing. This is a violin. He's thinking about playing the violin. [E: Turns out?] Then he plays the violin. [E: Feeling?] That he want to play the violin.

The narrator's comments about not knowing what something is because of the color suggest faulty understanding of the task and difficulty explaining the scene presented. Although initially baffled, he goes on to tell a simplistic story (boy wants to play the violin, then plays) with the help of prompts. The degree of concreteness coupled with the request for the more familiar colored pictures suggests impaired functioning.

Elizabeth, age 10-9, WISC-III IQ score of 100

Card 1. [Yells] I don't know! Ung . . . [E: Is this pretty tough?] Um-huh. [E: Well, why don't you start by telling me what is happening in the picture?] The

. . . person is thinking. [E: What was happening before?] I don't know . . . Maybe he's having trouble. [E: Turns out?] I don't know . . . [E: Well, the story is not in the picture, so it's up to you to make guesses.] No! I don't want to make guesses! [E: There are many ways to give right answers.] Uck . . . ckk . . . ckkk . . . ck . . . [E: What are some things he might be thinking?] I don't know! Feels very, very sad. [burps] [E: Turns out?] He's happy againnnnnnnahhhh!

The child's behavior during testing and style of not telling the story are important considerations. Elizabeth's expression of difficulty with the task by yelling and making random noises is not socially acceptable.

Johnny, age 9-2, WISC-III IQ score of 114

Card 1. A kid was making a violin [child dropped card] [E: That's okay.] and he was bored. He didn't know what to do with it. He didn't, he didn't know what to do with it. He was getting tired. It was almost his bedtime, and he wanted to know what to do with it but he didn't know what to do with it. He kept thinking of what to do. He didn't think of anything; he just sat there and thought of what to do. He didn't know what to do with the violin. He didn't know very much about music. It was getting dark, and he didn't know what to do so he just sat there and was thinking thinking. It was almost midnight. And he fell asleep before he could think of anything.

The sophistication required for "making a violin" is incongruous with being bored and with not knowing what to do with it. The character's having no idea of what to do with the violin that he made and his helpless (perseverative) immobility is paralleled by the narrator's inability to generate constructive coping responses to the task.

2. Rudimentary
Serious limitations in integrative reasoning are due to a highly simplified process of reasoning (deficit) indicated by any of the following:

1. Feelings or other inner states are not explained beyond simple connection to the stimulus or isolated event;
2. Causal inferences are minimal, extremely basic, or vague (e.g., "something bad happened");
3. Characters are distinguished by the way they look in the picture

("descriptive") or by outward actions without grasping differences in their intentions, feelings, history, or circumstances. Characters may focus on immediate or self-centered concerns and respond to situational provocation or vague emotions rather than being guided by deliberate intention or anticipation of realistic consequences;

4. Outcomes are vague, insufficiently related to a transitional process (means to ends), or fail to resolve the problem beyond the moment. Solutions to problems may be characterized by wishful (improbable but not impossible), or mildly unrealistic (naive) strategies or avoidance of conflict.

5. The narrator ignores important perceptual cues or leaves feelings or transitions unexplained with "gaps" in communication or understanding.

Consider again Jim's response to Card 1:

Jim, age 16, WAIS-R IQ score of 96, diagnosed with conduct disorder
    Card 1. He's looking at a violin. Probably bored, doesn't want to do. Somebody put it in front of him. Feeling angry and mad 'cause somebody asking him to do it. So he doesn't do it.

Jim's story illustrates two integration problems at this level: (a) He is "stuck" in the needs of one character's reaction to immediate circumstance or provocation without considering intentions or other contextual factors. Intentions are not attributed to the person looking at the violin or to the one who "put it [the violin] in front of him." Indeed, the identity of this person and the nature of the relationship between the person and the boy remain unknown; and (b) he fails to generate or follow through on strategies to meet demands, resolve problems, or anticipate negative consequences. Just as the character has no plans, the story progresses in piecemeal fashion without an overall plan on the part of the narrator. Lack of conceptual clarity is reflected in vagueness or fuzziness of story details and in the imbalance among feelings, actions, and thoughts. The boy's reaction ("doesn't do it") is prompted by boredom and anger without considering longer term strategies such as finding an alternative activity or compromise. These limitations in cognitive integration have hampered Jim's judgment and led to inappropriate behavior.

3. Superficial
The content of the stories is socially appropriate, but the narrative lacks "depth" and specificity. Reasoning coheres around relatively short-term pur-

poses or external demand, often in keeping with the cultural stereotypes or specific experiences of the narrator. The framework for understanding experience is dominated by naive, stereotyped or wishful thinking and superficial view of events or relationships. Characters are tuned in to external incentives or consequences with little satisfaction from intrinsic sources or from commitment to standards. Thus, instrumental actions are extrinsically driven rather than motivated by interest, curiosity, or enjoyment of the activity. Characters' actions are responsive to their needs and wants or to external pressure rather than directed by principle or long-term goals. Characters may want to alleviate their immediate distress or to obtain the usual things associated with the "good life" such as happiness, money, education, success, friends, or family. At the same time, characters may look for an "easy" course of action, or avoid age-appropriate responsibilities perceived as demanding. Therefore, actions and resolutions of tensions fail to balance long- and short-term perspectives, such as a stereotypic view of people and events or limited coordination of viewpoints of different characters. There may be a sense that the story is "borrowed" or "canned." The narrative may be based on a movie, a book, or a replay of actual experience without the flexibility to draw from various schemas to fashion an original narrative that fits the stimulus precisely.

Joe, age 10-3, above average IQ, diagnosed with Attention Deficit Hyperactivity Disorder (ADHD)

Card 1. Well, a kid joins violin, the strings, because he thought it would be easy and fun. But it wasn't because he had to make up all the homework he didn't do when he was in strings and the other kids were in class. When he found out they were having a concert, he hadn't practiced, so he tried to get out of it, but his parents wouldn't give him a note. They thought he should give it his best effort. Just before the concert, he broke the violin. He told his parents it broke accidentally, but they found out because he told his friends and their parents found out and told his parents. So they made him buy a new one. For the next two years he had to play violin, and he was bad at it, and he got really bad grades.

The kid who joined the band thinking that playing the violin would be easy and fun doesn't anticipate the frustrations, and when his parents refuse to let him out of his commitment, he breaks the violin. In covering up this action (tells parents it was an accident), the character is short-sighted, again failing to anticipate the consequences and suffers the price. The parents' intentions are given lip service (want son to give it his best effort), but parent-child perspectives are not co-ordinated (son deceives parents, gets punished, and gets bad grades). The narra-tor does connect actions with their consequences but views the negative outcomes as the culmination of a vicious cycle between the child and authority figures. This sequence of actions and reactions does not seem guided by under-lying principles such as intrinsic values or realistic problem solving.

4. Realistic

The framework for understanding experience is organized around realistic and practical considerations, with narrative construction guided by coherent prin-ciples rather than progressing by a series of actions and reactions (showing poor planning) or by borrowed details (stereotype, movie, book, or personal recollection). The story is conceptually clear and specific; the sequence of events reconciles inner states, actions, and outcomes and coordinates the in-dividuality of different characters. Characters act deliberately toward a clear purpose, although intrinsic sources of motivation or satisfaction (e.g., enjoying the task), the balance between long- and short-term perspectives, and the co-ordination of viewpoints across different characters are not as prominent or nuanced as at the highest level.

Ian, age 8-11, above average IQ, nonreferred, and well adjusted

Card 1. That's a violin? All right. Well, he came back from school and he didn't want to play the violin because he doesn't like it. Later, he'll probably play it because he wants to watch TV and do his homework and play.

The narrator's schemas include the setting of priorities and tolerance for unpleasant activities to meet responsibilities or goals. However, the storyteller doesn't reconcile the ultimate purpose or value of playing the violin in light of the boy's negative feelings about it.

5. Complex and Responsible

Multiple considerations are clearly differentiated and cohesively reconciled so that events are placed in a context that integrates various dimensions of the in-ner and outer worlds. Thus, feelings, thoughts, actions, and outcomes are well-coordinated within and across characters. Actions and concerns reflect long range interests, are precisely in accord with the stimulus, incorporate a well-conceptualized time frame, and show consideration for others. The narrative conveys an understanding of the complexities of the psychological world, including the intricacies needed to balance long- and short-term needs, aspirations, intentions, actions, and outcomes of various characters. Resolutions are mindful of the dignity of all parties and suggest flexible problem solving. Goals are more abstract than at the realistic level and may involve objectives such as self-development, consideration of other's feelings, or realistic desire to contribute to improving social conditions.

Benjie, age 9-11, nonreferred, well adjusted, very superior IQ (Other stories are discussed in Chapter 3, and the entire protocol is presented later in this chapter.)

Card 1. The boy has a violin except he can't play it very nicely. So he's kind of upset because he can't figure out how to play it well. You want to know what I think this thing is? [Points to the paper under the violin] [E: Up to you.] He's thinking whether he should keep trying or quit it because he doesn't know how to play it. [E: Turns out?] He gives up because he decides that he'll never be able to do it.

The boy's dilemma involves a decision about continued commitment to an activity that he cannot master according to his own standards. Unlike Ian's story, the meaningfulness of the activity is central to the decision. It is important to note that learning to play the violin is optional and, unlike other skills such as reading, is generally not considered essential for success. Therefore, it is socially acceptable for the child to a make a decision, and this process of decision-making is important for assigning the level of cognitive-experiential integration. The boy's decision is not based on momentary frustration with the task but on the conviction that he will never play the instrument up to his standards.

PRODUCTION OF IDEAS

The sequence of ideas in the evolving story is generated through a combination of two types of thought processes, *associative* and *rule-based*.

DON'T FORGET

The same behavior in a given situation may grow out of schemas that differ in their complexity. For example, some individuals may refrain from expressing anger because they anticipate a negative reaction, whereas others may refrain from venting because they understand its emotional impact on others.

Associative thoughts are characterized as automatic, and rule-based thoughts are characterized as deliberate (Sloman, 1996). The two systems of thought serve complementary functions. The associative system draws on the probabilistic structure of information, whereas the rule-based system specializes in analysis or abstraction and guides the focus of thinking to relevant features that can be logically examined. However, the complexities of the thought process are not adequately captured by dichotomizing rule-based versus associative thinking. Indeed, automatic thoughts are often rule-based for two reasons. First, the recurring patterns of experience have an inherent structure (e.g., the laws of nature) and, provided that they are coherently represented in memory, associative thought is logical and internally consistent. Second, rational inferences about the stream of experiences become automatic over time (Smolensky, 1988). Thus, rather than being devoid of logic, associative thoughts are typically sensitive to hierarchical and causal relations because they are based on representations of recurring events and experiences that are orderly or bound by cause-effect relations (Sloman, 1996). Accordingly, the associative thinking applied to the storytelling task is expected to be rule-based and logical. However, the logic and causal relations implicit in the sequence, content, and organization of associative ideas (automatic) may not be explicitly understood by the narrator (not subjected to rational analysis).

Associative paths may stimulate creativity, whereas logical analysis can direct thoughts toward goals. The combination of creativity and rigorous rule application is needed in all disciplines. Logical reflection on an inner world of richly elaborated and nuanced association is a source of "intuitive" wisdom. In daily life, individuals reconcile associations and rule-governed thought (Sloman, 1994) by establishing local (or explanatory) coherence or general (or conceptual) coherence. Local coherence applies rules and explanations to the temporary contents of working memory where individuals are more influenced by what they "see" than by what they "know." *Conceptual coherence* or framing current information in light of long-term knowledge is usually established selectively as deemed relevant. Thus, most individuals tend to explain their feelings or behaviors according to the peculiarities of the current predicament without reflecting on the possibility that their reaction is typical for them in a certain class of situations. Conceptual coherence may result if a disappointment spurred the individual to seek explanations that involve reflection on patterns of thoughts, feelings, and actions across time and settings.

≡Rapid Reference 4.5

Distractibility and Associative Thinking

Various sources of distractibility have been linked to attentional disorders (Levine, 1987):

1. Visual or auditory stimuli: detecting and responding to irrelevant visual and auditory information.
2. Appetite: the "insatiability" that is often said to describe attentionally disordered children.
3. Peers: responsible for difficulty focusing on class work.
4. Free-flight distractibility: tendency to free-associate so that the mental associations themselves become a source of distraction (e.g., daydreaming).

To meet the storytelling task demand, there must be some effortful coordination between being "reminded" (by the pictured cues) through an associative process and using deliberate thought to construct a logical story that explains the stimulus and satisfies the instructions. The question, when coding the level of associative thinking, is whether ideas are successive associations elicited by a previous thought, stimulus, feeling, specific experience, or stereotype, or whether ideas are guided by organized personal schemas that lend coherence to the story details. Problems organizing or inhibiting associations have been linked to distractibility (see Rapid Reference 4.5).

Five levels of associative thinking are described:

1. Tangential Association

The narrator makes up the story as one idea triggers another without apparent causal linkages and without anchorage to a central concept. Loose or tangential associations suggest difficulty focusing on relevant stimuli, a problem with flexibly changing mental sets, or a difficulty inhibiting strong associations not pertinent to the current task (Weiner, 1966). Poor control over the attentional and cognitive process interferes with strategic and organized integration of ideas. Therefore, content of stories may be highly idiosyncratic (out of tune with expected regularities in experience), irrelevant, personalized, overly specific, or unrelated to the picture. Responses may initially match the stimulus but subsequently veer away. The narrative creates the impression that thoughts are fluid as the storyteller moves from topic to topic without transition, seemingly carried away in the stream of thoughts or details. In the extreme, the narrator appears to slip into an inner world or lose the focus of the task. The narrative may be characterized by difficulty attending selectively to appropriate stimuli as the narrator may be vague or imprecise in gearing the story to the pictorial cues or may focus on irrelevant detail.

Adam, age 9-8, with high average IQ, referred to clarify the source of his resistance to going to school

Card 5. Okay, there's this plant. It's really weird. It's real small except whoever comes in the room they disappear. People started to go into the room and they disappear. Finally, this lady peeked in and saw plant eating people. Then she screamed and the plant ran around and ate her. Finally, it ate everyone in the house. Then it went to next house and next house and ate everyone. Then started having babies. They all spread out and ate everyone in the neighborhood. Then went to other states and countries. Soon there were no more people in world. The one plant this only plant started to take over world and now they did. So that's the end of the world.

Although this sequence may have been borrowed from a fictional plot, it meets the criteria for tangential association. The stimulus showing a woman looking into a room serves as a point of departure for a series of associations to a minor detail (plant). The ideas generated have no apparent causal connections to each other or to a unifying concept.

The following story, comprised of a series of personal associations evoked by the woman in the picture, does not satisfy the task demand.

Stephanie, age 7-8, Stanford Binet IQ score of 113

Card 5. Ooo, I got one. Once my grandmother and grandfather went to New Jersey to see my aunt, and then my aunt went to New York to see my other one, and then my aunt went to see my uncle in Annapolis, and then my uncle went to see my great-grandmother in New York, and then my great-grandfather went to see me and my mom and my mom and my dad and nobody, and then we went to see you. The end. But that's really not a true story. [E: Feeling?] Oh yeah. The grandmother feels okay even though she just had a cold and my grandfather has a pain in his leg so he doesn't feel so well, and he's going to the hospital . . . in 1997.

After considerable associative verbiage, the narrator realizes she didn't tell a "true story." This realization may be an important starting point for helping her develop strategies to organize ideas. However, in response to questions about feelings, she refers to physical discomfort pointing to problems understanding the inner world and providing a clue about the nature of her difficulty with this task.

2. Linear Association

Associations may be described as linear when each idea is triggered by the preceding ones rather than being woven around an implicit organizing framework or plan for accomplishing the task. Linear association reflects difficulty shifting from one dimension of experience to another. Thus, the ideas introduced have some causal link to the preceding and subsequent ideas but are not geared to support a larger pattern. Difficulty with shifting from one aspect of experience to another is evident when the narrator overelaborates one component as thoughts, feelings, or action without a cohesive balance among them or when the storyteller associates ideas to the stimulus, previous story event, or emotion rather than deliberately balancing various dimensions of the task demand. The story progression does not grossly violate logical expectations, but causal connections between proximal story details do not bring conceptual coherence to the narrative as a whole. The narrator may associate different possible explanations for what the picture might be (e.g., giving two or more possible scenarios), and various alternatives may remain undeveloped. Ideas may be introduced as piecemeal responses to the directions, thereby showing some attempt to deal with the task (albeit in an associative fashion).

Johnny, age 9-2, WISC-III IQ score of 114

Card 5. Once there was a woman who went in the bathroom to take a shower. She thought she heard a noise. The noise sounded like footsteps coming up the stairs. She got her bathrobe and went out of the shower to see what it was. And she said, "Anybody there?" But no one answered. Then she got back into the bath. Then she heard some more noise thought coming upstairs. Then the woman came back out of the shower and said, "I mean it, is anybody there?" Still she heard no answer. She got back into the shower, and she heard more creaking noises like it was coming up the stairs. And she, then she yelled, "I mean it, get out of here or I'll call the police." Then there was no answer again.

She got back into the shower, then she heard the noise coming to tops of steps, then she came out of shower the last time and it was just her dog Fido. The end.

The first action is tied to the woman hearing noises while taking a shower. However, the subsequent actions are perseverative associations with no revision in strategy. Logically, the sounds made by Fido should have been familiar to the woman. So the premise of the entire sequence of events is a bit "off." Having landed on a theme, the narrator repeated the ideas with only slight variation. Thus, the causal connections among the ideas are vague. Moreover, the stimulus is not a good match to the story. The narrator follows a linear track until he lands on a seemingly satisfactory end.

The narrative need not be long or rambling to be linearly associative as the following story told by Jeremy (age 12, with low average IQ score on the WISC-III) shows.

Card 5. She's going through the door; she finds the light on, okay, she cuts the light off.

This story is an example of linear association reflecting minimal efforts of the narrator, who provides simple associations to the stimulus that are sequentially organized but do not shift from one dimension of experience to another (thoughts, feelings, actions, outcomes). The woman "going through the door" does not think about why the light is on. She simply turns it off. The story is devoid of intentions or causal connections that would provide an organizational framework for the story. Proximal details such as finding the light on and turning it off have an associative connection. One thought simply leads to the next without an interconnected network of ideas.

3. Patterned Association

The narrator introduces ideas according to patterns of regularities in experience or prefabricated story lines. Thus, a ready-made schema (scripted or experienced) is reproduced without carefully calibrating the response to the task demand (instructions, nuances of the stimulus, active planning). Borrowing a sequence of ideas from a familiar source such as a story, movie, television show, or a literal replay of what is recalled from a previous experience is a strategy to deal with the task without having to generate an original story. Individuals who rely on such strategies tend to encode the regularities in the stream of events without actively organizing information. Thus, in responding to the TAT task, the individual searches his or her memory to find a "canned" narrative that fits the stimulus. Often this formulaic approach leads to the production of a "stereotypic" story with the feel of a bad movie that is lacking in depth and missing a sense of genuineness of the characters. The narrator may include unnecessary details or, conversely, the story may be sparse with few or vague details. The reasons for characters' actions and reactions and causes for events are at least superficially incorporated but may not be precisely understood. In effect, the patterns of events that easily come to mind (familiarity, salience) are related without actively monitoring the progression of the story and with limited understanding of social causality. In an attempt to reconcile the story with the stimulus, the logic may be mildly strained or the match with the picture may seem like a "stretch."

Micah, age 14, with a WISC-III Full Scale score of 105, was evaluated due to concerns about rages that he had been experiencing since the age of two. His parents wanted to understand what Micah needs to keep his anger from escalating.

Card 5. A man and a woman's son didn't come home one night, and they got really worried. So that night the sheriff came and started talking to the husband, and the woman kept on trying to come in and see what the heck was going on, but the sheriff kept telling her to get out, and the husband did too. And it turned out that the kid was kidnapped by some guy. And . . . I don't know . . . the son had been caught stealing something from the store, and the sheriff picked him up and brought him into jail, and so the lad . . . the husband and the wife went to go bail their kid out of jail, but they didn't have enough money, so the kid had to stay in jail for a couple of days. And the wife and the father were worried and upset that their son had done it, and mad at the son. [E: Ending?] Their son finally got out of jail and got grounded for a long time. [E: What are the parents thinking/feeling?] They were thinking that they were going to kill him or something . . . not literally kill him. Get him in a lot of trouble, but when they got to their son, they were just worried about him, wondering if he was okay. [E: What is the son thinking/feeling?] He was mad that he got caught, and he was sorry for what he did. He realized that it wasn't worth it. He was scared that his parents were going to get at him.

This story of parents concerned about their child's being arrested reflects Micah's recurring conflict with authorities. Micah's understanding of this conflict situation emphasizes immediate consequences (concerns about being caught and punished by his parents) instead of possible long-term impact of his arrest or the wrongness of his actions (except that it wasn't worth it given the consequences of getting caught). Micah acknowledged parental viewpoint by association rather than reflective understanding. Parents worry and bail out their son, but their good intentions are not meaningfully incorporated into the son's conclusions (emotional and cognitive) about the situation.

4. Logical Association

Logical associations involve active and organized processing of the ideas that enter awareness. Ideas are introduced in ways that suggest some anticipatory planning. Thus, the narrative includes details and transitions that tie various dimensions of experience as well as the stimulus cues into a common context. The focus of the narrative is evident—events, thoughts, feelings, actions, and outcomes are compatible with a central theme despite some possible tangents or overelaborations. Causal reasoning governing associations is grounded in sound logic. The story premises may be a bit naive or idealized, but not unrealistic.

Mathew, age 11-8, WISC-III IQ score of 126 (VIQ = 137; PIQ = 110)

Card 5. A boy promised his mother that he would clean up his room, which he hadn't done for quite a very long time. So, his mother felt very relieved that he comes to clean it up. But when she came to check, the room was even dirtier than before, and she feels very angry at him. She feels she's going to punish him, um, and her son had ran away for a little bit and when he came back she made him clean up not only his room but also several other rooms in the house because he had been bad.

The premise is that the child disappoints his mother by not keeping his promise. Expecting to be punished, the son runs away but "only for a little bit." This indication that the son's disappearance would be brief signals some planning of the story's progression as the narrator anticipates a reconciliation. Upon his return, the son realizes that he will have to pay the consequences for being "bad." This set of associations is logical but falls short of the highest level because the reason the son abandons his intentions to clean up his room ("dirtier than before") remains unclear.

5. Integrative Association

Story elements are cohesive and tightly organized around a central theme. Ideas shift conceptually in accord with well-integrated, complex, internalized representations that connect intentions, actions, and outcomes within and across characters. Given that the storytelling process and structure of narratives are related, this level presumes a high level of cognitive-experiential integration as described earlier. Although the level of associative thinking generally corresponds to the level of cognitive-experiential integration, they have distinct foci. Associative thinking focuses on the sequence of ideas in the developing story, whereas cognitive-experiential integration emphasizes the coordination of various dimensions of experience into a cohesive narrative structure.

At age 9, Benjie's story to Card 5, shown below, is not particularly dramatic or complex but evolves from establishing a purpose (looking for someone) to taking appropriate action (searching) with the expectation of a reasonable outcome (of finding the person because of the implicit premise that the person is at home). Despite the simplicity of the story, the schema is well developed in terms of the intention-action-outcome set and serves as an implicit organizational structure that guides the introduction of ideas.

Card 5. A lady comes home or rather she comes into a room and she's looking for someone so she searches the house and that's it. [E: Who?] Maybe someone else who lives in the house and maybe she wants something of that person. [E: Happens?] She keeps searching 'till she finds him.

The following story told by a student in kindergarten also develops through a set of integrative associations.

Subject 203 (#90)

Card 5. The mother comes looking for her little boy. And he wasn't there. He might of runned away because his mother told him she was going to spank him. His mother was sad when he ran away. He feels sad, too. She thinks something bad might have happened to him. He might of got lost. He finds a friend and his friend helps him and his mother. His mother gives him a spanking for

> ## DON'T FORGET
>
> Analysis of stories, particularly in the context of a comprehensive assessment, can clarify the nature and severity of impairments pertaining to the referral concerns or particular diagnosis. Problems with attention, for example, are associated with every diagnosis. Therefore, it is important to glean the precise nature and severity of the attentional difficulty in relation to the level of impairment in the process of reasoning and organization of experience.

running away. Then he doesn't do it anymore.

Despite the unsophisticated style of telling the story (e.g., age-appropriate language, sentence structure), the conceptualization of the details in relation to an underlying theme is quite mature. The ideas are logically linked and cohere into an organized schematic structure. In contrast to the story told by Mathew, this one provides a long-term resolution as the boy learns not to run away in the future. Both mother and son take responsibility for their own feelings and actions and appreciate the feelings of the other. Each feels sad about the situation and seems aware of these emotions in the other. This balance of viewpoints is the backdrop for seeking a third party to facilitate a reconciliation. Subsequently, the child accepts punishment for an impulsive action and learns a lesson. In contrast to the story told by Mathew, this one incorporates external provocation, inner states, actions, and resolutions.

CASE ILLUSTRATION

To provide opportunities to contrast two protocols on the coding dimensions presented in this chapter, Figure 4.1 illustrates the coding of stories told by Oscar (O) referred with attentional concerns whose protocol is discussed at length, and stories told by Benjie (B), a focused and attentive student similar in age to Oscar.

The figure comprises a set of worksheets summarizing the guidelines for coding the variables described in this chapter. These worksheets are designed to help the examiner organize the cognitive dimensions of the narrator's experiential schemas. For each card administered, the examiner (a) indicates the presence of the characteristic described and (b) assigns levels based on the cognitive variables indicated. Subsequently, the examiner uses the patterns noted in the worksheets to formulate explanations for story imports and to answer the referral questions. Worksheets pertinent to emotion, object relations, and motivation/self-regulation are presented respectively in Chapters 5, 6,

I. PERCEPTUAL INTEGRATION

A. Degree of Congruence with the Stimulus

(Check as many as apply for each story) Cards→	1	2	3	4	5	6	7	8	13			
There is disregard or misperception of basic emotions or relationships depicted (e.g., excluding a pictured character; tension is not related to scene).				O		O						
There is disregard or misperception of characters' ages.												
There is a focus on irrelevant stimulus details.												
The emphasis is perceptual rather than conceptual (focus on isolated stimulus elements without positing meaningful relationships among them).												
Unresolved vacillation or indecision about what the stimulus configuration means (not wondering what one object is).												
Interpretation of basic emotions and relationships is limited by being significantly at odds with contextual cues in the stimulus (e.g., disregard or misperception of major stimulus features) or by absence of clear connections with story events.		O	O		O			O				
Pictured elements are adequately related, but the fit between the story details and the stimulus configuration is not precise.	O											
There are meaningful and realistic relationships among various stimulus features that precisely capture the "gist" of the scene (e.g., understanding social causality and appreciating nuances of the stimulus).	B	B	B	B	B	B	B	B	B			

B. Levels of Perceptual Integration

Level One: Discrepant. The premise of the story is not appropriate to overall stimulus configuration due to any of the following: Emotions and relationships depicted are significantly misrepresented, ages and roles of characters don't match the stimulus, tensions are not recognized or completely misread.

Level Two: Literal. Primary misperception is in the *inferential* or *implicit* meaning of the stimulus. There is recognition of major elements (or emotions) without understanding the psychological process (e.g., emotions or actions are simplistic associations to the scene that may be vague, scripted, or stereotypic) and /or without grasping the nuances of contextual cues (e.g., relationship of foreground to background, implications of clothing).

Level Three: Imprecise. There are subtle distortions of tension state. The story generally captures the implications of the stimulus vis-à-vis emotions and relationships, but the fit is not precise (e.g., timing, cause–effect inference, or context is not precise). Major object ignored or misperceived but feelings or relationships are not.

Level Four: Accurate. All cues and subtleties are accounted for in the interpretation of feelings and relationships (despite possible omissions or misidentification of minor details or some perceptual emphasis).

(Choose one level for each story)

Card	1	2	3BM	4	5	6BM	7GF	8	13					
Oscar	3	3	2	1	2	1		2						
Benjie	4	4	4	4	4	4	4	4	4					

Figure 4.1 Cognition

and 7. Completing the worksheets is a challenging process at first, but after becoming familiar with the guidelines, the examiner may emphasize the variables that are most pertinent for a particular client.

Oscar

Oscar was referred for evaluation by his parents at the age of nine because of increasing concerns about behaviors suggestive of attentional problems

II. CONCRETE VERSUS ABSTRACT THINKING

A. Concrete Thinking

1. Formal Elements of Storytelling Process and Story Structure

(Check as many as apply for each story) Cards→	1	2	3	4	5	6	7	8	13			
Picture is taken literally. Events do not depart from immediate time frame depicted in stimulus; feelings emanate directly from the scene rather than from story events explaining the picture.												
Instructions are taken literally. Each component of the directions is addressed rather than telling a story (with or without prompting).												
There is a lack of understanding that the story is generated by the narrator rather than inherent in the picture.												
There is no change or insight, or there is an absence of transitional events for story resolution or altered feelings or circumstances.												

2. Formal Elements of Story Content

(Check as many as apply for each story) Cards→	1	2	3	4	5	6	7	8	13			
Concerns are extremely trivial or momentary; content emphasizes daily routines typically taken for granted (e.g., eating, sleeping, showering).												
Inner states, intentions, or motives are vague or not elaborated (e.g., causes, antecedents) beyond stimuli, superficial impressions, or stereotypes.	O	O	O	O	O	O		O				

B. Level of Abstraction in Explaining the Stimulus

(Degree of abstraction can be gleaned from the way that picture stimuli are described when the respondent is not able to develop a story)

Level One: Enumerative Description. Content is limited to naming or describing isolated or irrelevant details of the picture without relating various components to each other or to a common theme. Feelings are tied to the stimulus.

Level Two: Concrete Description. Content is tied to a more holistic view of the picture but doesn't incorporate inner purpose or motives of characters depicted. Emotions or intentions are tied simplistically to events.

Level Three: Interpretive Description. An "explanation" of the scene is provided in terms of inner attributes and outward appearance of characters (psychological process and events are distinct, yet cohesive).

(Choose the highest level applicable to each story)

Card	1	2	3BM	4	5	6BM	7GF	8	13				
Oscar	2	2	2	2	2	2		2					
Benjie	3	3	3	3	3	3	3	3	3				

Figure 4.1 (continued)

first noted when he was seven. Parents reported behaviors such as forgetting to do homework unless reminded and failure to turn in the work even if completed. His current and previous year's teachers also reported problems with completion of class work and homework. Despite Oscar's distractibility when doing school-related tasks, he has done well academically, having earned mostly A's.

III. INFORMATION PROCESSING

A. Use of Stimuli

(See Perceptual Integration and Degree of Abstraction in Card Description)

B. Planning and Monitoring

1. Formal Elements of Storytelling Process and Story Structure

(Check as many as apply for each story) Cards→	1	2	3	4	5	6	7	8	13			
Narrator gives irrelevant responses, silly content, and extraneous chatting while receiving instructions or narrating the story.												
Narrator complains about being bored or wants to stop ("how many more?").												
Narrator gives first-person stories or personalizations, suggesting inability to distance self from objective demands of the task.												
Narrator loses the set for telling the story (drawn away from initial focus by examiner's inquiry or personal associations).	O	O	O		O	O		O				
There are arbitrary shifts in perspective, inconsistencies, or contradictory details in the story.	O	O	O	O	O	O		O				
Causes for events or motives are poorly understood.	O	O	O	O	O	O		O				
No tension and/or no outcome. (If checked, ignore the two items below)												
Outcome or change occurs without adequate transition.												
Outcome does not adequately address the central conflict, tension, or dilemma as posed by the narrator.		O	O		O			O				

2. Formal Elements of Content

(Check as many as apply for each story)* Cards→	1	2	3	4	5	6	7	8	13			
Story characters don't care, are bored, engage in wishful thinking or short-term solutions.			O		O	O		O				
Characters emphasize immediate gratification or material gain.												
Characters act or react without clearly defining the problem or goal.	O	O	O	O	O	O		O				
Actions are haphazard and occur without planning or anticipation.		O	O	O	O	O		O				
Characters jump to inappropriate or premature conclusions, can't figure things out, fail to consider reasonable alternatives, or overreact.		O	O	O	O	O		O				
Characters desire to avoid or escape legitimate, age-appropriate restrictions/responsibilities considered unfair or incomprehensible.		O	O	O								
Characters continue to behave in ways that contradict how they think they "should" act.			O										

Content may be too limited for any to apply.

C. Time Perspective

(Check as many as apply for each story) Cards→	1	2	3	4	5	6	7	8	13			
Immediate time frame												
Unrealistic time frame		O	O	O	O	O		O				
Vague time frame	O											
Intermediate time frame												
Appropriate time frame	B	B	B	B	B	B	B	B				

Figure 4.1 (*continued*)

D. Process of Reasoning/Coherence of Story Structure

(Check as many as apply for each story) Cards→	1	2	3	4	5	6	7	8	13			
Disorganized narrative process with unfocused progression of ideas (personalized thoughts, perseveration, content discrepant from stimulus, or emotional reactivity to the picture).	O	O	O	O	O	O		O				
Socially unacceptable content or conviction (e.g., bizarre content; extreme hostility or violence).								O				
Incompatible levels of conceptualization (ideas don't "go together").					O	O		O				
Faulty logic; major contradictions; magical thinking; confusion; fragments of ideas left incomplete.								O				

E. Coordination of Inner and Outer Elements of Experience (Reflection)

(Check as many as apply for each story) Cards→	1	2	3	4	5	6	7	8	13			
Impetus for action of characters comes from external demand, greed, or rebellion rather than inner purpose.	O	O	O	O								
Characters act or react on the basis of vague emotions, wishful thinking, or previous story event, rather than purposeful, realistic attempts at problem resolution.	O	O	O	O	O	O		O				
Characters lack responsibility for actions, outcomes, or welfare of others (absence of moral standard or accountability).								O				
Self-presentation is not congruent with social conventions. Characters may be antisocial, morbidly helpless or significantly at odds with normal interpersonal demands or circumstances, and/or narrator's behavior during testing strains acceptable bounds.												
Wishes and fantasies are distinguished from realistic appraisal. Inner preoccupation is separated from reality (external demands or rules).	B	B	B	B	B	B	B	B	B			
Clear intentions (versus vague or stereotyped) are linked with appropriate actions and appropriate outcomes in keeping with a realistic grasp of social causality.	B	B	B	B	B	B	B	B	B			

F. Coordination of Perspectives of Different Individuals

(Check as many as apply for each story) Cards→	1	2	3	4	5	6	7	8	13			
Views and needs of all characters depicted in the stimulus or story are considered in the resolution rather than centering on only one character.	B	BO	B	B	B	B	B	B	B			
Characters are meaningfully related to one another rather than entrenched in separate concerns or insights that are not communicated.	BO	BO	B	B	B	B	B	B	B			
Characters retain their individuality (convictions, intentions, outcomes) while interacting in a mutually enhancing manner (in ways that precisely match the stimulus).	B	B		B		B	B		B			
Details and sequences support main concepts; relationships among characters are well-defined rather than vague or stereotypic.	B	B		B		B	B		B			

Figure 4.1 (continued)

G. Levels of Cognitive-Experiential Integration

Level One: Disorganized. This level is indicated by any of the following: implausible or grossly illogical events; discrepancy between the stimulus and story; bizarre, gruesome, socially unacceptable content; highly improbable, unrealistic sequence of events; abandonment of a character in an extreme state of helplessness or deprivation; highly idiosyncratic and/or illogical assumptions about the world including distorted understanding of cause-effect relationship; feelings, thoughts, and actions that are incongruous with each other and/or depart grossly from social expectation; socially inappropriate or disorganized thoughts (e.g., conceptually incompatible ideas, major contradictions).

Level Two: Rudimentary. Rather than idiosyncratic distortion, there is a markedly simplified process of reasoning (possibly a "descriptive flavor") incorporating minimal causal connections. Feelings or inner states are not explained beyond simple reactions. Causal inferences are nonexistent, extremely rudimentary, or vague. Characters are distinguished by the way they look in the picture (though important perceptual cues may be ignored) or by outward actions, with minimal differentiation in their intentions, feelings, history, or circumstances. Characters are tuned in to relatively immediate concerns and focus on short-term or self-centered outcomes. They respond to the situational provocations rather than deliberate intention or anticipation of realistic consequences. Outcomes are vague, insufficiently explained, or fail to resolve the problem beyond the moment. Solutions to problems or conflicts are characterized by wishful (improbable but not impossible) or unrealistic strategies or avoidance of conflict.

Level Three: Superficial. Narratives portray more complex coordination of ideas than Levels 1 and 2. The vagueness (lack of specificity) of story elements and superficial conformity with cultural "scripts" convey a stereotyped view of events or relationships. Relatively greater emphasis on external incentives or consequences than on inner life and lack of commitment to standards promote stereotypic view of events and actions that are geared toward needs and wants. Characters may want to alleviate their immediate distress or to obtain the usual things associated with the "good life" (feeling good, money, education, success, relationships). However, the narrative lacks "depth" or has "gaps" in understanding (e.g., disregarding some important aspect of the situation). Match with the stimulus may be imprecise.

Level Four: Realistic. Events depicted are realistic and convey coherence between inner states and external circumstances, both within a character and across different characters. Characters' durable intentions guide appropriate actions directed toward clear purposes or problem-resolution. However, the emphasis at this level is more on realistic and practical considerations than ideals, standards, principles, and/or intrinsic sources of satisfaction that characterize the highest level. Contextual cues may be ignored, but emotions and relationships are accurately interpreted.

Level Five: Complex and Responsible. The narrative conveys an understanding of complexities of the psychological world and flexible problem solving that balances long- and short-term needs and aspirations of various characters, as well as feelings, thoughts, intentions, actions, and outcomes within characters. Resolutions are mindful of the needs and rights of all parties, goals are more abstract than previous levels and may involve objectives such as self-development or realistic desire to contribute to improving social conditions. Story flows smoothly, depicts events in a conceptually clear and specific manner, and places events in a context that integrates multiple dimensions and perspectives. The inner and outer worlds are well-differentiated and well-coordinated. Actions and concerns reflect long-range interests, are in accord with subtleties of the stimulus, incorporate a well-conceptualized time frame, and show consideration among others.

(Choose one level for each story)

Card	1	2	3BM	4	5	6BM	7GF	8	13					
Oscar	3	3	2	2	2	2		1						
Benjie	5	5	5	5	4	5	4	5	5					

Figure 4.1 *(continued)*

During the testing sessions, Oscar was generally responsive and eager to complete tasks despite some difficulty maintaining his attention. When distracted (by a variety of stimuli), his attention was easily directed back to the task by a verbal prompt. He seemed more engaged and less distractible when performing the unstructured tasks such as drawing and storytelling than the structured academic type tasks. However, his actual performance was more organized with greater structure. His Full Scale IQ score on the WISC-III was in the high average range (114; 82nd percentile). There was no discrepancy be-

H. Production of Ideas/Levels of Associative Thinking

Level One: Tangential Association. Story rambles and is made up as one idea triggers another without apparent causal linkages to each other or to a central concept. Responses may initially match the stimulus but veer away subsequently. The content may be tangential to the stimulus and/or personalized.
Level Two: Linear Association. Ideas are introduced linearly in association to the stimulus, previous story event (e.g., repetitive elaborations on one idea such as series of actions), or emotion. Responses may center on addressing the specific components of the directions rather than the production of a "story." Narrator may try to connect proximal ideas but overall causal connections among the story details are nonexistent, vague, or implausible.
Level Three: Patterned Association. Ideas are introduced according to scripted regularities in experiences or cultural or subcultural stereotypes. The sequence of ideas is formulaic and may be borrowed (from a story, movie, or television show) or may be a literal replay of familiar, scripted experiences. The story progression is somewhat like a bad movie, lacking in depth or a sense of genuineness of the characters. Details that might be expected to be implicitly understood may be explicitly stated; few or vague details may be given. The superimposition of scripted patterns may involve some subtle distortion of the nuances of the stimulus or imprecise logic.
Level Four: Logical Association. Ideas are introduced in ways that tie various dimensions of experience into a common context. Logic and coherence of the narrative are evident (events, thoughts, feelings, actions, and outcomes are congruous). The story premises and supporting detail are clearly related.
Level Five: Integrative Association. Story elements are cohesive and tightly organized around a central theme with clearly prosocial and realistic convictions guiding the story progression. Ideas shift conceptually in accord with well-integrated, complex internalized representations. Well-developed schemas are implicit in the subtext of the story, which concludes without "loose ends."

(Choose one level for each story)

Card	1	2	3BM	4	5	6BM	7GF	8	13					
Oscar	2	2	2	2	2	2		1						
Benjie	5	5	5	5	4	5	4	5	5					

Figure 4.1 (continued)

tween Verbal and Performance Scale scores (117 versus 110). The Freedom from Distractibility Index (118; 88th percentile) was also high average. Scores on the Woodcock-Johnson Achievement Test–Revised ranged from average in broad written language to very superior in broad reading and broad math. Oscar completed the visual form of the Test of Variables of Attention–Revised (TOVA-R) as a measure of sustained attention. The TOVA is a computerized test presenting a series of stimuli in quick succession and requiring a response only to target stimuli. Although his performance was within the normal range, the rate of commission errors (incorrectly responding to the nontarget stimulus) increased significantly as the test session progressed. Elevated rates of commission errors suggest difficulty inhibiting responses to comply with the task demand. It should be noted that the TOVA was not designed to be used as the sole diagnostic criterion in determining the presence of attention deficit disorder.

Oscar's TAT protocol is examined in terms of the variables introduced in this chapter to address the referral issues. His stories, imports, and explanatory hypotheses are followed by a narrative summary.

Card 1. Um. Once upon a time, a boy was looking at his violin thinking that he would never be able to play it. Then his father came in and brought in a private music teacher to so she could teach him how to play his violin and . . . she said, "well, young man I see that you want to play the violin." And the boy said, "yes, I guess so," and the lady said, "well, I am your private music teacher, you can call me Ms. Bosh." And she gave him something to play and taught him the notes and then she asked him to play it. The song was "Twinkle, Twinkle, Little Star." And then she said, "that's the first basic violin music. Now, can you please play that?" And the boy played and made several mistakes and she said . . . made him practice until he got it perfect. He played over and over and over and over. And then he had to play so long that he went into overtime and the lady had to get paid extra. And so there was a recital coming up and the lady had told him . . . and Ms. Bosh had told him and then he . . . the boy started to practice very hard and then one day no, and then one week. One week, he was playing very well and then he was able to go on to another song. And she said, "you are doing very well for a beginner, how would you like to be the star of the beginning class." And he said, "would I ever!" And then she taught him even more music so he would know what to play for the upcoming program and then she also told him that it was a Christmas program. And he said, "Okay." And then he had to practice Christmas songs, like "Jingle Bells" and all those other songs. And then he had to be in . . . he had to be Joseph in a play and, no, he had to be baby Jesus and his parents were Mary and Joseph and after the play he had to play songs with the beginners. And then after the class . . . then after the recital . . . after the Christmas program, she made him advanced and after a while he became the top student in his advanced class. [E: Before?] Um, he was playing around and then his father came in, playing around with his toys, and his boats in the pond in his backyard . . . his pool in his backyard . . . playing with his toys . . . he was playing jump off the ship. [E: Feeling?] In the first part of the story, he was feeling depressed. Then, in the center, he started feeling better and then, at the end, he felt very good and proud of himself.

Content import: If a boy receives praise and recognition (to be the best), he is willing to work hard but needs others' help and support to overcome discouragement and lack of interest.

Process import: When telling a story about a picture, you rely on specific details from experience rather than on lessons or abstractions derived from them (this applies to all subsequent stories).

Explanatory hypotheses: After defining the tension in the scene, Oscar loses the focus of the task, replaying concrete details from memory as a script without giving them priority and without a plan for constructing the story. When redirected by the examiner ("what happened before?"), Oscar switched to a different train of thought without connection to the previous sequence of events (describing how the boy was playing around in the back yard). This pattern of stringing together the concrete details of his experiences through an associative process without organizing them conceptually to meet the requirements of the task suggests problems with deliberate organization of behavior in open-ended tasks or situations with few inherent guidelines.

Motivational and emotional issues are not covered in this chapter, but this story (and others in the protocol) gives no indication of intrinsic enjoyment of the task as the character seems motivated by recognition for doing well (becoming the star of the class). Possibly, praise and encouragement are effective extrinsic incentives in combination with guidance and structure to maintain attentional focus.

Card 2. This story is about a family trying to survive in the wild. Once upon a time, there was a man, a mother, and a daughter. They lived on a farm out in the mountains. The man was the farmer and he had to plant all the food and take care of the animals. The mother was the helper for the father and the daughter went to school and also helped her father. One day, on the daughter's way to school, she got lost and then she met a boy in the wild and he helped her out because he had lived in the wild for almost all of his life. And then he told her his story and he said that he used to live like her. Then on his way to school he got lost too and he ended up a green man. Green Man. And then he helped her back out of the wild and showed her the way from there to her school. And she got to school and then all day she was thinking about the boy and then all the time that she went back she was still thinking about him. Then she went out into the wild to visit him. And then when she got back home her father and mother were very angry. They said, "Rose," that was her name, "Rose, what were you doing out there so long?" And she said, "nothing, really" and then her father could tell that she was lying because her face always gets really red and she always has water dripping down when she's nervous and she's lying, and her father said, "Rose I can tell that you are lying. Now, tell me what, what happened out there." And she said, "Um . . . well, I was out in the wild . . ." And her father and mother cut her off right there and they said it at once, "What were you doing out in the wild?" And she said, "I gotta go inside and do my homework." And then they, her parents wouldn't let her inside and when they finally found out the truth they grounded her and "No more going to the wild. You can only go to school. We are going to be there every day for a month. And we are going to be there with you when you go to school too so we can make sure that you don't play in school, that you don't go to the wild, that you have no fun for a month." And she said, "That's not fair," and he said, and they said, "Rose, it doesn't matter if it's fair or not, we are trying to protect you." And she said, "That's so unfair" [unclear] and they said, "Rose, just go to your room." And she went to her room and laid down and started doing her homework and cried. Then later on after the month was done their parents felt very sad for what they did . . . they were ashamed of themselves and let her go out into the wild whenever she wanted to but they made one deal that they would have to supervise her. And she said, "Okay." And they lived happily ever after and they got to meet the boy and later on they got married [sings "Wedding March"] and that's the end. [In this story Oscar used different voices for the characters. The voice for the girl was high pitched and was difficult to understand on the tape in certain spots.]

Content import: If a girl violates parental rules, she temporarily accepts her parents' restrictions and supervision but assumes that they ultimately will let her do what she wants.

Explanatory hypotheses: The process of narrating the story is similar to that of Card 1, proceeding from statements about the stimulus to a story that develops through concrete details including verbatim exchanges between characters. Oscar's problems with monitoring and directing his own ideas and behaviors are evident in the story content and structure as well as narrative process. Just as the main character "got lost" on the way to school, Oscar seems lost in the details of his fantasy and dialogue. Parental supervision in the story likely compensates for the character's (and narrator's) difficulty with self-regulation but may not always be welcome (the character is happy when parents back away from their restrictions). Again, there is no indication of the girl's engagement in school work or devotion to a goal other than to live "happily ever after" with parents regretting their actions rather than the child being concerned about meeting expectations.

Card 3. Once upon a time, there was a little girl. Her name was Miss Latitia. And the people called her Miss Latonya because her full name was Latitia Latonya. And then after a while she had to go down the road to pick up some food and everyone kept saying, "Hello, Miss Latonya." And then she said, "Hello." And she had to pick up all of her groceries and she came back to her house and went outside. [E: Tell me what's happening in the picture.] Well, it looks like she's crying. [E: Are you telling me about the picture? Let's start over and tell me a story about what's in the picture.] Once upon a time, there was a lady named Miss Latitia and she was outside talking to her neighbors and then someone came up and started and said that the landlord came up and told her that she had a few days to pay the rent or else she would have to leave her house. And then she went back to her bedroom and started crying and she said, "What am I going to do? I don't have money. I don't have enough money." And then she started to look around in the city for a job. Then she found one. When she came back home she sat down on her bed and she sat down on the floor by her bed and said, "Oh, I have to start work tomorrow morning." And then, after a while, she thought, "I guess it is worth it because I do have to pay the landlord's rent and I think I would rather live in my home instead of living on the street." And so she went downstairs . . . she went down to the bank and begged the bank people for a few dollars. And they gave her twenty . . . a twenty-dollar bill out of their money, everyone each, and they had four . . . there was ten people there which means she got . . . a lot of money. And then the landlord asked for one thousand dollars and now she only had to pay eight hundred. And then the landlord said, "Do you have the rest of the money," and she said, "No, but I'm going to . . . but, I got a job so I could pay for it." And he said, "All right." And then he left and she said, "Whew." And the landlord said . . . then when the landlord was walking away he said, "That woman . . . she thinks it's no fun to work." And then she said, "Oh, am I ever going to think its fun to work?" And then she sat down by the side of her bed and started crying again. Then, after a few minutes, she got up and started lying down. And then she asked, she asked herself, "What have I gotten myself into? I could have gotten a job earlier and paid the landlord the money he wanted. But, now I have to pay him eight hundred dollars." And every year, the landlord would come around and demand four hundred dollars. No wait. All right, the landlord wanted one thousand two hundred and then she only had to pay one thousand and the landlord needed one thousand dollars more. And every year the landlord would come around and demand . . . , and the landlord would demand four hundred dollars. And she never paid and she kept saying, "I'll do it next year." And then after three of four years, she had to pay all the money and she said, "Oh, I was so careless, I could have paid so long ago." And then after a while, she ended . . . after three years, no, after five weeks, no, after eleven months, she was able to pay the landlord back. And she did. And she didn't re-alize that she paid the landlord more than enough. She had paid him five thou-sand dollars. The landlord gave her back her change and she said, "Thank you." Not knowing that it was her money still. And then . . . [E: If you feel like you are done just let me know.] Okay.

Content import: Without a plan for meeting life's burdensome obligations (keeping a job to pay the rent), a person relies on others not only for help in a crisis but for relief from ongoing responsibilities.

Explanatory Hypotheses: Oscar had to be directed to gear his story to what is happening in the picture just as the main character had to be reminded to pay the rent. The story is a repetitious series of associations with details not pro-viding a conceptual shift. Being carried away by the details and having no strat-egy for ending the story, Oscar abandoned the narrative as soon as the examiner hinted that he might wind it up. Again, the need for external direc-tion to organize ideas and behaviors is evident. Difficulty planning ahead is suggested by the manner of constructing the story and by the failure of the woman to anticipate the need for paying rent until she was in jeopardy of be-ing thrown out of her residence. The complicating factors are the characters' use of ineffective (reactive) strategies to deal with the situation (e.g., paying the wrong amount) and the view that work is "no fun."

Card 4. Once upon a time, there was a man named Rocky and his wife was called Lily. Then, after a few days, Rocky had to go to work and he said, "Gotta go Lily." And she said, "Okay. Have a good time dear." And he said, "Okay." And then after a while, Rocky got called to um, across the world and she said, "Rocky, when will you come back?" And he said "I don't know, maybe in a few months." And she said, "Oh, okay, have a good time dear." And he said, "Bye." And then he got called . . . after that he got called to China and he had to call his wife and said, and he said, "Honey, I'm gonna have to be here a little bit longer." And she said, "For how long?" And he said, "About a year." And she fainted and then she got off the phone and she said, "Bye, honey" and fainted.

And then he fainted. And then after a few minutes, they both got back up and Rocky had to help some Chinese kids because they were being attacked by some gangsters. And he saved their lives and ended up in the hospital. Then after a while, he called his wife and said, "Honey, I think . . . the doctor said that I shouldn't go anywhere now for a while, so I may be coming back home earlier than I expected." And she said, "That's great." And then she started planning a big surprise party for him. She invited everyone in her neighborhood. [Examiner prompts] I don't know how to describe this. [E: Feeling?] She was . . . in the beginning, she was feeling a little bit happy. And then, in the middle, she started to feel a little bit more sad. In the sort of end, she was feeling very sad. Then in the very end, she was feeling very happy. That's all I can think of.

Content import: One way for a husband to get out of his business responsibilities and return to his wife (and a surprise party) is to get hurt while doing something heroic.

Explanatory hypotheses: This meandering story is significantly out of tune with the stimulus (husband and wife amicably saying goodbye is not consistent with the pictured scene). Shifting external circumstances control the relationship between the husband and wife. Accordingly, a fortuitous opportunity to perform a heroic deed enables the characters to do what they want. On a more general level, the import of this story is that ordinary people have little free choice, but heroes do as they please. The happy ending (surprise party) seems a bit unrealistic considering that the husband is coming home because "the doctor said I shouldn't go anywhere for a while." Similar to previous stories, feelings are not interwoven with circumstances but added later in response to inquiry.

Card 5. Once upon a time, there was an old lady called Agatha. Agatha lived alone. She tried to keep her home as neat as possible. But, whenever . . . whenever someone in her apartment came over they always messed up her place because everyone besides her was sort of drunk. And Agatha said, "You people must stop drinking," and they said, "You know, we shouldn't, it's not like it's affecting us." And she said, "Yes, it is, see, you used to be nice and so did you." And then there was this man that was always mean to everyone. And she said, "Well, it's not affecting you, you were always mean." And then she said . . . after him she said, "You were nice too. Everyone except for him was nice. You guys have changed a lot ever since you started drinking. You guys must stop."

And then they tried to stop, but it wouldn't work. And then one of them started smoking. And then Agatha took . . . started making a . . . started making a vote for and it went worldwide for everyone that sells guns and everything like that and alcohol and stuff like that to shut their stores down, every store. As long as the alcohol doesn't . . . as long as the alcohol doesn't help people then they couldn't sell it anymore and it helped. People stopped selling guns and alcohol. And started selling good things like protein, juice, and calcium, and sodas and they were no longer selling guns. Instead of guns they were selling water guns. And then amazingly the rates of every store that stopped selling those things went up very high. Their rates went up quadrupled and then everyone wanted to thank her so they let her own their businesses. And then she was still old but she was, she was favored by everyone around the world. [E: Feeling?] In the beginning, she was feeling sad for the people. In the middle, she feeling a little bit angry and in the end, she was feeling very happy. [E: Before?] She, when she first moved in, she used to have it quiet and then after a week it started.

Content import: If one is concerned about a specific problem, one may go on a general crusade to tackle all the bad things in the world and become (unrealistically) a world-class hero.

Explanatory hypotheses: Rather than resolving the character's initial concern about keeping her apartment neat, the story proceeds as a flight of fancy where the character becomes a heroine. By now, the associative pattern of narrative development is familiar; the story progresses through a series of unlikely events with details that are poorly monitored. The details are incorporated as they come to mind rather than through the use of a more active process of selecting and subordinating the details in the interest of constructing a cohesive story to meet the task demand. Thus, ideas are associatively connected but not conceptually organized.

Card 6. Once upon a time, there was a man named George. He was a very tidy and clean man and he had . . . he . . . he was also rich but still kind. And then he had hired a maid and her name was Miss Phillips. And Miss Phillips was about I think . . . she was about fifty-six years old . . . now that's ancient. And she had said, "You are a very clean man Mr . . . Mr. George. Are you ever going to get a bigger house because you . . . you know that you have a wife and several children. Why you have more children than the Brady Bunch themselves." He said, "I know, I am not sure if I want to get a bigger house. I mean, all our memories are in this house. I'm thinking about it." And then she said, "You have to get a bigger house." He said, "I know but I am not sure if I want to leave this house." And after the next day, she said, "I have an idea, why don't you just take all of your valuables and take them and . . . take them with you . . . every single thing?" And he said, "But, but what about my memories?" And she said, "Your memories will live on with you; they won't be left in here, they will be with you." And he said, "Well, that's a good point." And then he said, "Okay, we'll start moving tomorrow." And she said, and then she said, "But how can you move that fast?" And he said, "Well, we'll get the fastest people in the universe to move us. And then on Earth . . . on the face of the planet to move us." And then, they did. They were moved in less than one day. They had moved to a big mansion. Bigger than this whole school complex. And after a while everyone said . . . after a while the kids finally found their parents and said, "Daddy, I, where's our bedrooms?" and they had been living there for three years. And he said, "I don't know, we'll have to get a . . . we'll have to put a map somewhere in here." And they said, "Yeah." And then after while, they had to post maps almost everywhere. And they did. The end. [E: Feeling?] In the beginning, the father was feeling a little bit sad and happy. And in the middle, the father was feeling okay, pretty good. And in the end, the father was feeling very happy, at the very end.

Content import: If a person is rich, he or she can make a fanciful decision such as moving his or her family to a mansion, but unexpected complications arise that are unrealistically resolved.

Explanatory hypotheses: Again, this is a far-fetched story beginning with a character's concern about neatness and ending with a family moving to a mansion and being so lost that it is necessary to post maps (external structure). As with previous stories, in the absence of planning or anticipation, events unfold through successive reactions to earlier events.

Card 8. Once upon a time, there was a young man and his father. The young man's father was very ill and they had to cut him open to see what was wrong with him. And they said, "Well, young man I don't think we should have cut your father open. The thing is he has an ulcer and also he had the flu, amnesia, and what's it called . . . cancer." And then he said, "What cancer, the flu, amnesia, and all those other things!" And then he said, "I'm afraid so." And then his father was just lying there. And then he said, "Dad, Dad, hello Dad." And then his Dad woke up and said, "Ah, what's the problem?" He said, "Dad you have several problems." And then he wouldn't tell him any more. Then, his father said, "Is he mad at me?" And then they said, "No sir, it's just a problem that we can't help." And he said, "What is the problem. Is it . . . is it something I got in trouble with?" And they said, "No, it's much worse than that, you may . . . you have the chance of dying." And he was like, "WHAT?" And then they were still cutting him open. I mean closing him. And then the guy was had a knife in his hand and accidentally ripped off all his stitches and he was like, "AHH!" And then they had to start all over with the stitching. And so, after a while his son had grown up and then his father died of natural . . . natural reasons. And also because that's the reason . . . and also because of the flu, cancer, and other things. And so he wished and wished and wished and wished that his father would come back. And then after a while they . . . during his father's burial the doctors ran up to the boy and said, "Hey kid, we had made a mistake, your father is not dead." And he said, "What?" And then he . . . and then they said, "He's just sleeping." And then he was like, "Then how come when he was awake he didn't he didn't realize that?" And they said, "Well, I don't know." And then he said, "Yes, my father's alive." And then when his father woke up and got out he said, then the boy said, "Hi dad, you're alive, you have no problems." And he was like, "Phew!" The end. [E: Feeling?] In the beginning, the boy was feeling sad. In the middle, the boy was feeling still sad. And in the end, the boy was feeling real happy.

Content import: When it is difficult to accept what seems inevitable, a boy gets his wish and finds out that there was a big mistake and everything is fine, after all.

Explanatory hypotheses: This story progresses like a bad movie with one-dimensional characters and unlikely sequences of events, including a magical ending. Not having planned ahead, Oscar comes to a point where he is not satisfied with the remaining possibilities for a logical ending to the story. So, he grants his character's wish by bringing his father back from the dead. As with previous stories, people do not face the consequences of their actions, and things turn out fine despite serious mistakes.

Narrative Summary

In constructing the TAT stories, Oscar enjoyed expressing his ideas as they entered his awareness without a plan for strategically subordinating the unfolding details to accomplish the task at hand. Sometimes, when the stimuli were particularly complex, the story content was not a good fit with the pictured scene, indicating that without clear guidelines, Oscar has difficulty gearing his responses to the cues in the surroundings. Oscar's difficulties monitoring the progression of the stories parallel the description of characters as requiring external supervision and guidance or as encountering problems meeting obligations or resolving their dilemmas due to lack of planning or anticipation. Characters who are heroic are exempt from life's humdrum requirements. These patterns are in line with Oscar's reported distractibility, inattention, and problems with organization. Oscar's tendency to get carried away with associated details (a style often characterizing individuals with attentional deficits) suggests significant distractibility. In contrast to Oscar's performance on more structured tasks where he was easily redirected, the examiner's prompts usually did not improve the story. Oscar's above average performance on the structured tasks contrasted with his relatively less organized performance on tasks such as the TAT that permitted him to set his own standards and goals for the product. Ironically, he enjoyed the less structured measures and experienced some boredom and frustration with the more structured academic tests.

Although Oscar's stories demonstrate some difficulty monitoring thought process and resisting the pull of less relevant ideas, content was generally socially appropriate. Moreover, Oscar's motivation to please others and to be recognized as successful was evident despite minimal indication of intrinsic investment in goal-directed activities. This motivational pattern, coupled with better performance on tasks with inherent structure and clearly designated response standards, suggests that Oscar will benefit from guidance (at school and at home) to complete assignments that involve planning and self-monitoring. Although at times Oscar perceives external limits as intrusive, he does respond to encouragement, praise, and recognition. Should recommendations discussed with the family and teachers prove insufficient, a trial of medication may be considered.

Benjie

The following stories told by Benjie are also coded in Figure 4.1:

Card 1. The boy has a violin except he can't play it very nicely. So he's kind of upset because he can't figure out how to play it well. You want to know what I think this thing is? [Points to the paper under the violin] [E: Up to you] He's thinking whether he should keep trying or quit it because he doesn't know how to play it. [E: Turns out?] He gives up because he decides that he'll never be able to do it.

Card 2. It looks like a family in the mid- to late 1800s, and there's the mother who looks like she's taking a rest and there's either one of the sons or the father who's taking the horse and one of the girls looks like she has just read a book and she's coming back to the house with the book she read. I'm not sure they let girls go to school at that time. Otherwise, I would have said she's coming home from school. [E: Anything going on in the family?] Just looks like they're trying to get the day's work done so they can make a living.

Card 3BM. There's a person, and she looks very tired or sad. I have to decide . . . sad, very sad. Someone close to her probably had something bad happen, and she's trying to get over it. Is that a gun? [E: Does it look like a gun to you?] No, a vague object, could be a gun. I don't know if she was depressed and shot herself but it looks like a vague object. That's why I asked because it could be a possibility. [E: What happened?] Maybe one of her family members died. [E: Ending?] She ends up getting over it. Lets out her grief and goes on with life.

Card 4. Well, there's a man that looks very mad at someone who annoyed or offended him, and his wife is trying to stop him from doing anything he'll regret such as attacking the person who was offending him. At the end, she'll restrain him and he'll stop and get over his anger.

Card 5. A lady comes home or rather she comes into a room and she's looking for someone so she searches the house and that's it. [E: Who?] Maybe someone else who lives in the house and maybe she wants something of that person. [E: What happens?] She keeps searching 'till she finds him.

Card 6BM. Have to think. [short pause] A grandmother's son just came home and told her some bad news that he was very sad about and she was both surprised and sad hearing this. That's it. [E: If making up story, what would be the news?] Well maybe . . . I don't really know, just something she's surprised and sad to hear. [E: Ending] She heard the bad news, and they're both a little sad and life goes on. I sound like a tv show.

Card 7GF. Okay. On the story before, I think they did let girls go to school . . . in a one-room schoolhouse. In this picture, the teacher is trying to teach the girl her lessons, but the girl doesn't seem very interested and the girl doesn't learn her lesson and whoever is teaching her gets mad for not paying attention to the lessons. [E: Happens eventually?] The teacher gets mad at her like I said. [E: Future?] Well, after she was scolded, she paid attention more to her lessons.

Card 7BM. A boy comes home with his report card and his father isn't very happy and he punishes him and the boy is very sad because of the punishment. [E: Then what happens?] Then he serves his punishment, and he's not very happy doing it but has to live with it.

Card 8BM. A boy, yeah a boy, more like an adolescent has to have surgery and he's dreaming about how it's going to be and he's a little scared so he's thinking how it's going to be. So he sees what's going to happen to him, and it makes him even more scared. I don't know why there's something that looks like a rifle there. [E: Ending?] He goes through it, and he realizes he was worried about nothing because he didn't even feel it.

Card 12M. A person is sick, and his grandfather comes to see him and his presence there helps the boy get better. [E: Grandfather think?] He's sad that the boy is sick and hopes that he can help in any way. Actually rather, his grandfather being there doesn't cure his illness but it makes him feel better that a person's there by his side.

Card 12BG. Looks like a field with trees and grass and lots of vegetation, river or stream winding through it and an old boat used once in a while if ever and looks like a peaceful place where a person would want to come when they're feeling depressed or stressed or when they just want peace and quiet. It's different from all the rest because there are no people.

Card 13B. There's a boy sitting outside of his log cabin and he looks bored and he's trying to figure out what to do and he's a little sad because he doesn't have anything to do and he can't find anything to do. [E: Ending?] He just doesn't get to do anything because he can't think of anything.

TEST YOURSELF

1. Which statement is not true of perceptual integration?

(a) It is unrelated to cognitive-experiential integration.

(b) It refers to the accuracy and precision in explaining the scenes in the pictures.

(c) A high level requires positing conceptual relationships among the perceptual elements.

(d) All of these are true.

2. Which statement does not characterize concrete thinking

(a) It is tied to immediate situational cues.

(b) It is closely linked to specific personal experiences.

(c) It fosters trial and error problem solving.

(d) All of these statements are true.

3. Which statement does not belong with cognitive-experiential integration?

(a) Integration of past, present, and future time perspectives.

(b) Organization of ideas according to causes and effects and other logical frameworks.

(c) Coordination of stimuli from the inner and outer worlds.

(d) All of these statements apply.

4. Why is time perspective important in TAT stories?

5. What are the essential differences between associative and rule-based thinking?

6. How do deficits and distortions in thinking manifest in TAT stories?

7. Disrupted schema development (due to attentional or other processing difficulties) is evident in TAT stories. True or False?

Answers: 1. a; 2. d; 3. d; 4. Instructions specifically cue time sequences, which are essential to the story structure. Moreover, time frame organizes thought; 5. Associative thinking refers to a stream of ideas that is not deliberately organized (automatic) but reflects the inherent regularities of experience, whereas rule-based thinking refers to deliberate analytical or logical thought process geared to a purpose; 6. Deficits are evident in what is left out or remains vague, whereas distortions manifest in content that is contradictory, illogical, or socially inappropriate; 7. True.

Five

ESSENTIALS OF TAT ASSESSMENT OF EMOTION

Picture stimuli, such as those in the TAT set that display dysphoric affect, require the respondent to demonstrate capacity to experience, modulate, express, and resolve negative emotion. Difficulty symbolizing and representing affect results in stories that minimize, overplay, or distort emotions by ignoring the emotionally charged aspects of the pictured stimuli, by overreacting to emotional cues, or by misperceiving the cues. The focus of this chapter is on the principles by which individuals conceptualize and regulate negative emotions. A situation that provokes a feeling activates both the emotion and its related cognitions (Bower, 1992) so that repeated experiences with specific affects, their associated situations, and actions become routinized into automatic cognitive patterns or schemas (e.g., Beck, 1976). These schemas link together the affective and cognitive aspects of mental representations with physiological reactions, as well as with expressive and instrumental behaviors (Lazarus, 1991a; Schwartz & Shaver, 1987). Any one of the elements in the network triggers the other elements to which it is associatively connected (Berkowitz, 1990). For example, negative affect tends to evoke physiological reactions, ideas, memories, and expressive motor reactions associated with that emotion as well as to prompt other negative feelings. The story form is a useful tool for assessing how emotions are organized within broader schematic networks.

As a result of becoming associated with cognitions, affective or somatic reactions develop into emotions. Thus, a "feeling" becomes an "emotion" when it is embedded in a network of justifying experiences that translates a physiological event into a "story." Shweder (1994) explains, "The 'emotion' is the whole story, the whole package deal—a kind of somatic event (fatigue, chest pain, goose flesh) and/or affective event (panic, emptiness) experienced as a kind of perception (of loss, gain, threat, possibility) and linked to a kind of plan (attack, withdraw, confess, hide, explore)" (p. 38). Accordingly, emotions are complex narrative structures that give shape to bodily (e.g., muscle tension) and affective (e.g., sadness) experiences by connecting the feelings to eliciting conditions and action plans.

Specific emotions are tied to specific appraisals according to an "if-

> **DON'T FORGET**
>
> Cognitive processing difficulties that interfere with an organized accounting of the emotions portrayed, and qualities of thinking about emotionally charged situations (such as the accuracy of sizing up the tensions) were presented in previous chapters.

then" formula whereby an individual perceiving a demeaning action will feel angry, and a person facing uncertainty or existential threat will feel anxious. However, if "anger" is a response to being demeaned, then the individual, in a given cultural milieu, must recognize the demeaning signals (Lazarus, 1994). The emotion "story" connects feelings to causes in ways that are governed by rules, and these rules are provided by culture (Lazarus, 1991c; Lutz & White, 1986). Yet, individual differences in emotionality influence the likelihood of appraising a certain event as demeaning or threatening. Through individualistic appraisal processes connected with the ebb and flow of pleasant and unpleasant affects, persons may develop highly idiosyncratic emotion stories that distort not only the perceived elicitors of feelings but also strategies for their regulation.

Problems with emotion regulation are at the core of child psychopathology (e.g., Cole, Michel, & Teti, 1994), being involved in both internalizing and externalizing disorders (Achenbach & Edelbrock, 1983). Regulation of emotion is necessary for the individual to monitor, evaluate, and modify emotional reactions over time to accomplish goals and maintain relationships (Thompson, 1994). Schemas that integrate information from the internal environment with cues from the external environment function as the individual's tools for cognitive control over emotions (Santostefano, 1991). Consider two children in the same family who responded differently to a canceled family outing. Josh, the 10-year-old, was angry about missing the trip and did not stop pouting until he was given a date when the trip would be rescheduled. His 8-year-old brother Joe was more concerned about the "baby" sister's sudden fever and did not express any disappointment about the trip. His "working model" of the situation allowed Joe to accept departures from expectations more easily than

Josh. Without such flexibility, expected behaviors (anniversaries, birthdays, holidays) or planned vacations may have the demanding flavor of a "contract" that must be fulfilled.

Three characteristics of schemas discussed to this point are pertinent to cognitive control of emotion (see Rapid Reference 5.1). The complexity and

---

≡ Rapid Reference 5.1

Schemas and Emotion Regulation

1. *Complexity and organization of schemas.* Two related sources of difficulty with self-regulation of emotion (including problems with recognition, interpretation, and expression) are lack of sufficient organization and complexity of the schemas (deficits) and dysfunctional organization (distortion). Deficits involve problems of regulation due to underdevelopment of control structures, whereas distortion involves problems of dysregulation due to maladaptive control structures that direct emotions toward inappropriate goals (Cicchetti, Ackerman, & Izard, 1995; Rubin, Caplan, Fox, & Calkins, 1995).

2. *Retrieval of schemas from memory.* Accessibility to prior experience from memory depends on the schemas that are activated. Emotions promote awareness of mood-congruent information through selective retrieval from memory (e.g., Blaney, 1986; Isen & Means, 1983) and selective processing of cues in the immediate surroundings (e.g., Bower, 1992; Mathews & MacLeod, 1994). Individuals sometimes have access to more wisdom when advising others than when facing such a situation themselves because what they know may not come to awareness in emotionally charged situations (Bower, 1981).

3. *Coordination of activated schemas with on-line information processing.* The individual's "on-line" problem-solving resources (e.g., attention, working memory) influence how schemas are confirmed or reshaped in light of the cues in the current situation. For example, individuals who ruminate on negative emotions rather than focusing on regulatory strategies are at greater risk for serious bouts with depression through the three following mechanisms (see Nolen-Hoeksema, 1999). First, ruminations encourage the dominance of awareness by negative thoughts that, in turn, exacerbate the negative affect, thereby increasing access to depressive thoughts and memories (schema activation). Second, the ruminative process drains energy and impairs concentration, thereby impeding more constructive thinking and problem solving (further disrupting "on-line" processing). Third, unsolved problems and failure to meet current expectations (due to problems with "on-line" processing) feed the vicious negative cycle.

organization of the schemas are critical in the appraisal of emotionally significant events and in generating coping responses (Frijda, 1986; Lazarus, 1991b).
At a relatively simplistic level, events are judged by their immediate emotional
impact on the perceiver without understanding causes (internal or external),
intentions, or perceptions of relevance to goals (immediate and long-term).
Such simplified appraisals spawn similarly simplified coping responses (e.g.,
exploding; fight/flight reactions elicited by fear). Complex appraisals enable
the individual to use broader motivational structures and long-term principles
to marshal strategies for handling the situation or managing the emotions.

EMOTIONS AND TAT STORIES

The appraisal of the sources of the negative affect displayed in TAT stimuli
and the mechanisms for coping are brought together in the "emotion story."
Although coping is conceptually distinct from appraisal, both simultaneously influence emotions. For example, the experience of anxiety involves
the appraisal that a situation is threatening and the perception that the person is unable to manage the situation (Beck & Weishaar, 1989). However, individuals typically do not pause to deliberate on their coping abilities but act
spontaneously on the basis of schemas connecting actions and expected outcomes. For this reason, the regulation of emotion occurs prior to as well as
subsequent to its onset (antecedent and response-focused regulation respectively; Gross, 1998). For instance, an individual hearing a loud and unexpected noise is likely to be startled. However, the startle response is
mitigated if the individual understands that the noise is harmless by seeing a
large book dropping.

Problems with coping may be confined to specific situations and represented in situation-specific schemas. Accordingly, self-defeating causal attributions of socially anxious and shy college students are restricted to situations
such as meeting new people where being shy is most troublesome (Teglasi &
Fagin, 1984; Teglasi & Hoffman, 1982). Indeed, coping behaviors are more accurately described as responses to specific stressors than as generalized coping
styles (Folkman & Lazarus, 1980; 1986; 1988). The coping responses seen in
stories about TAT pictures are built on the narrator's identification of the
problem prior to formulating a strategy. The storyteller's conceptualization of
the emotions as stemming from internal sources (psychological processes),

external provocation, or some combination influences strategies for coping with affective tensions.

Source of Affect

The regulation of distressing emotions depends on whether the individual attributes the feeling to specific external sources, to internally organized psychological processes, or to some combination. Logically, if affect is attributed entirely to external sources, then the only way to alter the feeling is to change the situation. In contrast, the internal organization of feelings would lend itself to internal regulation and to the distinction between the impact of an event and its intent. However, there are exceptions. For instance, depressed individuals judge their negative emotions as stemming from within but tend to rely on others to change them. The reluctance of depressed individuals to initiate behavior to alter their negative feelings may be due to a sense of hopelessness, lack of energy, or perceived inefficacy.

In a TAT story, differentiating between internally and externally organized emotions relies on the salience of intentions and purposes in the emotion-action-outcome connections. The basic question pertains to whether emotions are tied to a cohesive network of inner (intentions, shared psychological context) and outer (circumstances, consequences) considerations or pegged to external realities with possibly a rudimentary or stereotyped awareness of the inner world. Consider the following story to TAT Card 3: "He's sad because he was punished for doing something bad. [E: Ending.] He forgets about it." The affect is tied to the punishment, an external source, and not to the "meaning" or intent of the behavior (of the punished or punisher).

Stories told to TAT Card 2 by two 6th grade students participating in a study (Locraft & Teglasi, 1997) demonstrate a contrast between internal and external organization of feelings that were associated with low and high levels of empathy, respectively.

Card 2. A girl is walking to school and she's thinking she doesn't like living on a farm. She wants to be a great writer of books and write books about other countries like South America, Australia, and France. And maybe give speeches and maybe get invited to the White House. [E: Turns out?] Her dreams come true. It all happens like she thought and dreamed it would. [E: Feeling?] Wonderful.

The "girl" dreams of abandoning farm life for fame and glamour but only considers the external trappings. The narrator (rated by her teacher as low in empathy) pays no heed to the people in the background, associating positive emotions with an imagined "life style" but without a realistic process.

Card 2. It looks like she, the woman with the books, is going somewhere but she's watching her father work and she sees her mother relaxing before she works some more. She looks like she's upset about something . . . maybe they're poor and don't have enough money to send her to college. She thinks about it and it makes her sad. It turns out that she helps them with the work. They work well together because each of them has something they're good at doing and they enjoy working together. She helps them for a couple years and business gets better and they put away some money each month and after a few years she is able to go to college.

The "woman" in this story also sets goals that involve leaving the farm. However, unlike the "girl" in the previous story, she is grounded in the connection to her family and understands the reality of having to work toward her goal. More importantly, her emotions are assets that enable her to "enjoy" working with her family. In keeping with the general trend among the highly empathic children, this narrator's emotions are internally organized and woven together with cognitions into a rich and nuanced schema.

Internally organized emotions are grounded in the understanding that feelings endure beyond the precipitating event because they are sustained by memories (historical context) and intensified by prior feelings (the "last straw" phenomenon). In contrast, externally organized emotions are directly attributed to the situation without delving into the psychological world of motivation, intentions, principles, or relatedness.

Stories are coded according to sources of affect by choosing one of the categories listed below:

- *Unrecognized.* The tension depicted in the scene is not incorporated into the story.
- *Descriptive.* Emotion is tied directly to the cues in the picture (e.g., "this boy looks sad"). The feeling exists as an isolated reality tied to the stimulus without causal connection to thoughts or circumstances

beyond what is pictured in the scene. The sole basis for the identification of the emotion is the posture or facial expression of the characters portrayed or an association to the stimulus such as "this picture reminds me . . ." The word "because" may still indicate a descriptive conceptualization of affect as illustrated by the following excerpt from a story to Card 8BM: ". . . the boy [in front] is looking mad or angry, and the two men that have the knife are looking happy *because* they are killing someone." The response is based primarily on perception without interpretation (emphasis on what is seen versus what is known). Descriptive accounting of feelings also indicates assigning affect to external sources but relies more directly on the pictured cues than on the category below.

- *External.* The individual detects patterns and regularities between feelings and circumstances (and possibly actions) but is not aware of purposes and intentions. Feeling is virtually isomorphic with the circumstances (e.g., provoked by the situation or someone's action) without accompanying psychological process (e.g., goal, intention). The feeling is attributable to external source (e.g., blaming others) with a sense that the feeling would disappear with a change in the external conditions ("sad because someone yelled at him"). Internal states appear less salient than actual events or actions. Externally organized feelings are portrayed as (a) being tied concretely to the stimuli, (b) being tied directly to specific events or provocations, (c) being borrowed directly from "canned" stories (movies, TV, novels), (d) constituting vague or stereotypic notions about how one should feel, or (e) pertaining to the moment rather than organized into a cohesive framework of thoughts, actions, and outcomes.

- *Internal.* The source of feeling is internal if the emotions are cognitively organized inner states (e.g., "meaning," goals, ideals, values, standards) that are tied to eliciting circumstances (e.g., "sad because he can't play the violin nicely"). Thus, inner and outer worlds are balanced (conviction along with long-term meaning versus specific events). Feelings are implicitly understood as psychological processes associated with other dimensions of experience, such as thoughts and actions, as well as external circumstances. The key to locating the emotion as internal is the characters' "owning" the feeling. In contrast, the locus of the feeling is external if it is directly attributable to external sources.

Coping with Affective Tensions

In stressful situations, individuals employ some combination of *problem-focused* or *emotion-focused* coping strategies. The former subsumes efforts to solve specific problems, whereas the latter centers on behaviors and thoughts to overcome negative moods associated with an event. Problem-focused coping is an effective way to ameliorate negative affect (Folkman, 1984), provided that the adverse situation can be changed or avoided. Otherwise, there is little choice but to undertake strategies aimed at moderating the feeling. In those circumstances, emotion-focused coping may be the most appropriate strategy. Normal variation in emotional reactions and in sensitivity to stimuli according to temperamental dispositions (e.g., Watson & Clark, 1992) have implications for the appraisal of life events and the manner of coping with unpleasant emotions (see Carver, Scheier, & Weintraub, 1989). Individuals experiencing intense negative reactivity face greater difficulties regulating their emotions (see Rothbart & Jones, 1998) (see Rapid Reference 5.2).

TAT stories demonstrate three categories of coping: non-coping, immediate or partial coping, and long-term or problem-focused coping. For the purpose of coding, one of the three categories is designated first, followed by the selection of the specific subcategories.

1. Non-coping or Unrealistic Coping

The emotion is considered unregulated when (a) tensions are unrecognized, do not change, or become more extreme; or (b) coping strategies are nonexistent, magical, or highly unrealistic.

- *Unaware.* Negative emotions are not recognized. The narrator's failure to register tensions precludes the need to describe coping efforts by the characters.
- *Lacking change in affect.* The character is left in the original negative state without self-awareness or resolution. The final affect state may be explained by the picture.
- *Overwhelmed.* Extreme states of misery prevail, or negative affect escalates. Story character or narrator may engage in self-doubting or

☰ *Rapid Reference 5.2*

Temperamental Individuality and Emotion Regulation

Emotion regulation is multifaceted, involving inhibition of inappropriate behavior related to strong negative or positive affect, moderating physiological arousal induced by the strong affect, and refocusing attention to organize goal-directed activities (Guttman & Katz, 1989). Cognitive development and increasing regulatory control over attentional processes permit increased modulation of emotion (Cichetti et al., 1995). Thus, individual differences in attention influence emotion regulation abilities (see Eisenberg, Fabes, Murphy, & Maszk, 1995; Rothbart & Posner, 1985; Wilson & Gottman, 1996). An individual anticipating problems with regulating emotions in a particular situation is more likely to appraise that situation as threatening or as unpleasant. With the passage of time, affect and cognition reciprocally trigger one another (Terwogt, Kremer, & Stegge, 1991), as parts of the "emotion story" described earlier. Positive affective states facilitate access to positive cognitions ("stories or schemas"), whereas negative states promote access to negative cognitions (Grych & Fincham, 1990). Given that memory is encoded according to how it makes the individual feel, positive affect may have a buffering influence because it tends to bias interpretations and recall of social encounters toward a favorable direction (Isen, 1993). Such positive biases may be necessary to preserve optimal mental health (e.g., Taylor & Brown, 1988).

Dysphoric mood is associated with emotion-focused coping (Lazarus & Folkman, 1984) that is often short-sighted, as exemplified by depressed individuals' preference for more short-term rewards (Rehm & Plakosh, 1975; Schwartz & Pollack, 1977; Wertheim & Schwartz, 1983) over delayed but more substantial reinforcements and by the tendency of undergraduates prone to experience unpleasant emotions to seek ways to feel better rather than problem-solve (Westen, 1994).

other negative ruminations or display angry outbursts that serve no constructive purpose. Emotions may disrupt problem-solving efforts of characters or the narrator's attempts to develop the story. Character remains helpless, bereft of self-directed strategies to seek assistance or to resolve the feelings or adverse circumstances.

- *Reactive.* The story character or narrator may be reactive to feelings without a realistic strategy to deal with the emotion or the situation. For instance, characters lack perspective, are lost in feelings, or jump to premature conclusions. They may do or say things that aggravate the problem. Thus, characters are provoked to act without purpose or strategy.

- *Detached, resigned, or hopeless.* Despite registering the affective tensions, characters fail to produce any purposeful responses to regulate feelings because of a sense of futility or resignation.
- *Guilty, regretful.* The character wallows in unresolved guilt or regret.
- *Substantially unrealistic.* The tension is resolved without a realistic intervening process. Thus, affect changes without adequate transition. For example, characters may be content with unconvincing reassurance or may succeed as a result of a magical or improbable turn of events. The feeling is resolved through an unlikely turn of events (e.g., wins the war single-handedly; unrealistic demand is granted) or through dreaming or hoping (when action or request for help is warranted).

Immediate or Partial Coping

In contrast to long-term coping, which addresses the source of the feeling or problem, this immediate style is more oriented to doing whatever is expedient to manage the current feeling (minimize negative affect or enhance positive affect) than to attaining an enduring resolution. The emphasis may be either on changing the emotion without addressing its causes or on impulsive short-term actions to change the momentary situation provoking the feeling. If a feeling pertains to short-term issues, then short-term resolutions are warranted; however, short-term resolutions to durable feelings or problems constitute partial coping.

- *Decrease negative affect.* The primary aim is to alleviate the immediate emotional discomfort rather than to address enduring issues or causes. Examples include reducing anxiety by cognitive or behavioral avoidance, relying blindly on others for help or momentary reassurance, eradicating the negative affect through a change of circumstance that does not entail an instrumental or deliberate mediating process, and naively expecting that mistakes will be accepted by others upon less-than-convincing apologies.
- *Increase positive affect.* The primary aim is need gratification or reward seeking, particularly through unlikely means analogous to a gambler who might overlook realistic probability and relish the possibility of

winning the jackpot. Thus, stories may be overly optimistic with happy endings that are unlikely but not magical or highly implausible (non-coping). The narrator may tell a simplified story, overlooking some important issues. Positive feelings may prevail through a change in the external circumstance without an internally mediated process.

- *Excessive dependence on others.* Characters rely on others when it would be appropriate (given character's age and circumstances) to take actions or use other strategies.
- *Excessive independence from others.* Excessive independence is indicated when the strategy is not likely to resolve the problem in the long run without cooperation or communication with others.

Long-term or Problem-Focused Coping

Characters expend realistic efforts to address the source of the negative feeling or to promote durable positive states. Change is due to characters' initiative to address the source of the tension by planning ahead, altering circumstances, becoming self-aware, or realistically accepting or reframing the feeling. In other words, the narrator is capable of taking responsibility for the regulation of emotional tensions or enhancing emotional well-being in ways that balance long and short-term considerations.

- *Decrease negative affect.* Coping strategies address the source of the feeling as external (the actual situation) or internal (interpretation). Effective problem solving resolves tensions realistically for the long term, not just for the moment. However, sometimes the only realistic strategy is to accept the situation and deal with the feeling constructively, find meaning, or reframe it.
- *Increase or maintain positive affect.* The character uses problem solving, goal setting, or another strategy to promote positive experiences (e.g., goal attainment; relationship enhancement).
- *Realistic resolution of tension without seeking / receiving help or support.* Given the character's age and the dilemma posed, it is appropriate to resolve tensions without seeking or receiving help.
- *Realistic resolution of tensions with appropriate request for help or support (not passive, blind dependence).* The character does whatever is possible before seeking help.

- *Appropriate help, advice, or reassurance provided without specific request.* Natural and appropriate responsiveness of others enables the character to resolve the dilemma. Such help does not appear magically (others seem to "read" the character's mind or appear from nowhere) but occurs within a context of a mutually caring relationship.

EMOTIONAL MATURITY AND TAT

The concept of emotional maturity refers to the cognitive interpretation of affective experience. Certain ways of thinking about emotion are conducive to better reality testing and more effective emotion management. With increasing representational and cognitive development, global, vague, or polarized affects such as happiness or sadness become differentiated into more specific emotions such as pride, shame, gratitude, worry, or relief. As emotions become more nuanced and organized, the connection between eliciting circumstances and feelings becomes more complex (e.g., a child is unhappy when a friend "shows off" but doesn't dislike her in general). When emotions are not embedded in an organized network of cognitions, the individual lacks the tools to reflect on the causes of the feelings and strategies for their regulation. Thompson's (1986) application of the concept of affect maturity to the interpretation of TAT stories emphasizes two characteristics as the hallmarks of maturity: (a) The feeling is specific to a situation, person, or event rather than globally experienced (everything about a person is aversive versus one habit); and (b) the feeling is embedded in a cognitive network that includes specific understandings about feelings and ways to cope with or reframe them. These essential aspects of affect maturity are tied to two related concepts: the reality testing of emotions and the understanding that emotions are internal and separate from, though related to, the external circumstance (as discussed in the previous section).

Reality Testing of Affect

The key to reality testing emotions is in separating the individual's affective experience from the "objective" characteristics of the person or circumstance evoking the feeling. Without separating feelings from the actual characteristics of the persons or circumstances evoking them, the perceiver can only judge others negatively when experiencing discomfort. However, separation of the feeling as the property of the perceiver rather than as inherent to the target makes it possible to question the appropriateness of the feeling or to conceptualize alternative interpretations of an event or action (Thompson, 1986). It is the conceptualization of emotion as an internal process in relation to the eliciting context that permits the distinction between the psychological impact of actions and the intention of the actor. For example, the acknowledgment "When I feel vulnerable and you are preoccupied, I feel as if you are rejecting me" suggests such a separation. Otherwise, an individual who connects feelings only to external provocations might simply feel rejected without awareness of complexities such as psychological processes (preexisting feeling) and intent of others.

Causal understanding of emotions is not only important to the testing of reality but also to the regulation of the emotion. The conceptualization of affect as mediated by internal processes, including memories and preexisting feelings (Harris, Olthof, & Terwogt, 1981; Nannis, 1988), permits internally organized efforts to regulate the feeling. Otherwise, the individual "gripped" by the feeling state looks to a change in external events, remains helpless, or vacillates between opposite emotions (Thompson, 1986). Even when feelings or reactions are internally attributed, they are difficult to resolve if they are not adequately tested against reality. Feelings that are disconnected from or vaguely linked to causes or circumstances are not amenable to reformulation or constructive problem-centered resolution primarily because they are not sufficiently understood. Vague or impressionistic processing of information impedes reality testing as important details are overlooked, and affect is globally attributed. Alternatively, emphasis on detail without considering the broader perspective also impedes reality testing. Difficulty with differentiating durable emotions from transient reactions impedes the process of self-reflection.

Reality testing may be distorted in the service of controlling affect through the use of defense mechanisms such as denial, projection, and intellectualization (for coding defense mechanisms in TAT stories, see Cramer, 1991). Defensive strategies that reduce distress often do so at the cost of diminished accuracy in processing information about the self and the world. Within a schema framework, defense mechanisms constitute information processing styles that conserve preexisting schemas by distorting, discounting, or restricting the information that comes to awareness. To avoid becoming overwhelmed or disorganized, individuals may curtail cognitive activities in defensive ways or limit their engagement with tasks and activities to moderate the intensity of their emotions. Because defenses can distort perceptions of reality, they may hinder the development of accurate schemas about the self and the world. However, other defense mechanisms may be adaptive and may contribute to building a well-differentiated set of representations of the self in the world (Vaillant, 1977; 1992). In turn, complex and well-differentiated schematic structures permit the individual to respond to an event effectively even while experiencing unpleasant affect. For instance, an individual may tolerate higher levels of frustration if the unpleasant activity serves a larger purpose.

Disruption of cognitive processing of affect-laden information may be chronic or temporary due to the impact of intense emotions on previously organized cognitive networks (see Rapid Reference 5.3). Reality testing may improve when the intensity of the emotion subsides and the individual reflects on the emotion (applying previously organized schemas) or seeks out another opinion.

The distinction between the role of schema complexity and schema activation may explain the difference between two types of depression distinguished from TAT stories as "empty" and "guilty" (Wilson, 1988). The empty form is characterized by lack of inner resources to sustain interest (energy) in activities

DON'T FORGET

In a sense, all interpretive units apply simultaneously. Emotions that are significantly out-of-tune with circumstances in the story or discrepant from picture stimuli (see Chapter 4) suggest impaired reality testing.

CAUTION

The examiner should not assume a one-to-one correspondence between a particular story component and its interpretation. A response such as "This picture doesn't remind me of anything" may reflect the narrator's defense against anxiety by avoidance and blaming the stimulus (see Cramer, 1996) or the narrator's inability to develop a story around the scene presented. Likewise, stereotyped stories may be viewed as defensive strategies to regulate emotion by simplifying complex nuances that may be overwhelming (Cramer, 1996) or may be viewed as representing the narrator's characteristic style of information processing.

≡Rapid Reference 5.3

Emotions and Reality Testing

Emotions may interfere with reality testing by altering cognitions (Epstein, 1994; Thompson, 1986):

1. In the extreme, strong negative affect may promote inflexible or dichotomous thinking or even the loss of fundamental cognitive distinctions, thus making it difficult to evaluate the appropriateness of the feeling to the circumstance.

2. Affect may seem all-consuming and lead to the evaluation of others on the basis of emotion without further processing. Such simplified processing makes it difficult to judge the target of the affect apart from the feeling itself.

3. Affect may disrupt information processing about intentions or circumstances, resulting in the attribution of feeling to an entire person, group, or situation without making relevant cognitive distinctions.

4. Affect may lead to the perception of minor obstacles as insurmountable barriers to accomplishment as witnessed by the association of anxiety with avoidance, defensiveness, and lowering of aspirations.

5. Affect such as boredom and low arousal may lead to disinterest in processing subtle, interpersonal information, resulting in more simplistic, wishful, or stereotyped views (such as unfounded optimism in the face of failure or adversity).

Failure to make nuanced distinctions may lead to impulsive expression of feelings such as anger or blame or to the experience of threatening or painful global expectations (e.g., general expectations of being rebuffed or criticized rather than situation-specific determinations). Behaving inappropriately during testing constitutes a direct translation of feelings into action rather than managing the emotion or expressing it verbally.

or relationships, or to cope with challenges that would seem to be a function of impoverished schemas. The guilty form of depression may be related to ready activation of self-reproaching schemas by negative affect or social cues (see Rapid Reference 5.4). The empty form of depression develops early and is associated with more severe pathology than the later-appearing guilty form of depression (Kernberg, 1975a; 1975b).

Characteristics of TAT stories indicative of affect maturity include complexity and coherence of emotions, coordination of emotions, clarity and

≣Rapid Reference 5.4

TAT Indices of the Empty versus Guilty Forms of Depression

The empty form of depression, marked by insufficient internal structures to guide self-regulatory activity, manifests in TAT stories as (Wilson, 1988):

- themes of emptiness, unworthiness, loss, or loneliness. If the picture portrays a single character, the narrator's inability to introduce other characters leads to a focus on the person's isolation or loneliness.
- harsh criticism of the self or others rather than appropriate remorse or guilt
- description of characters as bored, apathetic, or feeling nothing
- explosive affect or impulsive action
- others characterized in relation to need gratification

The sense of "emptiness" is compatible with the inability to represent the support needed or with problems relying on these representations (inner resources) spontaneously (by introducing a helpful character not depicted in the scene or taking initiative to resolve the dilemma). Without resources of self-regulation that have been internally organized and represented, an individual may experience attempts by others to impose external sources of self-regulation as harsh and critical. The distinction between the "empty" and "guilty" forms of depression is an example of the usefulness of narrative techniques to examine schemas as adjuncts to the DSM criteria.

specificity in the identification of emotions, and levels of maturity in the conceptualization and resolution of emotional tensions.

1. Complexity and Coherence of Emotions (within One Individual)

- Affect pertains to characters' long-term interests or convictions rather than to immediate needs or provocations. Feelings are embodiments of durable inner motives and convictions (standard, goal, harmonious relationships) rather than reactions to the moment or to the stimulus or expressions of nonspecific distress.
- The affective impact of actions is distinguished from its intent. This distinction may be implicit rather than directly stated.
- Emotions, thoughts, actions, and outcomes are congruous with each other and in tune with social causality and stimulus configuration.

Thus, affect is attuned to the overall "message" of the scene (rather than being tied to a discrete part of the stimulus, isolated event, or preceding story detail), is meaningfully woven into the unfolding narrative, and changes as appropriate.

- Feelings seem to be drawn from the meaningful synthesis of the narrator's experience rather than being stereotypic, superficial, feigned, borrowed, or associative verbiage.

2. Coordination of Emotions (across Individuals)

- In defining the dilemma, the narrator coordinates feelings of all relevant characters into a shared context. The internal states of various characters are coordinated (explicitly or implicitly) rather than each being entrenched in a solipsistic view. The professional may infer such coordination, even if there is only one character, by the degree to which the character's activities are congruent with an implicit sense of consideration for others or commitment to standards or principles.
- In resolving the dilemma, the narrator reconciles viewpoints and needs of all relevant characters. The resolution reflects adequate understanding of causes and their effects.
- Internal and external reality are distinct. The narrator differentiates inner states from external provocation (e.g., distinguishes the emotion of the perceiver from the target or source of the feeling).
- The characters' feeling is appropriate (in nature and intensity) to the evoking circumstances described in the story and is based on accurate reading of the stimulus configuration.

3. Clarity and Specificity in the Identification of Emotions

- The narrator identifies events (evoking circumstances, broader context) and their relationship to a character's inner world (feelings, intentions) clearly and specifically instead of making vague connections, such as "feels sad because something bad happened."
- The narrator makes clear distinctions of different characters' feelings according to evoking circumstances or difference in personality or viewpoint. (If only one person is described, the above category applies.)

- The narrator clearly delineates the relationships of characters to each other vis-à-vis the feelings described.

4. Levels of Maturity in the Conceptualization and Resolution of Emotional Tensions

A comprehensive understanding of emotion involves the joint consideration of two related components: how it is conceptualized (internally organized versus externally provoked) and how it is resolved (immediate to long-term coping). The conceptualization of affect may be more sophisticated than the resolution but not vice versa. Generally, emotions that are poorly understood spawn coping efforts that are similarly unrealistic, vague, or short-sighted.

The five levels of affect maturity include both the conceptualization and resolution of emotions.

Level 1.

Conceptualization: disjointed.   Various indicators suggest that affect is tied in a disjointed way to stimuli or story events: (a) Feelings or circumstances are discrepant from the stimulus; (b) emotions, motives, or purposes do not reflect inner attributes but are specific descriptions of: the stimuli, global reactions to the feeling state in the stimulus, vague impressions, or unmodulated and inappropriate reactions to perceived provocations; and (c) intent is not separated from impact or circumstances associated with feelings are implausible.

Resolution: non-coping or immediate coping.   Feelings conceptualized at this level are not conducive to realistic resolutions nor amenable to constructive actions because they are neither internally organized nor realistically tied to events. The story concludes with a resolution that is inappropriate, highly maladaptive, or nonexistent (story ending is distinct from the resolution of tensions). The affect may be arbitrarily changed to its opposite, or the new feeling may contradict the preceding premises. The story ending may not resolve the problem posed, but constitutes a superimposed happy (just rode her bike and watched TV) or unhappy (he died) closure to the narrative process. Another possibility is that negative affect (fear/hostility/helplessness) intensifies as the situation deteriorates. Characters may remain in extreme states of deprivation, fear, confusion, or abandonment with no resolution or may manifest clearly antisocial actions or poor judgment.

Let's return to Aaron, age 8-3, with a Full Scale IQ score of 119 on the WISC-III, who was in a therapeutic program for children diagnosed with "emotional disorder."

Card 1. The guy that is, the kid that wanted to draw a picture with stuff that he didn't have. [E: What happened before?] He needed some ink and a pencil, but there was a crack in the paper and he didn't have any tape. [E: So what was he thinking?] He's thinking of drawing. [E: And how is he feeling?] Umm, umm, concerned because he thinks he'll mess up on the picture and everyone will laugh at him. [E: And how does it turn out in the end?] He got the tape and finished his picture.

In response to the examiner's query, the initial dilemma of not having the materials needed to carry out his intended activity escalates to a new concern that is left unresolved (messing up and being laughed at). The story concludes when the boy suddenly, without an explanation, gets only one of the needed objects ("tape" but not "ink and a pencil") and finishes the picture. Thus, the coping strategies are as fragmented as the conceptualization of the tensions.

Level 2.

Conceptualization: provoked.　　Emotions pertain primarily to momentary considerations (provocation, need, desire) and involve simplistic reasoning (e.g., linear rather than causal association between feelings and events). For example, feelings may be reactions to the last event or immediate need rather than being embedded in a series of events (cohesive historical context) or encompassing a long-term view (principles, ethics, goals, relatedness). Feelings may be reactions to unanticipated perceived threats to one's physical or psychological well-being, or they may stem from either getting and doing or not getting and doing what one wants in the moment. Feelings may be overly justified by the stimulus or immediate external circumstance.

Resolution: non-coping or immediate/partial coping.　　In this situation affect does not change, affective shifts are inadequately explained, or resolution addresses only part of the problem. Thus, feelings or events change without a clear and reasonable intervening process (e.g., change of affect or activity is the outcome; affect is ignored or the problem simply disappears). Actions are vague, do not constructively address the problem, or overlook the distinction between short- and long-term resolutions to affective tensions.

This level is illustrated by a kindergarten girl's story. Her teacher described her as low in empathy and social competence.

Card 1. He's feeling sad. He lost his mommy. He thinks she's sick, that's why he's sad. [E: Then what?] He's thinking what he's gonna do with his mommy. [E: Ending?] He does something. [E: What?] Don't know.

The feeling of concern for the well-being of the character's mother is tied to his sense of loss and immediate desire to do "something" with his mother. Likewise, the vague resolution ("does something") is not pegged to the mother's recovery (a longer-term concern). The child does not have an internal representation of the relationship with her mother that can "stand in" for the times that she is not physically present.

Level 3.

Conceptualization: externally organized.   Emotions are recognized as internal to the characters but are elicited by external sources such as evaluation of others (success, approval, criticism) or from self-evaluations that are referenced to perceived evaluation of others. Emotions may be tied to pressure to conform to external standards, obligations, or rules (but not to arbitrary or capricious demands). The distinction between intent and impact of other's actions and demands is at least superficially understood.

Resolution: non-coping or immediate/partial coping.   Affect shifts are tied realistically to external change in circumstances or intervention by others but do not demonstrate durable convictions or initiative to seek long-term solutions. Given conceptualization at this level, failure to resolve tension due to inaction (non-coping) may be interpreted as a need for an external agent. The character may take constructive action to meet perceived external demand, but the motive is either to obtain approval or reward or to avert consequences. Thus, the external source creates the change in affect (e.g., wrongdoing is regretted only because of external consequences; affect changes because others provide rewards or reassurance). Resolution of inner tensions is tied to the reactions of others rather than reliance on inner resources. Some incompatibility or ambivalence remains between short- and long-term resolutions or in dealing with internal and external sources of tension.

This level is illustrated by Jaime, a first grader.

Card 1. The boy lost his bow to his violin, and his mother came in and said, "Why aren't you fiddling?" "Because I lost the bow to my violin." She said, "You look for it and if you don't find it, you'll be in big trouble." Then the end. He found it, and his mother said, "Good, before you finish fiddling, I'm going to give you a treat." [E: Feeling? Thinking?] In the beginning, he's thinking, "Boy, I lost my bow, wait 'till my mom finds out." He's sad. At the end, he's thinking, "Oh goody, I'm getting a treat." End.

The boy takes no initiative to search for the missing bow until prompted by his mother. Thoughts and feelings center on external pressures or incentives.

Level 4.

Conceptualization: internally organized.   Problem definition or affect is in tune with the circumstances described in the story, and feelings are organized according to rules, values, or goals that are socially sanctioned and internalized. Thus, concerns are not trivial and reveal a balance between immediate and long-term perspectives and external and internal frames of reference. Moreover, emotions are assets that motivate and guide principled, deliberate, purposeful actions or decisions.

Resolution: long-term coping.   Characters take internal responsibility for regulating their feelings and actions. Negative emotion serves as a cue to identify the sources of tension as well as the potential obstacles to coping, followed by realistic strategies to manage them. Coping strategies give appropriate weight to both external factors and inner states of characters. The characters coordinate purposeful thought, planning, and action (where possible) to resolve negative feelings or promote positive states. If such proactive efforts are not possible, characters seek appropriate help and accept logical consequences or inevitable events. When little else can be done, characters resolve feelings by reframing them. Outcomes are appropriate to the problem set and effort expended. Moreover, the resolution reflects initiative in responding to both internal and external sources of tension.

This level is illustrated by a kindergarten girl's story. The girl was participating in a study and was rated by her teacher as high in empathy.

Card 1. A boy is looking at his violin. He's going to play. He doesn't like it. His mother told him to play it. He tells her he doesn't want to play. She says he can play it later. He puts it away. He plays it after dinner. Then he likes it. His mother likes it.

The story reconciles internal and external sources of tension. Initially, the boy doesn't want to play the violin as requested by his mother. After the boy informs his mother, they come to a mutually satisfactory compromise ("play it later") that encompasses a longer-term perspective. The final touch, indicating sensitivity to the feelings for both characters (". . . he likes it, his mother likes it"), demonstrates appreciation of the importance of feelings (not merely outward compliance). If the narrator had elaborated on the boy's goals or commitment to playing the violin, this story would be coded at the highest level.

Level 5.

Conceptualization: principled. Emotions stem from prosocial, self-defined standards and goals coupled with self-awareness and acceptance of boundaries and limitations. The narrator resourcefully incorporates nuances of the stimuli into the narrative.

Resolution: long-term coping. The abstract and mature conceptualization of the problem is linked with coping that is geared to "meaning," principles, or values (e.g., acting with integrity or courage; making thoughtful decisions) and is not exclusively directed toward attaining a desired outcome (e.g., maintaining or repairing a relationship, overcoming obstacles, or achieving success) or managing feelings.

Let's consider again Benjie's story.

Card 1. The boy has a violin except he can't play it very nicely. So he's kind of upset because he can't figure out how to play it well. You want to know what I think this thing is? [Points to the paper under the violin] [E: Up to you.] He's thinking whether he should keep trying or quit it because he doesn't know how to play it. [E: Turns out?] He gives up because he decides that he'll never be able to do it.

The dilemma is not framed in terms of external pressure or expectation but in terms of a boy's autonomous decision about whether to continue investment in an activity in which he falls short of his own standards. What is important here is not whether the boy chooses to play, but the process by which the decision is made. The reason the boy gives up the violin is not because of momentary frustration but because he concludes that he will "never" play well.

CASE ILLUSTRATION

Jane

At the time of the evaluation, Jane, a 13-year-old girl, was being homeschooled because the school setting was viewed as not suited to her needs. Her psychiatrist requested a psychological evaluation to obtain more information. Figure 5.1 displays the coding of Jane's stories according to the categories described in this chapter.

Card 1. This boy's mother always wanted him to take violin lessons and he was always sure that if he did start taking them, that he wouldn't live up to his mom's expectations. And so he went to take his lessons and his teacher was a lot more understanding than he thought he would be. But he had to take lessons after school and he was really tired. He's feeling right now he's about to go to his lesson and he's feeling too tired to go but he doesn't want to let his mom down, so he's going to.

Import: If a boy is convinced he will always fall short of his mother's standards, he will try not to disappoint her by struggling against discouragement and fatigue to do what is expected.

Explanatory hypotheses: This story accurately accounts for the stimulus configuration and differentiates between externally imposed standards and internally experienced pressure to meet them. Possible barriers to effective coping relate to the character's feeling discouraged (anticipation of negative events, though things turn out better than expected) and being tired (lacking drive and energy). The boy has no intrinsic desire to play the violin but is motivated by not wanting to disappoint others. In the process of trying to do what the boy thinks he should, he remains stuck in an unpleasant emotional state.

I. CONCEPTUALIZATION OF EMOTIONS

A. Sources and Regulation of Affect
Sources of Affect

(Check as many as apply for each story) Cards→	1	2	3BM	4	5	6BM	7GF	13BM			
Unrecognized (tension depicted is not recognized)											
Descriptive (refers to stimulus)											
External											
Internal	✓	✓	✓	✓	✓	✓	✓	✓			

B. Coping with Affective Tensions
(Choose among non-coping, immediate coping, or long-term coping styles for each story. Then check the most appropriate categories within each style.)

1. Non-Coping or Unrealistic Coping

(Check as many as apply for each story) Cards→	1	2	3BM	4	5	6BM	7GF	13BM			
Unaware (negative emotion is not recognized)											
No change in affect, self-awareness, or understanding	✓										
Overwhelmed (misery prevails or negative affect escalates)											
Reactive (provoked to act without purpose or strategy)			✓								
Detached, resigned, hopeless (fails to act or react, withdraws, gives in)											
Guilty, regretful											
Substantially unrealistic. Magical external intervention or unlikely turn of events (e.g., wins the war single-handedly; character is granted unrealistic demand); dreaming or hoping (when action is warranted)											

2. Immediate or Partial Coping

(Check as many as apply for each story) Cards→	1	2	3BM	4	5	6BM	7GF	13BM			
Decrease negative affect and/or deal with the dilemma without fully addressing the sources of the tension (e.g., avoidance, temporary reassurance, resolving to do something).		✓		✓		✓	✓	✓			
Increase or maintain positive affect and/or act on the situation without recognizing important issues.											
Excessive dependence on others		✓									
Excessive independence from others											

3. Long-Term or Problem-Focused Coping

(Check as many as apply for each story) Cards→	1	2	3BM	4	5	6BM	7GF	13BM			
Decrease negative affect by effective problem solving (e.g., addressing the source of the feeling or reframing).					✓						
Increase or maintain positive affect through long-term problem solving and goal setting.											
Realistic resolution of tensions without seeking or receiving help/support.											
Realistic resolution of tensions with appropriate request for help or support (not passive, blind dependence).											
Appropriate help, advice, or reassurance provided without specific request, enables the character to resolve the dilemma.											

Figure 5.1 Emotion

II. EMOTIONAL MATURITY

A. Complexity and Coherence of Emotions (Within One Individual)

(Check as many as apply for each story) Cards→	1	2	3BM	4	5	6BM	7GF	13BM			
Affects pertain to durable, inner motives, long-term interests or convictions (standards, goals, harmonious relationship versus reactions to momentary needs, immediate situational provocation, or nonspecific distress).	✓	✓		✓	✓	✓	✓	✓			
Affective impact of actions is distinct from its intent.	✓	✓		✓	✓	✓	✓	✓			
Emotions, thoughts, actions, and outcomes are congruous with each other, meaningfully woven into the unfolding narrative, and in tune with social causality and the stimulus.	✓	✓		✓	✓	✓	✓	✓			
Feelings appear to be drawn from meaningful synthesis of narrator's experience (versus scripted, superficial, feigned, or associative verbiage).	✓	✓		✓	✓	✓	✓	✓			

B. Integration and Coordination of Emotions (Across Individuals)

(Check as many as apply for each story) Cards→	1	2	3BM	4	5	6BM	7GF	13BM		
In *defining* the dilemma, feelings of all relevant characters are coordinated into a shared context.	✓	✓		✓	✓	✓	✓	✓		
In *resolving* the dilemma, viewpoints and needs of all relevant characters are reconciled (with understanding of social causality).	No	✓		No	✓	No	No	No		
There is separation of internal and external reality and differentiation of inner states from external provocation (i.e., the emotion of the perceiver is distinct from characteristics of the target or source of the feeling).	✓	✓		✓	✓	✓	✓	✓		
Feeling is appropriate (in nature and intensity) to the circumstances described in the story and is based on accurate reading of the stimulus.	✓	✓		✓	✓	✓	✓	✓		

C. Clarity and Specificity in the Identification of Emotions

(Check as many as apply for each story) Cards→	1	2	3BM	4	5	6BM	7GF	13BM		
Clear and specific identification of the circumstances vis-à-vis a character's feelings.	✓			✓	✓	✓	✓	✓		
Clear delineation of the relationships of characters to each other vis-à-vis the feelings described. *	✓	✓		✓	✓	✓	✓	✓		
Clear distinctions of different characters' feelings according to evoking circumstance or differences in personality or viewpoint.	✓	✓		✓	✓	✓	✓	✓		

*If only one person is described (assuming only one is pictured), the above category applies.

Figure 5.1 (continued)

Card 2. This one girl lives on a farm and she's [long pause] she's going to school in a couple of minutes and at first it was a hard decision for her because she had a lot of work to do around her house. But her family encouraged her to try and go but she was afraid because not a lot of her friends went. Um, this is the third day that she's going to school and every time she goes she feels nervous but her classmates treat her surprisingly well and so she's kind of looking forward to it. [E: How does it turn out in the end?] In the end, she . . . she comes back and she's learned a lot and she's even made some new friends that treat her well and she wants to go back soon.

LEVEL OF MATURITY IN THE CONCEPTUALIZATION AND RESOLUTION OF EMOTION

Level One: Conceptualization—Disjointed. Affect is tied in a disjointed way to stimuli or story events (e.g., situations associated with feelings are highly implausible; feelings or circumstances are poorly coordinated with the stimulus). Emotions, motives, or purposes do not reflect inner attributes but are specific descriptions of the stimuli, global reactions to the feeling state in the stimulus, vague impressions, or unmodulated and inappropriate reactions to perceived provocations. Intent is not separated from impact.

Resolution: Non-Coping or Immediate Coping. Feelings conceptualized at this level are not conducive to realistic resolutions because they are not internally organized nor realistically tied to events. The story may conclude with an inappropriate, highly maladaptive resolution or no resolution. Affect may be arbitrarily changed to its opposite so the new feeling contradicts the premises of the preceding story. Outcomes may reflect extreme helplessness, fear, hostility, and/or involve clearly antisocial actions or poor judgment. Affects may become more negative or more intense as the situation keeps deteriorating; characters may remain in extreme states of deprivation, confusion, or abandonment with no resolution.

Level Two: Conceptualization—Provoked. Emotions are poorly integrated into a larger context, pertaining primarily to immediate concerns (provocation, need, desire). Feelings are tied to events in ways that may be implausible, short-sighted, self-absorbed, simplistic, or extremely vague. Feelings may be reactions to the last event or immediate need rather than pertinent to a larger context or cohesive with a series of events. Feelings may be superficial, feigned, or overly justified by the stimulus or by immediate external circumstance. There is poor understanding of psychological process or of social-causality.

Resolution: Non-Coping, Immediate, or Partial Coping. Affect does not change or shifts are inadequately explained. Feelings or events change without a clear and reasonable intervening process or without considering important aspects of the stimulus or the dilemma (e.g., change of affect or activity is the outcome; affect is ignored or the problem simply disappears). Actions are vague or do not constructively address the problem. There is a lack of distinction between short- and long-term resolutions to affective tensions.

Level Three: Conceptualization—Externally Organized. Emotions are recognized as internal to the characters, but they are elicited primarily by external sources such as actions and reactions of others or by external feedback or demand but with at least a superficial distinction between intent and impact. Emotions may be tied to pressure to conform to legitimate external standards, demands, or rules (not someone's whims).

Resolution: Non-Coping, Immediate, or Partial Coping. Affect shifts are realistically tied to external change in circumstances or interventions of others but do not entail durable conviction or initiative of characters to seek long-term resolution or pursue goals. At this level, failure to resolve tensions due to inaction may be interpreted as need for an external agent. When constructive action is taken to meet legitimate external demand, the motive is to obtain approval or reward or to avert consequences. Thus, external source influences affect change (e.g., positive actions are valued because they bring reward or approval; wrongdoing brings external consequences only). Resolution of inner tensions depends on the reactions of others. Some incompatibility or ambivalence remains between short and long term resolutions or in dealing with internal and external sources of tension.

Level Four: Conceptualization—Internally Organized. Emotions are smoothly incorporated into the narrative in ways that are congruent with external circumstances and coordinated with motives and convictions, as well as with deliberate, purposeful actions. External and internal frames of reference are balanced, various perspectives are coordinated, and characters communicate appropriately and act constructively on their feelings. Problem definition or affect is in tune with the circumstances and respects the psychological integrity of all relevant characters. Emotional reaction to the problem or task is appropriate to the stimulus and story context. Concerns are not trivial, but represent a balance between immediate presses and long-term perspective.

Resolution: Long-Term Coping. Characters take responsibility for regulating feelings and action. They engage in realistic, planful, active problem-solving efforts (where possible) or resolve their negative feelings by accepting logical consequences or inevitable events. Resolutions are appropriate to problem set and effort expended and reflect initiative in responding to both internal and external sources of tension. External factors along with inner states of characters guide purposeful thought, planning, and actions.

Level Five: Conceptualization—Principled. Emotions stem from prosocial, self-defined standards and/or goals coupled with self-awareness and acceptance of boundaries and limitations. Nuances of the stimuli are resourcefully incorporated into the narrative.

Resolution: Long-Term Coping. The abstract and mature conceptualization of the problem is linked with coping that is geared to "meaning," principles, and values and not directed exclusively to regulation or management of feelings, maintaining or repairing a relationship, overcoming an obstacle, or achieving success.

(Choose the highest level applicable for each story)

Card	1	2	3BM	4	5	6BM	7GF	13BM					
Jane	3	3	2	3	4	3	3	3					

Figure 5.1 (continued)

Import: If a girl is apprehensive about going to school (without her friends), family encouragement motivates her to go, and she is surprised to find that she likes it (makes friends and learns).

Explanatory hypotheses: Again, the character is initially apprehensive (particularly about peer social support) but finds that things work out better than expected. At first, the girl considers the possibility of not going to school but accepts the challenge with family encouragement. An underlying issue is one of making choices to tolerate or avoid situations that are uncomfortable. There seems to be a desire (also seen in Card 1) to engage in socially sanctioned activities, but doing so comes at a high price in terms of stress.

Card 3BM. I'm going to assume this lady's sleeping. Okay. Um, this this lady is at the beginning of college and that she had to get up really early and when she went to class, no one was there and then she found out it had been like a closing day but the building was still open because they had work to do on it. So she was too tired to walk back to her car, so she thought she would just take a nap. And when she wakes up I guess she'll go back to her car. That's pretty bad but I guess that's it. What was she thinking? Well, when she went to sleep she thought that she would take a quick nap but when she got up she found out that it had been like four hours. She was embarrassed but no one seemed to mind so she was okay with it.

Import: Normal life demands are so exhausting that if given a respite from her obligations (class cancelled), a girl opts for instant relief (can't wait to take a nap) even at the risk of feeling embarrassed.

Explanatory hypotheses: The theme of fatigue seen in Card 1 resurfaces. In this story, the fatigue is so intense that the girl naps in the classroom before she goes home. There is an emerging sense that the narrator, experiencing nervousness and fatigue and anticipating negative events, struggles to balance her tolerance for stress with her desire to live up to social expectations. As she vacillates between accepting and avoiding difficult and burdensome expectations, she discovers that when she meets the challenge, things often turn out better than anticipated. However, in the face of such stress, it would be difficult to sustain positive action, and avoidant behavior is likely.

Card 4. When this guy got home from work he was in a bad mood because his boss is always giving him trouble . . . um . . . and he worked with computers and he felt like his boss was always being lazy because he would never do any work himself. And he . . . when he was driving home he almost got in a car accident and it made him feel even worse. And when he got home his wife didn't understand why he was upset and he was in too bad of a mood to explain it to her. But she wanted to help and he thought that maybe if he waited a little while to calm down then he'd be able to talk about it. But he was afraid that if he explained it to her now that he would be yelling at her and he didn't want to do that. So he feels he doesn't want to make his wife upset and he just wants to wait a little bit so he'll feel better about it and then he'll talk about it.

Import: If a man is intensely upset during the course of a routine day and it is difficult to explain his feelings without upsetting others (family members who want to help), he waits until he's calm before he will talk about it.

Explanatory hypotheses: Again, life is a hassle, and negative emotions build over the course of the day. Others, such as family members, want to help, but it may be hard for them to understand the emotional intensity. Uncomfortable emotions generated by daily hassles complicate relationships, and it is necessary to moderate emotional intensity to keep from upsetting others.

Card 5. This lady is a mother to a twelve-year-old boy and she thought she had heard him yelling for his mom, probably for a glass of water or something about an hour after she tucked him in. And the mother was . . . ah . . . knitting some things, so she decided to just come up and see what he wanted and when she came up to look in he looked really sick. And she asked him how he felt and he said he felt like he had a fever, so she took his temperature and it wasn't that bad. But she thought that she would take him to the doctor anyway. And, and when she took him to the doctor, they said that he just had the flu and that they would give him some medicine. So she was . . . she was happy that he was okay.

Import: When a 12-year-old boy is sick, his mother takes good care of him.

Explanatory hypotheses: Not only does the mother respond to what the child says, but she also uses her own judgment to notice that her son "looked really sick." There is a contrast between a child's being cared for when physically ill and otherwise struggling to meet demands.

Card 6BM. The man is from the police place. He's a a police officer and the lady he's standing next to is the mother of someone who died. And he was sent out to tell her, which is something he's never done before because he never likes dealing with their reactions. So he . . . he told his superior that he didn't want to go but he said that he had to. So he went to tell her . . . and when he told her that her son was dead she was really upset and couldn't believe it. But she didn't . . . like . . . she wasn't as . . . she didn't act like he would expect her to and he tried to make her feel better. And he wanted to say some things to make her feel better but didn't want to upset her more. So he just waited until she wanted to hear what he had to say.

Import: If a person dislikes having to deliver bad news and cannot avoid this responsibility, he or she will try to minimize the pain by waiting for the right time.

Explanatory hypotheses: This story captures the narrator's interpersonal sensitivity and the salience of feelings. The problem relates to difficulty facing intense emotions; the police officer's intense feelings jeopardize his carrying out his duties.

Card 7GF. This girl just turned ten years old. And her mom always bought her a doll for her birthday and she had gotten sick of them by then but she didn't want to say anything to hurt her mom's feelings, because she appreciated that she got gifts from her parents. And . . . um . . . one of the people who worked in her kitchen noticed that she was upset and wanted to help. So she tried talking to her but the girl didn't seem to want to talk about her own feelings. So the kitchen lady read her some stories that she wrote and it calmed the girl down . . . like . . . she thought about it and she was happy that her mom got her something and the end. Yeah.

Import: If someone is being nice to a girl (mother), but the girl is not satisfied, she does not express her true feelings and tries to appreciate what others are trying to do for her.

Explanatory hypotheses: As with the story to Card 6BM, this story shows a difficulty broaching emotionally sensitive topics. Rather than risk a potential confrontation that might hurt her mother's feelings, the girl keeps her dissatisfaction to herself. However, this is not a one-time event but one that is likely to recur ("always bought her a doll . . ."). Perhaps the intensity of the emotions (as seen in previous stories) makes it feel risky to express them.

Card 13BM. This boy's father, um, liked to work with his cattle 'cause they worked at a ranch and the boy always wanted to help him with the cattle. But his dad didn't want him getting close to them because he was afraid that because he was so little that he'd get trampled if he wasn't careful. And the boy was upset because he always felt like his dad was always leaving him out of things and not letting him participate in things that he thought he should. And so he just sat and watched his dad working and thought that maybe if he watched him for a long time he would learn how to do it, so if his dad ever let him help him he would be better at it than his dad would expect him to be. And how does it turn out? In the end he . . . he doesn't get to help his dad for several years but when he does he turns out to be a big help to his dad.

Import: If a boy's father prevents him from doing grown-up things, he feels left out but waits years to earn his father's trust and finally proves himself.

Explanatory hypotheses: The boy seems to make a prudent decision that is likely to work for the long term but remains "stuck" with his feelings of being left out. There is an understanding of short- and long-term considerations and an appreciation of the intention on the part of both characters (father and son). The son wants to help, and the father wants to protect the child from harm. However, the sense of optimism that a child can be a big help when he gets older is accompanied by the unresolved negative feelings. Again, the boy waits and observes without expressing his feelings of disappointment or working toward a compromise to address the gap between short- and long-term outcomes.

Narrative Summary

During the 8th grade (about a year prior to this evaluation), Jane had begun homeschooling due to various concerns summarized as a "poor match" between her and the school system. She was cooperative throughout the four evaluation sessions but was usually tired and lethargic, probably because the testing sessions took place in the morning, and Jane typically did not get up until mid-afternoon. When responding to the structured cognitive and achievement tasks, Jane had a tendency to get off track by giving unnecessary detail that was not pertinent to the question. Although Jane completed the academic tasks presented to her, she had a difficult time working for long periods, requiring a break after an average of 45 minutes.

Currently, Jane has poor sleeping habits and many somatic complaints. She experiences headaches and stomach aches when anticipating a stressful event, and these appear to subside after the event has taken place. Physical reactions such as stomach upset, irritability, sleep problems, and headaches have been evident from an early age. More recently, this stress cycle has become pronounced in connection to school attendance. Jane was described by her mother as a fidgety baby and as reactive to low level stimuli such as ordinary household noises as well as to social cues. Jane's current tendency to withdraw and protect herself from stimuli that are too intense to handle (e.g., avoiding relationships with friends her own age and wanting to leave school) is traceable to a history of being highly reactive and alert to the stimuli around her. Currently, Jane's irregular sleep habits interfere with her functioning. She is extremely lethargic in the morning, and her mother reports that it is difficult to get her up by two in the afternoon. Jane indicated that she feels sick to her stomach and light-headed when she wakes up. However, as the day goes on, the build-up of nervous energy results in Jane's being so keyed up that she stays awake until two or three in the morning and sometimes all night. Jane explained that she frequently worries at night, mostly about the small, mundane details of day to day life.

Jane's scores on structured cognitive and achievement tasks ranged from average to high average on the Wechsler Scales (WISC-III) and from average to very superior on the Woodcock-Johnson Test of Achievement–Revised). Jane's TAT stories are consistent with her spending so much of her energy coping with the everyday hassles of life that she is left without much energy to explore long-term goals or interests. Jane's stories indicated a coping style focused on the amelioration of immediate feelings without coming up with strategies to address more long-term issues. The characters' struggles to deal with their intense emotions and to manage their fatigue to meet demands of daily tasks and relationships are in accord with the daily dilemmas confronting Jane. The stories suggest a more sophisticated understanding of relationships and of social causality than of problem-solving strategies. At this point, so much of Jane's energies are consumed with managing her anxieties that she focuses on immediate relief from the pressures she experiences rather than on setting priorities for the long term. She would benefit from medication that would break the cycle of anxiety that tends to escalate over the course of the day. In conjunction with the reduction of anxiety and the establishment of a consistent sleep pattern, Jane may benefit from counseling to manage her sensitivities and reactions to daily hassles and to increase her resources to tackle more long-term issues including setting goals and pursuing interests.

🪶 TEST YOURSELF 🪶

1. **What is meant by an "emotion story?"**

2. **How does emotion influence the appraisal of events?**

3. **Which characteristics of schemas are relevant for emotion regulation?**

   (a) complexity

   (b) retrieval from memory

   (c) coordination with "on-line" cognitive processes

   (d) all of the above

4. **Which of the following pairs are least related to each other?**

   (a) appraisal and coping

   (b) positive affect and internal organization of emotion

   (c) emotional maturity and reality testing

   (d) defense mechanisms and cognition

5. **Appraisals that are _____ are most likely to result in the distinction between the intent and impact of actions.**

   (a) internally organized

   (b) vague

   (c) provoked

   (d) well-intentioned

6. **Define reality testing of emotions.**

Answers: 1. The emotion is connected to a network of justifying experiences, reactions, thoughts, plans, actions, and outcomes; 2. Appraisal of a particular event is influenced by the individual's current emotions and activated schemas representing prior experience (real or vicarious) in that situation. The qualities of schemas that influence appraisals—such as their complexity, organization, and activation—are shaped by the individual's regulation of emotional and attentional processes in the given situation. Finally, because memories are encoded according to their associated feelings, positive and negative emotions facilitate selective access to mood-congruent schemas; 3. d; 4. b; 5. a; 6. Separation of one's feelings from the objective characteristics of the target of those feelings to enable the individual to question the appropriateness of the emotional reactions.

Six

ESSENTIALS OF TAT ASSESSMENT OF OBJECT RELATIONS

S chema theory and object relations theory converge in their underlying assumptions. However, the latter is clinically rooted with more extensive documentation of its relevance to adjustment and psychopathology, as well as to treatment decisions (e.g., Bornstein & O'Neill, 1992; Leigh, Westen, Barends, & Mendel, 1992; Masling & Bornstein, 1994; Westen, 1993). Much like schemas, "object relations" represent the organization of accumulated experiences that function outside of awareness as templates for understanding interpersonal experiences. Internal images of both self and others are referred to as objects (Meissner, 1971, 1972). Object relations theory does not focus on the observable transactions among people but pertains to the manner in which actual interactions become subjectively represented within the individual in the process of development (Fairbairn, 1952; Klein, 1948; Winnicott, 1965). The importance of object relations theory lies in the contention that individuals relate to other people according to the internal patterning of self-other experiences. Thus, the subjective experience of relatedness is grounded in the content of memory regarding self and others and in processing current information in ways that support past perceptions.

Mirroring the developmental trends for schemas in general, internal representations (objects) become less grounded in the immediate situation, more symbolic or conceptual, and more consistent. Thus, more specific object representations transform into general principles of object relations (Greenberg & Mitchell, 1983). Object representations are tied directly to specific relationships, whereas object relations are abstract schemas embodying the principles and processes that organize the individual's conception of self and other people. Essentially, object relations (like all schemas) constitute an inner structure that enhances capacity for internal regulation by providing inner resources for organizing experiences in the absence of external support or guidance. The concept of internal objects, first postulated by Klein (1932), assumes that actual relationships become intrapsychic structures that enable individuals to feel connected to others even in their absence. These internal objects or object representations organize and direct the relationship between the inner and outer worlds. The object relations also contribute to the motivational system because the internalized psychic structures motivate the individual in ways that external relationships did previously. The creation of an "internal world" through a process of internalization (Meissner, 1981) promotes a sense of "true self," as compared to a superficial, "false," or inauthentic self that is oriented to external appearances (e.g., Guntrip, 1968; Kernberg, 1976; Kohut, 1977; Winnicott, 1965). The individual's "inner world" is the filter for understanding and orchestrating encounters with the external world.

Assessment of object relations provides a map of the inner world of relationships. The construct of "object relations" has been measured from various theoretical perspectives using diverse instruments including the Rorschach and several narrative techniques (such as stories told to thematic apperceptive stimuli), as well as analysis of dreams and early memories (for a review, see Stricker & Healey, 1990). The use of stories in response to pictures seems particularly suited to assess internal representations of relationships because the stories given ". . . provide considerable access to cognitive and affective-motivational patterns related to interpersonal functioning in intimate relationships" (Westen, 1991, p. 56). Bellak's scoring system for the TAT and CAT (Bellak, 1993; Bellak & Abrams, 1997) subsumes object relations under the general rubric of integration of the ego because object relations permit the ego to perform the self-regulatory functions previously provided by caregivers.

DEVELOPMENT OF OBJECT RELATIONS

The object relations model developed by Fairbairn (1954) and later elaborated by others (Guntrip, 1968, 1974; Kernberg, 1976; Kohut, 1977) attempts to correct some of the deficiencies of classical psychoanalytic theory by emphasizing interpersonal relatedness in understanding development and behavior. The development of self-representation and representation of others occurs in tandem (Sandler, 1992), and distinctions within the self are prerequisites to the differentiation of self from other (Meissner, 1981). As discussed previously, the infant's attributing intentionality to others hinges on awareness that his or her own behaviors are intentional. Infants as young as 18 months have been shown to imitate others' *intended* rather than their *actual* behaviors (Meltzoff, 1995). The general developmental course of object representation is paralleled by an increasing differentiation of self-representation. Consistent with schema development in general, the representation of self and others becomes more complex as a function of maturation and experience.

The development of object relations (see Rapid Reference 6.1) proceeds through increasing articulation of a sense of self as distinct from others through the separation-individuation process (Mahler, 1966; Mahler, Pine, & Bergman, 1975), delineating the growth of cognitive-affective mechanisms relating to the mental representations of self and other. The earliest representations of others correspond to the need satisfaction of the perceiver. But, as schemas about others are created apart from the individual's own needs, the

Rapid Reference 6.1

Development of Object Relations

The internalized images of self and other develop together through a progression that ranges from perception of objects as global or diffuse or as disconnected fragments to greater organization and coherence, resulting in more stable and consistent representation of self and others (Kernberg, 1976). At the highest developmental stage (ego identity), past experience has been consolidated into a system of values and abstract principles of conduct that transcend the specific objects to which they were previously attached. Failure of self-object differentiation and lack of self-cohesion make it impossible to appreciate characteristics of others apart from the needs of the self. The mechanism of splitting refers to dichotomously classifying experiences as either all good or all bad rather than integrating them into a more complex or abstract conceptualization (e.g., ambivalence). Such dichotomous thinking may occur in reaction to overwhelmingly intense emotions or because of difficulty integrating experience due to cognitive/attentional limitations. However, without coordinating various facets of experience, including pleasant and unpleasant encounters, the individual is confined to live in the present and to appreciate only what others provide in the moment. The individual remains trapped in the one-dimensional immediacy of the current experience without the capacity to coordinate self with other or "now" with "later."

characteristics of the inner and outer worlds become independently conceptualized. Nevertheless, the distinctions that are made among others depend on
cognitions and emotions of the perceiver. As discussed in earlier chapters, feelings influence judgments and guide attention to what is relevant or meaningful, and, in concert with cognitions, direct the structural organization of object
representations.

The development of increasingly complex self and other representations
and the acquisition of adaptive behavioral patterns through reinforcement follow different principles (e.g., Meissner, 1974; Raynor & McFarlin, 1986; Sandler & Rosenblatt, 1962). The continuing growth of inner structure increases
the capacity to sustain constructive behavior without extrinsic reinforcement
and the capacity to tolerate separation from others. Such development depends not so much on the acquisition of a repertoire of functional skills but
on the quality of relationships in terms of stability and affective involvement.
Accordingly, the learning paradigm in terms of specific reinforcements is subsumed by a larger framework of the object relation (Meissner, 1981). Internalization is a form of learning that makes it possible to shift from contingency-
based to self-directed behavior.

OBJECT RELATIONS AND ADJUSTMENT

Many psychoanalytic investigators link problems with object representation to
the severity and type of psychopathology (e.g., Blatt, Brenneis, Schimek, &
Glick, 1976; Blatt & Lerner, 1983; Bornstein & O'Neill, 1992; Mayman, 1967;
Procidano & Guinta, 1989; Spear & Lapidus, 1981; Stuart, Westen, Lohr, &
Benjamin, 1990). Such a connection seems logical for two related reasons.
First, difficulty organizing experience limits the capacity to engage in the complex integrative task of internalization. Second, problems with internalization
curtail the development of inner structures needed for self-regulation. Three
pathological modes of relating (see Rapid Reference 6.2) have been described
within the object relations framework (e.g., Kernberg, 1975, 1976; Kohut,
1971): (a) relating to others as "self-objects," (b) relating to others as "transitional objects," and (c) relating to others as "part objects." All three modes of
relating are appropriate during specific developmental moments but are
pathological if they persist (Klein, 1948; Mahler et al., 1975; Winnicott, 1971).

The actual qualities of others combine with individualistic styles of processing

≡Rapid Reference 6.2

Pathological Modes of Relating

1. Self object: a conceptualization of others only in terms of how the individual wishes or needs them to be. The attributes of others that do not pertain to the self are not valued or, perhaps, not even noticed. Such a solipsistic view has a distorting influence on the perception of others and precludes the possibility of appreciating their individuality. At the extreme, lack of self-cohesion and absence of self-other differentiation is associated with delusional distortion, fragmentation, or loss of cohesion of the self.

2. Transitional object relations (Winnicott, 1971): objects that are intermediate between an actual person and the internal representation of that person. Transitional objects serve an anxiety-reducing function much like a special blanket or teddy bear at bedtime provides comfort that comes from outside the self, though not directly from another human being. Rather than assuming the self-soothing or self-regulating functions through internal means, persons use other individuals the way a normal child uses transitional objects. Such individuals externalize responsibility from the self onto others, and this process detracts from stability in both self- and object representation.

3. Part-object relations (see Klein, 1948; Sullivan, 1953; Mahler et al., 1975; Kernberg, 1976): a view of others that is restricted to the function they provide. Accordingly, attributes of individuals that are not pertinent to carrying out specific functions remain unnoticed or unappreciated. The individual is evaluated only in terms of how he or she carries out specific functions. This type of interpersonal orientation could be due to a variety of factors such as inability to make the distinction, lack of interest, or fearful avoidance.

information to determine whether encounters are seen as damaging or harmful (versus rewarding, satisfying, or inspiring). The primary cognitive underpinning of object relations development is the complexity of information processing to differentiate nuances in self and others and to integrate these elements cohesively. Differentiation refers to noticing moods, values, preferences, points of view, and other qualities of the self and the other. Integration is the formation of linkages among the multiple dimensions that have been differentiated (Baker-Brown et al., 1992; Suedfeld, Tetlock, & Streufert, 1992). Complex mental representations permit a nuanced understanding of psychological processes (such as the relationship between enduring personality dispositions and transient states, conscious and unconscious) and of other influences on the current interpretation of events (such as prior history or personal meanings).

Emotions spur interest in processing intra- and interpersonal information by pointing to the particular distinctions that are relevant for the individual. Empathy and positive emotions sustain interest in processing the nuances of interpersonal information, thereby increasing the cognitive complexity of the representations as well as the likelihood that the qualities that are discerned are appreciated apart from the needs of the perceiver (Locraft & Teglasi, 1997). The regulation of emotion has emerged as an influential variable in empathy-related responding. Individuals experiencing problems regulating negative emotions respond to the suffering of others with personal distress rather than sympathy or empathy (for a review, see Eisenberg, Wentzel, & Harris, 1998). In turn, personal distress promotes behavior aimed at ameliorating one's own discomfort rather than helping the other. Thus, intense affect results in temporary loss of complex distinctions as well as increased concern for one's own state. By definition, empathy requires the accurate understanding of another's experience as different from that of the perceiver (Hoffman, 1982). The attribution of feelings to internal or external sources (discussed in Chapter 5) is also pertinent. An external perspective is compatible with an exchange orientation in relationships where the focus is not on shared understanding but the pattern of behavioral give-and-take. Such an orientation may be a function of limited insight into behavior or of limited emotional engagement.

MUTUALITY OF AUTONOMY

Mutuality of autonomy refers to interdependence and mutual respect among individuals who understand (on a continuum of complexity) and value each other's unique qualities. Only when autonomy is experienced within the self can it be granted to others. Thus, two important dimensions of the personality, the definition of the self and relatedness to others (Blatt, 1990), are developmentally linked to the concept of mutuality of autonomy. Individuals may emphasize one over the other such as by sacrificing self-definition to maintain relatedness or by being preoccupied by issues of self-definition (e.g., guilt, self-reproach). Both limit the capacity to experience mutuality of autonomy. If the self-definition is disconnected from lived experience, the sense of autonomy suffers, and relatedness with others seems inauthentic.

The assessment of mutuality of autonomy (Urist, 1977, 1980; Urist & Shill, 1982) has emphasized two separate but overlapping dimensions of object relations: (a) degree of self-object differentiation, and (b) degree of empathic relatedness. When differentiation is low, boundaries between self and others are blurred, and there is little or no sense of autonomy. When differentiation is high, definitions of self and others are clearly articulated with well-defined boundaries between separate and autonomous individuals and with relatively stable and unique psychological processes. When empathic relatedness is low, perceptions of others are determined by one's preoccupations. In contrast, high empathic connection is associated with views of others that are realistic, mutual, and respectful of individuality. Appreciation of individuality requires awareness that others have different values, opinions, or standards. Otherwise, principles that regulate the relationship between self and other may not stem from empathic understanding but from rigid reliance on duty or normative expectations. As Westen (1985) noted, a need-gratifying form of relatedness is difficult to separate from a need-gratifying view of morality. Thus, empathic relatedness and information processing are intricately tied to morality and concerns for others.

Westen and colleagues, arguing for the necessity to understand current and future interpersonal transactions to inform the psychotherapeutic process, constructed a procedure for interpreting TAT stories to assess various developmental levels of object relations in adults and children (Westen, Klepser, Ruffins, Silverman, & Boekamp, 1991). These levels (see Rapid Reference 6.3), which incorporate object relations theory, social cognition, and clinical observation, have been shown to relate to social adjustment and to predict criterion groups (Leigh et al., 1992; Westen, 1993).

Previous chapters in this volume explicate the cognitive and affective processes of differentiation and integration generally applied to social information processing and schema development. Biases or gaps in processing information noted earlier interfere with systematic development of object relations, depriving the individual of a valuable inner resource for self-regulation. The cognitive organization of emotions described in Chapter 5 plays a key role in the development of self and other representations. The "emotion story" expresses individual differences in the connections between the inner world of emotions, intentions, or goals and the outer world of reactions, actions, and consequences. Positive or negative emotions experienced as stemming from internal sources provide the foundation for intrinsic motivation, empathy,

≡Rapid Reference 6.3

Social Cognition and Object Relations Scales (SCORS; Westen et al., 1991; Westen, 1993)

Five levels are used to rate each of four dimensions of social cognition and object relations (see also Kelly, 1996, 1997):

1. *Complexity of representations of people.* This construct subsumes three developmental phenomena: (a) the capacity to differentiate between self and others, (b) the perception that self and others have stable, multidimensional dispositions, and (c) the awareness of complex motives and subjective experiences in self and other. The most mature level encompasses an understanding of the interplay between transient and enduring psychological experience. At the most primitive level, people and perspectives are not clearly differentiated.

2. *Affect tone of relationships.* Unlike the other three, this dimension does not assume a developmental progression with age. The quality of the representation of people and relationships ranges from the highest level (benevolence), where relationships are expected to be safe or enriching, to the lowest level (malevolence), where relationships are expected to be destructive.

3. *Capacity for emotional investment in relationships or moral standards.* This scale was designed to evaluate sources of moral concern such as orientation to reward or punishment versus guilt or meeting other's expectations. At the highest level, relationships are based on mutual care, appreciation of each other's attributes, and commitment to moral standards. At the lowest level, relationships are based on need gratification.

4. *Understanding social causality.* This dimension focuses on causal attributions about interpersonal behavior ranging from the highest level, where the multiply interacting dimensions of experience are well understood as explanations for social interactions, to the lowest level where causes are poorly understood with explanations being illogical, inappropriate, unlikely, or absent.

commitment to standards, and valuing others apart from one's needs. Alternatively, emotions experienced as prompted directly by external sources lay the groundwork for a focus on rewards or punishments and on need-gratifying relationships. Another dimension of the "emotion story" comprises the connections among intentions, means, and ends, which are, in turn, the cornerstones of autonomy defined as the individual's acting purposefully on intentions to attain goals.

The construct of mutuality of autonomy captures the essence of object relations because it combines the intra- and interpersonal worlds. Autonomy focuses on the intrapersonal world of intentions, goals, feelings, thoughts, and connections between actions and expectations (i.e., outcomes or reactions from others), whereas mutuality of autonomy acknowledges the complementary relationship between the intra- and interpersonal worlds of interacting individuals. Thus, the basis of mutuality of autonomy is the recognition that each person brings his or her representation of prior experience and current frame of mind to a given interpersonal encounter. Individuals relate to each other according to how they coordinate the inner and outer worlds (self in relation to the world, to generalized others, and to a specific other). Basically, object relations are interpersonal schemas that govern social information processing. A professional may apply qualities of schemas, such as their complexity, logic, and organization, to the assessment of object relations with thematic apperception techniques.

CODING OBJECT RELATIONS AS MUTUALITY OF AUTONOMY

The twin processes of differentiation and integration contribute to mutuality of autonomy. Differentiation entails the awareness of nuances of various dimensions of experience within and across individuals. Integration is the coordination of the dimensions that have been differentiated. Attributes that are differentiated occupy awareness, and the rules governing the integration of these distinctions dictate their relevance. The distinctions and connections made within the self (e.g., intention-action sequences) are amenable to generalization to others. Therefore, a nuanced awareness of one's own psychological world permits the understanding that others have their own perspectives, reasons, or motives for action. Characteristics of self and other (and world) that are salient for the individual are most prominently represented in the mental structures and stand out the most during interpersonal encounters as well as in stories told to picture stimuli. Thus, the narrative task brings to light qualities of persons and relationships that the individual is most likely to discern (e.g., inner or outer attributes) and the number of different dimensions considered (e.g., intent and impact). An individual may elaborate extensively on a given dimension of experience, such as action, without ties to other dimensions, such as thought. Moreover, an individual may offer intricate details about characters' appearance (clothing, age) or the background, but downplay feelings or intentions.

Coding object relations includes several dimensions: (a) differentiation of viewpoints and attributes within and across individuals, (b) integration of feelings, thoughts, actions, and outcomes within and across individuals, and (c) mutuality of autonomy as indicated by characters' mutual respect of each other's autonomy. The next section presents these three parameters of stories in check-list fashion and then distills them into five levels of object relations. Coding of the checklists and of the levels of object relations is not based on the words per se but on the extent to which the schema conveyed by all the story details (not in the additive fashion) correspond to a particular mode of relatedness in terms of the construct of mutuality of autonomy. The coding parameters that focus on object relations incorporate the basic cognitive and affective processes described in Chapters 4 and 5 and are informed by research on object relations and related constructs applied to the Rorschach technique (Blatt & Lerner, 1983; Urist, 1977, 1980) and TAT (DeCharms, 1992; Thompson, 1986; Westen, 1991).

1. Differentiation of Viewpoints and Attributes within and across Individuals

- Viewpoints of each character remain fuzzy. The views or needs of a single character are vague or virtually no distinction is evident between characters. The narrator does not recognize individuality within or across persons. Characters are not distinguishable in terms of their intentions, goals, actions, feelings, thoughts, or outcomes. (This is particularly problematic if their depiction in the stimulus warrants such distinctions.) The narrator may describe characters in ways that are too global (e.g., diffuse negative affect; pervasive sense of upset) or too specific (e.g., has an eyebrow; feeling the table).
- The narrator bases distinctions among characters on superficial, outward attributes (appearance, wealth) or how they look in the stimulus.
- The narrator bases distinctions on a simple, event-feeling connection

or a vague intention without grasping the psychological process (e.g., "crying because he fell" or "wants to find out what something is").

- The narrator bases distinctions on stereotypes or duty, such as carrying out a role as mother, husband, or friend.
- The narrator uses dichotomous distinctions (e.g., good versus bad, weak versus strong, threatening versus safe, special versus ordinary).
- Characters' attributes are seen only in relation to another's needs, desires, or preoccupations (e.g., emotions are misperceived; reasoning about interpersonal events is based on wishes, fears, preoccupations, or associations of the perceiver rather than realistic understanding of social causality).
- Characters differ in their needs, views, and actions, and these differences are seen as legitimate in a mutually respectful relationship.
- The narrator makes distinctions based on elaboration of characters' values, goals, principles, long-term investment, or purposeful, constructive actions.

2. Integration of Feelings and Perspectives within and across Individuals

- The narrator incorporates feelings, tensions, and conflicts into a meaningful context that relates perspectives across individuals (e.g., shared understanding, common goals) or within individuals (e.g., when only one character is portrayed, there are prosocial connections among intentions, actions, and outcomes).
- The narrator conveys a sense of continuity of inner life by reconciling positive and negative facets of characters or genuine connections among individuals (rather than focusing on isolated attributes or momentary concerns).
- The narrator differentiates the perspectives and needs of all characters and balances them by coordinating past, present, and future interests of all concerned.
- Individuals are not left to wallow in painful insight or an upsetting circumstance, nor is there a magical solution. Rather, characters communicate their ideas to others or engage in constructive actions motivated by purpose and principles, as well as mutual respect and understanding.

3. Mutuality of Autonomy

- The narrator gives characters autonomy, sense of initiative, conviction, and deliberate pursuit of realistic, goal-directed activities.
- All characters (in the picture or introduced in the story) are balanced in their respective sense of autonomy. Each is autonomous and appreciates the other's individuality apart from his or her own needs or feelings.
- Characters respond to an immediate situation, action, or demand without prior history or personal conviction (or investment), fail to act, or act without deliberate intention.
- The narrator evaluates people only in terms of what they provide. Characters relate in terms of what they do for or want from each other without recognition of one another's autonomy.
- The narrator presents an imbalance of autonomy where one character is competent, heroic, or intrusive while others are incompetent, helpless, or ignored. This code also applies when a character portrayed in the stimulus is left out of the story.
- The narrator evaluates people as obstacles or hindrances without mutual respect.

Levels of Object Relations (choose the one that fits best)

Many lines of research agree that information processing is more complex when the information is personally engaging or relevant (e.g., McArthur & Baron, 1983; Woike & Aronoff, 1992). For example, Locraft and Teglasi (1997) found that, for children in kindergarten to 6th grade, the complexity of representations on the TAT was much more closely related to children's empathy than chronological age. Although thematic apperceptive narratives reveal the individual's typical style of social information processing, they may not apply to all situations or types of relationships. Individuals who are capable of more nuanced awareness of relationships may choose to behave at lower levels. Some relationships are scripted encounters or functional by design. For example, people who arrange a carpool to transport their children may have no interest in relating to one another except for carrying out their agreed upon functions. Under stress, individuals may tune out the nuances of others' expe-

DON'T FORGET

In addition to content, structural attributes of the story, such as the appropriate match to the stimulus and logical sequence of events, are important in determining the level of object relations.

riences (by choice or necessity) as they focus on their own concerns. Rather than being general, blind spots in perceiving self and others may be limited to specific relationships or specific times when the individual feels jealous or threatened. The point of assessing levels of object relations is not to predict behavior in all relationships but to evaluate the distinctions within and connections among individuals that the narrator characteristically discerns.

Three of five levels of object relations are illustrated with stories discussed earlier to highlight the overlap between previously presented concepts and object relations are described below.

1. Disorganized or Detached Experience of Relatedness

The individual is devoid of resources to understand relationships and, therefore, experiences a severe imbalance of mutuality (e.g., helpless against the whims of controlling and powerful others), poor reality testing, or serious restrictions in autonomy. An impaired cognitive-emotional process (disorganized or highly simplified) disrupts the differentiation and integration of various perspectives (mutuality) and the sense of self-cohesion (autonomy). The individual's inner life is chaotic or globally diffuse, or he or she does not perceive individuality among others, resulting in undifferentiated or unclear boundaries between the inner (self) and outer (others) worlds. The individual may not distinguish thoughts, feelings, and actions among characters ("both feel same way") even when their postures and facial expressions in the picture are different. Autonomy is so limited, and disparity of power is so severe that characters either exploit, malign, or overpower others or feel similarly victimized. Characters show no remorse for hurtful actions or make unrealistic or unreasonable demands on one another. The narrative suggests impaired social reasoning stemming from problems integrating affect and thought or differentiating between wishes and realistic considerations (e.g., implausible sequence of events).

Three stories illustrating this level were told by Slade, age 15, with a Full Scale IQ score (WISC-III) of 113. Slade was undergoing a psychological evaluation in connection with his arrest for the seemingly premeditated murder of his parents. The entire protocol is presented later in this chapter.

Card 1. You want a story about this? Okay. I think the school's gonna have a concert, and he wants to be in it. He goes home gets Dad's old violin, looks at it, and tries to figure it out. Gets Dad to help him play it and learns how and gets in the concert. [E: Thinking?] That he doesn't know how to play and thinking how to learn. [E: Feeling?] Feels anxious, confused.

The premise of the story is unrealistic. The boy wants to attain something instantly (playing in a concert) that ordinarily takes years of preparation. Through a succession of unlikely events, he simply "gets" what he wants (Dad's old violin, Dad's help, and the opportunity to play in the concert) without considering the context (history with music) or purpose beyond participating in one concert. Analogously, the narrator's schema engenders quick solutions to complex and long-term problems.

Card 4. I think guy getting ready to go somewhere. Woman doesn't want him to go. Turns out he leaves. Man's feeling determined to leave. Woman feels alone 'cause he's leaving.

The narrator appears to construct the story in a rote fashion according to each component of the instructions and according to the characters' appearance in the picture. The story does not capture the intensity of the man's emotion nor the connection between the man and the woman (i.e., prior history or context). There is no concern about the inner world of intentions or motives. The harsh reality of Slade's schema is that people simply do as they desire without justification (beyond wanting to), and regardless of the feelings of others.

Card 8BM. Uh, think this boy's shot somebody . . . gun there. Looks like he did it on purpose . . . not a sorrowful look on his face. Imagining the guy getting surgery. [E: Future?] Guy's gonna live and he's gonna get charged with attempted murder. [E: Feeling?] Look like pretty mean.

This depiction of a boy who shot someone on purpose is cold and factual. The story is tied to the pictured cues and centers around social consequences ("gonna get charged with attempted murder"). However, there is no attempt to explain the motives or mitigating circumstances and no remorse. Throughout Slade's protocol, there is a marked absence of a moral rudder or empathic relatedness to steer his behavior.

2. Momentary Experience of Relatedness

A rudimentary sense of autonomy or limited mutuality exists in the moment and coincides with a self-absorbed or self-serving style of relatedness. The narrator notices characteristics of others as they pertain to immediate need states, so that perception of self and others shifts according to circumstances and without insight or reflection. Emotions are tied to immediate external considerations, and remorse is tied to consequences. Inner attributes are ill-defined (e.g., diffuse negative affect or global sense of upset) or are based on stereotypes (e.g., unconvincing verbalization about duty or blind obligation) without experiencing the personality as a continuous, cohesive whole. Interactions entail significant imbalance in mutuality of autonomy (e.g., emphasis on one perspective or disparity of status or of power) where individuals need others to foster self-cohesion. The narrator differentiates characters on the basis of momentary need or immediate gain without the sense that they are whole persons. Relatedness may be experienced only when the other is physically present (a single character feels alone, no one helps; concerns are basic revolving around needs for safety, survival, or protection). The relationship per se is unimportant, not durable, and interchangeable (e.g., no reference to shared experience; no stated or implied standards or principles). Fantasy may replace actual relations (e.g., characters are unreal such as actors). Characters may be passive or reactive, taking no responsibility for actions or outcomes.

Three stories told by Jim, age 16, with average IQ, illustrate this level. Prior to the evaluation, which took place in an inpatient setting, Jim had been diagnosed with Conduct Disorder.

Card 1. He's looking at a violin. Probably bored, doesn't want to do. Somebody put it in front of him. Feeling angry and mad 'cause somebody asked him to do it. So he doesn't do it.

The boy is reactive to his immediate feelings in response to an external demand, the purpose of which is unexplained. The "somebody" who put the violin in front of him is not seen as a whole person (with intentions, reasons, or even an identity).

Card 4. Don't know. I'm not good at these things. It's a man and a woman and she's trying to talk to him. Maybe they're arguing. I don't know. He's feeling, I don't know. She's feeling, I don't know, and he's trying to leave 'cause maybe he's angry, hurt, upset. Don't know. Probably stay and listen and then he leaves.

In contrast to Slade's story at the previous level, the two individuals are engaged (arguing) in an interaction that captures their depiction in the stimulus. However, their engagement is momentary as the man will go through the motions of listening, then leaves as he originally intended.

Card 8BM. Somebody got messed up so two people have to do surgery and person is on the table. Son's in the room. He's feeling scared 'cause maybe he, Dad, might die. He deals with it and waits to see what happens.

When someone gets "messed up," it is natural for others to try to save him. However, as the father's life hangs in the balance, the son "deals with" his own feelings (in the moment) and then "waits to see what happens to his father."

3. Functional Experience of Relatedness

Emphasis is on the duty or function served rather than the human connection. Reciprocity is recognized in the form of a rigid reliance on quid pro quo exchanges. Approval or disapproval, as well as rewards and punishments, contribute to the functional exchange. Individuals anticipate punishment for wrong-doing and feel genuine remorse. However, they do not set their own standards but attempt to conform to expectations. Obligation is not grounded in internal forces (such as ethical principles) but constitutes a give-and-take response or duty as dictated by societal mores. Thus, obligation or reciprocity is not valued as an end (i.e., a matter of principle) but as instrumental to something else (i.e., reciprocal functions).

Three stories told by Jaime, age 10-9 with Stanford-Binet IQ score of 138, illustrate this level. At the time of the evaluation, teachers described her as "very smart" but often "spacey" and "inattentive."

Card 1. Okay. This boy, he is sad because before his mother told him that he had to practice violin, otherwise he would be in trouble. Now the boy doesn't like to practice violin, and he's mad at his mother. And he wants to break the violin except it's an expensive violin and his grandfather gave it to his mother and his mother gave it to him so he knows he shouldn't break it. So he practices, but it's without heart and soul.

The narrative smoothly incorporates the directions and stimulus cues. The boy in the story is resentful of family pressure (at least two generations) to pursue an activity that he doesn't like but succumbs to this extrinsic source of motivation. He suppresses his anger and complies, playing without "heart" to avoid getting into trouble. Jaime has a longer-term view than Jim and understands the intentions of others. She, like her character, goes through the motions of what she is supposed to do. Difficulty with sustained attention or disinterest in the activity may be contributing to the tension ("doesn't like to practice").

Card 4. This guy is a cop, spy, and he goes to meet people, does spy work. And his wife is worried about him because this is one of his most dangerous things. He wants to go out, and she won't let him. He breaks free and tells her it is for the good of the country and he leaves. The end.

There is acknowledgment of the good intention of the other (wife is worried) and a context for the disagreement. Yet, the man's function as a "spy" is carried out with only lip service to the relationship ("tells her it's for the good of the country"). Duty to one's country could have been balanced with responsiveness to the wife's concern, for example, promising to be careful or to keep in contact. Again, we see that Jaime discerns others' good intentions and wants to stay within conventional bounds (do her duty). However, her character, similar to the boy in the previous story, acts without "heart" by not reciprocating the emotional engagement of his wife. Being a "spy" is an exciting activity that would appeal to an individual who has difficulty sustaining attention in more routine situations.

Card 8BM. This little boy is hoping that his father will come out of surgery healthy. His father had internal bleeding, and the doctor said it could be fatal. He doesn't want his father to die because his father is his only living relative besides his grandparents who are so old and frail and wouldn't be able to take care of him. His mom was killed when she gave birth to him because the doctor made a mistake and cut something that killed her. After a few weeks, the doctors say the boy's father will be able to go home in a matter of days. The boy is extremely happy for two reasons. One the doctors say his father will be able to go home soon and the doctors also say that he won't have another fatal sickness for a long time. The end.

The boy's concern for his father is linked to his function as the only living relative who is capable of taking care of him.

4. Reciprocity and Standards are Basic to Relatedness

Autonomy and relatedness are governed by a strong sense of fair play or prosocial standards. These values promote continuity and consistency in relations with others and within the self. Reciprocity is not perceived as quid pro quo but as a natural mode of relating among individuals who care about each other. The narrator clearly differentiates the characters and gives them internalized standards and rules of conduct that are sufficiently flexible to permit appropriate compromise.

The following three stories were told by #203, a kindergarten participant in a research study, rated by his teacher as high in empathy. (All participants had a verbal IQ of average or higher.)

Card 1. He feels sad. Then he still's sad. He can't . . . doesn't know how to play it. He tries to play it but it sounds squeaky and ugly. [E: Thinking?] How would it sound if he knew how to play it. Then he tries again and then he does it good.

The character is sad because the violin sounds squeaky and keeps working to attain an implied standard (to improve from sounding squeaky to good). The boy's effort is sufficient for the goal and outcome; trying to make a nice sound (a process goal) can be accomplished relatively easily (compared to the dilemma presented in Slade's story of getting into a concert without knowing how to play). Although no other character is introduced, there is a clear sense of internalized standards that "stand in" for external relationships. The next story, told to an interpersonal scene, reveals this generalized connection in the context of a specific interaction.

Card 4. There is a man sick and there's a woman taking care of him. He does want to do something but she won't let him because she knows he is sick. And he was almost ready to do it but she did not let him. He didn't do it because she didn't want him to. She's thinking if she had let him do it, what would have happened. He was thinking what would happen if he didn't do it. [E: Feeling?] Sorta happy because he didn't do it. Maybe at that moment he wanted to kill a snake.

A man refrains from doing something he wants because a caring woman insists that this will jeopardize his health. There is no threat of disapproval or other form of coercion, hence no major disparity of power. At the end, the man is glad he listened.

Card 8BM. The boy is having an operation. And he's asleep. He gets a big cut. [E: Before?] He got in a accident on a wedding day. That's the same boy after the operation [boy in the front of the picture]. After the operation that's what he looks like. He feels sad because he has his operation. [E: Turns out?] It turns out okay, the doctors help him, and he gets better.

This story is about a boy thinking back on his surgery that was necessitated by an accident. He recovers and goes on with his life. Despite the unsophisticated language, this narrative is a resourceful explanation of the relationship between foreground and background in the stimulus and depicts an autonomous character who recovers from adversity.

5. Relatedness through Mutuality of Autonomy

This level is characterized by full appreciation of uniqueness and individuality, apart from needs or requirements of social exchange or conventional morality. The narrative conveys an awareness of the relationship between transient and enduring psychological experience and of complex motives in self and others. The narrator portrays the inner lives and concerns of all characters in accord with their depiction in the stimulus and in ways that entail mutual respect for individualistic styles, together with appreciation of subtle intra- and interpersonal nuance. Characters value societal rules or obligations in the context of mutual care and commitment to moral standards. Mutuality of autonomy is far removed from the concept of rugged individuality or extricating oneself from the web of community. Indeed, the ties are so strong that they transcend the other's immediate presence. There is a fine-tuned understanding of multiply interacting dimensions of experience such that the concerns of one character seamlessly incorporate the views of the others or balance short- and long-term considerations.

Three stories told by Benjie, age 9-11, Stanford–Binet IQ score of 140, illustrate this level. Benjie was participating in a research study and was described by his teacher as being intrinsically motivated by standards rather than by grades and highly esteemed by classmates.

Card 1. The boy has a violin except he can't play it very nicely. So he's kind of upset because he can't figure out how to play it well. You want to know what I think this thing is? [Points to the paper under the violin] [E: Up to you.] He's thinking whether he should keep trying or quit it because he doesn't know how to play it. [E: Turns out?] He gives up because he decides that he'll never be able to do it.

The boy makes an autonomous decision, not in the spur of the moment nor in response to frustration, but after concluding that he will never succeed at the particular activity. He does not seek help, advice, or approval because the decision is his to make. The feeling of "upset" is caused by the boy's perception of being unable to meet his own standard for playing "nicely." There is no hint of external pressure; the boy simply assumes that others would respect his (well-reasoned) decision.

Card 4. Well, there's a man that looks very mad at someone who annoyed or offended him, and his wife is trying to stop him from doing anything he'll regret such as attacking the person who was offending him. At the end, she'll restrain him and he'll stop and get over his anger.

Mutuality of autonomy is demonstrated by the wife's trying to stop the husband from doing anything "he'll regret." Therefore, she does not impose her own standards but realizes that her husband is blinded by his anger and offers a rational perspective. In turn, the husband understands the force of his anger. After he listens to his wife, he takes responsibility for his feelings and "gets over his anger." Short and long-term psychological processes are nicely balanced in this story. The inner and outer worlds of both characters are differentiated and coordinated.

Card 8BM. A boy, yeah a boy, more like an adolescent has to have surgery, and he's dreaming about how it's going to be, and he's a little scared so he's thinking how it's going to be. So he sees what's going to happen to him, and it makes him even more scared. I don't know why there's something that looks like a rifle there. [E: Ending?] He goes through it, and he realizes he was worried about nothing because he didn't even feel it.

There is a nuanced understanding that dwelling on an anxiety-provoking event is counterproductive, particularly if nothing can be done about it. Sometimes, the worry is more scary than the reality. Again, this is a nice portrayal of time sequence and a resourceful accounting of the stimulus.

CASE ILLUSTRATION

Slade

Slade, a 15-year-old, was evaluated to understand his frame of mind pursuant to being charged with the premeditated murder of his parents. Professionals administered various assessment tools, including the TAT, the Rorschach, and Wechsler scales. Though he was generally cooperative during the evaluation, Slade was constantly drumming his fingers on the table and, at times, laughed inappropriately. Figure 6.1 displays the coding of Slade's protocol on the variables introduced in this chapter.

Card 1. You want a story about this? Okay. I think the school's gonna have a concert and he wants to be in it. He goes home, gets Dad's old violin, looks at it, and tries to figure it out. Gets dad to help him play it and learns how and gets in the concert. [E: Thinking?] That he doesn't know how to play and thinking how to learn. [E: Feeling?] Feels anxious, confused.

Import: A person can get what he or she wants even if it is unrealistic (to play in the concert without going through the normally time-consuming process).

Explanatory hypotheses: In this story, the narrator expresses the conviction that quick and easy solutions are attainable for complex and long-term problems. The story shows a lack of understanding of "how" things happen and

I. DIFFERENTIATION, INTEGRATION, AND MUTUALITY OF AUTONOMY

A. Differentiation of Viewpoints and Attributes Within and Across Individuals

(Check as many as apply for each story) Cards→	1	2	3BM	4	5	6BM	8BM	13BM	13MF	17BM
Viewpoints of different characters (or single character) remain fuzzy. Little or no distinction is evident.	✓		✓	✓		✓		✓	✓	✓
Distinctions among characters are based on superficial, outward attributes (lifestyle, possessions) or how they look in the stimulus.		✓	✓	✓		✓	✓	✓	✓	
Distinctions are based on simple event-feeling connections (e.g., crying because he fell) or vague intentions (wants to find out what something is) without grasping the psychological process.						✓				
Distinctions are based on stereotypes or duty in carrying out roles as parent, spouse, child, or friend.										
Distinctions are dichotomous (e.g., good vs. bad; weak vs. strong; threatening vs. safe; special vs. ordinary).					✓					
Characters' attributes are seen only in relation to another's needs, desires, or preoccupations (e.g., emotions are misperceived; reasoning about interpersonal events is based on wishes, fears, or preoccupations of the perceiver rather than realistic understanding of social causality).	✓	✓		✓			✓		✓	
Characters differ in their needs, views, and actions, and these differences are seen as legitimate in a mutually respectful relationship.										
A character is committed to principles and is invested in a relationship or in prosocial goal-directed activities (not just wanting an outcome).										

B. Integration of Feelings and Perspectives Within and Across Individuals

(Check as many as apply for each story) Cards→	1	2	3BM	4	5	6BM	8BM	13BM	13MF	17BM
Feelings, tensions, and conflicts are incorporated into a meaningful context that relates perspectives across or within individuals.										
Sense of continuity of inner life is conveyed by reconciling positive and negative facets of characters (e.g., realistically managing emotions) or by genuine connections among individuals (versus isolated attributes or momentary concerns).										
The perspectives and needs of all characters are balanced by coordinating past, present, and future interests of all concerned.										
Characters communicate their ideas to others and their actions are based on mutual understanding and respect.										

C. Mutuality of Autonomy

(Check as many as apply for each story) Cards→	1	2	3BM	4	5	6BM	8BM	13BM	13MF	17BM
A character shows autonomy, sense of initiative, conviction, or a deliberate pursuit of realistic, prosocial, or goal-directed activities.										
All characters are balanced in their respective sense of autonomy. They respect and appreciate each other's individuality (e.g., intentions, feelings, thoughts, actions, outcomes) apart from their own needs or feelings.										
Characters respond to an immediate situation, action, or demand without prior history, conviction, or investment; they fail to act or act without deliberate intention.	✓	✓	✓	✓	✓	✓	✓	✓	✓	
People are evaluated only in terms of what they provide. Characters relate in terms of what they do for or want from each other without recognizing one another's autonomy.	✓	✓	NA	✓	NA	✓	✓	NA	✓	
There is an imbalance of autonomy where one person is competent, heroic, or intrusive, while others are incompetent, helpless, or ignored.	✓	✓		✓	✓		✓			
People are viewed as obstacles or as harmful.		✓			✓		✓			

Note: The above qualities may be implicit, particularly when only one character is depicted.

Figure 6.1 Relationships

simplistic reasoning. First, wanting and getting to be in a school concert without a prior history of playing or practicing with the band violates basic tenets of social causality. The expectation that a boy would learn a complex skill (by getting his father's violin and help) in the time between the announcement of a concert and the actual performance indicates a failure to grasp the process

D. Levels of Object Relations

Level One: Disorganized or detached experience of relatedness. Disorganized or highly simplified thought process disrupts the differentiation and integration of various perspectives (mutuality) and the sense of self-cohesion (autonomy). This level is characterized by impaired social reasoning where the individual is devoid of resources to understand relationships and, therefore, experiences a severe imbalance of mutuality (e.g., helpless against the whims of controlling and powerful others or detached from relationships) and/or serious restriction of autonomy or poor reality testing (e.g., unrealistic expectations). Individuality (in circumstance, emotion, intention, thought) is not salient, resulting in lack of differentiation or responsiveness across individuals and unrealistic coordination between the inner and outer worlds within individuals.

Level Two: Momentary experience of relatedness. Personality is not experienced as a continuous, cohesive whole, and there is rudimentary recognition of individuality. Therefore, self-esteem and relationships with others exist in the moment. Limited autonomy pulls for differentiating others on the basis of momentary need or the immediate situation without the sense that they are whole persons. Therefore, characteristics of others are salient if they pertain to immediate needs or wants (character's portrayal in the stimulus may not even be noticed). Feelings are tied to immediate external demands or circumstances, and remorse is tied to consequences. Perception of self and others shifts (dichotomously) according to circumstances and without insight or reflection. Characters' inner attributes and individual differences are ill-defined, dichotomous, or are based on stereotypes. An imbalance of mutuality of autonomy and/or a disparity of status or of power may be explicit or implicit.

Level Three: Functional experience of relatedness. Emphasis is on the function served rather than on enduring connection with reliance on rigid quid pro quo exchanges. Approval or disapproval as well as reward or punishment contribute to the functional exchange. Characters attempt to conform to each other's expectations rather than engage in autonomous goal-directed activities or efforts to meet standards. They appear to take turns in carrying out their functional roles, and this exchange is the foundation for the relationship. Attributes that pertain to character's functions are most salient. Characters show remorse and accept punishment for wrongdoing.

Level Four: Relatedness through reciprocity and standards. A sense of fair play dictates expectations in relations with others and in self-evaluation. Reciprocity is not perceived as quid pro quo but as a natural mode of relating among individuals who care about each other. Characters are clearly differentiated, autonomous, and have internalized standards and rules of conduct that permit appropriate compromise.

Level Five: Relatedness through mutuality of autonomy. There is full appreciation of uniqueness and individuality, apart from the perceiver's needs or requirements of social exchange. Inner life and concerns of all characters are portrayed in ways that show full mutuality of autonomy and appreciation of subtle intra- and interpersonal nuance, in keeping with the stimulus cues. A fine-tuned understanding of multiply interacting dimensions of experience includes a distinction between transient and enduring psychological experience, balance between the inner and outer worlds of self and others, and coordination of long- and short-term considerations.

(Choose one level for each story)

Card	1	2	3BM	4	5	6BM	8BM	13B	13MF	17BM	
Slade	1	1	2	1	1	1	1	1	1		

Figure 6.1 (continued)

involved. There is a sense that the narrator's judgment disregards the constraints of social reality. Second, there is no explanation for why the boy wants to be in the concert (i.e., interest in music, being with friends). In fact, when asked how the boy feels, Slade focuses on the stimulus (negative emotion) without connecting the feeling to the happy events in the story.

Card 2. I draw a blank. All right. I think her father wants her to do work. [E: What kind?] On farm. She wants to go to school and learn something good. Family wants her to work on farm. She's trying to decide. Looks like she goes to school, walkin' away. [E: Feeling?] Concerned, little worried, unsure.

Import: If a girl's family wants something different from what she wants, she will do as she pleases without considering their reasons or intentions and without any communication.

Explanatory hypotheses: Simplified reasoning and either/or thinking are evident in the girl's decision-making process. In delineating the central problem as a dichotomy between what is wanted by the family and girl, there is a sense of detachment as though each encounter is split from the others (no relationship, no historical context). The central character does what she wants without heeding the needs of others or recognizing her place in the family. The girl's decision also fails to include implications for the future and is only vaguely connected to her own intentions or goals ("learn something good"). One wonders what this girl did yesterday and what she will do tomorrow. As in the previous story, the emotions and actions refer back to the stimulus (girl looks as if she is walking away) rather than being incorporated meaningfully into the narrative progression.

Card 3BM. What's that by the foot? Don't know if boy or girl. [E: Doesn't matter.] This person, uh, don't know, maybe he/she drunk. Trying to decide whether to drive or not and thing by leg is keys to car. Doesn't want to drive 'cause afraid will crash car.

Import: A person who is drunk thinks about driving (without a destination) but decides against it only because he or she is afraid of crashing the car.

Explanatory hypotheses: Again, reasoning is simplified and is restricted to the immediate considerations with no history or aim. The premise of the story (to drive or not to drive while drunk) has no tie to past events that might provide a reason to drive to a particular destination or explain why the character might be drunk. Hence, the character's dilemma has no context in external circumstances or inner psychological processes. The outcome is a decision provoked by fear of consequences without reference to the character's intention in wanting to drive in the first place.

Card 4. I think guy getting ready to go somewhere. Woman doesn't want him to go. Turns out he leaves. Man's feeling determined to leave. Woman feels alone 'cause he's leaving.

Import: If a man wants to leave a woman, he will do so knowing that she will feel alone.

Explanatory hypotheses: The interaction is understood simplistically without any sense of relatedness between the man and woman or durable intentions for actions. Characters' intentions or history of prior interactions seems irrelevant, and there is no communication, compromise, or concern for others. Likewise, a person has no larger, internal purpose for actions; the man just wants to leave. The emotions are ignored, and there is no glue that sustains long-term interests or binds people together, even for a moment. The message here (as in Card 2) is that if people want different things, they just go their separate ways without caring about each other and without any particular reason for leaving.

Card 5. Don't know. She gets home and window broken and door open. Just walkin' in to the living room looking to see what's missing. Safe been broken open and all the money's gone. [E: Feeling?] Scared all stuff stolen and don't know if burglar still in the house or not.

Import: If someone (an older woman) is a victim, she remains at the mercy of others without taking constructive action.

Explanatory hypotheses: Following a burglary, a frightened woman, concerned about the loss of her possessions, is left vulnerable to revictimization without acting or seeking help to protect herself (e.g., calling the police, leaving her house). The narrator seems to feel no inclination to bring closure to the woman's predicament, leaving her afraid and not knowing if she is safe from the burglars who may still be lurking. The character's emotion fails to spur appropriate action, and the narrator is too detached to provide an ending that ties up loose ends and removes the woman from danger.

Card 6BM. I think man just told mother he's going off to war. She looking out window contemplating what's going to happen. Turns out he goes to war and comes home safely. Got to tell one that's different.

Import: When a man tells his mother that he's going off to war, he gets no response, but he does return safely.

Explanatory hypotheses: This is no ordinary good-bye scene as mother and son seem disconnected emotionally. The son brings seemingly distressing news about having to go off to war, yet the emotional impact of this information is lost (the mother distantly contemplates what will happen in the future). The story is bound to a stilted and literal reading of the picture without any hint of relatedness between mother and son.

Card 8BM. Uh, think this boy's shot somebody . . . gun there. Looks like he did it on purpose . . . not a sorrowful look on his face. Imagining the guy getting surgery. [E: What happens in the future?] Guy's gonna live and he's gonna get charged with attempted murder. [E: Feeling?] Look like pretty mean.

Import: When a person shoots someone on purpose, he doesn't regret it, and because the "guy" lives, he only gets charged with attempted murder.

Explanatory hypotheses: Taking his cues from the picture, Slade describes a shooting done on purpose without remorse because "not a sorrowful look on his face." The act of shooting someone would normally beg for an explanation rather than being accepted as a routine occurrence. However, Slade does not provide a socially acceptable reason for the shooting. He matter-of-factly concludes the story with the boy's being charged with attempted murder. Again, the reasoning is simplified; the presence of the gun and the boy's facial expression automatically "add up" to a shooting done on purpose, without prior history, reason, or moral feelings. Analogously, Slade is likely to act on the basis of highly simplified reasoning that is detached from moral emotions, interpersonal connections, or durable intentions. Even his awareness of possible consequences seems detached from its implications. There is no hint here that Slade regards human life as intrinsically valuable.

Card 13B. Think he's living on a farm and growing up farm life. He's just sittin' in the sun. [E: In the future?] Grows up, becomes a farmer. [E: Thinking? Feeling?] Seems concerned about something, looks a little troubled, maybe he's worried about the livestock.

Import: If a boy lives on a farm, he grows up to be a farmer (without his own thoughts or feelings).

Explanatory hypothesis: Like the other stories, this one is a product of simplistic reasoning. Slade uses the pictured cues to construct a simple story line that ignores the boy's inner life and does not introduce any other characters. Rather than dealing with the boy's current thoughts and feelings, the narrator takes a big jump in time (boy grows up to be a farmer). In response to inquiry, Slade describes the boy as concerned with livestock, a vague and seemingly associative connection to farm life that is not quite appropriate to the child's age.

Card 13MF. Think they're both drunk. At a party and had sex. He wake up not knowing who she was. He's kind of in a stupor. [E: Thinking?] Worried, unsure of surroundings.

Import: After getting drunk at a party and having sex with a woman he doesn't know, a man is disoriented and unsure of his surroundings.

Explanatory hypotheses: In a matter-of-fact way, Slade describes a man thinking only of himself and of his situation in the moment. Again, intentions, prior events, relatedness, or future consequences do not factor into Slade's thinking.

Card 17BM. Uh, looks like he's climbing a rope. Maybe a construction dude, but not wearing shoes, pants. Happy, naked guy climbing a rope. [E: Thinking?] Climb rope. [he laughs] Being a monkey. [E: In the future?] He ends up here [referring to the institution in which he is confined].

Import: If a man does strange things, he ends up in a psychiatric institution.

Process import: Without understanding emotions or intentions, a person cannot explain this situation so he or she laughs it off.

Explanatory hypotheses: Unable to delve into motives or intentions, Slade cannot explain what is happening in the scene and basically describes the stimulus. Though he recognizes consequences, he fails to experience their emotional impact.

Narrative Summary

The simplified process of reasoning and concrete thinking reflected in Slade's stories contrast with his performance on more structured tests. Focusing on external appearances, Slade describes what is happening in the pictured scenes without tying the current situation to past or future events or to an inner world of emotions or durable intentions. His characters are frozen according to their portrayals in the stimulus, without meaningful relationships to one another and without emotional engagement in long-term pursuits. When prompted to include feelings (because he does not do so spontaneously), Slade's tendency is to refer back to how the characters looked in the stimulus, thus, divorcing the character's experiences (story events) and their actions from their feelings. Although Slade is able to provide a label for the feelings portrayed in the picture, he does not grasp their psychological significance in sustaining relationships or formulating intentions. Actions and reactions are based on momentary considerations that do not have a realistic link to the past or future and are not meaningfully integrated with feelings or intentions. Slade's judgments and expectations fail to incorporate a realistic understanding of social causality or consideration for others. When responding to situations, he is not guided by interpersonal connections, long-term goals, or durable intentions. Rather, he is preoccupied with what he wants in the moment and does not grasp any links between the current circumstances, prior history, and implications for later. Moreover, on an emotional level, he sees no connection between himself and others, nor is he invested in concerns beyond the moment. His focus on isolated events that are disconnected from the multiple dimensions of human experience is consistent with the detached demeanor he exhibited during the evaluation and with the general impressions that he lacks remorse.

🖋 TEST YOURSELF 🖋

1. **Object relations theory**
   (a) focuses on observable transactions among people.
   (b) focuses on early memories.
   (c) overlaps with schema theory.
   (d) all of the above.

2. **Explain why *object relations* is to *object representations* as *abstract* is to concrete.**

3. **The process by which individuals learn skills for daily functioning is essentially the same as the process of "internalization" that leads to the development of psychic structure.** True or False?

4. **Define each of the following three pathological modes of relating described within the object relations framework: (a) self-object, (b) transitional object, (c) part-object.**

5. **How are autonomy and mutuality of autonomy pertinent to object relations?**

6. **How are positive emotions, empathy, and emotion regulation pertinent to level of object relations?**

Answers: 1. c; 2. Object relations and abstract schemas embody principles that organize conceptions of self and other, whereas object representation is directly tied to a specific relationship; 3. False; 4. (a) Self-object relations: failure to notice characteristics of others apart from one's own feelings or preoccupations. (b) Transitional object relations: valuing others only in terms of the comfort they provide. (c) Part-object relations: restriction of interest in others to the function they serve; 5. Autonomy refers to the connections between the inner and outer worlds within a single individual, and hence to the representation of the self in relation to external circumstances. The more autonomous an individual, the more he or she can value the autonomy of others (mutuality of autonomy) and appreciate others apart from self-interest; 6. Poor emotion regulation is associated with focus on one's own discomfort in response to others' distress and disrupts empathy. Positive emotions and empathy spur interest in characteristics of others, resulting in more complex processing of interpersonal information.

Seven

ESSENTIALS OF TAT ASSESSMENT OF MOTIVATION AND SELF-REGULATION

Motivation and self-regulation are reciprocally linked: Goals serve regulatory functions, and performance of goal-directed activities requires self-regulation. The field of motivation addresses the twin questions of *what* moves individuals to act and *how* they pursue their intention. Thus, motivational schemas include the desired goals (what) and the means to attain them (how). Once goals have been solidified, they become sources of self-regulation because they (a) selectively orient attention to information in the surroundings or in memory, (b) influence choices of tasks or activities, and (c) energize effort in the pursuit of purposeful activities (Gollwitzer & Moskowitz, 1996; McClelland, 1987). In turn, the implementation of instrumental actions to pursue intentions and to subordinate immediate preferences to long-term commitment requires two types of self-regulatory processes (Kuhl, 1984, 1992): *action control,* to maintain intentions in the face of competing motivational tendencies from internal forces or distraction by external sources, and *performance control* to carry out the intended action. Thus, motivated behavior entails not only the setting of goals but also the resources to pursue and maintain intentions over time or in the face of external or internal barriers. Indeed, the field of motivation highlights the self-regulatory functions of goals and the self-regulatory processes needed to pursue goals.

Self-regulation itself is an important goal that influences other goals. The disciplines of temperament and personality acknowledge the centrality of self-regulation but differ in their emphases. The field of temperament focuses on the regulation of basic processes, such as maintaining optimal levels of stimulation or emotional intensity, that are grounded in a set of neurobiological systems (Rothbart, Derryberry, & Posner, 1994; Strelau, 1994). The study of personality emphasizes structures or processes (i.e. an "executive" or "ego") that perform self-regulatory functions by orchestrating and balancing the individual's various tendencies to meet adaptive demands or attain specific purposes (see Karoly, 1993 for a review). Individuals with greater temperamental reactivity face greater self-regulatory challenges to allay fears, control their irritability, put their negative and positive emotions in perspective, and keep unwelcome, ruminative thoughts at bay (e.g., Henderson & Fox, 1998; Rothbart & Bates, 1998).

Any given behavior may be the product of flexible compromises between short-term self-regulatory demands and long-term goals or may constitute aimless reactions to external stimuli or short-sighted efforts to reduce negative emotions (anxiety, boredom, tension, emptiness). For instance, those with high reactivity in novel situations may haphazardly avoid unfamiliar situations or develop various strategies to deal with the feelings such situations elicit (plan ahead, prepare, practice). Thus, the *what* of motivation may range from attempts to cope with immediate preoccupations and temperamental exigencies to the pursuit of well-articulated goals and principles. The *how* of motivation may range from being reactive and haphazard to being planful and organized.

In a sense, temperamental self-regulation is a building block of personality-based self-regulation. Motivation, for instance, has been characterized according to how individualistic temperamental inclinations are balanced with social expectations in the formulation and pursuit of goals (see Rapid Reference 7.1). Individuals who expend a great deal of energy to keep from being overcome by negative affect may be limited in focusing on long term interests and may favor coping strategies geared to immediate relief. Those who often engage in activities that are at odds with temperamental predispositions may pay a heavy price in stress (Strelau, 1983). A comprehensive theory of motivation would identify the psychological processes, both conscious and uncon-

DON'T FORGET

The various temperamentally rooted regulatory systems influence one another. For instance, problems with attention regulation (e.g., poor control over intrusively ruminative thought) detract from affect regulation by limiting flexibility in shifting attention to other information with more positive affect tone or to considerations that would bring to awareness contextual factors that might mitigate the emotion (Derryberry & Rothbart, 1988; Martin & Tesser, 1989; Rothbart, Ziaie, & O'Boyle, 1992).

≡Rapid Reference 7.1

Intrinsic and Extrinsic Sources of Motivation

- *Introjection* is a process of "taking in" rules for actions by referencing external authority (approval or disapproval) and involves the underlying subjective experience of being controlled by rules and expectations of others (punishment) or by inner forces acting on the individual (threat of guilt, promise of self approval, pressure based on self-esteem). *Integration,* on the other hand, is a process in which a person identifies with and values an activity, accepting full responsibility for the behavior and its outcome. The subjective experience entails a greater sense of consistency and coherence between the person's behavior and inner states (Deci & Ryan, 1985; Ryan & Connell, 1989).

- The terms self-control and self-regulation have been applied to goal-directed behaviors that are outgrowths of introjection and integration, respectively (Kuhl & Fuhrman, 1998). *Self-control* refers to the pursuit of goal-directed activities that are imposed by significant others or assumed by the adoption of cultural values but are not supported by the individual's preferences. The self-control mode of pursuing goals involves a great deal of conscious effort to overcome personal proclivities in a struggle to keep going against the temperamental grain. In contrast, *self-regulation* refers to the pursuit of goal-directed activities that are in accord with the person's short- and long-term inclinations and are congruent with an integrated sense of self.

scious, that influence goal setting and shape goal-directed actions, as well as the impact of goals on cognition, emotion, and behavior (see Cantor & Sanderson, 1999).

TAT AND MOTIVATION

Various motives such as achievement, power, or affiliation are typically studied separately with TAT stories (see Smith, 1992). However, persons often balance individualistic aspirations and interpersonal goals with concerns for the welfare of others, and their relative emphases may differ according to culture (Suarez-Orozco, 1989). More importantly, regardless of the specific motive, a generic structure comprised of the connections among goals, actions, and outcomes underlies all types of motivational concerns, including individualistic achievement, interpersonal relationships, moral decision-making, and coping with adverse circumstances (Arnold, 1962). The "import" of the story detailed in Chapter 3 captures the narrator's ability to formulate intentions and generate appropriate means to pursue them. Goals motivate behavior regardless of whether they focus on self-development (e.g., seeking fulfillment, overcoming feelings of inferiority through work), lifestyle (e.g., earning a living, overcoming poverty, being like everyone else), relationships (e.g., avoiding rejection, gaining friendship, earning freedom from control of others), feeling good (e.g., avoiding fear or anxiety, seeking enjoyable activities), or striving for accomplishment. The variables that are most clinically relevant to motivation are (a) formulating and sustaining an intention; (b) planning and implementing steps to pursue goal-directed activities; (c) anticipating consequences; and (d) formulating implications for self-evaluation. Therefore, the level of motivation is based on the import derived from the connections among goals or intentions, actions, and outcomes.

Before designating the levels derived from TAT stories, the next section introduces the central components of motivation: (a) *goal formulation,* which describes the manner in which the problem, goal, or dilemma is delineated, (b) *reaction to the goal,* which includes emotions or complications engendered by the goal, and (c) *the actions and reactions,* which are steps taken in pursuit of intentions.

Goal Formulation

Once goals are solidified, they function like other mental representations that are activated automatically by environmental cues or internal processes and serve as regulators of cognition, affect, and behavior (see Bargh & Chartrand, 1999; Gollwitzer, 1999 for a review). The nature of the goals pursued by individuals, the degree of risk undertaken to pursue goals, and the type of feedback sought depend on the perceived conditions under which the self is viewed as worthy or unworthy, competent or incompetent (see Rapid Reference 7.2).

Generally, TAT pictures suggest a goal or dilemma to be incorporated into the narrative. Provided that a goal has been set, and regardless of whether it is imposed or self-initiated, the nature of the goal may be characterized by narrative structure and process or content.

≡Rapid Reference 7.2

Learning Goals versus Performance Goals (Dweck, 1986, 1996)

Goals are set depending on whether self-evaluation centers on internal standards versus external feedback or consequences (Gollwitzer & Kirchof, 1999; Raynor & McFarlin, 1986):

1. *Learning goals* are set by those who are motivated by their own self-evaluation and who prefer to undertake challenges that maximize learning and seek realistic feedback.
2. *Performance goals* are set by those who are more concerned with the favorable judgment of others and who emphasize outcomes rather than investment in the task and strive to enhance a sense of competence by seeking positive or by avoiding negative feedback.

Narrative Structure and Process

- The narrator offers clear and appropriate definition of the central problem, tension, or dilemma, given the stimulus. Problem definition implies cause-effect understanding rather than a vague, nonspecific intention or tension.
- The story is logical and proceeds without irrelevant or contradictory details. Reasoning is realistic, and sequence of events is plausible.

Content

- A realistic, prosocial goal is imposed by others but accepted willingly by a character. The goal is in accord with socially accepted roles and responsibilities and not coerced by others' whims.
- Characters set a realistic, prosocial goal or seek to resolve a conflict or dilemma rather than react to the provocation or desire of the moment (such as wanting to get a toy or to play) or engage in routine activities.
- Characters exhibit interest, curiosity, pride, concern, empathy, and a commitment to standards or ideals that foster achievement or prosocial activity.
- Characteristics of goals for each story may be noted as Clear/vague or absent; self-initiated/imposed; long-term/short term; prosocial/

antisocial; realistic/unrealistic; process/outcome; attainment of positive/aversion of negative; interpersonal/task; substantial/trivial; idealistic/concrete; fulfillment of inner standards/fulfillment of demands or expectations.

Goal Maintenance

To sustain goal-directed activities, the individual must maintain intentions in the face of competing motivational tendencies and distraction from external sources (action control) as well as possess the competencies to carry out the intended actions (performance control) (see Kuhl, 1984, 1992).

In TAT stories, complications in the plot, perceived competency to attain the goal, external barriers, or changing conditions flesh out the narrator's motive-related schemas. The character's reaction may reveal problems sustaining the goal (e.g., abandoning the goal, changing the goal, facing conflicting goals), anticipating obstacles or supports from the environment, difficulties implementing goal-related activities (e.g., experiencing boredom or lack of confidence), or other complexities. The following characteristics of narrative pertain to the maintenance of goals:

Narrative Structure and Process
- The story proceeds according to a plan rather than made up detail by detail.
- The narrator incorporates all parts of the instructions with or without inquiry. If prompted, the response enhances the story rather than being minimal or repetitive.

Content
- Goals are attuned to the inner world (what is wanted) and to external realities. Accordingly, characters display foresight, plan ahead, set priorities, or anticipate consequences for self, others or both. Characters realistically appraise external or internal barriers to goal attainment (they do not engage in ruminative preoccupation) without abandonment of the goal. For example, characters may choose a realistic alternative rather than opt for an "easy" goal.
- Characters perceive the pursuit of the goal as interesting, desirable, enjoyable, or relevant rather than feel pressured or rely on external

incentives. They desire to engage in goal-related activity rather than procrastinate or avoid the demand or responsibility (not a vague wish but clear intention).

Pursuit of Goals

Actions in pursuit of goals are more likely to be sustained if (a) the individual possesses cognitive, attentional, and emotional resources discussed in previous chapters, and (b) the individual relies less on effortful self-control strategies and maximizes the use of the automatic, self-regulatory mode, thereby freeing up resources for complex and long-term endeavors (see Rapid Reference 7.3). In any given situation, the sense of competence to pursue intentions is undermined when the individual cannot meet the information processing, emotional, or behavioral demands. Individuals who tune out information that is relevant to daily decision-making will err in judgment, and individuals who cannot sustain action based on long-term investment will abandon their goals. The struggle to meet temperamental self-regulatory demands may deplete the individual's resources, and stress or frustration may temporarily restrict the ability to initiate or sustain goal-directed behavior.

Efforts to pursue intentions involve some combination of actions, plans, or decisions. Actions may emphasize control over the external world or changing the inner world to exert more effective control over the outer world or adjust to the inevitable. In TAT stories, three characteristics of actions are relevant: (a) *deliberateness of the actions,* such as actions directed toward a goal versus aimless, haphazard, unplanned, or provoked behaviors; (b) *intent of the actions,* such as a routine action or an action taken solely to satisfy a need (eat, shower, go to bed) versus instrumental action; and (c) *breadth of perspective of the action,* such as reaction to immediate need, provocation, or stimuli versus a broader perspective, including a longer time frame that includes the interests of self and other. Additionally, the quality of goal-directed mental effort, such as deliberate planning and thought versus ruminative mental process, follows the patterns of these distinctions. Actively making a decision or resolution in a thoughtful, self-directed way may be considered independently from the actual decision.

Several characteristics of narratives pertain to the narrator's schemas for active pursuit of intentions.

≣Rapid Reference 7.3

Factors that Enhance the Pursuit and Attainment of Goals

1. *Coordination of conflicting goals or resistance of distraction from environmental sources to meet long-term goals (Cantor & Blanton, 1996).* Self-regulation involves proactive and reactive modes of control (Bandura, 1988, 1989). Proactive control rests on the capacity to downplay immediate pulls or short-term gain in favor of long-term goals and future considerations. Reactive control is the modulation of behavior according to input from external sources, and this type of control is necessary for the execution of a skill or application of knowledge to changing cues and circumstances.

2. *Formulation of goals that are grounded in realistic appraisal of resources and interests (Deci & Ryan, 1991).* Individuals are severely limited in their conscious, deliberate self-control resources and quickly become depleted by such efforts (e.g., Muraven et al., 1998). Excessive reliance on self-control is associated with the subjective experience of stress and may jeopardize the individual's physical and psychological well-being (Deci & Ryan, 1991). Nevertheless, self-control may be necessary when short-term inclinations are likely to result in adverse consequences in the future. Ideally, self-control is temporary until the activity in question becomes emotionally satisfying.

3. *Strategies to increase reliance on automatic schemas by bridging the gap between effortful control over goal-directed actions and automatic control.* The transition from conscious and effortful control over goal-directed behavior to reliance on well-developed schemas is facilitated if the individual can become automatically guided by selected environmental cues. The individual can accomplish this shift by formulating *implementation intentions* that specify when, where, and how to engage in goal-directed behavior (Gollwitzer, 1993, 1996). In this way, the initiation of goal-directed behavior is placed under the control of situational cues, rather than requiring effortful control. For example, specific plans for a morning routine become automatically cued (e.g., alarm clock ringing signals preparation to shower), enabling the sequence of activities to proceed without thought, rather than each requiring an act of will. The individual is more likely to reach goals that are specified as such rather than goals that remain vague (Locke & Latham, 1990).

Narrative Structure and Process

- Story includes appropriate transitional events or means-ends connections, suggesting that the narrator can maintain self-directed activity and follow through on intentions.

Content

- Actions are prosocial, realistic, and sufficient for the expected outcome.
- The character values responsible, goal-directed actions or decisions as distinct from outcomes. Characters are aware of the implications of their actions for others and assume appropriate responsibility for self-regulation and principled choices.
- Characters realistically balance inner motives and external constraints with regard to the connections between means and ends. Characters anticipate and deal with potential barriers to actions and are sensible in their outcome expectations.
- Characteristics of actions for each story may be noted as present/absent; planful/haphazard; realistic/unrealistic; reliance on self/reliance on externals; prosocial/antisocial; proactive/reactive; search for positive/avoidance of negative; goal-directed/aimless; enjoyable/burdensome.

Level of Motivation

Narratives provide a vehicle for understanding the integration of human action with intention in reference to anticipated outcomes. While each of the components of motivation (goal formulation, reaction to goal, instrumental action and outcome) may be examined separately, the narrator's schemas about the conditions for happy or unhappy outcomes (imports) are inferred from their combination. Therefore, the four levels of motivation are keyed to the import of the story (see Chapter 3) rather than to the sum of the discrete components such as goals or actions identified above as pertinent to motivation. Moreover, units introduced in earlier chapters elucidate the narrator's understanding of causality and other thought processes inherent to the import.

Levels of motivation are determined not by happy or unhappy endings but according to the convictions expressed primarily through the intentions-

DON'T FORGET

Story analysis seeks answers to the "what" and "how" of motivation and of self-regulation

1. What information about self, other, and the world is of interest to the individual?
2. What makes the person happy or unhappy? What does the person want? What is valued about accomplishments (e.g., outcomes, process, standards, harmonious relationships)?
3. What does the individual seek when choosing tasks, activities, goals, and risks?
4. What are the individual's priorities in balancing different goals such as short- versus long-term or implicit versus self-attributed?
5. What are the individual's expectations about support or hindrance from others and about the likelihood of accomplishing goals or getting what he or she wants?
6. How cohesive and realistic are the various elements of motivation-related intentions, feelings, thoughts, actions, and anticipated outcomes?
7. How organized and planful are the actions in the pursuit of intentions?

means-ends connections. Thus, happy outcomes represent positive convictions only when they are realistic and result from appropriate actions or attitudes. Unhappy outcomes also represent positive convictions when the import is prosocial and realistic (e.g., "crime does not pay" or "lack of effort leads to failure"). For example, if the narrator offers a negative outcome in a story about a theft, he or she communicates the moral that one should not steal, and this conviction is positive for the long-term interest of the individual and from society's views on morals. The four levels of motivation described next are pegged to the import representing the narrator's schema and not to the immediate outcome for the story characters.

1. Extremely Poor Motivation
This level is characterized by unrealistic or illogical connections among goals, actions, and outcomes, or a lack of connection among these components. For example, "success occurs without goals or efforts" or "failure follows hard work."
Positive Outcome:
- *Intentions/Goals* are vague, ill-intended, unrealistic, unstated, inadequately defined, trivial, or extremely lofty.

- *Reactions* include boredom, obvious lack of interest or inability to withstand setback or frustration, or negative attitudes toward effort or success.
- *Actions* include absence of effort; aimless activity; blind dependence on, rebellious defiance of, or humiliation by others; unlikely or anti-social means; nonconstructive actions; or wishful thinking with no realistic basis.

Import: One can attain success or happiness without clear or realistic goals, long-term investment or interest, or active effort, or one can attain it through unrealistic or antisocial means.

Negative Outcome:
- *Intentions/Goals* are unclear, unstated, inappropriate or unrealistic.
- *Reactions* include expectation of failure, in spite of active effort or self-determined choices or because of difficulty with understanding or meeting demands; a need to blame failure on others or a feeling that efforts are misunderstood; a feeling that failure or adversity cannot be overcome but leads to despair, frustration, inaction, confusion, feelings of inadequacy, hopelessness, pretense, deceit, escape, fantasy, dream, or sleep.
- *Actions* include positive effort that may be misunderstood or thwarted by circumstances, or absence of constructive action due to discouragement, lack of goals, or confusion.

Import: A person should expect negative outcomes in spite of good intentions, realistic goals, and active effort, or because of confusion or disorganization. Challenges or setbacks may lead to despair, frustration, or inaction.

Illustration: Stories told by Aaron, age 8-3
Card 1. The guy that is, the kid that wanted to draw a picture with stuff that he didn't have. [E: What happened before?] He needed some ink and a pencil, but there was a crack in the paper and he didn't have any tape. [E: Thinking?] He's thinking of drawing. [E: Feeling?] Umm, urnm, concerned because he thinks he'll mess up on the picture and everyone will laugh at him. [E: Ending?] He got the tape and finished his picture.

Card 2. The old barn that had a big plowing field. [Short pause] The, the farm didn't have any money, so they couldn't buy any tools but they did have a plow and a horse too. The man who had a horse, the horse was fifty years old and the girl, she always carries a book in her hand, and she wraps her hand around it, and she always wears her same clothes every day, and she wears her hair down really great, and she likes plowing the field, and she lives in the field farm with all the hay and animals, and she lived happily ever after. [E: Thinking?] They are thinking and having a great time with lots of money and they can buy anything they want. [E: Feeling?] They feel, well, they got some money and they feel very, very happy.

Card 7GF. The old woman. The old woman was, is always sitting in bed for hours and hours. She always knits, always sits there doing nothing but knitting, knitting, knitting. But she was a knitting and knitting. She knitted socks and shirts and sometimes did. One day she did a great knitting job on her thing. The little girl was so proud of doing her work. She always wore a big, big, big frown. And carried a baby in her hands. She always weared her happy shoes. She always carried the baby and she always loved to go on her bike. The old lady, she can't move. She'll never move. And she was thinking about she'll move again, then she will go around doing, getting the mail.

2. Poor Motivation

At this level, the narrator displays some understanding of what is needed to produce desired outcomes but has not incorporated the self-reliance needed for independent achievement. Characters attain success with easier goals that are whimsically substituted or success follows upon reluctant or insufficient actions. Failure is due to barriers that are not clearly understood.

Positive Outcome:

- *Intentions/Goals* may be clearly stated and prosocial or remain vague.
- *Reactions* include optimism without adequate reasons—a character simply forgets a problem, makes the best of it, or is happy having tried; the feeling that success is empty or unrewarding and leads to tension.
- *Actions* are not directly pertinent to the task at hand or taken reluctantly; means to goals are vague or the character expends less effort than is required; actions are undertaken for approval, recognition, conformity, or self-centered motives; the character hopes for success or thinks about the problem; actions taken without commitment or interest; the character displays passive dependence on help or advice.

Import: A person can attain success despite actions that are reluctant, not directly pertinent to the goal, not fully adequate, or by setting "easy" goals.

Negative Outcome:

- *Intentions/Goals* may be clearly stated and prosocial or remain vague.
- *Reactions* include frustration, boredom, or anger; external barriers preclude sufficient action or interfere with engaging in expected behaviors.
- *Actions* include thinking and planning but no direct effort; interference of extraneous factors; and tolerance of adversity or failure, though action is possible.

Import: A person fails or is unhappy (when goals are prosocial) because of inadequately defined goals, internal or external barriers, or insufficient action, despite planning and thinking. The causes for failure or unhappiness are not clearly understood by the character or narrator.

Illustration: Stories told by Theodore, age 13-9.

Card 1. So I just tell a story about the picture? [E: Yes.] Okay. The boy has a violin. And he can't play it so he feels sad, and he wishes that he would be able to play it, but he can't so he just sits there and stares at it. [short pause] That's all.

Card 2. Okay, there's a girl, and she lives on a farm. And she doesn't want to be a farm person anymore, and she wants to go to school and become like a lawyer or a business person or something. So she decides to leave the farm. And that's all I got.

Card 7GF. There is a girl, and her family is rich and they're trying to make her be tutored or go to school and she doesn't want to. She just wants to play, and she's feeling very bored and staring out the window. [short pause] [E: Thinking?] That this is boring. And she wanted to play outside. [E: Turns out?] She's just sitting there staring at the window watching the other children play outside. [Theodore leans back in chair and looks away.]

3. Mildly Positive Motivation

At this level, the narrator appropriately recognizes difficulties involved in goal attainment and the need for compensatory action, revision of goals, or seeking of assistance. If barriers or adverse conditions cannot be overcome by sustained effort or other appropriate means, the result is failure or unhappiness (with appropriate responsibility taken). If there are realistic compensatory strategies to overcome obstacles, then success may follow. The linkages among the motivational elements reflect adequate understanding of causality. Success is proportionate to the goals set and strategies used (becoming world famous requires extraordinary commitment). The motivational and volitional aspects of intentions or schemas are present or strongly implied. The goals are evident, but reaction to the goal may be mixed. The need for planning and instrumental activity is recognized, but implementation of the intention poses difficulties.

Positive Outcome:

- *Intentions/Goals* are prosocial and adequately articulated but involve mixed feelings, are difficult to achieve, or are modest.
- *Reaction* is mixed or ambivalent, and the character actively seeks extra help or advice before doing everything possible. However, the character does not show blind dependence, and judges advice on its merits; others provide adequate support or inspiration. Some temporary tension or loss is associated with success.
- *Action* is maintained despite obstacles or initial discouragement; the character expends effort, but the outcome may be uncertain, conditional, or viewed as a possibility; the character continues constructive action despite disapproval or temporary setback.

Import: A person attains success or happiness (possibly conditionally or after initial discouragement) with goals that are modest or with help from others prior to doing everything possible but still through realistic means.

Negative Outcome:

- *Intentions/Goals* are prosocial, realistic, and clearly stated.
- *Reactions* include a grasping of the implications of characters' lack of planning, mistakes, procrastination, negative attitudes or poor organization as well as of excessive independence or refusal to heed sound advice.
- *Actions* include insufficient strategic effort (though planning may have taken place).

Import: Insufficient planning or effort leads to appropriate negative consequences and the character learns the lesson. The story is well-constructed, conveying the sense that the narrator both possesses and can use this insight.

Illustration: Stories told by Mathew, age 11-8, WISC-III IQ score of 126 (VIQ = 137; PIQ = 110).

Card 1. A boy wanted a violin, wanted it a lot so he asked his parents to get him one and they said no. He kept asking them, and, finally they thought he really wanted it so finally they got him one. Now that he has one, he doesn't know what to do with it. He's thinking about maybe he didn't really want it after all. Eventually, he learns how to play and he feels good about himself and becomes a famous violinist.

Card 2. A girl did want to go to school, but she can't go to school because there is no school around and she wanted for a long time there to be a school, and finally there was one. Now that she is going to school for the first time. At school she learns a lot of stuff and it's not quite what she thought, but she likes it. After a while she graduates. [E: Feeling?] She was very glad that she finally got to go to school.

Card 7GF. A girl found, umh, a cat on the street and took it home and left the cat but her mother didn't want the cat, and she's telling the girl that she has to take the cat out and basically throw it away and not take care of the cat anymore. The girl doesn't listen and eventually the girl though the girl gets to keep the cat. The mother doesn't like that though, and the girl is very happy.

4. High Motivation

At this level, the narrator operates from a framework of personal and social responsibility and articulates a realistic understanding of connections among circumstances (pictured stimuli and story events), goals, intentions, actions, and outcomes. The narrator's schema clearly and cohesively represents the various elements needed to sustain long-term, motivated action.

Positive Outcome:

- *Intentions/Goals* are realistic, clearly articulated, and reflect long-term purpose.
- *Reactions* reflect interest, principles, standards, and realistic self-confidence. Characters display self-determination but are able to seek advice after doing everything possible and accept legitimate demands. They exhibit a positive attitude toward work and show pref-

erence for values that are abstract, ethical, and altruistic rather than materialistic or expedient.

- *Actions* are autonomous, prosocial, respectful of others, sufficient for stated goals and outcomes, and reflect principles.

Import: Realistic goals or self-determined, principled actions lead to success, satisfaction, happiness, or harmonious relationships.

Negative Outcome:

- *Intentions/Goals* include ill intent, self-glorification, self-centered goals, or mistaken action.
- *Reactions* include recognizing the inappropriateness of blaming failure on others and understanding the negative implications of boredom, disinterest, inadequate means, or impulsive action. The narrator recognizes other factors such as blind dependence, defiance, and refusal to seek or accept reasonable help or advice as contributing to negative outcomes.
- *Actions* are cohesive with outcomes, and intention-action-outcome sequences are compatible with each other and with the outcome. Thus, inaction, unreasonable action, or action based on bad intentions associated with negative outcomes represent a prosocial conviction and cohesion of elements.

Import: Ill-intended actions or inadequate means (e.g., "too little, too late") lead to failure, unhappiness, or disrupted relationships. Ill-intended actions, even if accompanied by success, are punished. Again, there is a sense that the narrator possesses and can use this insight.

Illustration: Stories told by #14, age 9-7

Card 1. What's that thing right there? Hmmm. Ah, this boy wants to take an instrument lesson. He wants to take piano, and his mom wants him to take violin. So she signed him up for violin lessons. So he's looking at the violin feeling sad. [E: Turns out?] Then on his first violin lesson it turned out that he liked it.

Card 2. Okay. A long time ago there was a teenager that lived on a farm with her father, brother, and mother. She liked reading books, but there weren't many books, and they were very expensive. So she would walk a long way just to get books from her neighbors, like Abe Lincoln.

Card 7GF. Once there was a girl and she had a learning problem. And her mother made her a little doll. And she would carry the doll around wherever she went and thought about going home. But her mother got a tutor to come for her and she couldn't pay attention. So the mother took away the doll and said if she paid attention she would get the doll back. So she worked hard all year and her mother gave her the doll.

TAT AND SELF-REGULATION

Three increasingly complex self-regulatory mechanisms, self-monitoring, self-direction, and self-determination, manifest themselves in storytelling.

Self-monitoring

The modulation and calibration of responses to changing cues in the current situation enables the individual to function in the moment and comprises a basic adaptive repertoire. An individual may monitor actions to be appropriate in the immediate context but may not necessarily gear behavior to a purpose beyond the short-term. General indicators of adequate self-monitoring of ideas, of affective expression, and of other behaviors to the requirements of the immediate situation include (a) exhibiting appropriate behavior during the evaluation, such as attempting to modulate speed of telling the story with the examiner's writing pace, maintaining eye contact, and engaging in reciprocal conversation with the examiner; and (b) demonstrating basic narrative competencies, such as accurately interpreting the pictured stimulus and staying within the bounds of basic logic and social acceptability of story content.

Behavior During the Evaluation

When self-presentation is inappropriate, either in terms of behavior during the assessment (irrelevant conversation, unacceptable or unusual behavior) or in content of the story (gruesome, hostile, sadistic, bizarre), the individual is not using organized schemas to monitor thought processing or actions to social expectations.

Use of the Stimulus

Self-monitoring requires the individual to size up the relevant information in the surroundings. This awareness is indicated by the narrator's grasping the "gist" of the pictured scene.

Internal Logic of the Story

A narrative that is socially appropriate, free from contradictory details, perseverations, or clearly illogical ideas suggests that the narrator has listened to and remembered the unfolding story details.

Basically, self-monitoring entails the essential skills to gear actions and reactions to situational expectations. Going beyond self-monitoring requires not only continuous evaluation of the individual's activities over time but also increasing differentiation and integration of schemas to organize the immediately available environmental cues from lessons drawn from the past and according to implications for the future.

Self-Direction

Self-direction involves shifting attention and effort away from current situational pulls to more distant concerns. Self-monitoring and self-direction correspond to a general distinction between *intentionally controlled* behavior, which is guided by goals, versus *stimulus controlled* behavior, which is organized by elements of the context (Ford, 1994). The internal organization of behavior permits individuals to extricate themselves from the draw of the immediate situation to pursue long-term adaptive demands. Self-direction entails prioritizing, sustaining, and monitoring behavior over time to resolve problems or deal with adverse situations, generate strategies and maintain efforts to accomplish tasks and to carry out a complex sequence of behaviors, and meet long-term social expectations rather than attending only to current external presses. Self-monitoring is reactive to the immediate environment, whereas self-direction is more proactive and requires greater internal control of behavior. Various levels of difficulty maintaining intentionally controlled behavior are implicated in most DSM disorders such as Attention Deficit Hyperactivity Disorder (ADHD), mood disorder, and schizophrenia, as well as various conduct and character disorders (Frick & Lahey, 1991). For example, attentional deficits have been described as the control over attention by external contingencies rather than by the individual's goals (Barkley, 1997).

In the storytelling task, self-monitoring and self-direction parallel the distinction between stimulus control and intentional control over behavior. Self-monitoring, in the absence of self-direction, is reflected in stories that are organized around stimulus features, directions, external demands, or stereotypes. Self-direction is demonstrated by the portrayal of characters who direct actions toward a prosocial purpose, goal, or expectation beyond the provocation of the immediate circumstance depicted in the picture or described in the narrative. Furthermore, the narrative is actively and planfully constructed, transcends the stimulus pull, and smoothly incorporates storytelling directions.

Self-Determination

The field of motivation has postulated various constructs to distinguish between the pursuit of goal-directed activities that are intrinsically valued versus those that are socially promoted. Self-determination involves decisions, goals, or actions that balance the inner and outer aspects of experience, such as self-presentation with feelings, actions with intrinsic satisfaction, values or standards, and immediate demands with long-term aspirations. Self-determined behavior is based on a cohesive set of priorities and values that gives purpose and meaning to the individual's endeavors. A subjective sense of self-determination, competence, and pride in accomplishment is linked with higher levels of motivation and self-regulation (Deci, Eghrari, Patrick, & Leone, 1994). Not surprisingly, self-determination involves (a) integrative information processing in which decisions and behaviors are predicated on multiple considerations (e.g., self and others, now and later, outcome and process, expedience and principles), and (b) investment in standards and prizing of instrumental behaviors in which the individual stays the course despite temporary frustration or the draw of other activities. When the investment is coupled with realistic self-awareness, the individual may seek help as needed, modify plans or goals, and rebound from failure or disappointment.

Self-determination in the storytelling task is reflected by characters who show deliberate, purposeful, and organized action based on an integrated, well-elaborated inner life and reliance on internal standards or motives beyond successful outcomes. In addition to incorporating the characteristics of self-monitoring and self-direction, self-determination is exhibited by stories that coordinate the inner and outer worlds of various characters and realistically balance short- and long-term considerations. Accordingly, character's actions are guided by self-investment and intrinsic motivation, such as enjoyment of the challenge, with priorities balanced between the process and outcome.

Levels of Self-Regulation

Self-regulatory processes are characterized along a continuum of complexity, proceeding from the very basic level of reacting to the incoming stimulation to the strategic pursuit of long-term goals or ideals in ways that simultaneously serve immediate and long-term functions. Increasing complexity of information processing permits multiple considerations to guide self-regulation, and well-developed schemas reduce the effort of processing information by providing templates that automatically organize the cues in the surroundings in relation to the individual's goals, standards, or principles. The five levels of self-regulation presented in this section synthesize all the coding dimensions described earlier (see Rapid Reference 7.4).

Given that schemas are triggered by external cues, internal states (motives, feelings), or both, different schemas may be activated at different times. Thus, an individual's level of self-regulation may vary according to the demands of the situation. A person who functions well under some conditions (e.g., structured or low risk) may become indecisive and disorganized when faced with more complex challenges. It is not unusual for individuals to function below customary levels under the influence of intense emotions or during times of stress or transition. In such circumstances, the individual may be less responsive to the needs of others and more focused on the immediate pressures. In the face of stress or other negative emotions, integrated schemas about the self and the world may not be activated (Gray, 1987; Kuhl, 1996).

1. Dysregulation

Form and content of stories reflect fragmentation in processing life experience associated with impairment in thought organization or affect modulation. These impairments are reflected in problems with reality testing, with formulation of intentions, and with establishing relationships. The individual reacts

≋Rapid Reference 7.4

Self-Regulation: Convergence of Cognition, Emotions, Relationships, and Motivation (see also Bassan-Diamond, Teglasi, & Schmitt, 1995; Teglasi, 1993)

- *Cognition.* Higher levels of self-regulation entail not only more precise reality testing in terms of accurate and nuanced awareness of self, others, and the world, but also an increased organization of what is perceived, in line with dictates of logic, and of social causality. Higher levels are characterized by applying greater synthesis to the organization of experience, whereas lower levels entail grasping reality by stringing together islands of experience that are not cohesively related to the past or future or to organizing convictions or principles. Serious problems with self-regulation are evident when the narrator has difficulty keeping track of ideas (contradictions, excessive repetition, logical fallacies) or keeping content within the bounds of social acceptability (extreme violence, morbid helplessness).

- *Organization of emotions and relationships.* At higher levels of self-regulation, increased organization of inner life governs actions and standards for evaluation of self and others rather than reaction to external events or anticipation of external consequences. Increasingly integrative information processing is reflected in the description of characters with well-elaborated and cohesive inner states who possess the perspective and insight necessary to modulate short-term reactions or overreactions and to put events and feelings into an appropriate intra- and interpersonal context (i.e., balance self-other interests and compromise among conflicting goals or motives).

- *Motivation.* Higher levels of self-regulation involve increased emphasis on well-organized concerns, goals, or principles that are pursued proactively and planfully. Reactive, haphazard, or unplanned actions or decisions prompted by immediate needs, wishes, or provocations represent lower levels of self-regulation than those that involve more distant goals, foresight, or commitment to principles or values.

to faulty perceptions and cognitions such as a focus on minute, irrelevant considerations or is driven by intense emotions such as fear, panic, terror, or rage. The individual does not integrate relevant components of the immediate situation, and he or she has difficulty monitoring routine behavior without clear guidelines. Narratives may focus on isolated aspects of experiences (e.g., centering narrowly on elements of the picture without capturing the meaning of the stimulus) or global impressions (e.g., expressing global reactions to the scene as a whole). Five story characteristics, in addition to highly inappropriate behavior during the evaluation, suggest this level:

1. The narrator perseverates or overelaborates certain feelings and details or includes fragments of ideas that are not pertinent to the story as a whole.
2. The narrator shows faulty logic or contradictory or grossly incompatible ideas (e.g., at different levels of abstraction).
3. The narrator shows faulty interpretation of the pictured scene.
4. The story contains implausible, socially inappropriate, or bizarre content.
5. A character acts or reacts on the basis of highly idiosyncratic views of causes and effects (e.g., remains in an extreme state of helplessness or deprivation).

At this level, the narrator's schemas fail to provide an accurate map to size up how the various cues in the immediate surroundings "go together." Because the need for well-organized schemas is minimized in highly structured situations (that do not require the appraisal of ambiguous information), individuals who tell stories at this level may perform within the highest ranges on some achievement and intellectual tests, yet function with little awareness of the implications of actions for others and for the self, even in familiar situations.

This level of self-regulation is illustrated by the following stories told to Cards 1 and 2 by Aaron, age 8-3, who is receiving special educational services for an emotional disability.

Card 1. The guy that is, the kid that wanted to draw a picture with stuff that he didn't have. [E: What happened before?] He needed some ink and a pencil, but there was a crack in the paper and he didn't have any tape. [E: Thinking?] He's thinking of drawing. [E: Feeling?] Umm, urnm, concerned because he thinks he'll mess up on the picture and everyone will laugh at him. [E: Turns out?] He got the tape and finished his picture.

Aside from being discrepant from the contextual cues depicted in the stimulus, the story lacks cohesion due to arbitrary shifts in perspective (e.g., from being preoccupied with lack of tools for drawing to concern about being laughed at) and the introduction of ideas that don't fit well together (e.g., the boy needed some "ink and a pencil"). The initial premise of not having the materials with which to draw is rather trivial especially in comparison to the more serious issue of the boy's concern about messing up the picture and being laughed at (i.e., juxtaposition of ideas at incompatible levels of conceptualization). This seemingly more serious twist in the story is casually introduced and then abandoned (i.e., introduction of ideas left incomplete) as if the narrator did not understand its significance. At the end, the boy "got the tape and finished the picture" but the narrator offers no explanation as to how ("ink and pencil" are still missing).

Card 2. The old barn that had a big plowing field. [short pause] The, the farm didn't have any money, so they couldn't buy any tools but they did have a plow and a horse too. The man who had a horse, the horse was fifty years old and the girl, she always carries a book in her hand, and she wraps her hand around it, and she always wears her same clothes every day, and she wears her hair down really great, and she likes plowing the field, and she lives in the field farm with all the hay and animals, and she lived happily ever after. [E: Thinking?] They are thinking and having a great time with lots of money, and they can buy anything they want. [E: Feeling?] They feel, well, they got some money and they feel very, very happy.

A shift in perspective from the personification of the farm ("the farm didn't have any money") to the people in the scene ("so they couldn't buy any tools . . .") gives the story an "odd" quality. Eventually, thoughts about being rich make the characters happy; however, this is an unrealistic connection between means and ends. The description of the scene is unusual because it weaves together details that are at different levels of conceptualization ("the girl, she always carries books in her hand and she wraps her hand around it"). "Carrying books" is a more meaningful description than the trivial observation of "wrapping her hand around it." Other details such as the age of the horse or the girl's wearing the same dress every day are irrelevant to the story as a whole. The narrator ignores more substantial considerations such as the feelings or intentions of the people portrayed in the scene and the relationships among them.

2. *Immediacy*

Information processing and behavior center on the feelings or concerns of the moment without adequate reflection on prior events, future consequences, or implications for others. Judgments and actions are based on what immediately dominates awareness without relating salient aspects of the current situation to the past or future. Therefore, actions are reactive to the situation and are aimed at seeking immediate gain or relief without adequate reflection on future consequences or implications for self or others. Interpersonal information processing is distorted by selective attention to characteristics of others that serve the individual's wants or needs in the moment without attending to other pertinent considerations. The individual's self-presentation may pass muster in the moment, but over time behavioral inconsistencies become obvious to others, and the individual's lack of enduring commitments hampers adjustment. Long-term self-regulation is constrained by the individual's inability to sustain interest in situations that do not contribute to the immediate sense of well-being.

Emotions, intentions, thoughts, actions, and outcomes simply do not "add up" with respect to time perspective or intra- and interpersonal context but are not as jarringly incompatible or illogical as the previous level. Thus, content is not bizarre nor socially inappropriate, but the narrator demonstrates poor understanding of cause-effect relationships vis-à-vis the long term. Lack of specificity in the description of inner states such as thoughts, feelings, or intentions may contribute to the impression of poor understanding of social causality. Five story characteristics pertain to this level:

1. The narrator relies exclusively on external or concrete cues to read emotion because of difficulty reading internal states; emotions are generated by a stimulus, unexpected event, or provocation (lack of anticipation) that is not clearly tied to a context.
2. Characters relate to each other based on their momentary affective impact without considering their intentions or circumstances. Thus, intent is not separated from impact.
3. Information processing is determined by what the individual desires rather than by realistic considerations.
4. Goals emphasize short-term relief from unpleasant affective states

or avoidance of conflict, or characters act or react without a plan or consideration of context.

5. Problem conceptualization is limited by focusing on the immediate.

Jim, age 16 and diagnosed with conduct disorder illustrates this level in his stories about TAT cards 1 and 2.

Card 1. He's looking at a violin. Probably bored . . . doesn't want to do. Somebody put it in front of him. Feeling angry and mad 'cause somebody asked him to do it. So he doesn't do it.

The entire story occurs in the "moment" as captured by the picture without meaningful consideration of preceding context ("somebody puts it in front of him") and without regard to intention or rationale behind the vague request "to do it." Thus, understanding of social causality and separation of intent and impact are minimal. Poor understanding of social causality is also suggested by the seeming absence of consequence for noncompliance ("so he doesn't do it"). The boy's (and narrator's) awareness is dominated by immediate cues and feelings, and this style guides behavior that is reactive to the moment.

Card 2. Okay. This is a farm. Hmm, girl's coming home from school. Her mother and father is on the farm doing work. She has to do homework. She acts like she's going to do it but doesn't do it. . . . What I do? [E: Feeling?] Probably mad 'cause has to do homework but she's not going to do it.

There is an effort to avoid the burdens of work by pretending to do it. Again, pretending may work for the moment but does not serve longer purposes. In this story and the one above, the character is angry, and information processing and behavior are reactive to this feeling to the exclusion of other considerations.

3. External Direction
Various elements of the current situation, including relationships, are more realistically appraised, but information processing and behavior are externally guided by imposed standards and feedback. At this level, the story content revolves around more long-term expectations and more general, less narrow

concerns, such as conformity to more complex external demands (grades, rules, stereotyped social expectation), rather than the momentary provocation, whim, or avoidance of socially expected activity (e.g., going to school) characterizing the previous level. Nevertheless perceptions of self and others are not differentiated, and flexibility is limited by reliance on rigid quid pro quo reciprocity. Emotions attributed to characters have a superficial, stereotypic flavor. Thus, characters suffer the consequences of ill-advised action but do not dwell on the intentions or on feelings of remorse.

At this level, the individual needs external feedback or bolstering to initiate or sustain independent, instrumental behavior, even when the tasks and goals are accepted as legitimate or self-imposed. The individual may be aware of the struggle to meet expectations or of problems prioritizing seemingly conflicting demands, which results in a sense of pressure to conform to acknowledged standards of conduct. Emotional and cognitive impediments to self-regulation may contribute to difficulty giving inner direction to sustained efforts without external validation or sources of motivation. The need for external sources of regulation may be rooted in mild problems with sustaining attention, regulating emotion, or organizing ideas. The individual may perceive day to day expectations as legitimate but burdensome, and self-direction is vulnerable to derailment. Six characteristics of stories apply to this level:

1. The narrator is aware of inner motives and separation of impact from intent but places emphasis on external events rather than insight or inner direction.
2. Perceived norms or consequences guide behavior rather than personal commitment. Characters do the right thing due to external pressure, approval, duty, or reward or to avert potential negative consequences.
3. Characters may have problems carrying out intentions or acting constructively on insight.
4. Limited intrinsic motivation places burdensome demands on characters to meet legitimate external demands or attain goals and aspirations without external incentive.
5. The narrator may emphasize the details of the picture to bolster judgment but is able to get beyond the cues provided.
6. Characters may need external support due to affective sensitivity

(e.g., tendency to experience anxiety and/or frustration) in response to performance demands.

Stories told by Jaime, age 10-9, with a very superior IQ score, illustrate this level. Her teacher describes her as doing very well academically but experiencing some difficulty with interpersonal relationships.

Card 1. Okay. This boy, he is sad because his mother told him that he had to practice violin otherwise he would be in trouble. Now, this boy doesn't like to practice violin, and he's mad at his mother. And he wants to break the violin except it's an expensive violin and his grandfather gave it to his mother and his mother gave it to him so he knows he shouldn't break it. But he practices but without heart and soul.

The boy is aware of the meaning that the violin has for his family but does not share this connection with the family tradition. He feels stuck with his resentment and plays without heart and soul. The boy regulates behaviors to the demands of the family but he requires the threat of external consequences to do so. The source of motivation and regulation is extrinsic.

Card 2. Can I study the picture for a little? Okay, this will be funny. In the picture there is a big farm and no civilization around for twenty miles. The girl's mother is pregnant and the girl's mother has some books on how to give birth and the little girl has to study it so she could help her mother give birth. The man is her brother, and he wants a boy except the girl wants a sister and they fight about it. A few weeks later the mother gives birth to twins, a boy and a girl. So both kids are satisfied. Oh, I forgot to say that the reason the man couldn't help the mother give birth is that he had to attend to the farm work.

The narrator resourcefully pulled together the apparent pregnancy of the woman with the girl carrying the books. In contrast to the solitary activity needed to comply with family expectations in Card 1, Jaime is more comfortable and resourceful when called on to assume an important helping role. Jaime's external orientation is evident in the nature of the conflict between the brother and sister and its external resolution (birth of twins). The reason given for the man's inability to help was possibly based on an inflexible adherence to the stimulus ("had to attend to the farm work") or difficulty balancing activities or collaborating. It would not be unreasonable to temporarily set aside farm work to attend to a pressing need. However, external demands seem to take priority over internally organized actions, cooperation, or compromise.

4. Internal Direction

Information processing and behavior are guided by internal representations of standards and values. Action at this level is proactive, modulated, and internally organized, but emphasizes cultural values or standards rather than personal commitment to principles. Characters' actions and reactions are set in a reasonable context that is consistent with but transcends the immediate environmental pull or provocation. A greater sense of competence than at the previous level imparts more initiative and persistence of goal-directed behavior as appropriate for desired ends. Task engagement and interpersonal reciprocity no longer have the demanding flavor of the previous level. Nevertheless, the thoughts, feelings, and behaviors, though cohesive and oriented to the long-term, are organized around meeting adaptive demands or goals rather than emphasizing investment in a standard or commitment to principles. Persons operating at this level may be vulnerable to experiencing a relatively mild duality between their behaviors spurred by self-attributed motives (internalized standards not fully supported by temperamentally based preferences) and implicit motives.

The individual displays more self-reliance in the pursuit of long-term interests and maintains more durable interpersonal connections than at the previous level. Despite some specific blind spots, individuals functioning at this level are able to balance specific goals with concerns for family and friends and coordinate long- and short-term considerations. The narrative is well-organized, and characters anticipate, plan, and gear their efforts toward prosocial ends.

This level is illustrated by #203, a student in kindergarten participating in a research study.

Card 1. He feels sad. Then he still's sad. He can't . . . doesn't know how to play it. He tries to play it but it sounds squeaky and ugly. [E: Thinking?] How would it sound if he knew how to play it. Then he tries again and then he does it good.

The boy begins the process of playing the instrument by taking initiative to change the "squeaky" sound, and then "he does it good." The language is simplistic, as appropriate for a 5-year-old, but the schema is sophisticated.

Card 2. What's happening here is this girl has her books in her hands. There's a farm, too. There's a boy with his horse. There is a lady by a tree. They are sad because they don't have food. They try to grow food. All of them work together and they make the food grow and they are happy.

At first, the narrator merely described stimulus elements then tells a simple story about a family that works together to meet a common goal. At the end, the family is happy having resolved the problem by growing the food that they need.

5. Self-Determination

A complex and well-integrated inner framework for information processing is evident in the cohesiveness among the described circumstance and characters' thoughts, feelings, actions, and outcomes. Multiple considerations are seamlessly integrated within and across perspectives. The narrator incorporates the nuances of the stimuli without glossing over the intense negative emotions depicted. Thoughts, feelings, actions, sequence of events, and views of various characters are well-coordinated in relative emphasis, context, and time frame. Characters engage in deliberate, planful, volitional, autonomous, and purposeful action or decision with realistic outcomes. They are highly invested in the process of these activities, with outcomes being important but secondary. The combination of complex information processing and a balance between relatedness and autonomy permit the evaluation of people as they are, apart from the feelings or needs of the perceiver.

Besides having all the characteristics of the pervious level, stories at this level indicate (1) inner standards for self-evaluation or conduct (explicit or implied) in the story content and structure, (2) abstract aims or principles that give coherence to the stream of events or govern behavior, and (3) a valuing of the process as intrinsically satisfying or serving a purpose distinct from the outcome. Self-determination involves an intrinsic drive to meet standards or goals that are valued beyond their connection to desired ends. The instrumental activities themselves are sustaining to the individual, sometimes even at the expense of the outcome. Even at the highest levels of self-regulation, there may be temporary or situation-specific lapses of self-monitoring or self-direction due to stress, fatigue, or intense emotion.

This level is illustrated by stories told by Benjie, age 9–11, described by his teachers as highly motivated, empathic, and respected by his peers.

Card 1. The boy has a violin except he can't play it very nicely. So he's kind of upset because he can't figure out how to play it well. You want to know what I think this thing is? [Points to the paper under the violin] [E: Up to you.] He's thinking whether he should keep trying or quit it because he doesn't know how to play it. [E: Turns out?] He gives up because he decides that he'll never be able to do it.

The boy is upset because he can't figure out how to play the violin well. This is an inner concern having to do with standards and not a reaction to external demand. Given the premise that this is a voluntary activity, the tension shifts to the process of making a decision about whether the boy should continue with the violin or quit. The autonomous decision is not a reaction to frustration but made according to a deliberate process of concluding that the boy will "never be able to do it."

Card 2. It looks like a family in the mid- to late 1800s, and there's the mother who looks like she's taking a rest, and there's either one of the sons or the father who's taking the horse, and one of the girls looks like she has just read a book, and she's coming back to the house with the book she read. I'm not sure they let girls go to school at that time. Otherwise, I would have said she's coming home from school. [E: Anything going on in the family?] Just looks like they're trying to get the day's work done so they can make a living.

In describing the farm, Benjie is concerned with interpreting the stimulus in the proper historical context (the 1800s). Thus, in processing information, he goes well beyond immediate considerations, even struggling with whether "they let girls go to school at that time." The narrator is too concerned with being precise to make up just any story that seems logical by today's standards. He finally tells a simple story about a family trying to get their work done so they can make a living. Benjie's previous story also hints at his precision and high standards.

This seemingly simple story might be coded at Level 4, except for two considerations that bring it up to Level 5. First, the effort to give a historical context and the precision to keep story details compatible with the social realities of the time and pictured cues suggest a sophisticated approach to information processing and self-regulation. (Message: Whatever the historical time and place, family members work together to earn a living.) Second, the implied understanding of individuality in the context of a common goal indicates a complex and sophisticated schema. (Message: Individuals are free to pursue their interests, such as "reading books," while cooperating to "make a living.")

CASE ILLUSTRATIONS

Sandra

The TAT stories of Sandra, a 19-year-old college student, demonstrate that for the purpose of intervention, it is important to understand the gap between a person's intentions and the self-regulatory resources to pursue them. Figures 7.1 to 7.3 exhibit the coding of the protocol according to the variables introduced in this chapter. Sandra was evaluated at the request of her therapist because of an impasse after six months of regular attendance of sessions. Sandra's participation in therapy was at the insistence of her parents who were concerned because she seemed to have "no direction in life." As part of the evaluation, the professional administered the TAT, the Wechsler Adult Intelligence Scale Revised (WAIS-R), and the Rorschach technique.

Card 1 . . . Don't like pictures. Not all of them . . . Umm . . . like story, like once upon a time. This is a boy . . . He's . . . okay, he . . . is it a violin? I don't know. Can I say two things? [E: Whatever you want.] He's either frustrated because he can't play it or he's sad because he's not allowed to play it anymore. He wants to play it but for some reason he can't . . . [stares at picture] [E: Turns out?] He becomes a great, did I say that was a violin?, violin player, and he's happy. [E: Okay, I think you have the idea.]

Import: Even if a person has trouble setting and pursuing goals, that person simply assumes that someday he or she will be very successful and happy.

Sandra is put off by the task and vacillates in her interpretation of the pic-

Card	Import of Story	Choose Level of Motivation	
		Positive Outcome	Negative Outcome
1	Even if a person has trouble setting and pursuing goals, that person simply assumes that someday he or she will be very successful and happy.	1	
2	When a person sees the humdrum life of others, that person is reminded to go to school and get a good education so he or she does not have to be like them.	2	
3BM	Without structure, it's hard to know what's going on, but if a person looks for clues in the environment and asks for help, things will work out eventually (though that person is stuck for the moment).	2	
4	Even when the problem between two people remains unclear and unresolved, if they try to work things out, they can live happily ever after.	2	
5	If a person intends to do one thing but does something that is related, it's just as well, and things work out.	2	
6BM	If a man explains why he must leave his mother (job transfer), she understands, and despite her sadness, "gives her blessing."	3	
7GF	In a difficult situation, if someone doesn't want to deal with the tensions, he or she can simply pretend that things are not the way they seem.	1	
8BM	When a boy's father is shot in the woods, others will come on the scene to do what is necessary to save his life while the son prays, and later the father expresses gratitude.	2	

Note: If a meaningful import cannot be extracted from the story content, it may be derived from formal qualities of the narrative process or structure.

Figure 7.1 Import and Motivational Level

tured scene as she does in her own intentions. The story content is appropriate to the stimulus, but Sandra cannot determine whether the boy is experiencing internal (frustration) or external (not allowed) barriers to achievement. In any case, the narrator takes no heed and describes the boy as becoming a great violinist, seemingly without effort. This lack of connection between means and outcomes parallels Sandra's own difficulties with clearly defining goals, overcoming obstacles, and taking the necessary steps to accomplish her intentions.

Card 2. God! These things are . . . Okay, there's . . . [stares] . . . this girl on her way to school, she's walking to school, and she sees this man working in the field, and that's his wife watching him. His wife's talking to him I guess, may be talking to him. He's working with his horse on the farm, and she's thinking that

	Positive Story Outcome	**Negative Story Outcome**
Level One: **Extremely Poor Motivation**	**Intentions/Goals.** They are vague, ill-intended, unrealistic, trivial, unstated, inadequately defined, or extremely lofty. **Reactions.** They include boredom, obvious lack of interest or inability to withstand setback or frustration, negative attitude toward effort or success. **Actions.** They include absence of effort, aimless activity, blind dependence on, rebellious defiance of, or extreme pressure by others, unlikely, antisocial, or nonconstructive actions, wishful thinking with no realistic basis. **Conviction.** Success or happiness can be attained without clear/realistic goals, long-term investment or interest, or active effort, or through unrealistic or antisocial means.	**Intentions/Goals.** They are unclear, unstated, inappropriate, or realistic and socially appropriate. **Reactions.** They include expecting failure despite active effort or self-determined choices or because of difficulty with understanding or meeting demands. Failure or adversity cannot be overcome, is blamed on others, leads to despair, frustration, inaction, hopelessness, pretense, deceit, escape, fantasy, dream, sleep, inadequacy, or confusion. **Actions.** Positive effort may be misunderstood or thwarted by circumstance or absence of constructive action due to discouragement, lack of goals or confusion. **Conviction.** Negative outcomes are expected despite good intentions, realistic goals, and active effort or because of confusion or extreme disorganization.
Level Two: **Poor Motivation**	**Intentions/Goals.** They are clearly stated and prosocial or vague. **Reactions.** Optimism without adequate reasons; character forgets, makes the best of it, is happy having tried; success is empty or unrewarding and leads to tension. **Actions.** Actions are not directly pertinent to the task at hand or taken reluctantly; means to goals are vague or less-than-required effort is expended. Actions are undertaken for approval, recognition, conformity, or self-centered motives; character hopes for success or thinks about the problem; actions are taken without commitment or interest; passive dependence on help or advice. **Conviction.** Success or happiness can be attained despite actions that are reluctant, not directly pertinent to the goal or fully adequate. Success can be attained by setting "easy" goals.	**Intentions/Goals.** They are clearly stated and prosocial or vague. **Reactions.** Frustration, boredom, anger, or external barriers preclude sufficient action or expected behavior. **Actions.** Thinking and planning have occurred, but no action is taken; extraneous factors have interfered; adversity or failure is tolerated, though action is possible. **Conviction.** Failure or unhappiness (when goals are prosocial) may be due to internal or external barriers or insufficient action, despite planning and thinking. (The causes for failure or unhappiness are not clearly understood by the character or narrator.)
Level Three: **Mildly Positive Motivation**	**Intentions/Goals.** They are prosocial and adequately defined but modest, very difficult, and/or involve mixed feelings. **Reactions.** They may be mixed or ambivalent; character actively seeks extra help or advice before doing everything possible. Dependence on others who provide adequate support or inspiration, but dependence is not blind as advice is judged on its own merits; some temporary tension or loss is associated with success. **Actions.** Actions are maintained despite obstacles or initial discouragement; effort is expended but the outcome may be uncertain, conditional, or viewed as a possibility. **Conviction.** Success or happiness are attained (possibly conditionally), perhaps after initial discouragement or with help from others prior to doing everything possible through realistic means.	**Intentions/Goals.** They are prosocial and adequately defined. **Reactions.** Narrator grasps implications of character's lack of planning, mistakes, procrastination, negative attitudes, or poor organization as well as excessive independence or refusal to heed sound advice. **Actions.** There is insufficient strategic effort (though planning may have occurred). **Conviction.** Insufficient planning or effort leads to appropriate negative consequences and lesson learned. (The story is well-constructed, conveying a sense that the narrator possesses and can utilize this insight.)
Level Four: **High Motivation**	**Intentions/Goals.** They are realistic, clearly articulated, and reflect long-term purpose. **Reactions.** They include interest, principles, standards, and realistic self-confidence. Self-determination, but able to seek advice after doing everything possible; acceptance of legitimate pressure. Positive attitude toward work; preference for values that are abstract, ethical, or altruistic rather than materialistic or expedient. **Actions.** Actions are autonomous, prosocial, respectful of others, sufficient for stated goals and outcomes, or maintain principles. **Conviction.** Realistic goals, self-determined, principled actions lead to success, happiness, or harmonious relationships.	**Intentions/Goals.** These include ill intent, self-glorification, self-centered goals, or mistaken action. **Reactions.** The narrator recognizes inappropriateness of characters' intentions or prior action (e.g., inadequate or impulsive). **Actions.** Actions and outcomes are cohesive and convey prosocial principled conviction. **Conviction.** Ill-intended actions or inadequate means (e.g., "too little, too late") lead to failure, unhappiness, or disrupted relationships. Ill-intended actions, even if accompanied by success are punished. (Again, there is a sense that the narrator possesses and can utilize this insight.)

Figure 7.2 Levels of Motivation in Relation to Outcome

I. GOAL FORMULATION

A. Structure and Process

(Check as many as apply for each story) Cards→	1	2	3BM	4	5	6BM	7GF	8BM				
There is clear and appropriate definition of central problem, tension, or dilemma, given the stimulus (versus vague, non-specific intention or tension).			✓			✓		✓				
Story is logical and proceeds without irrelevant or contradictory detail; reasoning is realistic, and sequence of events is plausible.		✓				✓						

B. Content

(Check as many as apply for each story) Cards→	1	2	3BM	4	5	6BM	7GF	8BM				
A realistic, prosocial goal or dilemma is imposed by others but accepted by a character.						✓						
Characters set a realistic, prosocial goal, conflict, or dilemma.	✓		✓	✓		✓						
Characters exhibit interest, curiosity, pride, concern, empathy, and commitment to standards, ideals, task, or prosocial activity.						✓						

C. Characteristics of Goals *(Check for each story)*:

absent-vague / clear
long-term / short-term
process / outcome
substantial / trivial

self-initiated / imposed
prosocial / antisocial
idealistic / materialistic
attainment of positive / aversion of negative

realistic / unrealistic
interpersonal / task
meeting of inner standards / meeting of demands or expectations

II. REACTION TO THE GOAL, DILEMMA, OR STORYTELLING TASK

A. Structure and Process

(Check as many as apply for each story) Cards→	1	2	3BM	4	5	6BM	7GF	8BM				
Story proceeds according to a plan rather than made up detail by detail.						✓						
Narrator incorporates all parts of the instructions with or without inquiry. Prompted responses enhance the story (versus providing minimal or repetitious responses).		✓	✓	✓		✓		✓				

B. Content

(Check as many as apply for each story) Cards→	1	2	3BM	4	5	6BM	7GF	8BM				
Characters acknowledge possible external obstacles or internal limitations without being stymied; they set priorities, display foresight, plan ahead, and anticipate consequences.												
Characters perceive the goal-related activities as interesting, desirable, or relevant, rather than feel pressured, rely on external incentives, or avoid the demand or responsibility.												

III. GOAL-DIRECTED ACTIONS

A. Structure and Process

(Check as many as apply for each story) Cards→	1	2	3BM	4	5	6BM	7GF	8BM				
Appropriate means-ends connections suggest that the narrator can maintain self-directed activity and follow through on intentions.												

Figure 7.3 Motivation and Self-regulation

B. Content

(Check as many as apply for each story) Cards→	I	2	3BM	4	5	6BM	7GF	8BM					
Actions are prosocial, realistic, and sufficient for the expected outcome.						✓							
Responsible, goal-directed actions or decisions are valued as distinct from outcomes.						✓							
Characters' inner motives and external constraints are realistically balanced in the intention-action-outcome set.						✓							

C. Characteristics of Actions *(Check for each story)*:

present / absent
prosocial / antisocial
goal-directed / aimless

planful / haphazard
proactive / reactive
reliance on self / reliance on externals

realistic / unrealistic
search for positive / avoidance of negative
enjoyable / burdensome

LEVELS OF SELF-REGULATION

Level One: Dysregulation. Form and content of stories reflect fragmentation in processing life experience associated with impairment in thought organization (e.g., ideas out of context, implausible sequence of events, illogical or bizarre ideas, inconsistent level of conceptualization; perseveration). The person reacts to faulty perceptions provoked by minute, irrelevant considerations or is hopelessly immobilized. The respondent may focus narrowly on elements of the picture without capturing the meaning or may express global reactions to the stimulus as a whole. Characters act and react without awareness of causes and effects, or the narrator's behavior during the evaluation is clearly inappropriate. Relevant components of the immediate situation are not integrated, and the individual has difficulty monitoring routine behavior without clear guidelines.

Level Two: Immediacy. Information processing and behavior relate to the moment, without adequate reflection on prior history, future consequences, or implications for others. Judgments and actions are based on what immediately dominates awareness, without organization or integration of salient aspects of the current situation that have important but remote implications. Self-monitoring may pass muster in the moment, but self-direction in the longer term is hampered by inability to maintain interest in situations that do not contribute to immediate sense of well-being. Actions are aimed at seeking immediate gain or relief. Feelings are not regulated internally but evoked by immediate external circumstances. Thus, intentions behind actions are not clearly distinct from their impact.

Level Three: External Direction. Information processing and behavior are guided by externally imposed standards, feedback, or necessity (e.g., adverse event) rather than by the provocation or whim of the moment. Various elements of the current situation and relationships are more realistically assessed than at previous levels (including a distinction between intent and impact, awareness of rules and expectations, quid pro quo reciprocity). Story content revolves around more long-term expectations and more general, less narrow or trivial concerns, but might be mildly unrealistic or naive because perceptions of self and others are not well-differentiated. There may be a sense of pressure to meet demands of others or to conform to acknowledged standards of conduct rather than be directed by inner values or standards. External sources of motivation or reassurance are needed to tolerate frustration and persist in long-term instrumental action.

Level Four: Internal Direction. Information processing and behavior are implicitly guided by standards and prosocial values that are internally represented and that the individual feels competent to attain. The individual can balance personal concerns with needs of family and friends and coordinate short- and long-term considerations. Task engagement and interpersonal reciprocity do not have the demanding flavor of the previous level but lack the personal conviction of the highest level. There is more initiative and greater organization of thoughts, emotions, and behaviors. Initiative and effort are appropriate for desired ends and for meeting adaptive demands (well-organized and long-term).

Level Five: Self-Determination. Information processing is complex and responsible, as indicated by stories that elaborate inner experience within or across characters in ways that are cohesive with the stimulus, described circumstance, actions, and outcomes. Thus, characters' intentions, thoughts, feelings, actions, outcomes, and story events are well-coordinated in relative emphasis, context, and time frame. Characters are invested in planful, autonomous, socially responsible, and purposeful action and are dedicated to enduring principles. Information processing is more complex than the previous level, incorporating multiple dimensions of experience and perspectives of relevant others over the long term. Therefore, people and events may be evaluated as they are, apart from the feelings or needs of the perceiver. Standards or goals are valued beyond their connection to desired ends; the instrumental activities themselves are sustaining to the individual.

(Choose one level for each story)

Card	I	2	3BM	4	5	6BM	7GF	8BM
Sandra	2	3	2	2	2	3	2	3

Figure 7.3 (continued)

she doesn't want to look like that when she gets older, like the lady. She doesn't want to live on the farm. She feels sorry for that lady, for both, for the lady. So she goes to school to get an education so she's not like them.

Import: When a person sees the humdrum life of others, that person is reminded to go to school and get a good education so he or she doesn't have to be like them.

The girl goes to school to avoid becoming what she fears, not because she is interested in learning. Sandra gives lip service to the importance of education, but her implicit schema does not imbue learning or the effort involved with positive affect. In general, Sandra does not delve into the inner world of characters but relies on the stimulus or external appearances ("doesn't want to look like the lady"), and social conventions (getting an education). Thus, external structure and supports guide her goal-directed actions.

Card 3BM. Don't know what this is . . . umm . . . guess it's a girl. A boy or girl, either sleeping, crying, or . . . umm . . . [frustrated] don't even know what. [Examiner repeats directions.] I guess she's crying because . . . okay, this doesn't make sense though. [stares as if answer is in the card] I think they're car keys. No idea. This is dumb. She's crying because . . . what is that thing is . . . someone stole her car. She has no way home from this place. So then she calls the police and tells them that her car is missing. Eventually they find her car, and then she's happy. Can you tell me what that is? [E: It can look like different things to different people.]

Import: Without structure, it's hard to know what's going on, but if a person looks for clues in the environment and asks for help, things will work out eventually (though he or she is stuck for the moment).

Sandra doesn't feel comfortable making decisions without clear expectations. She initially vacillates before settling on a plot. In the process, she became frustrated, stating that the task was dumb, but she responded to encouragement. This tendency to blame outside factors is consistent with her reliance on the environment to regulate her behavior. The character's calling the police is a quick and conventional reaction to the stolen car and doesn't address the other problem of having "no way home from this place." Thus, Sandra does not invest sufficient energy into the task to tie up the loose ends, and the character resolves only part of her problem. Sandra's incomplete processing of information (only dealing with part of the problem) and limited resources (no internal representation of possible sources of support, obvious frustration with the task, and unsystematic approach to narrating the story) suggest why she has difficulty regulating her behavior to accomplish long-term purposes (in the absence of supportive structures).

Card 4. Okay, . . . this is a man and a woman who . . . they either just had a fight, or he wants to go somewhere, and she doesn't want him to go. Okay, she's trying to persuade him either not to go or to forgive her. And then, I guess eventually he does it, he forgives her or he doesn't, or he might go, or he'll stay. And they live happily ever after.

Import: Even when the problem between two people remains unclear and unresolved, if they try to work things out, they can live happily ever after.

Process Import: You are determined to give this conflict a happy outcome, but you are not clear about the process.

Again, Sandra cannot commit to one story line. Her vacillation about what's going on in the picture (noted in several cards) suggests that she feels uncertain of her judgment in situations that are somewhat ambiguous and depends on external cues and supports. The story ends happily but without a resolution to the dilemma. As with previous stories, the connection between means and ends is limited.

Card 5. Okay, can you make up people who aren't there? This is a lady who is coming to tell her children it's time for their nap. So she sticks her head in and says it's dinner time, and all the kids come to dinner. Everybody eats dinner, and kids go back and play. In the library, den, I think it's supposed to be the library.

Import: If a person intends to do one thing but does something that is related, it's just as well, and things work out.

Process Import: When you are not guided by structures and lose your train of thought, things work out if you find a familiar track.

The lady is coming to tell her children it's time for their naps but calls them to dinner instead. This twist in the story suggests that Sandra is not monitoring the details (also seen in other stories) and has difficulty sustaining her own intentions in the absence of support. Her query about introducing additional characters also points to her need for external guidance.

Card 6BM. This man and his mother . . . Okay . . . laugh . . . he's coming to tell her he's moving away [laugh] cause of his job he was transferred somewhere, and she's upset. Doesn't want him to go. She's looking out the window wondering what she'll do without him around and . . . [asks to read story] he explains to her that he has to go. Well, then she understands his reasoning but she still doesn't want him to go, but she understands it's the best thing for him so she lets him go, not not lets him, she's not angry 'cause he can do whatever he wants. She gives him her blessing, "do you know what I mean?" But she's still upset, no hard feelings. They say goodbye. How many more?

Import: If a man explains why he must leave his mother (job transfer), she understands and despite her sadness, "gives her blessing."

This story provides more cohesive connections among the narrative elements (circumstances, intentions, actions, and outcomes). However, no real action is required—one character simply needs to understand the other. The son explains that he has to go, and the mother understands. Still, the conventional goodbye seems a bit abrupt as no plans are made to ease the separation.

Card 8BM. Weird! I don't know what this kid's doing. Okay. Is this . . . Oh, you can't tell me. The man has been shot and two men, possibly doctors, but I doubt it. The two men are trying to remove the bullet and save his life—his son . . . daughter, don't know . . . son is praying that his father will live and survive this awful tragedy . . . and . . . okay, then it turned out, seems they're lost in the woods . . . ok, they fix him up, these men, and then they get him to a hospital, and he survives and thanks these men for saving his life.

Import: When a boy's father is shot in the woods, others will come on the scene to do what is necessary to save his life while the son prays, and later the father expresses gratitude.

After the father is shot, the two rescuers appear on the scene without any initiative on the part of the son. Sandra perceives others as helpful in playing out their conventional roles, but the characters facing the dilemma have limited resources.

Card 7GF. Oh God . . . [laughs] . . . okay. [turns it over, chews finger, makes faces] Okay, this girl . . . in with her mother or teacher . . . wait. This lady is reading to this little girl, a sad story. What else should I say? The girl doesn't look like she's paying attention, but she really is. She's amazed by the story. She's gonna drop this kid, that's how shocked she is. It's a baby doll, not real.

Then she finishes the story, and the child leaves. [pauses] Hated it. Glad it's over. I don't understand how you can make anything from that.

Process Import: In a difficult situation, if you don't want to deal with the tensions, you can simply pretend that things are not the way they seem.

The narrator side-stepped the tension in this picture by describing the girl, who seems not to be paying attention, as being so engrossed that she fails to hold on to the baby who (fortunately) turns out to be a doll. Sandra's coping strategy of avoiding tension or unpleasantness is evident in other stories that conclude happily but without the necessary intervening processes. Analogously, her characters are limited in their instrumental actions to resolve the problems or dilemmas set before them. For Sandra, the TAT task was frustrating and onerous. Her discomfort with the ambiguity of the pictures and the task, coupled with her reliance on external cues rather than on her own resources, made it difficult for her to settle on one explanation of the scene.

Narrative Summary

Sandra appears to be floundering in the campus setting because she is not intrinsically invested in the learning process and because she has not developed the resources necessary to regulate her behavior in the unstructured environment of a large university. She wants to stay in school because she believes that her future well-being depends on getting an education. However, she is not able to invest herself in the process of learning and has difficulty keeping a schedule for eating, sleeping, and attending classes. She told her examiner that in high school, she also experienced difficulty getting up and would miss school on the average of once a week. Moreover, she rarely studied, cheated to get by, and admitted having significant involvement with drug abuse since the fifth grade. Sandra characterized her therapist (who had requested the evaluations) as not providing direction during the sessions and indicated that she did not discuss important issues because she wasn't asked about them. As a result, she just talked about meaningless topics. Sandra was clear about her desire to succeed academically, but at the same time, she acknowledged that she found school work aversive and recognized that she was not achieving her goals.

Sandra's scores on the structured Wechsler Scales were in the high average range and were otherwise unremarkable. However, the TAT provided many clues to explain Sandra's predicament. First, though Sandra was generally able to recognize the conflict or tension in stimuli, she had difficulty sticking to one explanation, mirroring the discomfort she feels in making judgments or decisions without clear external guidelines. The task itself was frustrating and burdensome, and without additional direction from the examiner, Sandra looked to the external cues. In doing so, she had difficulty developing the themes that she introduced, placing relatively greater emphasis on explaining the stimulus (external) than on elaborating feelings, thoughts, or intentions (internal). Moreover, the stories produced positive outcomes without sufficient plans, actions, or initiatives on the part of characters facing a dilemma, suggesting these resources are not available to guide Sandra's daily behavior.

Sandra needs more directive therapeutic interventions to help her put the external structures and supports in place. Subsequent to the evaluation Sandra worked on identifying and seeking the external structures that would prompt her to engage in behaviors to meet her goals (e.g., entering a sorority so she could join peers at regular meals; planning a realistic schedule and developing routines to enable her to get ready in the morning, be on time for classes, and study). Sandra responded quickly to these external structures and began to feel increased control over her life. Subsequent sessions focused on ways to make these routines automatic and to examine the factors that impeded the development of connections between intentions, actions, and outcomes.

🪶 TEST YOURSELF 🪶

1. **Motivation and self-regulation are related because**
   (a) goals regulate thoughts, feelings, and behaviors.
   (b) self-regulation is an important goal that influences other goals.
   (c) both "a" and "b."
   (d) neither "a" nor "b."
2. **How is an "import" linked to motivation?**
3. **Motivation that is congruent with temperamental inclinations is associated with which of the following terms?**
   (a) introjection
   (b) integration
   (c) implementation intentions
   (d) self-control

(continued)

4. The designation of levels of motivation does not include

(a) goal setting.

(b) goal maintenance.

(c) the specific goal.

(d) means to attain goals.

5. How do the levels of self-regulation incorporate all previous coding dimensions?

6. To be rated at the highest level of motivation, a story must have a happy ending. True or False?

7. Self-regulation is characterized as optimal when the individual frequently engages in behaviors that go against the temperamental grain. True or False?

Answers: 1. c; 2. incorporates the key components of motivation; 3. b; 4. c; 5. Cognitive, emotional, and motivational processes contribute to the development of broader self-regulatory schemas that guide perceptions of self, others, and the world; 6. False; 7. False.

Eight

All thematic apperception techniques are grounded theoretically in the proective hypothesis, use pictures to elicit stories, and require trained professionals to interpret the responses. The essential differences across methods reside in the specific pictures presented and the particular approaches used to analyze the stories. The development of storytelling tools subsequent to the introduction of the TAT has proceeded through the delineation and validation of various approaches for interpreting stories told about TAT pictures, the introduction of new sets of pictures without additional interpretive procedures, as exemplified by the Children's Apperception Test (CAT), and the packaging of new sets of pictures with interpretive criteria, such as the Roberts Apperception Test for Children (RATC) and Tell-Me-A-Story (TEMAS). The name of the test is typically associated with the set of pictures and not the interpretive method. Without question, the TAT has been the most popular storytelling instrument in clinical use with adults (e.g., see Gieser & Stein, 1999) and also useful with children and adolescents (Teglasi, 1993). This chapter describes three storytelling tests developed specifically for use with children or adolescents. In-depth coverage of every storytelling measure is unnecessary, as a solid grounding in one narrative technique should generalize to others (Russ, 1998).

CHILDREN'S APPERCEPTION TEST

The introduction of the Children's Apperception Test (CAT) was based on the premise that children between the ages of 3 and 10 would identify more with animal than with human figures (Bellak & Bellak, 1949, 1952). However, subsequent research did not support the contention that the CAT would be superior to the TAT and, where differences were found, the data pointed in favor of pictures with human figures (Holt, 1958; Light, 1954; for a review, see French, Graves, & Levitt, 1983). Indeed, it has been suggested that the CAT pulls for regressive content (Eagle & Schwartz, 1994; Schwartz & Eagle, 1986) and may be less useful than the TAT, except possibly with the youngest children, ages 3 and 4.

In response to studies questioning the superiority of animal figures over those depicting humans, the Bellaks published the CAT-H, substituting human characters for the animal figures in the original CAT (Bellak & Bellak, 1965). In developing the human version, the authors aimed to make the two sets equivalent, but it was not possible to retain the same level of ambiguity in regard to age, gender, and cultural attributes of some of the figures. Although the Bellaks continued to prefer the original CAT, they acknowledged that the CAT-H may be more suitable with children between the ages of 7 and 10 or with highly intelligent younger children (who may find the animal figures to be "childish"). Studies comparing responses elicited by the CAT and CAT-H were not remarkably different (Gardner & Holmes, 1990; Haworth, 1966; Myler, Rosenkrantz, & Holmes, 1972; Neuringer & Livesay, 1970) and differences generally indicated that human cards were either equal or superior to the animal cards in evoking psychologically meaningful material. This conclusion held across various ages (preschool to 6th grade) and populations (well-adjusted, emotionally disturbed, intellectually retarded, or gifted). Other authors review the history of the CAT and CAT-H in greater depth (see Bellak & Abrams, 1997).

Despite the failure of research to support the superiority of CAT stimuli with children, it is important to remember that the cards (the original CAT and CAT-H) pull for specific themes (see Rapid Reference 8.1). Clinicians deal with individuals and the usefulness of specific thematic cards depends on the case. For instance, clinicians have noted the advantage of using the CAT with certain adult personality types (Kitron & Benzimen, 1990). The authors and others have considered use of the CAT animal figures to be advantageous (Kline & Svaste-Xuto, 1981) because of gender neutrality and cross-cultural applicability. In an attempt to make the CAT administration more engaging for children, Hoar and Faust (1973) developed a jigsaw-puzzle version of the CAT cards. Thus, the CAT and its variations provide still another tool for the practitioner.

Each of the 10 CAT cards depicting animal figures in human-like situations was designed to clarify children's problems around various issues: eating, relating to parental figures as individuals and as a couple (primal scene, Oedipal feelings), fears of loneliness, sibling rivalry, toilet training, mastery, aggression, and

◤Rapid Reference 8.1

CAT Cards

1. Chicks are seated around a table upon which a large bowl of food has been set. Off to one side is a large chicken, dimly outlined.

2. One bear pulls a rope on one side while another bear and a baby bear pull on the other side.

3. A lion with a pipe and cane sits in a chair. In the lower right corner a little mouse appears in a hole.

4. A kangaroo with a bonnet on her head carries a basket with a milk bottle. In her pouch is a baby kangaroo with a balloon. On a bicycle is a larger kangaroo child.

5. The card shows a darkened room with a large bed in the background and a crib (with two baby bears) in the foreground.

6. The card shows a darkened cave with two dimly outlined bear figures in the background and a baby bear in the foreground.

7. A tiger with bared fangs and claws leaps at a monkey that is also leaping through the air.

8. Two adult monkeys sit on a sofa drinking from tea cups. One adult monkey is in foreground sitting on a hassock and talking to a baby monkey.

9. A darkened room is seen through an open door from a lighted room. The darkened room contains a child's bed in which a rabbit sits up looking through the door.

10. A baby dog lies across the knees of an adult dog, both figures show a minimum of expression in their features. The figures are set in the foreground of a bathroom.

acceptance by the adult world (see Rapid Reference 8.1). Whereas the authors designed the CAT stimuli to elicit content pertaining to universal issues according to a psychoanalytic view of development, they introduced a supplemental set of stimuli, the CAT-S (Bellak & Bellak, 1952), to learn about specific problems (see Rapid Reference 8.2). The examiner may select any single picture or combination from the supplemental set in addition to the CAT stimuli.

Administration of the CAT

The administration procedures described in Chapter 2 apply to all storytelling methods. However, cards selected and the specific wording of the instructions

═Rapid Reference 8.2

CAT Supplementary Cards

1. Four mouse-children are on a slide. One is just sliding down, one is about to start the slide, and two are climbing up the ladder. Numbers one and three suggest males; two and four suggest females (skirts, bows in hair).

2. The card shows a classroom situation with three little monkeys. Two sit at typical school desks, one stands with a book in hand while one of the seated monkeys holds his tail.

3. Mouse-children are "playing house." "Father mouse" wears eyeglasses that are much too big for him and obviously belong to an adult, and is receiving a beverage from "Mother mouse" while toys and a baby doll in a carriage are dispersed about them.

4. A big bear sits crouched forward, holding a baby bear on its lap and in its arms.

5. A kangaroo is on crutches and has a bandaged tail and foot.

6. A group of four foxes (two male and two female) are in a race with the goal in sight, and one male is closest to it.

7. A cat stands before a mirror looking at its image.

8. A rabbit doctor is examining a rabbit child with a stethoscope; some bottles of medicine are visible in the background.

9. A grown deer is taking a shower and is half hidden by a shower curtain. A small deer is looking toward the larger figure. An enema bag hangs against the wall.

10. An obviously pregnant cat stands upright, with a large belly and apron askew.

vary across techniques. The authors of the CAT suggest that all 10 cards be administered in numerical order. However, if the child becomes restless, the clinician may present fewer cards with selections based on the themes elicited by the cards. The following instructions to the CAT differ from those of the TAT by introducing the task as a game and by not directing the narrator to tell what the characters are thinking and how they are feeling:

"This is a story game. There are ten pictures altogether. When I show you each picture, the idea is for you to try to make up a make-pretend story for the picture. Tell what is happening in the picture, then what happens next, and how the story ends. Another way is you can make up what you think happened before, then tell what's happening in the picture, and then put an ending to it. We are interested in how you make up a story with a beginning, middle, and an end from your own imagination. Okay, here is the first picture" (p. 3).

If the child has described the picture but is having trouble continuing, the examiner may prompt by saying, "That's a good beginning to the story. Now can you tell me what you think is going to happen next?" If the child does not put an ending to a story, the examiner may prompt with, "Now, how does the story end?" If necessary, the examiner may read the story back to the child (noting it on the transcript).

Interpretation of the CAT

When the authors introduced the CAT stimuli and its variations, the pictures were not accompanied by new interpretive procedures, and methods for interpreting stories told to TAT cards were applied. However, others subsequently introduced interpretive units specific to CAT stimuli (e.g., Haworth, 1963) or adapted units previously used with TAT pictures (e.g., Chandler, Shermis, & Lempert, 1989). Bellak and Abrams (1997) indicate some minor differences between interpreting the TAT and CAT, noting the lack of systematic research delineating specific differences in responses of children and adults to the TAT or year-by-year changes in responses of children. Haworth (1966) provides some examples of normal CAT stories at various ages and reviews some developmental trends from preschool to age 10 (see Rapid Reference 8.3).

Bellak's (revised, 1992) Short Form for analyzing stories is intended for use with both the TAT and the CAT stimuli. The examiner who is familiar with the theoretical underpinnings of the Form uses it to organize the narrator's responses by scrutinizing each story according to the 10 variables listed: the main theme, the main hero, the main needs of the hero, conception of the environment, interpersonal object relations, significant conflicts, nature of anxieties, main defenses against conflicts and fears, adequacy of superego, and integration of the ego. The interpreter pulls the variables considered for each story into a summary analysis based on the interpreter's familiarity with and endorsement of the psychoanalytic perspective for content interpretation. Bel-

≡Rapid Reference 8.3

Age-Related Shifts in Perceptions Have Been Noted in CAT Stimuli*

1. At younger ages (6 and below) children may not be aware of small details such as the mouse in Card 3 or the pouch and baby in Card 4. Therefore, expectations for eliciting content such as father/child relations in Card 3 cannot be met if the narrator does not take note of the much smaller mouse figure. In the human version of this stimulus, the child is much more prominent and difficult to ignore.

2. By age 7, there are few omissions (mean = 1.4) of pictured characters.

3. The figures that are omitted, particularly at ages 5 and below, are very small, vague, or blurred.

*See Haworth (1966).

lak's suggestion that clinicians analyze the 10 variables to find patterns and trends rather than judge from a single isolated story is shown in the case example presented in Chapter 10. The form also includes a section for rating each of 14 ego functions (see Rapid Reference 8.4).

Other interpretive procedures for stories told to CAT stimuli were developed specifically for use with the CAT pictures or were adapted from the TAT. The Schedule for the Analysis of the CAT (Haworth, 1963), intended primarily as an aid for the qualitative evaluation of the stories and secondarily as a rough quantitative index for within-subject and group comparison, includes three broad categories: (a) defense mechanisms such as reaction formation, undoing and ambivalence, isolation, repression and denial, deception, symbolization, and projection and introjection; (b) phobic, immature, or disorganized responses indicating fear or anxiety, regression, or weak or absent controls; and (c) gender identification rated as adequate (same gender) versus confused or opposite gender. Critical "scores" calculated for each category have been found to differentiate between clinical and school samples. More recently Cramer (1991) extensively studied three mechanisms of denial, projection, and identification with both the TAT and CAT.

Byrd and Witherspoon's (1954) classification of CAT responses as enumerative (naming of objects), descriptive (qualities of objective stimulus features), and apperceptive (interpretation beyond the objective features of the picture)

≡Rapid Reference 8.4

Ego Functions Assessed with CAT and TAT

1. *Reality testing*—distinction between inner and outer stimuli; accuracy of perception; reflective awareness

2. *Judgment*—anticipation of consequences and the emotional appropriateness of this anticipation

3. *Sense of reality*—extent of derealization or depersonalization; clarity of boundaries between the self and the world

4. *Regulation and control*—regulation of drives, affects, and impulses; directness of impulse expression; effectiveness of delay mechanisms

5. *Object relations*—degree and kind of relatedness (e.g., extent to which objects are perceived independently of oneself; primitiveness of the perception)

6. *Thought process*—memory, concentration, attention, and conceptualization; primary and secondary process

7. *Adaptive regression in the service of the ego*—creativity such as formation of new cognitive configurations

8. *Defensive functioning*—adaptiveness or maladaptiveness of defenses

9. *Stimulus barrier*—threshold for reacting to stimuli and effectiveness of strategies for managing excessive stimulus input

10. *Autonomous functioning*—freedom from impairment in managing everyday life tasks

11. *Synthetic-integrative functioning*—extent to which the narrator actively relates events to each other or reconciles incongruities

12. *Mastery-competence*—effectiveness in mastering the environment

13. *Superego*—strength and adaptiveness of conscience (e.g., too strong, too weak, inconsistent)

14. *Drive*—strength and adaptiveness of drives (e.g., too strong, too weak, inappropriate, too aggressive or impulsive)

gave credit to the highest level. In Picture 1, "chicks" are seen as enumerative, "sitting" is rated as descriptive, and "eating something, mother hen is feeding them" is apperceptive. Apperceptive responses may be further classified according to the underlying dynamic such as sibling rivalry, fear, or aggression (Bellak & Bellak, 1952).

Associative Elaboration and Integration Scales (Slemon, Holzwarth, Lewis,

CAUTION

The units for CAT interpretation have not been normed, and inter-rater reliability for various scoring systems has been sketchy. Therefore, the instrument has been described as theoretically, but not psychometri-cally, valid (Hatt, 1985).

& Sitko, 1976) introduced for use with TAT pictures have been applied to the CAT (Schroth, 1977). The Associative Elaboration Scale, intended to measure the tendency to embellish stories with details beyond what is suggested by the card, is scored on a 10-point scale based on the number of interpretive comments. The Integration Scale, intended to measure the degree to which the narrator brings together the story details into a cohesive plot, is scored on a 6-point scale, ranging from no theme or pure description to a complete and integrated story with no irrelevancies. In applying these scales to the CAT, Schroth found interrater correlations sufficiently high for clinical settings. Children 8 to 10 years of age had significantly higher Associative Elaboration and Integration scores than those aged 6 and 7. The correlation between IQ scores and Associative Elaboration (.13) and Integration (.03) were not significant.

The Transcendence Index, originally devised for use with the TAT (Weisskopf, 1950), has been applied to the CAT (Armstrong, 1954; Budoff, 1960; Haworth, 1963; Weisskopf-Joelson & Lyn, 1953; Weisskopf-Joelson & Foster, 1962). The Transcendence Index is the number of statements that either go beyond pure description of the stimulus or are independent of what is actually shown in the picture. Despite the fact that any frequency count is subject to the undue influence of story length, this index has been popular as a measure of productivity because it includes elaborations of the characters' inner worlds (emotions, thoughts) and events that occur prior or subsequent to the pictured scene. However, the Transcendence Index does not take into account either the cohesiveness among these components or their compatibility with the stimuli.

TELL-ME-A-STORY (TEMAS)

In an effort to develop a thematic apperception test that is useful for minority children, the authors of the Tell-Me-A-Story (TEMAS) designed two parallel sets of pictures depicting minority and nonminority children interacting in urban settings and provided population-specific norms for designated scoring criteria

(Constantino, Malgady, & Rogler, 1988). The authors reasoned that the context depicted in the pictured scene should be closer to the experience of the narrator (see Rapid Reference 8.5). Otherwise, interest and responsiveness to the stimuli are minimal, and the resulting data are insufficient and unreliable.

Stimuli

The authors contend that the pictures in the TEMAS set are particularly relevant to poor, urban, Black, and Hispanic children, but also useful with White and middle-class

> ≡ *Rapid Reference 8.5*
>
> ### Picture Content, Race, and Culture
>
> 1. Situation may be unfamiliar to the child due to cultural influences.
> 2. A child may not identify strongly with individuals from another cultural or racial background.
> 3. The same stimulus situation may be interpreted differently due to cultural experiences or norms.
> 4. Presenting all White figures may interfere with rapport when administering the test to minority children.

children. The test includes two parallel sets of pictures, one for minorities and another for nonminorities, with normative data for both populations. The TEMAS pictures, like the TAT, depict conflictual interpersonal situations but, unlike the TAT, these stimuli present two sides of a conflict, with most pictures resembling a split screen that represents opposite sides of an antithetical situation or inner dilemma. Thus, the TEMAS stimuli are highly structured and familiar, and presentation of both sides of a conflict provides clear expectations of what narrators should include in the story. The scoring identifies adaptive and maladaptive responses to these conflict situations.

Each version of the TEMAS, designed to elicit identical themes, includes 23 pictures, with the minority set featuring predominantly Hispanic and African American characters in urban environments and the nonminority set depicting predominantly nonminority characters in an urban environment. Both versions have a short form composed of nine cards. Of the short form, four cards are given to both genders and five are specific to gender. Of the 23 in the long form, 12 are used for both genders and 11 are specific to gender. Only one is age-specific (Card 22, adolescent girls or boys). The set includes four that depict pluralistic characters that can be used for either minority or nonminority groups. The cards for the short form are described in Rapid Reference 8.6, and the reader is invited to consult the Manual (Constantino et al., 1988) for further detail.

≡Rapid Reference 8.6

TEMAS Stimuli Included in the Short Form

Card 1B. A mother is giving a command to her son. A father is in the background. Friends are urging the boy to play basketball with them. (Theme: interpersonal relations and delay of gratification)

Card 1G. A mother is giving a command to her daughter. A father is in the background. Friends are urging the girl to jump rope with them. (Theme: interpersonal relations and delay of gratification)

Card 7. An angry mother is watching her son and daughter argue over a broken lamp. (Theme: interpersonal relations, aggression, and moral judgment)

Card 10B. A boy is standing in front of a piggy bank holding money while imagining himself looking at a bicycle in a shop window and buying an ice cream cone. (Theme: delay of gratification)

Card 10G. A girl is standing in front of a piggy bank holding money while imagining herself looking at a bicycle in a shop window and buying an ice cream cone. (Theme: delay of gratification)

Card 14B. A boy is studying in his room. A group of boys and girls is listening to music in the living room. (Theme: interpersonal relations, achievement motivation, and delay of gratification)

Card 14G. A girl is studying in her room. A group of boys and girls is listening to music in the living room. (Theme: interpersonal relations, achievement motivation, and delay of gratification)

Card 15 (minority version). A policeman is giving an award to a group of Police Athletic League (PAL) baseball players. A policeman is arresting a group of three boys and one girl who have broken a window and stolen merchandise. (Theme: interpersonal relations, aggression, achievement motivation, and moral judgment)

Card 15 (nonminority version). A policeman is giving an award to a group of soccer players. A policeman is arresting a group of three boys and one girl who have broken a window and stolen merchandise. (Theme: interpersonal relations, aggression, achievement motivation, and moral judgment)

Card 17B. A boy is studying and daydreaming about receiving an A from his teacher and receiving an F from his teacher. (Theme: anxiety/depression, achievement motivation, and self-concept)

Card 17G. A girl is studying and daydreaming about receiving and A from her teacher and receiving an F from her teacher. (Theme: anxiety/depression, achievement motivation, and self-concept)

Card 20. A youngster is in bed dreaming of a scene showing a horse on a hill, a river, and a path leading to a castle. (Theme: anxiety or depression)

Card 21. A youngster is in bed dreaming of a monster eating something and of a monster making threats. (Theme: aggression, anxiety/depression, and reality testing)

Card 22B. A boy is standing in front of a bathroom mirror, imagining his face reflected in the mirror with attributes of both sexes. (Theme: anxiety/depression, sexual identity, and reality testing)

Card 22G. A girl is standing in front of a bathroom mirror, imagining her face reflected in the mirror with attributes of both sexes. (Theme: anxiety/depression, sexual identity and reality testing)

Administration

The entire protocol of 23 cards or a subset of 9 cards may be administered to any given child. The clinician chooses the set of cards (minority or nonminority) that corresponds to the racial or cultural identification of the child. The manual provides detailed instructions: "Initially, the examiner says: 'I'd like you to tell me a story. I have a lot of interesting pictures that I'm going to show you. Please look carefully at the people and the places in the pictures and then tell me a complete story about each picture—a story that has a beginning and an end'" (p. 19).

After showing the first picture to the child, the examiner provides a temporal sequence to structure events in the story by saying, "Please tell me a complete story about this picture and all the other pictures I will show you. The story should answer three questions: (1) What is happening in the picture now? (2) What happened before? (3) What will happen in the future?" These instructions may be repeated for each card.

After giving the instructions for temporal sequencing, the examinee is given the opportunity to tell the story spontaneously. The story is considered complete, and no further inquiry is necessary, if it includes the temporal sequence and addresses the six areas listed in Rapid Reference 8.7. Because the requested story elements are scored, the respondent may be unduly penalized if the examiner fails to inquire. At the completion of each story, the examiner first addresses the temporal sequence of the events as needed, followed by the remaining six story elements. Generally, the examiner should encourage the child to complete ideas (or sentences) and to clarify and explain characters' motives and behaviors. The examiner may ask such clarifying questions as the story is being narrated and should indicate them parenthetically, such as "(?)." Clarifying questions are not analyzed in the scoring system but may be clini-

≡ *Rapid Reference 8.7*

Six Areas to be Queried

1. (a) Who are these people? Do they know each other?
   (b) Who is this person?
2. (a) Where are these people?
   (b) Where is this person?
3. (a) What are these people doing and saying?
   (b) What is this person doing and saying?
4. (a) What were these people doing before?
   (b) What was this person doing before?
5. (a) What will these people do next?
   (b) What will this person do next?
6. (a) What is this person (main character) thinking?
   (b) What is this person (main character) feeling?

cally useful. The examiner makes structured inquiries after the story has been told and records these inquiries parenthetically by the number used (e.g., "1a").

Examiners use a stopwatch to record both the reaction time and the total time. The examiner starts the stopwatch when handing the picture to the child and stops it the moment the child begins to respond. This latency time is the reaction time recorded at the beginning of each story. If the story is complete the examiner stops timing. If not, the stopwatch remains running until the inquiry has been completed. The examiner encourages the child to speak for at least 2 minutes per story by using prompts such as, "Tell me what is happening in this picture," or, "Tell me what you see." The test allots a maximum time of 5 minutes for each story and, if the respondent is overly verbose, he or she is prompted to complete the story after 4 minutes (e.g., "How does your story end?").

Interpretation

The TEMAS measures 18 cognitive functions, nine personality functions, and seven affective functions, and includes three qualitative indicators (see Rapid Reference 8.8 to 8.11). The authors indicate that the test can be interpreted normatively and clinically for children aged 5 to 13 and clinically for children aged 14 to 18. The norms provided are to be used with children who are co-

≡Rapid Reference 8.8

Cognitive Functions

1. *Reaction Time**—elapsed time between presentation of the picture and start of the narration

2. *Total Time**—elapsed time between start of story and conclusion of the inquiry

3. *Fluency**—number of words in the story

4. *Total Omissions**—number of characters, events, and settings depicted but not mentioned in the story

5. *Main Character Omissions****—failure to mention principal character or characters in the story

6. *Secondary Character Omissions****—failure to mention figures other than main character or characters in the story

7. *Event Omissions****—failure to identify what is happening in the picture

8. *Setting Omissions****—failure to identify the location of the event

9. *Total Transformations***—the number of perceptual distortions of characters, events, and settings depicted

10. *Main Character Transformations****—incorrect identifications of main figures

11. *Secondary Character Transformations****—incorrect identifications of secondary figures

12. *Event Transformations****—incorrect identification of what is happening in the picture

13. *Setting Transformations****—incorrect identification of location

14. *Inquiries***—number of questions, including clarifications and structured inquiry

15. *Relationships***—identification of the characters and their relationships to each other

16. *Imagination***—content that goes beyond descriptive details about characters, events, and settings

17. *Sequencing***—relation of past, present, and future events

18. *Conflict***—recognition of the conflict depicted as polarities

*Quantitative scale
**Qualitative scale
***Optional scale

Rapid Reference 8.9

Personality Functions

The nine personality functions are assessed along an adaptive-maladaptive continuum that is defined according to psychosocial criteria.

1. *Interpersonal relations*—ability to synthesize the polarities of dependence/individuation, respect/disrespect, and nurturance/rejection

2. *Aggression*—direct verbal or physical expression of intent to harm self, other, or property

3. *Anxiety/depression*—irrational fears or worries about the current situation or about the future or pervasive unhappiness, psychosomatic symptoms, suicidal thoughts, feelings of worthlessness, and a tendency to cry or feel shy and withdrawn

4. *Achievement motivation*—the desire to attain a goal or to succeed in an endeavor that is related to some standard of excellence

5. *Delay of gratification*—the foregoing of an immediate reward in favor of delayed but more substantial reward or gratification

6. *Self concept*—realistic self-perception of intellectual, social, physical, and vocational abilities and mastery over the environment

7. *Sexual identity*—realistic perception of roles appropriate to gender

8. *Moral judgment*—ability to tell right from wrong and to act accordingly, to accept responsibility for wrongdoing, and to experience appropriate guilt for improper action

9. *Reality testing*—ability to distinguish between fantasy and reality, to recognize problematic situations, and to anticipate the personal and social consequences of behavior

operative and understand the requirements of the task, and who are able to communicate a sequence of events. Interpretations are based on a dynamic cognitive model incorporating the theoretical frameworks of ego psychology, interpersonal psychology, social learning theory, cognitive psychology, and motivational psychology (see the *Manual*).

As a first step, the interpreter follows a systematic sequential analysis of the scores on the cognitive, personality, and affective functions. Raw scores are converted to normalized T scores ($M = 50$; $SD = 10$), and each function is examined in terms of high and low scores (one standard deviation above or below the mean). The authors caution against interpreting functions in isolation, advocating for establishing meaningful patterns of quantitative and

≡Rapid Reference 8.10

Affective Functions

Seven distinct moods or affects are attributed to the main character or characters following the resolution of the tensions depicted in the scene:

1. *Happy**—contentment following a satisfactory resolution of the dilemma depicted in the scene
2. *Sad**—discontent associated with resolution of the conflict
3. *Angry**—strong displeasure associated with the conflict
4. *Fearful**—feeling of impending danger associated with the resolution of the conflict
5. *Neutral*—emotional indifference to the resolution of the conflict
6. *Ambivalent*—emotional indecision associated with the resolution of the conflict
7. *Inappropriate affect*—incongruence between mood state of main character or characters at the resolution of the conflict and earlier behavior in the story

*Quantitative scales

qualitative data across and within the cognitive, affective, and personality functions.

All nine personality functions are qualitatively scored on a scale of 1 (most maladaptive) to 4 (most adaptive). In addition, if a personality function is not pulled (N) as part of the content of a TEMAS story, it signifies a serious omission, denoting maladaptive selective attention to the specific function. The N cutoff is at or above the 15th percentile. Due to limited variability, 14 cognitive functions and three affective functions were not converted into T scores. Cut-off scores were designated at the 90th percentile.

≡Rapid Reference 8.11

Unscored Qualitative Indicators

1. Observed Test Behavior
2. Rejection of Cards
3. Content Analysis of Stories

CAUTION

The limitations of the TEMAS include geographically narrow standardization samples and little research other than studies conducted by the authors (Flanagan & DiGiuseppe, 1999).

ROBERTS APPERCEPTION TEST FOR CHILDREN

The authors' (McArthur & Roberts, 1982) rationale for developing the Roberts Apperception Test for Children (RATC) was based on dissatisfaction with currently available stimuli for use with children and the absence of an agreed-upon scoring system. They noted that the use of animal figures in human situations was not appropriate for most school-age children. Moreover, though they acknowledged that the TAT was designed for use with children and adults, with more than half the cards deemed appropriate for use with children (Murray, 1943), the authors observed that few cards actually depict children. In the absence of an agreed-upon system for scoring the content and structure of stories, the authors proposed an interpretive approach along with a new set of stimuli. According to the *Manual*, several characteristics of the RATC distinguish it from other commonly used thematic apperception tests (see Rapid Reference 8.12).

Administration

The test is administered individually. All 16 cards should be administered in numerical order using the version appropriate to the subject's gender and following the instructions in the standardization procedures:

≡Rapid Reference 8.12

Features of the RATC

1. The cards were designed for use with children and adolescents between the ages of 6 and 15, to assess perceptions of common interpersonal situations as an aid to general personality description and clinical decision-making with the projective hypothesis remaining the underlying theoretical framework.

2. The stimuli depict children in all 16 stimulus cards, and each emphasizes everyday interpersonal events. The pictures pull for themes of parent-child relationships, sibling relationships, aggression, mastery, parental disagreement, parental affection, observation of nudity, and school and peer relationships. Four of the cards depict aggressive situations and require the demonstration of strategies for coping with aggressive provocation.

3. The stimuli are consistent in their presentation, showing realistic drawings of children and adults.

4. Scoring criteria are objective and yield high interrater agreement.

5. The test provides normative criteria for a sample of 200 well-adjusted children, aged 6 to 15, to aid in the clinical interpretation of test results.

"I have a number of pictures I am going to show you one at a time. I want you to make up a story about each picture. Please tell me what is happening in the picture, what led up to this scene, and how the story ends. Tell me what the people are talking about and feeling. Use your imagination and remember that there are no right or wrong answers for the picture." If necessary, the examiner may add, "I want you to tell me a story with a beginning, middle, and end. Tell me what the people are doing, feeling and thinking." (p. 7)

If elements are missing from the story, the examiner may ask any of the following questions: (a) What is happening? (b) What happened before? (c) What is he or she feeling? (d) What is he or she talking about? (e) How does the story end? These questions may be used freely during the stories told to the first two cards but should be used sparingly thereafter. The child's consistent omission of certain story elements requested by the instructions is relevant information. The examiner may inquire as needed to clarify responses. Examples include asking the child to identify who is meant by "he" when a pronoun may refer to more than one character. The examiner should indicate the point in the story where an inquiry was used to distinguish spontaneous responses from those that were cued. A child who is unable to tell a story may be encouraged to "say something about the picture."

Stimuli

The 27 stimulus cards in the standard set depict common situations, conflicts, and stresses in children's lives. Of the 27 cards, 11 have parallel male and female versions, indicated by the letter "B" and "G" on the back of the card. Therefore, only 16 of the cards may be administered to each child (see Rapid Reference 8.13).

Interpretation

The measures include indices of adaptive and maladaptive functioning. There are eight adaptive scales, five clinical scales, and three critical indicators that occur rarely among well-adjusted children. Additional scales are Interpersonal Matrix, Ego Functioning Index, Aggression Index, and Level of Projection Scale (see Rapid References 8.14 to 8.18). To increase rater agreement, the

≡ Rapid Reference 8.13

The RATC Stimuli Were Designed to Elicit the Following Themes:

Card 1B/G: Family confrontation

Card 2B/G: Maternal support

Card 3B/G: School attitude

Card 4: Child support/aggression

Card 5B/G: Parental affection

Card 6B/G: Peer/racial interaction

Card 7B/G: Dependency/anxiety

Card 8: Family conference

Card 9: Physical aggression toward peer

Card 10B/G: Sibling rivalry

Card 11: Fear

Card 12B/G: Parental conflict/depression

Card 13B/G: Aggression release

Card 14B/G: Maternal limit-setting

Card 15: Nudity/sexuality

Card 16B/G: Parental support

≡ Rapid Reference 8.14

Eight Adaptive Scales of the RATC

1. *Reliance on others*—character reaches out to others for help

2. *Support (other)*—character gives others assistance, emotional support, or material objects

3. *Support (child)*—character shows self-reliance, assertiveness, positive emotion, perseverance, delay of gratification

4. *Limit setting*—parental or other authority figures correct the behavior of the character or set limits or expectations

5. *Problem identification*—character states a problem, confronts an obstacle, experiences inner conflict, or shows difficulty meeting others expectations

6. *Resolution 1*—character tends to seek easy or unrealistic solutions to problems, as seen in magical or wish-fulfilling resolutions, without mention of appropriate mediating steps

7. *Resolution 2*—character finds a constructive resolution to a problem (external or intrapsychic) that is limited to dealing only with the immediate situation and without indication of having "worked through" the problem

8. *Resolution 3*—character finds a constructive resolution that goes beyond the immediate concern and that fully explains the problem-solving process or shows new awareness or insight on the part of the character (is scored as an indicator and not a profile scale for children aged 6 to 12)

Rapid Reference 8.15

Five Clinical Scales of the RATC

1. *Anxiety*—character is apprehensive, fearful, self-doubting, guilty, or remorseful, or themes focus on death, illness, or accidents
2. *Aggression*—character feels angry, attacks verbally or physically, destroys objects or constructively expresses anger
3. *Depression*—stories contain sadness, despair, or physical symptoms of depression such as fatigue, apathy, or sleeplessness
4. *Rejection*—stories contain themes of separation, jealousy, discrimination, or feelings of being left out
5. *Unresolved*—the characters are not able to resolve the problem set before them in the story (there is an emotional reaction left hanging or there is no outcome to the story)

Rapid Reference 8.16

Three Indicators of the RATC (though lacking psychometric properties, they may be clinically useful)

1. *Atypical response.* The narrator displays extreme deviation from the usual themes or evidence of primary process thinking by distorting stimulus figure, distorting theme or emotion, denying obvious aspects of the card, telling an illogical story, stating homicidal or suicidal ideation, describing the death of a main character depicted in the card, or describing any form of child abuse.
2. *Maladaptive outcome.* The outcome is associated with characters' acting in socially unacceptable ways (withdrawing, manipulating, deceiving), contributing to an unresolved conflict, or using inappropriate defense mechanisms (denial, phobic, or hysterical behaviors).
3. *Refusal.* This is scored when a child refuses to give a response to a card or starts to tell a story but suddenly stops. None of the children in the well-adjusted sample rejected any of the 16 cards.

Rapid Reference 8.17

The Interpersonal Matrix

A grid summarizes the various scales and indicators in relation to the figures identified by the child, such as themes of aggression being connected with father figures. This matrix is used as a supplement to the profile scales and indicators.

CAUTION

The standardization sample includes a small number of children per age group.

examiner is cautioned to score only manifest content from the words and to use inferences only for qualitative assessment. The interpretation proceeds by converting raw scores for each scale (not the critical indicators) to normalized T scores for four age groups (6 to 7, 8 to 9, 10 to 12, and 13 to 15) and examining the profiles on various scales, along with qualitative analysis.

Rapid Reference 8.18

RATC Supplementary Measures (designed primarily as research tools for future validation)

1. *Ego Functioning Index.* Each of the following four categories incorporates two levels to make a total of eight points on the index: (1) distorted response (bizarre/atypical or misidentified), (2) mildly disturbed response (confused, unresolved), (3) stereotyped response (extremely stereotypic, mildly stereotypic), (4) creative response (moderately creative, exceptionally creative).

2. *Aggression Index.* The Aggression Index is divided into four categories, with three levels in each, to make a total of nine levels: (1) destructive aggression (physical attack on individuals or animals, verbal attack on individuals or animals, destruction of objects), (2) indirect or psychologically mediated aggression (aggression turned inward, displacement or projection of aggressive feelings to source outside self), (3) constructive use of aggression (release of aggressive feelings in socially acceptable ways, constructive or creative resolution of aggressive feelings).

3. *Level of Projection Scale.* Four distinct categories are divided into two levels to make a total of eight possible levels: (1) description (description of people or objects, description of present action), (2) ascription (projected action or conversation and projected feelings or motivations), (3) explanation (incomplete story and incomplete story with feelings, thoughts, motivations explained), (4) integration (complete story and expanded complete story).

TEST YOURSELF

1. **Subsequent to the introduction of the TAT, innovations in storytelling assessment involved**

   (a) introducing new stimuli without additional interpretive procedures.

   (b) developing new ways to interpret existing picture sets.

   (c) proposing new sets of stimuli along with interpretive criteria.

   (d) all of the above.

2. **What was the rationale for introducing the CAT, CAT-H, and CAT-S?**

3. **CAT administration differs from TAT administration because the CAT**

   (a) does not request the inclusion of thoughts and feelings.

   (b) introduces the task as a game.

   (c) both "a" and "b."

   (d) neither "a" nor "b."

4. **What was the rationale for developing the TEMAS?**

5. **What was the rationale for developing the RATC?**

Answers: 1. d; 2. The rationale behind CAT was that young children would identify more with animal than with human figures; furthermore, there was a perceived need for a set of stimuli designed to study specific developmental issues. The rationale for CAT-H was the need for a parallel set with human figures because research did not support the superiority of animal figures. Also, some children age 7 and older thought that the animal stimuli were "childish." The rationale for the supplemental stimuli in CAT-S was to learn about specific clinically relevant problems; 3. c; 4. TEMAS stimuli were introduced in an effort to make the storytelling technique more suitable for minority children by depicting urban settings, parallel sets showing minority and nonminority characters, and population-specific norms; 5. RATC stimuli were designed to portray children in contrast to the TAT set, which contains few cards depicting children. Moreover, in the absence of an agreed-upon scoring system, the authors proposed an interpretive approach along with new stimuli.

Nine

STRENGTHS AND WEAKNESSES OF STORYTELLING ASSESSMENT TECHNIQUES

Storytelling makes a unique contribution to a comprehensive assessment. However, in the absence of an agreed-upon interpretive system that is sufficiently comprehensive for clinical use, professionals are left to cobble together various approaches that match their theoretical framework. The dilemma for the field is that the technique's versatility and richness, which constitute its greatest assets, are also the sources of its greatest liability. A chief advantage of storytelling is its capacity to go beyond the content of cognitions, such as a tally of anxiety-related thoughts, to reveal the process of thinking, reasoning, and developing ideas. Reducing rich and complex narrative data to simple units that are normatively and psychometrically evaluated may undermine the strength of the method. As with any other assessment procedure, storytelling must be used in accord with its purpose and with acknowledgment of its strengths and limitations.

UNIQUE CONTRIBUTION OF STORYTELLING TO A COMPREHENSIVE ASSESSMENT

Storytelling techniques may be viewed as performance tests of personality (Teglasi, 1998) that reveal the narrators' thought processes and problem-solving strategies in managing the task as well as the schemas for organizing the inner world in relation to the external environment. This dual nature makes it possible both to compare story production with performance on other tasks in the assessment battery that measure cognitive or academic functioning and to self-report tests of personality. As a performance measure, storytelling is unique in that it predicts resources for organizing responses to situations without clear performance standards, whereas performance on the more structured cognitive tests (measures of intelligence or achievement) predict competence in similarly structured situations (see Teglasi, 1993, 1998). Storytelling also clarifies schemas about the self and the world in ways that differ from self-report.

Comparison with Other Performance Tests in the Battery

Similar to life situations, performance tests vary in terms of the amount of structure, cues, or prompts provided for response and in the amount of organization required for adequate performance. Generally, cognitive measures, such as tasks on the Wechsler scales, provide more structure than do conditions encountered in everyday situations. For example, verbally communicated problems tend to contain words that act as cues for accessing relevant knowledge, whereas daily judgments and decisions require spontaneous use of prior knowledge. Knowledge that is available when prompted by specific questions but is not sufficiently organized to be used in problem-solving situations has been described as "inert" (Bransford, Franks, Vye, & Sherwood, 1989). Typically, correlations between cognitive test scores and real-life accomplishments are no better than about .30 (e.g., Deary & Stough, 1996; Hunt, 1980). Limitations on generalizing from responses to structured tasks to real-life conditions are understandable in terms of the attributes that these measures do not assess. These include being aware that a problem exists or that a task needs to be done; recognizing and responding to implicit or subtle cues; setting priorities and planning toward their implementation; taking necessary initiative to pursue intentions; organizing, pacing, and monitoring responses; seeking or utilizing feedback; and sustaining long-term investment in relationships and independent activities. These competencies, traditionally viewed as pertaining to the personality domain, are needed for everyday functioning. Yet, they are not assessed when tasks are highly structured (see Rapid Reference 9.1).

Comparison to Self-Report

Despite their many advantages, self-report inventories have significant limitations (for a review, see Glass & Arnkoff, 1997), and there is an increasing awareness of the need to combine self-report measures with other approaches

≡Rapid Reference 9.1

Contrast between Structured Performance Measures and Storytelling

Structured Performance Measure	Storytelling
• Provides the verbal cues to access specific information or models that guide problem solving.	• Entails spontaneous use of schemas to interpret the scene, recognize that a problem exists, and formulate a resolution.
• Elicits knowledge in piecemeal fashion without revealing the process involved in learning or using it (Spitz, 1988).	• Reveals the synthesis of ideas in accord with characteristic style of organizing experiences.
• Specifies a single correct solution.	• Sets general performance criteria, such as coherence, logic, and match-with-stimulus, in line with many acceptable ways to accomplish the task.
• Predicts performance in familiar, scripted situations.	• Predicts adjustment in novel, stressful, or complex situations.
• If complex, the task may require planning multiple steps.	• Reveals planning over time to anticipate likely outcomes and pursue intentions.
• Is the product of logical learning and analysis.	• Is the product of reciprocal encounters with the world and logical reflection.

to assess personality. Paper-and-pencil measures, open-ended interviews, and other procedures for obtaining verbal self-descriptions all require respondents to give a conscious accounting of their concepts of self, others, and the world. However, considerable research indicates that people are not aware of many of their own cognitive processes (e.g., Kihlstrom, 1987). To the extent that schemas operate outside awareness, they are not amenable to assessment via self-report, but are inferred by others. Storytelling brings to light the cognitive-emotional contents and structures comprising schemas that operate outside awareness, whereas self-report questionnaire methods clarify the characteristics that are attributed to the self (see Rapid Reference 9.2).

≡Rapid Reference 9.2

Contrast between Self-Report and Storytelling

Self-Report	Storytelling
• Provides information that the individual has verbally organized (self-attributed) and wishes to share.	• Reveals understandings that may not be incorporated into the individual's conscious self-concept (implicit) and that thus are not amenable to assessment with self-report.
• Is amenable to defensive distortion and faking to present a socially desirable account of oneself.	• Works around the problem of faking by assessing schemas that operate outside awareness.
• Predicts immediate choices, particularly if cued by the situation.	• Predicts spontaneous and sustained preferences (Spangler, 1992).
• Does not capture the idiosyncratic nature of thoughts, because concerns are not tied to information processing or coping.	• Reveals the content of thoughts and manner of processing information (problem identification, reasoning).
• Reveals controlled reflections that may not be sensitive to automatic cognitive processing. Such cognitions may change with intervention (e.g., cognitive therapy) but do not mediate other changes (Hollon & Kendall, 1980; Hollon, Kendall, & Lumry, 1986).	• Reveals functional structures that organize ideas and connect intentions, actions, and outcomes, and other aspects of information processing.

Versatility as Both a Strength and a Liability

Storytelling provides rich and complex information that is difficult to obtain in other ways and is particularly useful in assessing clients' resources in unfamiliar, complex, or stressful situations. Systematic use of the technique requires labor-intensive interpretation by highly trained professionals. However, training generalizes to other interactions, such as interviews, where clinicians make judgments about communication, speech patterns, and the reality base of clients' thought processes. Given the inherent drawbacks of reducing multifaceted data into "scores," professionals have different opinions as to the

≡Rapid Reference 9.3

Strengths and Weaknesses of the TAT

Strengths	Weaknesses
• Instrument is popular, widely researched, and valued by clinicians, and distinguishes between referred and nonreferred groups.	• There is little consensus about interpretive approaches and absence of a comprehensive set of norms.
• Interpretation requires advanced training and complex judgment that enrich other areas of practice.	• The need for training and the labor-intensiveness of the method run counter to a penchant for quick and easy solutions.
• Many proponents claim that it is not necessary or even desirable to apply strict psychometric criteria to the TAT.	• Detractors are not comfortable with reliance on clinical judgment in the absence of norms and other psychometric data.

need for precise psychometric documentation in contrast to continued reliance on general interpretive guidelines and performance standards for storytelling (see Rapid Reference 9.3). Other sources of information compensate for gaps left by storytelling and vice versa.

The storytelling task has the advantage of going beyond the content of cognitions by establishing functional interpretive units that combine structure, process, and content of responses. Indeed, counting specific cognitions apart from their contexts would violate narrative assumptions. As Cramer (1996) put it, "scoring schemas that rely on checklists to characterize what the storyteller did and did not say overlook the important qualities that make one story different from another—different, not because of using different words but because the words are arranged in different ways to convey different meanings" (p. 33). The problem is not with the use of checklists per se but with how they are used. Checklists that segment words from the whole distort the psychological process of the narrator. Some authors advocate that raters stay close to the actual words to minimize inference and increase rater agreement. However, increasing the "objectivity" of coding by relying on the words ignores the implicit understandings conveyed by the juxtaposition of ideas and runs the risk of sacrificing validity (see Rapid Reference 9.4). For example, in the com-

≡Rapid Reference 9.4

Cautions about Validation

1. Validity must be demonstrated separately for each set of stimuli, interpretive system, and procedure for administration.

2. Validity must be documented for each professional, and each professional must have intensive training. The quantification of rich qualitative data is possible but requires trained inferences.

3. Validating units of content in isolation, particularly if coded directly from the words, has not been clinically useful. More promising approaches consider clusters (of content, structure, and narrative process) pertaining to a particular psychological construct.

4. Validation studies are often conducted through group comparison, yet clinical decisions are made for individuals.

5. Currently available instruments that provide norms are not supported by adequate research and normative samples are too limited to be used reliably (see Kroon, Goudena, & Rispens, 1998, for a review).

6. The selection of external criteria for validation should be guided by constructs common to storytelling and the chosen criteria (see Teglasi, 1998).

7. Thematic apperception techniques, even those that provide norms, generally encourage qualitative interpretation.

parison between referred and nonreferred children reported in the RATC *Manual,* there were no differences in the clinical scales of anxiety, depression, and aggression. The meaning of a character's expression of anxiety-related thoughts, such as "worry," depends on how the character copes with the feeling or situation and on the role of the stimulus in eliciting the content. Using stories to assess relevant psychological processes requires inferences and judgment about the connections of parts to each other and to the whole.

Predicting behavior from TAT responses is a complex endeavor (see Rapid Reference 9.5). The clinical value of the TAT is not in the prediction of specific actions but in the explanation of the behaviors that are of concern by clarifying how the individual thinks about the self and the world. Thus, although the TAT may suggest that an individual has the resources to plan ahead, actual adjustment will depend on how the environment responds to the individual's initiative. Temperamental qualities also play an important role. An individual who misreads social cues in the TAT pictures but has an easygoing temperament

≋ Rapid Reference 9.5

Pitfalls of Predicting Aggressive Behavior from Story Content

1. Individuals who exhibit aggressive behavior do not necessarily express aggressive content in stories. Hence, simple frequency counts are not only misleading but fail to capitalize on the capacity of storytelling to assess social information processing that may explain aggressive behavior.

2. Interpretation must take into account the nature of stimuli, such as their ambiguity and presentation of aggressive cues. Aggressive children were less likely to include aggressive content to stimuli depicting aggression (reported in the RATC *Manual*).

   • Pictures that pull for aggression bring to light factors that mitigate against its expression, whereas aggressive themes told to nonaggressive stimuli signal problems inhibiting aggressive thoughts and or actions (Salz & Epstein, 1963).

   • Aggressive children assume hostile intent in ambiguous situations (Crick & Dodge, 1996); hence the importance of stimulus ambiguity.

3. Interpretation of aggressive content must take into account the

   • pull of the stimulus.

   • justification for the aggression.

   • perceived benefits and consequences of aggressive behavior.

   • factors that inhibit aggressive actions, such as anxiety about aggression, anticipation of consequences, reasoning about the intent of actions (not just their impact), social information processing, and empathy.

   • the level at which aggression, such as thoughts, feelings, actions, or some combination of these, is expressed. When making predictions, thoughts correspond to thoughts, feelings foretell emotions, and behaviors forecast actions (Tomkins, 1947).

will behave differently than an individual who similarly misreads social cues but is highly reactive and easily provoked.

Future Directions

Two general trends regarding assessment with storytelling techniques are (a) the broadening of theoretical perspectives from a domination by the psychodynamic orientation to the inclusion of various views of cognitive and social/emotional development, and (b) the increasing call for standard scoring criteria with documented reliability, validity, and normative data.

Psychometric documentation of a clinically useful scoring system would have to focus on structural characteristics of narratives and principles abstracted from content rather than on content coded directly from the words. In clinical use, formal or structural variables

CAUTION

Because reliability, validity, and norms for storytelling are established for a particular set of stimuli, method of administration, and interpretive procedure, it would be unwise to undertake large-scale, normative studies prior to arriving at some consensus about clinically valid units of interpretation and a set of agreed-upon stimuli.

have greater empirical support than tallies of content (e.g., McGrew & Teglasi, 1990). Moreover, certain formal characteristics of narrative come up in many studies with variations only in name or slightly different coding criteria. This may be the right time to systematize these structural qualities by establishing general criteria, such as accuracy and complexity in the identification of the

≡Rapid Reference 9.6

Steps in Clinical Use of Storytelling

1. Use a system to organize relevant information conceptually. This step may or may not include the consideration of formal normative data. If it does not, the examiner must be aware of the types of responses expected, given the respondent's age and other characteristics. This step requires knowledge of the specific storytelling method.

2. Translate the data into frameworks, such as a particular psychological process which in turn, may be viewed in terms of a particular theoretical orientation (e.g., psychodynamic theory). This step requires knowledge of development, psychopathology, and personality.

3. Synthesize conclusions drawn from storytelling with other sources of information. This requires knowledge of other tests in the battery and an understanding of the client's circumstances and sociocultural context.

4. Answer the referral questions and plan interventions. This requires an understanding of the complexities of the presenting problem (or diagnosis) and of the process of change and development.

problem portrayed and constructiveness of its resolution. However, to capture the unique concerns of the individual, these formal components will still have to be integrated with qualitative analysis of content. Even when norms are available, they are not sufficient for an adequate "interpretation," which entails a recursive, multistep process (see Rapid Reference 9.6).

🖎 TEST YOURSELF 🖎

1. **The richness and versatility of storytelling assessment methods have complicated the process of documenting its psychometric properties.** True or False?

2. **Storytelling differs from performance tasks such as the Wechsler scales by setting general performance criteria rather than designating a single correct solution.** True or False?

3. **Self-report differs from storytelling in all but *one* of the following:**

   (a) Self-report is easier to fake.

   (b) Self-report may not be sensitive to automatic cognitive processing.

   (c) Self-report usually captures the idiosyncratic nature of thought processes.

   (d) Self-report may change with intervention but may not mediate other changes.

4. **For clinical purposes, methods of coding stories that stay close to the words to minimize inference tend to be**

   (a) more reliable.

   (b) less valid.

   (c) both "a" and "b."

   (d) neither "a" nor "b."

5. **When predicting aggressive behavior from story content, which of the following statements is not a pitfall?**

   (a) Simple frequency counts of aggressive content fail to consider information that may mitigate against its expression.

   (b) Depending on the stimulus, aggressive individuals are reportedly less likely to include aggressive content.

   (c) Prediction is complicated by the expression of aggressive content through thoughts, feelings, or actions.

   (d) All of the above are pitfalls.

Answers: 1. True; 2. True; 3. c; 4. c; 5. d.

Ten

ILLUSTRATIVE CASE REPORT

This chapter illustrates the use of storytelling in a comprehensive evaluation. The author's student conducted the assessment, using the TAT in writing the report. At the author's request, the student administered the CAT several months later. Both protocols are presented to allow the reader to compare conclusions drawn from two different storytelling methods.

The next section presents DM's TAT stories at chronological age 6-4, followed by conclusions based on coding of the cognitive variables included in chapter 4 (see Rapid Reference 10.1). The section then moves on to DM's CAT stories told five months later, along with conclusions based on Bellak's 10 variables (see Rapid Reference 10.2). As the reader will note, the major conclusions from the two procedures are virtually identical.

STORYTELLING METHODS COMPARED

TAT Stories

Card 1. Him thinkin' of that . . . the fiddle, and he's lookin' at it . . . [E: Before?] I think it's broken. [E: Feeling?] Sad . . . [E: Happens?] He'll cry . . . [E: And in the end?] Nothin'.

Import: When someone is sad that something is broken, he or she cries and nothing happens.

Notes: External events (broken violin) evoke sadness and crying without initiative to act or seek assistance. The story departs minimally from the moment depicted in the scene as there are neither context of previous events nor guiding intentions, and no other character is introduced to give relief.

≡Rapid Reference 10.1

Conclusions from the TAT, Organized According to Variables in Chapter 4.

- *Perceptual Integration.* DM responds to isolated stimulus features interpreted literally rather than conceptually. About half of the stories are significantly discrepant from the emotions and relationships depicted.

- *Level of Abstraction.* Stories are characterized by descriptions that are enumerative (naming or describing isolated or irrelevant stimulus detail) or concrete (no inner world or simplistic tie between events and feelings).

- *Planning and Monitoring.* Poor understanding of social causality leads to difficulty anticipating the outcomes of his actions or the reactions of others, resulting in a tendency to act or react without defining goals or purposes. DM's inability to figure things out or consider alternatives further limits goal-directed thoughts or actions.

- *Time Perspective.* DM's thought processes, feelings, and actions are rooted in the immediacy of the moment.

- *Process of Reasoning/Coherence of Story Structure.* Narratives provide numerous examples of disorganized thinking, faulty logic, and poor understanding of how ideas "go together."

- *Coordination of Inner and Outer Elements of Experience.* DM doesn't imbue his characters with intentions, standards, or psychological processes. Lack of cohesion between the inner and outer worlds makes it difficult for DM to reflect on his behaviors to separate fantasy from reality. Without a durable or cohesive sense of self in relation to others, DM needs routines, clear expectations, and direct signals of acceptance. Otherwise, he reacts to isolated cues or provocations with confusion, fear, or anger.

- *Coordination of Perspectives of Different Individuals.* Not understanding the inner world of thoughts, feelings, or intentions, DM has difficulty organizing the postures, facial expressions, and relationships portrayed in the pictures. He notices aspects of outward appearance according to their implications for basic needs for routine, safety, and acceptance. (Coding object relations, not shown here, indicates problems with relatedness influenced by difficulties with information processing and affect regulation.)

- *Level of Cognitive-Experiential Integration.* Numerous instances signaling disorganized processing of information and poor reality testing (including difficulty sizing up emotions as well as situational and interpersonal cues) characterize DM's functioning (Level 1).

- *Level of Associative Thinking.* The progression of DM's ideas is tangential or linear, with minimal causal connections (Levels 1 and 2). Ideas are evoked as reactions to the stimuli or to his emotions and show no apparent organization.

≡Rapid Reference 10.2

Conclusions from the CAT, Organized According to Bellak's Short Form

- *Unconscious Structure and Drives* (based on main themes, main hero, and main needs and drives of hero). DM sees familiar situations, such as a family eating dinner, talking, or bathing routines, as happy. Otherwise, DM feels helpless and confused, afraid, and needing but unable to seek reassurance and security.

- *Conception of Environment.* DM has difficulty understanding the nuances of the environment, leading him to a dichotomous construction of the world with familiar, routine situations associated with happy feelings and other situations eliciting feelings of vulnerability and confusion. DM is highly reactive to what he perceives as threatening, frightening, or provoking aspects of the environment.

- *Interpersonal Object Relations.* DM construes parental or family figures as supportive and reassuring and other figures as neutral or overpowering. DM does not infer relatedness when it is not directly portrayed in the stimulus.

- *Significant Conflicts.* No inner conflicts are apparent.

- *Nature of Anxieties.* DM's primary fears are of being left alone to suffer physical harm and of being helpless against powerful others.

- *Main Defenses against Conflicts and Fears.* Few defenses are apparent (mostly denial).

- *Adequacy of Superego.* Descriptive stories are not sufficiently elaborated to note expectations about being punished for wrongdoing.

- *Integration of the Ego.* Concrete thinking and unrealistically happy outcomes, along with hero's inability to deal with adverse situations, suggests impaired ego functioning and difficulty meeting age-appropriate expectations for autonomous behavior.

Card 2. She's holdin' the bible. And that man up there is carrying a horse, holding the horse. And the lady is standing by the tree, and she's lookin' at the lady ... [E: Thinking?] She's thinkin' about Jesus ... [E: Feeling?] Happy, 'cause she's thinkin' about Jesus. [E: Happens next?] That she will say Alelulia! [E: End?] She get, gives some money to them people that's poor. We have all them pages to do? All them?

Import: When you don't understand the whole picture, you focus on something safe to feel happy but you are still overwhelmed.

Notes: Difficulty pulling together the parts of this relatively complex stimulus is not unusual at this age. However, DM's poor reality testing of the perceptual cues (e.g., the man is "carrying a horse" corrected to "holding the horse") is unexpected. Given the difficulty of the task for DM, an expression of anxiety about having to produce more stories is understandable.

Card 3BM. He's cryin', she's crying. I mean she looks like she's dead, 'cause the knife is right there. [points] [E: Happened before?] Somebody put a knife in her. . . . [E: Why?] I don't know. That's why she's crying. That's number 3.

Process Import: If it is hard to figure out what is going on, you react to isolated cues and are left scared and confused.

Notes: DM's inflexibility and problems with causal understanding (e.g., inability to consider intentions) leads to reliance on simplistic associations (e.g., one-to-one correspondence between objects such as knife and events). Again, his uncertainty and anxiety about this task prompts him to check the numbers of the cards.

Card 4. She's lookin' at that man. That's her husband. And she hug him. [E: Feeling?] Happy. [E: Which one?] She's happy . . . [E: Him?] He's sad. [E: Why?] I don't know . . . [Examiner encourages him to make up the story.] . . . Somebody killed his grandmother. [E: Thinking?] Nothing. [E: End?] Them hug. She gives him a hug. That's one, two, three, four. . . . [counts cards in stack].

Process Import: If you don't understand emotions and relationships you react to parts of what you see without grasping how the parts go together.

Notes: At first, DM focuses on one character, ignoring the feelings of the other, in keeping with his tendency to react to parts of the information without connecting the pieces. When specifically asked, he recognizes that the husband feels differently than his wife. However, describing the wife as happy and the husband as sad is discrepant from the pictured scene.

Card 5. She lookin' at the lamp, and she's lookin' at the flower that is broke. It needs some water. And she needs something to drink. [E: Thinking?] She's thinking about the different colors. [E: Where?] Right here . . . the books. [E: Feeling?] Happy. [E: End?] Don't know . . . don't know. [Examiner reads his story.] She puts water in there.

Process Import: A situation or task is hard to understand because you consider only what you see without bringing an organized base of understandings that connect what you see in the moment with what you know from prior experience.

Notes: The woman has no particular goals or intentions but feels happy looking at the various objects portrayed in the scene or thinking about the different colors (which are actually variations in shades of black and white). Her need for a drink seems on par with the flower's needing a drink. It appears that, in the absence of specific cues that elicit unhappy emotions, when characters are engaged in routine activities, DM associates happy emotions.

Card 6BM. He's lookin' over there, and the woman is lookin' over there to see if her car is . . . is . . . um is . . . fixed. And then he hugs her. [E: Feeling?] Happy, happy . . . [points] Both are happy. What's that number? [points to story number in examiner's notes]

Import: It is hard to understand feelings and relationships, but hugs bring happiness.

Notes: DM superimposes affection and happiness on a tense scene without a logical explanation.

Card 7GF. She is carryin' the baby and her mom says, "Don't hold it down 'cause she can fall!" And then she, the daughter, punched her in the mouth, [E: Punched who?] Her mother . . . and the baby. [E: Feeling?] They're feelin' happy. What's that spell, F G? That's six! [looks on back of previous card turned down]

Import: If a parent admonishes her daughter, the child will lash out by punching everyone around but they all end up happy.

Notes: The story is consistent with DM's tendency to overreact to information that is not well understood with externalizing behavior. Being corrected seems to set him off.

Card 8BM. Oh, she's stickin' a knife at him, putting it in him, *stick* a knife in him. . . . But the boy is not doin' nothin'. The boy is just happy. And the boy killed that man, them [points to men in back], them that's putting the knife in his father. And then him lived happily ever after . . . and the father too, and the boy.

Process Import: You react to information literally without understanding it.

Notes: DM superimposes the familiar story structure where everyone lives happily ever after but without the logical ties to story events. DM is not able to synthesize experiences and grasps at fragments of information without connections.

Card 13B. That's number what? He's thinkin' about his mom, but his mom died. And his grandma's takin' care of him, and he's thinkin' about his friends. [E: Feeling?] Happy. [E: Happens?] He gets somethin' to drink, and then his school bus came and then he went on the school bus.

Import: As long as a person has someone to take care of him or her and he or she is participating in the familiar daily routine, that person is happy.

Notes: Concerns center on maintaining sources of need satisfaction and salience of the routine activities.

Summary of Imports

Overall, there is a sense that DM is very reactive to faulty perceptions about the world and needs a highly structured and predictable environment. Without access to organized schemas for understanding social causality, he has difficulty sizing up situations and either feels helpless or acts in a rote and inflexible manner. Because he has no goals or plans that would organize an enduring set of responses, DM's actions are guided by external triggers (Rapid Reference 10.1). He is particularly vulnerable to lashing out or behaving inappropriately when he feels confused or provoked (e.g., admonished).

CAT Stories

Card 1. Looks like they're eating soup . . . [E: Feeling?] Happy . . . [E: Thinking?] Don't know . . . maybe about them mom. [E: Thinking about her?] Don't know . . . [E: Turns out?] Good, good, good . . . [E: What happens?] Them play.

Import: When children in a family are eating, they are happy and play later.

Notes: The narrative style is similar to that of stories told to the TAT pictures. Specifically, DM needed prompting for each component of the story and had difficulty describing the inner world of intentions, emotions, and thoughts. Because the TAT cards show negative emotions, the narrator is expected to introduce some tension and to resolve the dilemma prior to concluding that the characters are happy. In contrast, happy emotions are not out of tune with this stimulus.

Card 2. Them pullin' a rope . . . And he's fallin' down. [points to figure on left] He's scared . . . And he's tired [points to middle], and he's pullin' it [points to right] . . . [E: Why's he scared?] Scared him bump his head. [E: Happens?] Don't know . . . mmm . . . bump his head and lay down.

Import: When pulling a rope with others, a person is scared that he or she may get hurt and then does get hurt.

Notes: The depiction of characters as "pulling a rope" rather than engaged in a purposeful activity is a literal translation of the picture, reminiscent of TAT responses. Moreover, each character has his own feeling or activity unrelated to the others.

Card 3. He's sittin' down. He's an old lion . . . And that's a mouse. And that's his cave . . . and this is a board. [points to background] This is his pipe . . . and this is flowers. [points to floor] [E: Feeling?] Sad. [E: Why?] 'Cause he don't . . . really don't have no friends . . . [E: End?] And then he had friends.

Import: If one feels sad without friends, one gets a friend without understanding how.

Notes: In response to inquiry after enumerating the characters and objects in the stimulus, DM describes the lion as sad because he has no friends. When pressed for an ending, the lion magically has friends. Though the mouse is noticed, there is no attempt to relate the mouse to the lion. This lack of coordination among characters is common in DM's responses to both the CAT and TAT stimuli. In both sets of stories, DM also lists external attributes of characters or labels objects without a priority in emphasis.

Card 4. That's the baby kangaroo [points to one on bike], and this is the wheel and the other wheel, and they drivin' a bike . . . No, this is the, the *big* baby and that's the little one, the little baby. [points to one in pouch] Them goin' to a picnic. And she's wearin' a hat. And this is a tree and another tree, and smoke . . . [E: Feeling?] Happy. [E: Happens?] They sit down and have them picnic.

Import: It is difficult to distinguish what is important from what is not, but when a family has a picnic they are happy.

Notes: An inability to prioritize elements of the pictured scene (i.e., the inanimate objects and characters are not differentiated in relative importance) and to develop ideas apart from associations with the immediate surroundings (also evident in TAT stories) suggests that DM does not use an organized set of schemas to interpret the cues in his environment.

Card 5. The bears is layin' down. And this is a bed and this is a . . . uhm . . . crib. This is a window and the blinds. And this is the light and this is the floor. [E: That's a good description. Now tell me a story] I don't know . . . from being tired and pulling a rope. [E: End?] Them get up.

Process Import: You notice what is around you on a literal level but can't interpret what is happening.

Notes: When pressed to tell a story after providing a description, DM explains that two bears are lying down because they are tired "from pulling a rope" (an association to a previous story). Unable to use previously organized schemas to understand the current situation, DM grasps at isolated ideas from the immediate surroundings.

Card 6. This is the big bear. This is the little bear . . . And this is the rock and this is a tree and stuff. [E: Bears thinking?] Sad. [E: Why?] They probably, the family got killed. [E: Turn out?] Don't know . . . them cryin'.

Process Import: When the situation is hard to understand, you helplessly assume the worst (i.e., family killed).

Notes: DM has problems organizing this stimulus, and a sense of uncertainty evokes fears of being left alone.

Card 7. Ugh!!! I don't like that one. It's too scary. I don't like this one. [E: Just look at it for a minute. Take your time.] Them tryin' to eat the gorilla . . . for his dinner, and the gorilla climbin' up and that's the tree. And him stripes. [E: Turn out?] He got ate up! And the family was sad.

Import: If a smaller animal gets eaten by a bigger one, his family is sad.

Notes: The narrator's fear of this picture is stylistically similar to his reactivity to the knife in the TAT cards. Furthermore, DM's failure to give priority to different levels of detail ("climbing up" and "him stripes") shows evidence of problems with conceptual organization.

Card 8. I don't like that one! . . . [E: Just look at it for a minute.] . . . It's funny! That's the mother and that's the Dad . . . other mom and the boy. This is the chair and couch. That's the baby [points to picture in background], and that's the door. . . . [E: Happening?] Them happy. . . . [E: Doing?] Them's talkin' to each other . . . in secrets. [E: Turn out?] Good. [E: What happens?] Don't know. . . . Climb trees.

Import: When people are talking together, they are happy.

Notes: Again, DM notices minute features of the scene, equating major and minor aspects of the stimuli (inanimate objects such as the chair and couch are enumerated along with characters; the picture of the baby in the background is listed along with the prominent figures). As with the other cards, DM can't "explain" what is happening in the picture or predict what might happen later (other than "happy").

Card 9. The baby carrot . . . [E: Baby what?] . . . carrot. No, baby rabbit. Sittin' in his bed. That's the mirror, the light, window, shade . . . This the door . . . the floor. And then he gets up from his nap. [E: Feeling?] Sad. [E: Why?] 'Cause he can't go out yet. [E: When?] After his nap.

Import: If a baby rabbit gets up from his nap, he's sad because he can't go out yet.

Notes: When the narrator is asked when the rabbit can go out, the response is when he gets up from his nap. Just as DM lives in the moment, the character reacts emotionally (sad) to his immediate situation rather than anticipating that he can go out soon.

Card 10. This is a dog, and that's the little dog, and that's his mother givin' him a bath. And his mother is on a chair. This is a bathroom, and the toilet, and that's the towel, and that's the garbage can, and that's the wall. He's happy, the baby. [E: Mom doing?] Petting him. [E: End?] Then he, um, makes food for his mom.

Import: The baby is happy being bathed and petted by his mother and later makes his mother something to eat.

Notes: DM tends to tell happy stories when the activity is familiar (eating, picnic). However, he has no resources to deal with novel, complex, or unhappy pictures (see Rapid Reference 10.2).

PSYCHOLOGICAL EVALUATION

Name: DM   School: G. Center
Dates of Evaluation: 11/17/99, 11/18/99,   Grade: 1
   11/30/99, & 1/4/00
Date of Birth: Age: 6-4

Tests Administered

Wechsler Intelligence Scale for Children–Third Edition (WISC-III)
Bender Visual Motor Gestalt Test (Bender-Gestalt)
Child Behavior Checklist (CBCL), Parent and Teacher Report Forms
Thematic Apperception Test (TAT)
Rorschach Inkblot Technique
Sentence Completion Task
Projective Drawings

Reason for Referral and Background Information

DM, a 1st-grade male student age 6-4, was recently transferred from out of state to a center serving children diagnosed with emotional disabilities, and this is where the current evaluation was conducted. From his first day at G. Center (9/20/99), DM demonstrated overactivity, impulsivity, defiance, and aggressive behavior, which the staff could not successfully handle even in this structured setting. He regularly shouted obscenities, verbally threatened staff, sexually touched and grabbed adults, and displayed physical aggression by kicking, biting, and spitting. On 9/27, DM verbalized self-degrading remarks and suicidal thoughts, at which time staff members alerted his mother and made a referral to the S. Mental Health Center. As an outcome of that outpatient mental health evaluation, DM started taking Ritalin on 10/19/99 to address symptoms of previously diagnosed ADHD, and he has been participating in therapeutic counseling. DM's behavior as charted by his teachers during the period from 10/13 through 12/6/99, in relation to the implementation of various interventions, showed that negative behavior decreased over time. Teachers discontinued recording after significant improvements in behavior. As a result of more positive behaviors, DM started successfully mainstreaming into a language arts class for 45 to 50 minutes per day, 3 days each week. When DM returned from winter break on or about 1/6/00, the negative behaviors resurfaced for approximately two weeks despite all interventions remaining in place. The individualized education program (IEP) team agreed that a thorough psychological and educational evaluation, as well as a comprehensive social history (Social/Cultural Report, not included), would assist in better understanding and educationally serving this child.

Background information on DM is incomplete despite brief reports on file from the School District of P. (4/98) and Family Resources, Therapeutic Parents and Children's Center, P. (4/98). DM and his mother had recently moved to this area from P., where DM had an IEP for special education services as a student with emotional disabilities. According to the evaluation by the School District of P., although DM refused to attempt most of the tasks, those portions he did complete suggested average learning ability, vocabulary, quantitative reasoning, and short-term memory. That evaluation refers to a diagnosis of ADHD and Oppositional Defiant Disorder; although the primary source of this diagnosis is not available, it does concur with two of the provisional diagnoses suggested in the S. Mental Health evaluation (10/1/99).

Behavior Observations

DM was pleased to participate in testing and to receive special attention from an adult. He enjoyed social conversation and participated in an age-appropriate manner, except for his inability to inhibit some sexual content. He worked to the best of his abilities on most tasks, for example, persevering for nearly 11 minutes on one puzzle until he completed it correctly. At the same time, on other tasks he did not enjoy or found extremely difficult, he would start to whine, fuss, cry, and seek distractions to avoid the work.

DM had been taking Ritalin for approximately one month when testing was started. This medication clearly improved his availability for testing, because with frequent redirection, he was able to work in this optimal one-on-one situation for up to one hour per session. At the same time, there were still extreme indications of attentional difficulties. His responses were consistently impulsive and associative, lacking evidence of planful and flexible thought. He often started tasks before instructed and had difficulty following directions. He required frequent directions to watch and listen to the examiner and additional training or examples to teach a task before he could perform correctly. Similar patterns in both verbal and nonverbal tasks suggested that this is an attentional problem more than possible deficits in the auditory channel. For example, on a verbal item, when asked to name three coins, his immediate association was to the pictures of presidents on U.S. coins, and he named "Abraham, Lincoln, and George Washington." While it was clear that he understood the question and had significant knowledge of coins, his impulsive response was not correct. Furthermore, he was unable to reflect upon or monitor his response and had no conception that he had made a mistake. He was usually unable to change his strategy if his initial impression was incorrect, and this pattern, observed throughout testing, is an indication of cognitive inflexibility.

Discussion of Test Results

DM's impulsive response style, which resulted in many incorrect answers despite apparent knowledge, suggests that he has not learned how to take time to think (i.e., to ponder the meaning of a question, consider alternatives, and plan his best response). His attentional problems clearly affected his performance on the cognitive measure. While these results are a fair indication of his present level of functioning, they are likely an underestimate of his true ability.

On the WISC-III, DM obtained a Full Scale IQ of 82, suggestive of cognitive ability in the low average range, at the 12th percentile compared with children his age. Significant scatter among the subtest scores, particularly within the verbal domain, suggests learning difficulties. The following section lists results of the WISC-III, with subtest scores of 8 to 12 representing the average range.

Verbal Tests	Scaled Scores
Information	6
Similarities	7
Arithmetic	2
Vocabulary	10
Comprehension	8
(Digit Span)	(5)

Performance Tests	Scaled Scores
Picture Completion	6
Coding	9
Picture Arrangement	8
Block Design	7
Object Assembly	9

Composites	Scores
Verbal IQ	81 ± 8
Performance IQ	86 ± 9
Full Scale IQ	82 ± 7
Verbal Comprehension Index	88
Perceptual Organization Index	86
Freedom from Distractibility Index	64
Processing Speed (not calculated)	

On the verbal tasks, DM performed at the 10th percentile compared to his peers, a score strongly affected by his associative thinking and impulsive responding. On the Arithmetic subtest, for example, on items of counting with one-to-one correspondence, DM was able to answer two additional items correctly when they were readministered with additional direction at the end of testing; thus, he possesses greater quantitative reasoning than this score reflects. DM's struggle to hold and repeat numbers back to the examiner, particularly in reverse order, show difficulties in concentration and working memory. When tasks requiring greatest attention and concentration are removed from the factor, DM's ability in the verbal domain appears stronger, as evidenced by the higher Verbal Comprehension Index of 88. His relatively strong skill in vocabulary (solidly average) is readily apparent to any observer. Hence, he comes across as a much more capable child than his present overall level of functioning.

DM enjoyed the nonverbal tasks more than the verbal and was able to concentrate fairly well without as much external structure. On these tasks of visual processing, organizing, and planning, and nonverbal learning and memory, he scored in the 18th percentile compared with other children his age. On many of these activities, the examiner noticed a pattern where DM tended to focus on one detail or clue, such that his attention was "stuck," and he failed to explore all information provided. This is an example of the cognitive inflexibility mentioned earlier. He had difficulty differentiating essential from nonessential details, impulsively and inflexibly focusing on that which first caught his attention.

When asked to copy nine geometric designs of the Bender Visual Motor Gestalt Test, DM approached the task impulsively, without planning or monitoring his work. He filled three pages with his large and, at times, perseverative drawings, clearly using the edge of the paper for structure and boundaries. This approach is often associated with impulsiveness, low frustration tolerance, and acting out behavior in children. DM completed the task in 4 minutes, 30 seconds, quicker than most children his age. It was not surprising that the quality of his drawings suffered, and he scored 14 Koppitz developmental errors, which translates to an age equivalent of 5-0 to 5-5 and a standard score of 75. It cannot be stated that all of his errors were due to his impulsive style, for some of the rotation and distortion errors were quite significant indicators of developmental delay. His fine motor skills should be closely monitored and reassessed, should these not improve along with his attention, concentration, and behavior as a result of ADHD medication. DM was able to recall five of the figures, again expanding his effort onto three sheets of paper. This is indicative of average to above average incidental visual memory.

DM's mother and classroom teacher completed the Child Behavior Checklist (CBCL; Achenbach, 1999). Mrs. M answered this questionnaire twice, according to her perception of his behavior both before and after he started medication for ADHD. His teacher completed the questionnaire after DM began medication and before his negative behaviors resumed early in January. Results are reported in *T* scores with a mean of 50. Scores below 67 are considered to be within the normal range. Scores followed by an asterisk (*) are in the borderline clinical range, and scores followed by a double asterisk (**) are in the clinically significant range, (i.e., they represent a high level of maladjustment).

Total Score	Before Meds (mother's response)	After Meds (mother's response)	After Meds (teacher's response)
Internalizing Behavior	77**	53	48
Withdrawn Behavior	66	51	43
Somatic Complaints	58	50	50
Anxiety/Depression	50	50	50
Externalizing Behavior	72**	57	50
Delinquent Behavior/ Aggressive Behavior	82**	53	46
Social Problems	85**	51	50
Thought Problems	73**	64	51
Attention Problems	67*	50	50
Sex Problems	88**	70**	50

The difference in DM's behavior before and after ADHD medication is striking. Before medication, Mrs. M endorsed items such as "Argues a lot," "Can't concentrate," "Can't pay attention for long," "Can't get his mind off certain thoughts: sexual obsessions," "Destroys things," "Disobedient at home and school," "Doesn't seem to feel guilty after misbehavior," "Impulsive acts without thinking," "Lying and cheating," and "Stealing." After medication, Mrs. M did not see most of these behaviors, or at least did not observe them to the same degree. However, DM's sexual obsessions remained an issue. The teacher's views are similar. With medication she observed normal classroom behavior. When commenting on DM's behavior before medication, her narrative (dated 11/1/99) stated, "frequently refuses to do work, needs one-on-one attention to complete any task, physical aggression (hitting, kicking), inappropriate language, sexual verbalizations, and sexual touching."

DM's social-emotional functioning was further evaluated through projective techniques. On all of these unstructured tasks DM experienced great difficulty, suggesting a need for clear task expectations and supports to keep him on track and set boundaries/limits for appropriate behavior. DM's TAT responses are characterized as concrete, often at odds with the stimulus, and lacking logical progression, with numerous examples of faulty thinking. His poor understanding of social causality leaves him feeling vulnerable and helpless without the resources to assess accurately and to respond to situations that depart from the familiar routine. For example, in two of his TAT stories, after seeing a knife, DM assumed that someone would "put" or "stick" the knife into one of the characters without a specific purpose or intention. DM's disorganized ideation is often confusing to himself and others. He has difficulty separating reality from fantasy, and he therefore clings rigidly to the limited schemas he has, even when they do not fit the circumstances. His schemas for understanding himself and others do not include intentions or psychological processes and fail to connect causes and effects. This extent of impaired cognitive functioning is likely the culmination of severe attentional problems as well as intrusive ideation from affective concerns.

Similar to his responses to the TAT, DM's responses to the Rorschach show that he tends to get lost in perseveration and tangential details and inappropriate integration of ideas. Moreover, the content of the Rorschach percepts suggests that he is unusually preoccupied with his body and bodily functions. At home this manifests in unusual urination and bowel habits. Both at home and at school DM is obsessed with sexual innuendo and language. This bodily preoccupation appears to stem from an image of himself as a fragile and vulnerable person. In his TAT stories, when DM perceives a negative stimulus (e.g., a knife or a gun) he assumes that someone controlling or powerful will use it against someone who is helpless or defenseless. His sentence completions also support this feeling of vulnerability (e.g., "What I want to happen most is . . . be a superhero and save all the kids"). When children experience such imbalance of autonomy (such that some people are intrusive and overpowering, while others are helpless and controlled), many cope through distance and detachment in relationships. The characters in DM's stories relate like robots, without individuality or emotion. For example, in one story, "somebody put a knife in her," and in another, "She punched her mother in the mouth . . . and the baby. They're feelin' happy." He is confused even about the concept of family, for when asked to draw a picture of his family (examiner confirmed "family" as DM began), he drew himself, a friend, and a girl, "I don't know her name." He appears devoid of inner resources to understand relationships and guide social behavior. He is lacking age-appropriate schemas that are built upon a child's subjective experiences, suggesting that he either has not been exposed to these experiences or he has not been cognitively and emotionally available to learn from them.

Summary and Recommendations

DM is a 6-year-old, 1st-grade student at G. Center, having transferred into F. County Public Schools as an emotionally disabled student from the School District of P. Due to the difficulty he was having in his adjustment to school this year, and due to limited information regarding prior evaluations, the IEP team decided to proceed with a full evaluation at this time. Testing suggests cognitive functioning in the low average range, a possible underestimate of his true ability. Struggling with ADHD in these early years of development has likely limited his availability to observe, process, and store knowledge typically held by other children his age. Additionally, although he recently started medication to improve his attention and decrease impulsivity, behavior during testing suggested that cognitive processing patterns related to attention deficit (e.g., associative thinking) have not yet changed, and this has further depressed scores. Difficulty in visual-motor integration was noted; however, impulsivity confounds the issue of a developmental delay in processing. Further evaluation for learning disabilities is recommended in approximately one year.

While DM's behavior has clearly improved since he started taking medication for ADHD symptoms, there remain issues of disorganized ideation that preclude his ability to size up a situation accurately (e.g., confusing reality with fantasy) and plan or solve simple social encounters (faulty judgment). Testing, interview, and observation further suggest that significant problems with relationships underlie DM's behavioral concerns. He anticipates victimization by controlling and powerful others, which results in his feelings of helplessness (regarding realistic resolution) and detachment. The combination of impaired information processing and poor relational development begins to explain

DM's acting out behavior. He has not developed a sufficient (age-appropriate) schematic framework from which he can accurately interpret and understand his surroundings and by which he can guide his own behavior. He is presently in need of external structure and clear guidelines set by others to maintain his behavior. Continued therapeutic counseling to address underlying relationship concerns is strongly recommended.

Test results will be used along with all other current assessment data to determine the most appropriate educational plan for DM at this time.

Lauren B. Lohr, MA   *Mila French, PhD*
NCSP School Psychologist   *NCSP School Psychologist*
Examiner   *Supervisor*

Appendix

COGNITION

I. PERCEPTUAL INTEGRATION

A. Degree of Congruence with the Stimulus

(Check as many as apply for each story) Cards→	I	2												
There is disregard or misperception of basic emotions or relationships depicted (e.g., excluding a pictured character; tension is not related to scene).														
There is disregard or misperception of characters' ages.														
There is a focus on irrelevant stimulus details.														
The emphasis is perceptual rather than conceptual (focus on isolated stimulus elements without positing meaningful relationships among them).														
Unresolved vacillation or indecision about what the stimulus configuration means (not wondering what one object is).														
Interpretation of emotions and relationships is limited by being at odds with important contextual cues (e.g., disregard or misperception of major stimulus features) or by inadequate connection with story events.														
Pictured elements are adequately related, but the fit between the story details and the stimulus configuration is not precise.														
There are meaningful and realistic relationships among various stimulus features that precisely capture the "gist" of the scene (e.g., understanding social causality and appreciating nuances of the stimulus).														

B. Levels of Perceptual Integration

Level One: Discrepant. The premise of the story is not appropriate to overall stimulus configuration due to any of the following: Emotions and relationships depicted are significantly misrepresented, ages and roles of characters don't match the stimulus, tensions are not recognized or completely misread.

Level Two: Literal. Primary misperception is in the *inferential* or *implicit* meaning of the stimulus. There is recognition of major elements (or emotions) without understanding the psychological process (e.g., emotions or actions are simplistic associations to the scene that may be vague, scripted, or stereotypic) and /or without grasping the nuances of contextual cues (e.g., relationship of foreground to background, implications of clothing).

Level Three: Imprecise. There are subtle distortions of tension state. The story generally captures the implications of the stimulus vis-à-vis emotions and relationships, but the fit is not precise (e.g., timing, cause–effect inference, or context is not precise). Major object ignored or misperceived but feelings or relationships are not.

Level Four: Accurate. All cues and subtleties are accounted for in the interpretation of feelings and relationships (despite possible omissions or misidentification of minor details or some perceptual emphasis).

(Choose one level for each story)

Card	I	2												

II. CONCRETE VERSUS ABSTRACT THINKING

A. Concrete Thinking

1. Formal Elements of Storytelling Process and Story Structure

(Check as many as apply for each story) Cards→	I	2											
Picture is taken literally. Events do not depart from immediate time frame depicted in stimulus; feelings emanate directly from the scene rather than from story events explaining the picture.													
Instructions are taken literally. Each component of the directions is addressed rather than telling a story (with or without prompting).													
There is a lack of understanding that the story is generated by the narrator rather than inherent in the picture.													
There is no change or insight, or there is an absence of transitional events for story resolution or altered feelings or circumstances.													

2. Formal Elements of Story Content

(Check as many as apply for each story) Cards→	I	2											
Concerns are extremely trivial or momentary; content emphasizes daily routines typically taken for granted (e.g., eating, sleeping, showering).													
Inner states, intentions, or motives are vague or not elaborated (e.g., causes, antecedents) beyond stimuli, superficial impressions, or stereotypes.													

B. Level of Abstraction in Explaining the Stimulus

(Degree of abstraction can be gleaned from the way that picture stimuli are described when the respondent is not able to develop a story)

Level One: Enumerative Description. Content is limited to naming or describing isolated or irrelevant details of the picture without relating various components to each other or to a common theme. Feelings are tied to the stimulus.
Level Two: Concrete Description. Content is tied to a more holistic view of the picture but doesn't incorporate inner purpose or motives of characters depicted. Emotions or intentions are tied simplistically to events.
Level Three: Interpretive Explanation. An "explanation" of the scene is provided in terms of inner attributes and outward appearance of characters (psychological process and events are distinct, yet cohesive).

(Choose the highest level applicable to each story)

Card	I	2											

III. INFORMATION PROCESSING

A. Use of Stimuli

(See Perceptual Integration and Degree of Abstraction in Card Description)

B. Planning and Monitoring

I. Formal Elements of Storytelling Process and Story Structure

(Check as many as apply for each story)　　　　Cards→	I	2										
Narrator gives irrelevant responses, silly content, and extraneous chatting while receiving instructions or narrating the story.												
Narrator complains about being bored or wants to stop ("how many more?").												
Narrator gives first-person stories or personalizations, suggesting inability to distance self from objective demands of the task.												
Narrator loses the set for telling the story (drawn away from initial focus by examiner's inquiry or personal associations).												
There are arbitrary shifts in perspective, inconsistencies, or contradictory details in the story.												
Causes for events or motives are poorly understood.												
No tension and/or no outcome. (If checked, ignore the two items below)												
Outcome or change occurs without adequate transition.												
Outcome does not adequately address the central conflict, tension, or dilemma as posed by the narrator.												

2. Formal Elements of Content

(Check as many as apply for each story)*　　　　Cards→	I	2										
Story characters don't care, are bored, engage in wishful thinking or short-term solutions.												
Characters emphasize immediate gratification or material gain.												
Characters act or react without clearly defining the problem or goal.												
Actions are haphazard and occur without planning or anticipation.												
Characters jump to inappropriate or premature conclusions, can't figure things out, fail to consider reasonable alternatives, or overreact.												
Characters desire to avoid or escape legitimate, age-appropriate restrictions/responsibilities considered unfair or incomprehensible.												
Characters continue to behave in ways that contradict how they think they "should" act.												

*Content may be too limited for any to apply.

C. Time Perspective

(Check as many as apply for each story)　　　　Cards→	I	2										
Immediate time frame												
Unrealistic time frame												
Vague time frame												
Intermediate time frame												
Appropriate time frame												

D. Process of Reasoning/Coherence of Story Structure

(Check as many as apply for each story) Cards→	1	2											
Disorganized narrative process with unfocused progression of ideas (personalized thoughts, perseveration, content discrepant from stimulus, or emotional reactivity to the picture).													
Socially unacceptable content or conviction (e.g., bizarre content; extreme helplessness, hostility, or violence).													
Incompatible levels of conceptualization (ideas don't "go together").													
Faulty logic; major contradictions; magical thinking; confusion; fragments of ideas left incomplete.													

E. Coordination of Inner and Outer Elements of Experience (Reflection)

(Check as many as apply for each story) Cards→	1	2											
Impetus for action of characters comes from external demand, greed, or rebellion rather than inner purpose.													
Characters act or react on the basis of vague emotions, wishful thinking, or previous story event, rather than purposeful, realistic attempts at problem resolution.													
Characters lack responsibility for actions, outcomes, or welfare of others (absence of moral standard or accountability).													
Self-presentation is not congruent with social conventions. Characters may be antisocial, morbidly helpless or significantly at odds with normal interpersonal demands or circumstances, and/or narrator's behavior during testing strains acceptable bounds.													
Wishes and fantasies are distinguished from realistic appraisal. Inner preoccupation is separated from reality (external demands or rules).													
Clear intentions (versus vague or stereotyped) are linked with appropriate actions and appropriate outcomes in keeping with a realistic grasp of social causality.													

F. Coordination of Perspectives of Different Individuals

(Check as many as apply for each story) Cards→	1	2											
Views and needs of all characters depicted in the stimulus or story are considered in the resolution rather than centering on only one character.													
Characters are meaningfully related to one another rather than entrenched in separate concerns or insights that are not communicated.													
Characters retain their individuality (convictions, intentions, outcomes) while interacting in a mutually enhancing manner (in ways that precisely match the stimulus).													
Details and sequences of events are cohesive; relationships among characters are well-defined rather than vague or stereotypic.													

G. Levels of Cognitive-Experiential Integration

Level One: Disorganized. This level is indicated by any of the following: implausible or grossly illogical events; discrepancy between the stimulus and story; bizarre, gruesome, socially unacceptable content; highly improbable, unrealistic sequence of events; abandonment of a character in an extreme state of helplessness or deprivation; highly idiosyncratic and/or illogical assumptions about the world including distorted understanding of cause-effect relationship; feelings, thoughts, and actions that are incongruous with each other and/or depart grossly from social expectation; socially inappropriate or disorganized thoughts (e.g., conceptually incompatible ideas, major contradictions).

Level Two: Rudimentary. Rather than idiosyncratic distortion, there is a markedly simplified process of reasoning (possibly a "descriptive flavor") incorporating minimal causal connections. Feelings or inner states are not explained beyond simple reactions. Causal inferences are nonexistent, extremely rudimentary, or vague. Characters are distinguished by the way they look in the picture (though important perceptual cues may be ignored) or by outward actions with minimal differentiation in their intentions, feelings, history, or circumstances. Characters are tuned in to relatively immediate concerns and focus on short-term or self-centered outcomes. They respond to the situational provocations rather than deliberate intention or anticipation of realistic consequences. Outcomes are vague, insufficiently explained, or fail to resolve the problem beyond the moment. Solutions to problems or conflicts are characterized by wishful (improbable but not impossible) or unrealistic strategies or avoidance of conflict.

Level Three: Superficial. Narratives portray more complex coordination of ideas than Levels 1 and 2. However, lack of specificity (vagueness) and conformity with cultural "scripts" convey a stereotyped view of events or relationships. Relatively greater emphasis on external incentives or consequences than on inner life and lack of commitment to standards promote actions that are geared toward needs and wants. Characters may want to alleviate their immediate distress or to obtain the usual things associated with the "good life" (feeling good, money, education, success, relationships). The narrative lacks "depth" and specificity, suggesting a stereotypical or superficial view with possible "gaps" in understanding (e.g., disregarding some important aspect of the situation). Match with the stimulus may be imprecise.

Level Four: Realistic. Events depicted are realistic and convey coherence between inner states and external circumstances, both within a character and across different characters. Characters' durable intentions guide appropriate actions directed toward clear purposes or problem-resolution. However, the emphasis at this level is more on realistic and practical considerations than ideals, standards, principles, and/or intrinsic sources of satisfaction that characterize the highest level. Contextual cues may be ignored, but emotions and relationships are accurately interpreted.

Level Five: Complex and Responsible. The narrative conveys an understanding of complexities of the psychological world and flexible problem solving that balances long- and short-term needs and aspirations of various characters, as well as feelings, thoughts, intentions, actions, and outcomes within characters. Resolutions are mindful of the needs and rights of all parties, goals are more abstract than previous levels and may involve objectives such as self-development or realistic desire to contribute to improving social conditions. Story flows smoothly, depicts events in a conceptually clear and specific manner, and places events in a context that integrates multiple dimensions and perspectives. The inner and outer worlds are well-differentiated and well-coordinated. Actions and concerns reflect long-range interests, are in accord with subtleties of the stimulus, incorporate a well-conceptualized time frame, and show consideration among individuals.

(Choose one level for each story)

Card	1	2											

H. Production of Ideas/Levels of Associative Thinking

Level One: Tangential Association. Story rambles and is made up as one idea triggers another without apparent causal linkages to each other or to a central concept. Responses may initially match the stimulus but veer away subsequently. The content may be tangential to the stimulus and/or personalized.

Level Two: Linear Association. Ideas are introduced linearly in association to the stimulus, previous story event (e.g., repetitive elaborations on one idea such as series of actions), or emotion. Responses may center on addressing the specific components of the directions rather than the production of a "story." Narrator may try to connect proximal ideas but overall causal connections among the story details are nonexistent, vague, or implausible.

Level Three: Patterned Associations. Ideas are introduced according to scripted regularities in experiences or cultural or subcultural stereotypes. The sequence of ideas is formulaic and may be borrowed (from a story, movie, or television show) or may be a literal replay of familiar, scripted experiences. The story progression is somewhat like a bad movie, lacking in depth or a sense of genuineness of the characters. Details that might be expected to be implicitly understood may be explicitly stated; few or vague details may be given. The superimposition of scripted patterns may involve some subtle distortion of the nuances of the stimulus or imprecise logic.

Level Four: Logical Association. Ideas are introduced in ways that tie various dimensions of experience into a common context. Logic and coherence of the narrative are evident (events, thoughts, feelings, actions, and outcomes are congruous). The story premises and supporting detail are clearly related.

Level Five: Integrative Association. Story elements are cohesive and tightly organized around a central theme with clearly prosocial and realistic convictions guiding the story progression. Ideas shift conceptually in accord with well-integrated, complex internalized representations. Well-developed schemas are implicit in the subtext of the story, which concludes without "loose ends."

(Choose one level for each story)

Card	1	2												

EMOTION

I. CONCEPTUALIZATION OF EMOTIONS

A. Sources and Regulation of Affect
Sources of Affect

(Check as many as apply for each story) Cards→	I	2											
Unrecognized (tension depicted is not recognized)													
Descriptive (refers to stimulus)													
External													
Internal													

B. Coping with Affective Tensions

(Choose among non-coping, immediate coping, or long-term coping styles for each story. Then check the most appropriate categories within each style.)

1. Non-Coping or Unrealistic Coping

(Check as many as apply for each story) Cards→	I	2											
Unaware (negative emotion is not recognized)													
No change in affect, self-awareness, or understanding													
Overwhelmed (misery prevails or negative affect escalates)													
Reactive (provoked to act without purpose or strategy)													
Detached, resigned, hopeless (fails to act or react, withdraws, gives in)													
Guilty, regretful													
Substantially unrealistic. Magical external intervention or unlikely turn of events (e.g., wins the war single-handedly; character is granted unrealistic demand); dreaming or hoping (when action is warranted)													

2. Immediate or Partial Coping

(Check as many as apply for each story) Cards→	I	2											
Decrease negative affect and/or deal with the dilemma without fully addressing the sources of the tension (e.g., avoidance, temporary reassurance, resolving to do something).													
Increase or maintain positive affect and/or act on the situation without recognizing important issues.													
Excessive dependence on others													
Excessive independence from others													

3. Long-Term or Problem-Focused Coping

(Check as many as apply for each story) Cards→	I	2											
Decrease negative affect by effective problem solving (e.g., addressing the source of the feeling or reframing).													
Increase or maintain positive affect through long-term problem solving and goal setting.													
Realistic resolution of tensions without seeking or receiving help/support.													
Realistic resolution of tensions with appropriate request for help or support (not passive, blind dependence).													
Appropriate help, advice, or reassurance provided without specific request, enables the character to resolve the dilemma.													

II. EMOTIONAL MATURITY

A. Complexity and Coherence of Emotions (Within One Individual)

(Check as many as apply for each story) Cards→	1	2											
Affects pertain to durable, inner motives, long-term interests or convictions (standards, goals, harmonious relationship versus reactions to momentary needs, immediate situational provocation, or nonspecific distress).													
Affective impact of actions is distinct from its intent.													
Emotions, thoughts, actions, and outcomes are congruous with each other, meaningfully woven into the unfolding narrative, and in tune with social causality and the stimulus.													
Feelings appear to be drawn from meaningful synthesis of narrator's experience (versus scripted, superficial, feigned, or associative verbiage).													

B. Integration and Coordination of Emotions (Across Individuals)

(Check as many as apply for each story) Cards→	1	2											
In defining the dilemma, feelings of all relevant characters are coordinated into a shared context.													
In resolving the dilemma, viewpoints and needs of all relevant characters are reconciled (with understanding of social causality).													
There is separation of internal and external reality and differentiation of inner states from external provocation (i.e., the emotion of the perceiver is distinct from characteristics of the target or source of the feeling).													
Feeling is appropriate (in nature and intensity) to the circumstances described in the story and is based on accurate reading of the stimulus.													

C. Clarity and Specificity in the Identification of Emotions

(Check as many as apply for each story) Cards→	1	2											
Clear and specific identification of the circumstances vis-à-vis a character's feelings.													
Clear delineation of the relationships of characters to each other vis-à-vis the feelings described. *													
Clear distinctions of different characters' feelings according to evoking circumstance or differences in personality or viewpoint.													

*If only one person is described (assuming only one is pictured), the above category applies.

LEVEL OF MATURITY IN THE CONCEPTUALIZATION AND RESOLUTION OF EMOTION

Level One: Conceptualization—Disjointed. Affect is tied in a disjointed way to stimuli or story events (e.g., situations associated with feelings are highly implausible; feelings or circumstances are poorly coordinated with the stimulus). Emotions, motives, or purposes do not reflect inner attributes but are specific descriptions of the stimuli, global reactions to the feeling state in the stimulus, vague impressions, or unmodulated and inappropriate reactions to perceived provocations. Intent is not separated from impact.

Resolution: Non-Coping or Immediate Coping. Feelings conceptualized at this level are not conducive to realistic resolutions because they are not internally organized nor realistically tied to events. The story may conclude with an inappropriate, highly maladaptive resolution or no resolution. Affect may be arbitrarily changed to its opposite so the new feeling contradicts the premises of the preceding story. Outcomes may reflect extreme helplessness, fear, hostility, and/or involve clearly antisocial actions or poor judgment. Affects may become more negative or more intense as the situation keeps deteriorating; characters may remain in extreme states of deprivation, confusion, or abandonment with no resolution.

Level Two: Conceptualization—Provoked. Emotions are poorly integrated into a larger context, pertaining primarily to immediate concerns (provocation, need, desire). Feelings are tied to events in ways that may be implausible, short-sighted, self-absorbed, simplistic, or extremely vague. Feelings may be reactions to the last event or immediate need rather than pertinent to a larger context or cohesive with a series of events. Feelings may be superficial, feigned, or overly justified by the stimulus or by immediate external circumstance. There is poor understanding of psychological process or of social-causality.

Resolution: Non-Coping, Immediate, or Partial Coping. Affect does not change or shifts are inadequately explained. Feelings or events change without a clear and reasonable intervening process or without considering important aspects of the stimulus or the dilemma (e.g., change of affect or activity is the outcome; affect is ignored or the problem simply disappears). Actions are vague or do not constructively address the problem. There is lack of distinction between short- and long-term resolutions to affective tensions.

Level Three: Conceptualization—Externally Organized. Emotions are recognized as internal to the characters, but they are elicited primarily by external sources such as actions and reactions of others or by external feedback or demand but with at least a superficial distinction between intent and impact. Emotions may be tied to pressure to conform to legitimate external standards, demands, or rules (not someone's whims).

Resolution: Non-Coping, Immediate, or Partial Coping. Affect shifts are realistically tied to external change in circumstances or interventions of others but do not entail durable conviction or initiative of characters to seek long-term resolution or pursue goals. At this level, failure to resolve tensions due to inaction may be interpreted as need for an external agent. When constructive action is taken to meet legitimate external demand, the motive is to obtain approval or reward or to avert consequences. Thus, external source influences affect change (e.g., positive actions are valued because they bring reward or approval; wrongdoing brings external consequences only). Resolution of inner tensions depends on the reactions of others. Some incompatibility or ambivalence remains between short- and long-term resolutions or in dealing with internal and external sources of tension.

Level Four: Conceptualization—Internally Organized. Emotions are smoothly incorporated into the narrative in ways that are congruent with external circumstances and coordinated with motives and convictions, as well as with deliberate, purposeful actions. External and internal frames of reference are balanced, various perspectives are coordinated, and characters communicate appropriately and act constructively on their feelings. Problem definition or affect is in tune with the circumstances and respects the psychological integrity of all relevant characters. Emotional reaction to the problem or task is appropriate to the stimulus and story context. Concerns are not trivial, but represent a balance between immediate presses and long-term perspective.

Resolution: Long-Term Coping. Characters take responsibility for regulating feelings and action. They engage in realistic, planful, active problem-solving efforts (where possible) or resolve their negative feelings by accepting logical consequences or inevitable events. Resolutions are appropriate to problem set and effort expended and reflect initiative in responding to both internal and external sources of tension. External factors along with inner states of characters guide purposeful thought, planning, and actions.

Level Five: Conceptualization—Principled. Emotions stem from prosocial, self-defined standards and/or goals coupled with self-awareness and acceptance of boundaries and limitations. Nuances of the stimuli are resourcefully incorporated into the narrative.

Resolution: Long-Term Coping. The abstract and mature conceptualization of the problem is linked with coping that is geared to "meaning," principles, and values and not directed exclusively to regulation or management of feelings, maintaining or repairing a relationship, overcoming an obstacle, or achieving success.

(Choose the highest level applicable for each story)

Card	1	2											

RELATIONSHIPS

I. DIFFERENTIATION, INTEGRATION, AND MUTUALITY OF AUTONOMY

A. Differentiation of Viewpoints and Attributes Within and Across Individuals

(Check as many as apply for each story) Cards→	I	2											
Viewpoints of different characters (or single character) remain fuzzy. Little or no distinction is evident.													
Distinctions among characters are based on superficial, outward attributes (lifestyle, possessions) or how they look in the stimulus.													
Distinctions are based on simple event-feeling connections (e.g., crying because he fell) or vague intentions (wants to find out what something is) without grasping the psychological process.													
Distinctions are based on stereotypes or duty in carrying out roles as parent, spouse, child, or friend.													
Distinctions are dichotomous (e.g., good vs. bad; weak vs. strong; threatening vs. safe; special vs. ordinary).													
Characters' attributes are seen only in relation to another's needs, desires, or preoccupations (e.g., emotions are misperceived; reasoning about interpersonal events is based on wishes, fears, or preoccupations of the perceiver rather than realistic understanding of social causality).													
Characters differ in their needs, views, and actions, and these differences are seen as legitimate in a mutually respectful relationship.													
A character is committed to principles, and is invested in a relationship or in prosocial goal-directed activities (not just wanting an outcome).													

B. Integration of Feelings and Perspectives Within and Across Individuals

(Check as many as apply for each story) Cards→	I	2											
Feelings, tensions, and conflicts are incorporated into a meaningful context that relates perspectives across or within individuals.													
Sense of continuity of inner life is conveyed by reconciling positive and negative facets of characters (e.g., realistically managing emotions) or by genuine connections among individuals (versus isolated attributes or momentary concerns).													
The perspectives and needs of all characters are balanced by coordinating past, present, and future interests of all concerned.													
Characters communicate their ideas to others and their actions are based on mutual understanding and respect.													

C. Mutuality of Autonomy

(Check as many as apply for each story) Cards→	I	2										
A character shows autonomy, sense of initiative, conviction, or deliberate pursuit of realistic, prosocial, or goal-directed activities.												
All characters are balanced in their respective sense of autonomy. They respect and appreciate each other's individuality (e.g., intentions, feelings, thoughts, actions, outcomes) apart from their own needs or feelings.												
Characters respond to an immediate situation, action, or demand without prior history, conviction, or investment; they fail to act or act without deliberate intention.												
People are evaluated only in terms of what they provide. Characters relate in terms of what they do for or want from each other without recognizing one another's autonomy.												
There is an imbalance of autonomy where one person is competent, heroic, or intrusive, while others are incompetent, helpless, or ignored.												
People are viewed as obstacles or as harmful.												

Note: The above qualities may be implicit, particularly when only one character is depicted.

D. Levels of Object Relations

Level One: Disorganized or detached experience of relatedness. Disorganized or highly simplified thought process disrupts the differentiation and integration of various perspectives (mutuality) and the sense of self-cohesion (autonomy). This level is characterized by impaired social reasoning where the individual is devoid of resources to understand relationships and, therefore, experiences a severe imbalance of mutuality (e.g., helpless against the whims of controlling and powerful others or detached from relationships) and/or serious restriction of autonomy or poor reality testing (e.g., unrealistic expectations). Individuality (in circumstance, emotion, intention, thought) is not salient, resulting in lack of differentiation or responsiveness across individuals and unrealistic coordination between the inner and outer worlds within individuals.

Level Two: Momentary experience of relatedness. Personality is not experienced as a continuous, cohesive whole, and there is rudimentary recognition of individuality. Therefore, self-esteem and relationships with others exist in the moment. Limited autonomy pulls for differentiating others on the basis of momentary need or the immediate situation without the sense that they are whole persons. Therefore, characteristics of others are salient if they pertain to immediate needs or wants (character's portrayal in the stimulus may not even be noticed). Feelings are tied to immediate external demands or circumstances, and remorse is tied to consequences. Perception of self and others shifts (dichotomously) according to circumstances and without insight or reflection. Characters' inner attributes and individual differences are ill-defined, dichotomous, or are based on stereotypes. An imbalance of mutuality of autonomy and/or a disparity of status or of power may be explicit or implicit.

Level Three: Functional experience of relatedness. Emphasis is on the function served rather than on enduring connection with reliance on rigid *quid pro quo* exchanges. Approval or disapproval as well as reward or punishment contribute to the functional exchange. Characters attempt to conform to each other's expectations rather than engage in autonomous goal-directed activities or efforts to meet standards. They appear to take turns in carrying out their functional roles, and this exchange is the foundation for the relationship. Attributes that pertain to character's functions are most salient. Characters show remorse and accept punishment for wrongdoing.

Level Four: Relatedness through reciprocity and standards. A sense of fair play dictates expectations in relations with others and in self-evaluation. Reciprocity is not perceived as *quid pro quo* but as a natural mode of relating among individuals who care about each other. Characters are clearly differentiated, autonomous, and have internalized standards and rules of conduct that permit appropriate compromise.

Level Five: Relatedness through mutuality of autonomy. There is full appreciation of uniqueness and individuality, apart from the perceiver's needs or requirements of social exchange. Inner life and concerns of all characters are portrayed in ways that show full mutuality of autonomy and appreciation of subtle intra- and interpersonal nuance, in keeping with the stimulus cues. A fine-tuned understanding of multiply interacting dimensions of experience includes a distinction between transient and enduring psychological experience, balance between the inner and outer worlds of self and others, and coordination of long- and short-term considerations.

(Choose one level for each story)

Card	I	2											

MOTIVATION

I. GOAL FORMULATION

A. Structure and Process

(Check as many as apply for each story) — Cards→	1	2											
There is clear and appropriate definition of central problem, tension, or dilemma, given the stimulus (versus vague, nonspecific intention or tension).													
Story is logical and proceeds without irrelevant or contradictory detail; reasoning is realistic, and sequence of events is plausible.													

B. Content

(Check as many as apply for each story) — Cards→	1	2											
A realistic, prosocial goal or dilemma is imposed by others but accepted by a character.													
Characters set a realistic, prosocial goal, conflict, or dilemma.													
Characters exhibit interest, curiosity, pride, concern, empathy, and commitment to standards, ideals, task, or prosocial activity.													

C. Characteristics of Goals (Check for each story):

absent-vague / clear   self-initiated / imposed   realistic / unrealistic
long-term / short-term   prosocial / antisocial   interpersonal / task
process / outcome   idealistic / materialistic   meeting of inner standards / meeting of demands or expectations
substantial / trivial   attainment of positive / aversion of negative

II. REACTION TO THE GOAL, DILEMMA OR STORYTELLING TASK

A. Structure and Process

(Check as many as apply for each story) — Cards→	1	2											
Story proceeds according to a plan rather than made up detail by detail.													
Narrator incorporates all parts of the instructions with or without inquiry. Prompted responses enhance the story (versus providing minimal or repetitious responses).													

B. Content

(Check as many as apply for each story) — Cards→	1	2											
Characters acknowledge possible external obstacles or internal limitations without being stymied; they set priorities, display foresight, plan ahead, and anticipate consequences.													
Characters perceive the goal-related activities as interesting, desirable, or relevant, rather than feel pressured, rely on external incentives, or avoid the demand or responsibility.													

III. GOAL-DIRECTED ACTIONS

A. Structure and Process

(Check as many as apply for each story) Cards→	I	2											
Appropriate means-ends connections suggest that the narrator can maintain self-directed activity and follow through on intentions.														

B. Content

(Check as many as apply for each story) Cards→	I	2											
Actions are prosocial, realistic, and sufficient for the expected outcome.														
Responsible, goal-directed actions or decisions are valued as distinct from outcomes.														
Characters' inner motives and external constraints are realistically balanced in the intention-action-outcome set.														

C. Characteristics of Actions (Check for each story):

present / absent   planful / haphazard   realistic / unrealistic
prosocial / antisocial   proactive / reactive   search for positive / avoidance of negative
goal-directed / aimless   reliance on self / reliance on externals   enjoyable / burdensome

LEVELS OF MOTIVATION IN RELATION TO OUTCOME

	Positive Story Outcome	Negative Story Outcome
Level One: **Extremely Poor Motivation**	**Intentions/Goals.** They are vague, ill-intended, unrealistic, trivial, unstated, inadequately defined, or extremely lofty. **Reactions.** They include boredom, obvious lack of interest or inability to withstand setback or frustration, negative attitude toward effort or success. **Actions.** Actions include absence of effort, aimless activity, blind dependence on, rebellious defiance of, or extreme pressure by others, unlikely, antisocial, or nonconstructive actions, wishful thinking with no realistic basis. **Conviction.** Success or happiness can be attained without clear/realistic goals, long-term investment or interest, or active effort, or through unrealistic or antisocial means.	**Intentions/Goals.** They are unclear, unstated, inappropriate, or realistic and socially appropriate. **Reactions.** They include expecting failure despite active effort or self-determined choices or because of difficulty with understanding or meeting demands. Failure or adversity cannot be overcome, is blamed on others, leads to despair, frustration, inaction, hopelessness, pretense, deceit, escape, fantasy, dream, sleep, inadequacy, or confusion. **Actions.** Positive effort may be misunderstood or thwarted by circumstance or absence of constructive action due to discouragement, lack of goals or confusion. **Conviction.** Negative outcomes are expected despite good intentions, realistic goals, and active effort or because of confusion or extreme disorganization.
Level Two: **Poor Motivation**	**Intentions/Goals.** They are clearly stated and prosocial or vague. **Reactions.** Optimism without adequate reasons; character forgets, makes the best of it, is happy having tried; success is empty or unrewarding and leads to tension. **Actions.** Actions are not directly pertinent to the task at hand or taken reluctantly; means to goals are vague or less-than-required effort is expended. Actions are undertaken for approval, recognition, conformity, or self-centered motives; a character hopes for success or thinks about the problem; actions are taken without commitment or interest; passive dependence on help or advice. **Conviction.** Success or happiness can be attained despite actions that are reluctant, not directly pertinent to the goal, or fully adequate. Success can be attained by setting "easy" goals.	**Intentions/Goals.** They are clearly stated and prosocial or vague. **Reactions.** Frustration, boredom, anger, or external barriers preclude sufficient action or expected behavior. **Actions.** Thinking and planning have occurred, but no action is taken; extraneous factors have interfered; adversity or failure is tolerated, though action is possible. **Conviction.** Failure or unhappiness (when goals are prosocial) may be due to internal or external barriers or insufficient action, despite planning and thinking. (The causes for failure or unhappiness are not clearly understood by the character or narrator.)
Level Three: **Mildly Positive Motivation**	**Intentions/Goals.** They are prosocial and adequately defined but modest, very difficult, and/or involve mixed feelings. **Reactions.** They may be mixed or ambivalent; character actively seeks extra help or advice before doing everything possible. Dependence on others who provide adequate support or inspiration, but dependence is not blind as advice is judged on its own merits; some temporary tension or loss is associated with success. **Actions.** Actions are maintained despite obstacles or initial discouragement; effort is expended but the outcome may be uncertain, conditional, or viewed as a possibility. **Conviction.** Success or happiness are attained (possibly conditionally), perhaps after initial discouragement or with help from others prior to doing everything possible through realistic means.	**Intentions/Goals.** They are prosocial and adequately defined. **Reactions.** Narrator grasps implications of character's lack of planning, mistakes, procrastination, negative attitudes, or poor organization as well as excessive independence, or refusal to heed sound advice. **Actions.** There is insufficient strategic effort (though planning may have occurred). **Conviction.** Insufficient planning or effort leads to appropriate negative consequences and lesson learned. (The story is well-constructed, conveying a sense that the narrator possesses and can utilize this insight.)
Level Four: **High Motivation**	**Intentions/Goals.** They are realistic, clearly articulated, and reflect long-term purpose. **Reactions.** They include interest, principles, standards, and realistic self-confidence. Self-determination, but able to seek advice after doing everything possible; acceptance of legitimate pressure. Positive attitude toward work; preference for values that are abstract, ethical, or altruistic rather than materialistic or expedient. **Actions.** Actions are autonomous, prosocial, respectful of others, sufficient for stated goals and outcomes, or maintain principles. **Conviction.** Realistic goals, self-determined, principled actions lead to success, happiness, or harmonious relationships.	**Intentions/Goals.** These include ill intent, self-glorification, self-centered goals, or mistaken action. **Reactions.** The narrator recognizes inappropriateness of characters' intentions or prior action (e.g., inadequate or impulsive). **Actions.** Actions and outcomes are cohesive and convey prosocial principled conviction. **Conviction.** Ill-intended actions or inadequate means (e.g., "too little, too late") lead to failure, unhappiness, or disrupted relationships. Ill-intended actions, even if accompanied by success are punished. (Again, there is a sense that the narrator possesses and can utilize this insight.)

IMPORT AND MOTIVATION LEVEL

Card	Import of Story	Choose Level of Motivation	
		Positive Outcome	Negative Outcome
1			
2			

Note: If a meaningful import cannot be extracted from the story content, it may be derived from formal qualities of the narrative process or structure.

SELF-REGULATION

LEVELS OF SELF-REGULATION

Level One: Dysregulation. Form and content of stories reflect fragmentation in processing life experience associated with impairment in thought organization (e.g., ideas out of context; implausible sequence of events, illogical or bizarre ideas, inconsistent level of conceptualization, perseveration). The person reacts to faulty perceptions provoked by minute, irrelevant considerations or is hopelessly immobilized. The respondent may focus narrowly on elements of the picture without capturing the meaning or may express global reactions to the stimulus as a whole. Characters act and react without awareness of causes and effects, or the narrator's behavior during the evaluation is clearly inappropriate. Relevant components of the immediate situation are not integrated, and the individual has difficulty monitoring routine behavior without clear guidelines.

Level Two: Immediacy. Information processing and behavior relate to the moment without adequate reflection on prior history, future consequences, or implications for others. Judgments and actions are based on what immediately dominates awareness without organization or integration of salient aspects of the current situation, with important but remote implications. Self-monitoring may pass muster in the moment, but self-direction in the longer term is hampered by inability to maintain interest in situations that do not contribute to immediate sense of well-being. Actions are aimed at seeking immediate gain or relief. Feelings are not regulated internally but evoked by immediate external circumstances. Thus, intentions behind actions are not clearly distinct from their impact.

Level Three: External Direction. Information processing and behavior are guided by externally imposed standards, feedback, or necessity (e.g., adverse event) rather than by the provocation or whim of the moment. Various elements of the current situation and relationships are more realistically assessed than at previous levels (including a distinction between intent and impact, awareness of rules and expectations, quid pro quo reciprocity). Story content revolves around more long-term expectations, and more general, less narrow or trivial concerns, but might be mildly unrealistic or naive because perceptions of self and others are not well differentiated. There may be a sense of pressure to meet demands of others or to conform to acknowledged standards of conduct rather than be directed by inner values or standards. External sources of motivation or reassurance are needed to tolerate frustration and persist in long-term instrumental action.

Level Four: Internal Direction. Information processing and behavior are implicitly guided by standards and prosocial values that are internally represented and that the individual feels competent to attain. The individual can balance personal concerns with needs of family and friends and coordinate short- and long-term considerations. Task engagement and interpersonal reciprocity do not have the demanding flavor of the previous level but lack the personal conviction of the highest level. There is more initiative and greater organization of thoughts, emotions, and behaviors. Initiative and effort are appropriate for desired ends and for meeting adaptive demands (well-organized and long-term).

Level Five: Self-Determination. Information processing is complex and responsible, as indicated by stories that elaborate inner experience within or across characters in ways that are cohesive with the stimulus, described circumstance, actions, and outcomes. Thus, characters' intentions, thoughts, feelings, actions, outcomes, and story events are well-coordinated in relative emphasis, context, and time frame. Characters are invested in planful, autonomous, socially responsible, and purposeful action and are dedicated to enduring principles. Information processing is more complex than the previous level, incorporating multiple dimensions of experience and perspectives of relevant others over the long term. Therefore, people and events may be evaluated as they are, apart from the feelings or needs of the perceiver. Standards or goals are valued beyond their connection to desired ends; the instrumental activities themselves are sustaining to the individual.

(Choose one level for each story)

Card	1	2										

References

Abelson, R. P. (1976). Script processing in attitude formation and decision making. In J. S. Carroll & J. W. Payne (Eds.), *Cognition and social behavior* (pp. 33–46). Hillsdale, NJ: Erlbaum.

Abelson, R. P. (1981). Psychological status of the script concept. *American Psychologist, 36,* 715–729.

Achenbach, T. M. (1999). The Child Behavior Checklist and related instruments. In M. E. Maruish (Ed.), *The use of psychological testing for treatment planning and outcomes assessment* (2nd ed.). Mahwah, NJ: Erlbaum.

Achenbach, T. M., & Edelbrock C. (1983). *Manual for the Child Behavior Checklist/4–18 and Revised Child Behavior Profile.* Burlington: University of Vermont.

Alexander, J. E. (1988). Personality, psychological assessment and psychobiography. *Journal of Personality, 56,* 265–294.

Alvarado, N. (1994). Empirical validity of the Thematic Apperception Test. *Journal of Personality Assessment, 63,* 59–79.

Anderson, J. (1990). *The adaptive character of thought.* Hillsdale, NJ: Erlbaum.

Applebee, A. N. (1978). *The Child's Concept of Story; Ages two to seven.* Chicago: The University of Chicago Press.

Arboleda, C., & Holzman, P. S. (1985). Thought disorder in children at risk for psychosis. *Archives of General Psychiatry, 42,* 1004–1013.

Archer, R. P., Marnish, M., Imhof, E. A., & Piotrowski, C. (1991). Psychological test usage with adolescent clients: 1990 survey findings. *Professional Psychology: Research and Practice, 22,* 247–252.

Armstrong, M. A. (1954). Children's responses to animal and human figures in thematic pictures. *Journal of Consulting Psychology, 18,* 67–70.

Arnold, M. B. (1962). *Story sequence analysis: A new method of measuring motivation and predicting achievement.* New York: Columbia University Press.

Aronoff, J., & Wilson, J. P. (1985). *Personality in the social process.* Hillsdale, NJ: Erlbaum.

Astington, J. W. (1991). Intention in the child's theory of mind. In D. M. Frye & C. Moore (Eds.), *Children's theories of mind: Mental states and social understanding* (pp. 157–172). Hillsdale, NJ: Erlbaum.

Atkinson, J. W. (1992). Motivational determinants of thematic apperception. In C. P. Smith (Ed.), *Motivation and personality: Handbook of thematic content analysis* (pp. 21–48). New York: Cambridge University Press.

Atkinson, R. C. (1964). *Studies in mathematical psychology.* Stanford, CA: Stanford University Press.

Bailey, B. E., & Green, J. (1977). Black Thematic Apperception Test stimulus material. *Journal of Personality Assessment, 41,* 25–30.

Baker-Brown, G., Ballard, E. J., Bluck, S., de Vries, B., Suedfeld, P., & Tetlock, P. E. (1992). The conceptual integrative complexity scoring manual. In C. P. Smith (Ed.),

Motivation and personality: Handbook of thematic content analysis (pp. 401–418). New York: Cambridge University Press.

Baldwin, M. W. (1992). Relational schemas and the processing of social information. *Psychological Bulletin, 112,* 461–484.

Bandura, A. (1977). *Social learning theory.* Englewood Cliffs, NJ: Prentice-Hall.

Bandura, A. (1988). Self-regulation of motivation and action through goal systems. In V. Hamilton, G. H. Bower, & N. H. Frijda (Eds.), *Cognitive perspectives on emotion and motivation* (pp. 37–61). Dordrecht, Netherlands: Kluwer Academic Publishers.

Bandura, A. (1989). Human agency in social cognitive theory. *American Psychologist, 44,* 1175–1184.

Bargh, J. A., & Chartrand, T. L. (1999). The unbearable automaticity of being. *American Psychologist, 54,* 462–479.

Barkley, R. A. (1997). Behavioral inhibition, sustained attention, and executive functions: Constructing a unified theory of ADHD. *Psychological Bulletin, 121,* 65–94.

Barlow, D. H. (1988). *Anxiety and its disorders: The nature and treatment of anxiety and panic.* New York: Guilford Press.

Baron-Cohen, S. (1991). Do people with autism understand what causes emotion? *Child Development, 62,* 385–395.

Baron-Cohen, S., Leslie, A. M., & Frith, U. (1986). Mechanical, behavioral, and intentional understanding of picture stories in autistic children. *British Journal of Developmental Psychology, 4,* 113–125.

Bassan-Diamond, L. E., Teglasi, H., & Schmitt, P. (1995). Temperament and a story-telling measure of self-regulation. *Journal of Research in Personality, 29,* 109–120.

Beck, A. T. (1976). *Cognitive therapy and emotional disorders.* New York: International Universities Press.

Beck, A. T., & Clark, D. A. (1997). An information processing model of anxiety: Automatic and strategic processes. *Behavior Research and Therapy, 35*(1), 49–58.

Beck, A. T., & Weishaar, M. E. (1989). Cognitive therapy. In R. J. Corsini & D. Wedding (Eds.), *Current psychotherapies* (4th ed.). Itasca, IL: Peacock.

Beckwith, R. T. (1991). The language of emotion, the emotions and nominalist bootstrapping. In D. Frye & C. Moore (Eds.), *Children's theories of mind: Mental states and social understanding* (pp. 77–96). Hillsdale, NJ: Erlbaum.

Bellak, L. (1975). *The TAT, CAT, and SAT in clinical use.* New York: Grune & Stratton.

Bellak, L. (1986). *The TAT, CAT, and SAT in clinical use* (4th ed.). Orlando, FL: Grune & Stratton.

Bellak, L. (1992). *Short Form TAT, CAT, & SAT Blank.* San Antonio, TX: Psychological Corporations.

Bellak, L. (1993). *The TAT, CAT, and SAT in clinical use* (5th ed.). Boston: Allyn & Bacon.

Bellak, L., & Abrams, D. M. (1997). *The Thematic Apperception Test, the Children's Apperception Test, and the Senior Apperception Technique in clinical use* (6th ed.). Boston: Allyn & Bacon.

Bellak, L., & Abrams, D. M. (1998). *A manual for the Children's Apperception Test (animal figures).* Larchmont, NY: C.P.S., Inc.

Bellak, L., & Bellak, S. S. (1949). Children's Apperception Test. Larchmont, NY: C.P.S., Inc.

Bellak, L., & Bellak, S. S. (1952). The supplement to the Children's Apperception Test (CAT–S). Larchmont, NY: C.P.S., Inc.

Bellak, L., & Bellak, S. S. (1965). The Children's Apperception Test. Larchmont, NY: C.P.S., Inc.

Bellak, L., & Bellak, S. S. (1973). *Manual: Senior Apperception Test.* Larchmont, NY: C.P.S., Inc.

Berkowitz, L. (1990). On the formation and regulation of anger and aggression: A cognitive-neoassociationistic analysis. *American Psychologist, 45,* 494–503.

Biernat, M. (1989). Motives and values to achieve: Different constructs with different effects. *Journal of Personality, 57,* 69–95.

Blaney, P. H. (1986). Affect and memory: A review. *Psychological Bulletin, 99,* 229–246.

Blankman, C., Teglasi, H., & Lawser, M. (2000, August). *Story telling and literacy.* Poster presented at the American Psychological Association Annual Convention, Washington, DC.

Blatt, S. J. (1990). Interpersonal relatedness and self definition: Two personality configurations and their implications for psychopathology and psychotherapy. In J. L. Singer (Ed.), *Repression and dissociation: Implications for personality theory, psychotherapy and health* (pp. 299–335). Chicago: University of Chicago Press.

Blatt, S. J., Brenneis, C. B., Schimak, J. G., & Glick, M. (1976). Normal development and psychopathological impairment of the concept of the object on the Rorschach. *Journal of Abnormal Psychology, 85,* 364–373.

Blatt, S. J., & Lerner, H. (1983). The psychological assessment of object representations. *Journal of Personality Assessment, 47,* 7–28.

Blum, G. S. (1950). *The Blacky Pictures.* New York: Psychological Corporation.

Bornstein, R. F., & O'Neill, R. M. (1992). Parental perceptions and psychopathology. *Journal of Nervous and Mental Disease, 180,* 475–483.

Bower, G. H. (1981). Mood and memory. *American Psychologist, 36,* 129–148.

Bower, G. H. (1997). How might emotion affect learning? In S. A. Christianson (Ed.), *Handbook of emotion and memory* (pp. 3–31). Hillsdale, NJ: Erlbaum.

Bower, G. H., & Cohen, P. (1982). Emotional influences in memory and thinking: Data and theory. In M. Clarke & S. Fiske (Eds.), *Affect and cognition* (pp. 291–331). Hillsdale, NJ: Erlbaum.

Bransford, J. D., Franks, J. J., Vye, N. J., & Sherwood, R. D. (1989). New approaches to instruction: Because wisdom can't be taught. In S. Vosniadou & A. Ortony (Eds.), *Similarity and analogical reasoning* (pp. 470–497). New York: Cambridge University Press.

Bretherton, I. (1987). New perspectives on attachment relations: Security, communication, and internal working models. In J. D. Osofsky (Ed.), *Handbook of infant development* (pp. 1061–1100). New York: John Wiley & Sons.

Bretherton, I. (1990). Open communication and internal working models: Their role in the development of attachment relationships. In R. A. Thompson (Ed.), *Nebraska Symposium on Motivation, 1988: Socioemotional development* (pp. 57–113). Lincoln: University of Nebraska Press.

Bretherton, I. (1991). Intentional communication and the development of an understanding mind. In D. Frye & C. Moore (Eds.), *Children's theory of mind: Mental states and social understanding* (pp. 49–76). Hillsdale, NJ: Erlbaum.

Bretherton, I., & Breghly, M. (1982). Talking about internal states: The acquisition of an explicit theory of mind. *Developmental Psychology, 18,* 906–921.

Broughton, J. M. (1981). The divided self in adolescence. *Human Devleopment, 24*(1), 13–32.

Bruhn, A. (1990). Cognitive-perceptual theory and the projective use of autobiographical memory. *Journal of Personality Assessment, 55,* 95–114.

Bruhn, A. (1992). The early memories procedure: A projective test of autobiographical memory, Part 2. *Journal of Personality Assessment, 58,* 326–346.

Bruner, J. (1986). *Actual minds, possible worlds.* Cambridge, MA: Harvard University Press.

Bruner, J. (1990). *Acts of meaning.* Cambridge, MA: Harvard University Press.

Budoff, M. (1960). The relative utility of animal and human figures in a picture-story test for young children. *Journal of Projective Techniques, 24,* 347–352.

Byrd, E., & Witherspoon, R. L. (1954). Responses of preschool children to the Children's Apperception Test. *Child Development, 25,* 35–44.

Cantor, N., & Blanton, H. (1996). In P. M. Gollwitzer & J. A. Bargh (Eds.), *The psychology of action: Linking cognition and motivation to behavior* (pp. 338–359). New York: Guilford Press.

Cantor, N., & Sanderson, C. A. (1999). Life task participation and well-being: The importance of taking part in daily life. In D. Kahneman & E. Diener (Eds.), *Well-being: The foundations of hedonic psychology* (pp. 230–243). New York: Russell Sage Foundation.

Caplan, R., Guthrie, D., Fish, B., Tanguay, P. E., & David-Lando, G. (1989). The Kiddie Formal Thought Disorder Rating Scale: Clinical assessment, reliability and validity. *American Academy of Child and Adolescent Psychiatry, 28,* 408–416.

Carlson, R., & Arthus, N. (1999). Play therapy and the therapeutic use of story. *Canadian Journal of Counseling, 33,* 212–226.

Carver, S., Scheier, M. F., & Weintraub, J. K. (1989). Assessing coping strategies: A theoretically based approach. *Journal of Personality and Social Psychology, 56,* 267–283.

Chandler, L. A., Shermis, M. D., & Lempert, M. E. (1989). The need threat analysis: A scoring system for the Children's Apperception Test. *Psychology in the Schools, 26,* 47–54.

Cicchetti, D., Ackerman, B. P., & Izard, C. E. (1995). Emotions and emotion regulation in developmental psychopathology. *Development and Psychopathology, 7,* 1–10.

Clark, D. A., Beck, A. T., & Alford, B. A. (1999). *Scientific foundations of cognitive theory and therapy of depression.* New York: John Wiley & Sons.

Cohen, H., & Weil, G. R. (1975). *Tasks of emotional development: A projective test for children and adolescents.* Boston: Tasks of Emotional Development (T.E.D.) Associates.

Cole, P. M., Michel, M. K., & Teti, L. O. (1994). The development of emotion regulation and dysregulation: A clinical perspective. *Monographs of the Society for Research in Child Development, 59,* 73–100.

Constantino, G., & Malgady, R. C. (1983). Verbal fluency of Hispanic, Black and White children on TAT and TEMAS, a new thematic apperception test. *Hispanic Journal of Behavioral Sciences, 5,* 199–206.

Constantino, G., Malgady, R. C., & Rogler, L. H. (1988). *Tell-Me-A-Story, Manual.* Los Angeles: Western Psychological Services.

Constantino, G., Malgady, R. C., Rogler, L. H., & Tsui, E. C. (1988). Discriminant analysis of clinical outpatients and public school children by TEMAS: A thematic apperception test for Hispanics and Blacks. *Journal of Personality Assessment, 52,* 670–678.

Cooper, A. (1981). A basic TAT set for adolescent males. *Journal of Clinical Psychology, 37,* 411–415.

Cornblatt, B. A., & Erlenmeyer-Kimling, L. (1985). Global attentional deviance in children at risk for schizophrenia: Specificity and predictive validity. *Journal of Abnormal Psychology, 94,* 470–486.

Cramer, P. (1987). The development of defense mechanisms. *Journal of Personality, 55,* 597–614.

Cramer, P. (1991). *The development of defense mechanisms: Theory, research, and assessment.* New York: Springer.

Cramer, P. (1996). *Storytelling, narrative and the Thematic Apperception Test.* New York: Guilford Press.

Crick, N. R., & Dodge, K. A. (1994). A review and reformulation of social information processing mechanisms in children's adjustment. *Psychological Bulletin, 115,* 74–101.

Crick, N. R., & Dodge, K. A. (1996). Social information processing mechanisms in reactive and proactive aggression. *Child Development, 67,* 993–1002.

Dana, R. H. (1982). *A human science model for personality assessment with projective techniques.* Springfield, IL: Charles C. Thomas.

Dana, R. H. (1996). Culturally competent assessment practice in the United States. *Journal of Personality Assessment, 66,* 472–487.

Deary, I. J., & Stough, C. (1996). Intelligence and inspection time: Achievements, prospects, and problems. *American Psychologist, 51,* 599–608.

DeCharms, R. (1992). Personal causation and the origin concept. In C. P. Smith (Ed.), *Motivation and personality: Handbook of thematic content analysis* (pp. 325–333). New York: Cambridge University Press.

Deci, E. L., Eghrari, H., Patrick, B. C., & Leone, D. R. (1994). Facilitating internalization: The self-determination theory perspective. *Journal of Personality, 62,* 119–142.

Deci, E. L., & Ryan, R. M. (1985). *Intrinsic motivation and self-determination in human behavior.* New York: Plenum Press.

Deci, E. L., & Ryan, R. M. (1991). A motivational approach to self: Integration in personality. In E. Dienstbier (Ed.), *Nebraska symposium on motivation* (pp. 237–288). Lincoln: University of Nebraska Press.

Demorest, A. P., & Alexander, I. E. (1992). Affective scripts as organizers of personal experience. *Journal of Personality, 60,* 645–663.

Denckla, M. B. (1994). Measurement of executive function. In G. R. Lyon (Ed.), *Frames of reference for the assessment of learning disabilities: New views on measurement issues* (pp. 117–142). Baltimore, MD: Brookes.

Derry, S. J. (1996). Cognitive schema theory and the constructivist debate. *Educational Psychologist, 31,* 163–174.

Derryberry, D., & Rothbart, M. K. (1988). Arousal affect and attention as components of temperament. *Journal of Personality and Social Psychology, 55,* 958–966.

Doane, J. A., Miklowitz, D. J., Oranchak, E., & Flores de Apodaca, R. (1989). Parental communication deviance and schizophrenia: A cross-cultural comparison of Mexican- and Anglo-Americans. *Journal of Abnormal Psychology, 98,* 487–490.

Dodge, K. A., & Price, J. M. (1994). On the relation between social information processing and socially competent behavior in early school-aged children. *Child Development, 65,* 1385–1897.

Downey, G., Lebolt, A., Rincon, C., & Freitas, A. L. (1998). Rejection sensitivity and children's interpersonal difficulties. *Child Development, 69,* 1074–1091.

Dunn, J. (1991). Young children's understanding of other people: Evidence from observations within the family. In D. Frye & C. Moore (Eds.), *Children's theory of mind: Mental states and social understanding* (pp. 97–114). Hillsdale, NJ: Erlbaum.

Dweck, C. S. (1986). Motivational processes affecting learning. *American Psychologist, 41,* 1040–1048.

Dweck, C. S. (1996). Implicit theories as organizers of goals and behaviors. In P. M. Gollwitzer & J. A. Bargh (Eds.), *The psychology of action: Linking cognition and motivation to behavior* (pp. 69–90). New York: Guilford Press.

Eagle, C. J., & Schwartz, L. (1994). *Psychological portraits of adolescents.* New York: Lexington Books.

Ehrenreich, J. H. (1990). Quantitative studies of responses elicited by selected TAT cards. *Psychological Reports, 67,* 15–18.

Eisenberg, N., Fabes, R. A., Murphy, B., & Maszk, P. (1995). The role of emotionality and regulation in children's social functioning: A longitudinal study. *Child Development, 66,* 1360–1384.

Eisenberg, N., Wentzel, N. M., & Harris, J. D. (1998). The role of emotionality and regulation in empathy-related responding. *School Psychology Review, 27,* 506–521.

Elias, M. J., & Tobias, S. E. (1996). *Social problem solving: Interventions in the schools.* New York: Guilford Press.

Epstein, S. (1994). Integration of the cognitive and psychodynamic unconscious. *American Psychologist, 49,* 709–724.

Epstein, S., & Pacini, R. (1999). Some basic issues regarding dual-process theories from the perspective of cognitive-experiential self-theory. In S. Chaiken & Y. Trope (Eds.), *Dual process theories in social psychology* (pp. 462–482). New York: Guilford Press.

Fairbairn, W. R. D. (1952). *Psychoanalytic studies of the personality.* New York: Basic Books.

Fairbairn, W. R. D. (1954). *An object-relations theory of the personality.* New York: Basic Books.

Fish, S., & Ritvo, E. R. (1979). Psychoses of childhood. In J. D. Noshpitz (Ed.), *Basic handbook of child psychiatry* (pp. 249–304). New York: Basic Books.

Fiske, A. P., Haslam, N., & Fiske, S. T. (1991). Confusing one person with another: What errors reveal about the elementary forms of social relations. *Journal of Personality and Social Psychology, 60,* 656–674.

Fiske, S. T., & Taylor, S. (1991). *Social cognition* (2nd ed.). New York: McGraw Hill.

Fitzgerald, B. J., Pasewark, R. A., & Fleisher, S. (1974). Responses of an aged population on the Gerontological and Thematic Apperception Tests. *Journal of Personality Assessment, 38,* 234–235.

Flanagan, R. E., & DiGiuseppe, R. (1999). Critical review of the TEMAS: A step within the development of thematic apperception instruments. *Psychology in the Schools, 36,* 21–30.

Flavell, J. H. (1963). *The developmental psychology of Jean Piaget.* Princeton: Van Nostrand.

Flavell, J. H. (1988). The development of children's knowledge about the mind: From cognitive connections to mental representations. In J. W. Astington, P. L. Harris, & D. R. Olson (Eds.), *Developing theories of mind* (pp. 244–267). New York: Cambridge University Press.

Foa, E. B., & Kozak, M. J. (1991). Emotional processing: Theory, research, and clinical implications for anxiety disorders. In J. D. Safran & L. S. Greenberg (Eds.), *Emotion, psychotherapy, and change* (pp. 21–49). New York: Guilford Press.

Folkman, S. (1984). Personal control and stress and coping processes: A theoretical analysis. *Journal of Personality and Social Psychology, 46,* 839–852.

Folkman, S., & Lazarus, R. S. (1980). An analysis of coping in a middle-aged community sample. *Journal of Health and Social Behavior, 21,* 219–239.

Folkman, S., & Lazarus, R. S. (1986). Stress processes and depressive symptomatology. *Journal of Abnormal Psychology, 95,* 107–113.

Folkman, S., & Lazarus, R. S. (1988). The relationship between coping and emotion: Implications for theory and research. *Social Science and Medicine, 26,* 309–317.

Ford, D. H. (1994). *Humans as self-constructing living systems: A developmental perspective on behavior and personality* (2nd ed.). State College, PA: Ideals.

Frank, L. D. (1939). Projective methods for the study of personality. *Journal of Psychology, 8,* 389–413.

Frank, L. D. (1948). *Projective Methods.* Springfield, IL: Thomas.

French, L. A. (1993). Adapting projective tests for minority children. *Psychological Reports, 72,* 15–18.

French, J., Graves, P. D., & Levitt, E. E. (1983). Objective and projective testing of children. In C. E. Walker & M. C. Roberts, *Handbook of clinical child psychology* (pp. 209–247). New York: John Wiley & Sons.

Freud, S. (1952). *A general introduction to psychoanalysis.* New York: Washington Square Press.

Freud, S. (1961). The ego and the id. In J. Strachey (Ed. and Trans.), *The standard edition of the complete psychological works of Sigmund Freud* (Vol. 19, pp. 3–66). London: Hogarth Press. (Original work published 1923).

Frick, P. J., & Lahey, B. B. (1991). The nature and characteristics of Attention-deficit Hyperactivity Disorder. *School Psychology Review, 20,* 163–173.

Frijda, N. H. (1986). *The emotions.* Cambridge: Cambridge University Press.

Frye, D. (1991). The origin of intention in infancy. In D. Frye & C. Moore (Eds.), *Children's theories of mind: Mental states and social understanding* (pp. 15–38). Hillsdale, NJ: Erlbaum.

Gardner, D. R., & Holmes, C. B. (1990). Comparison of the CAT and CAT-H with third grade boys and girls. *Psychological Reports, 66,* 922.

Gardner, H. (1991). *The unschooled mind: How children think and how schools should teach.* New York: Basic Books.

Gardner, R. A. (1971). *Therapeutic communication with children: The mutual story telling technique.* New York: Science House.

Gieser, L., & Stein, M. I. (Eds.). (1999). *Evocative images: The Thematic Apperception Test and the art of projection.* Washington, DC: American Psychological Association.

Glass, C. R., & Arnkoff, D. B. (1997). Questionnaire methods of cognitive self-statement assessment. *Journal of Consulting and Clinical Psychology, 65,* 911–927.

Goldfried, M. R., Greenberg, L. S., & Marmar, C. (1990). Individual psychotherapy: Process and outcome. *Annual Review of Psychology, 41,* 659–688.

Gollwitzer, P. M. (1993). Goal achievement: The role of intentions. In W. Stroebe & M. Hewstone (Eds.), *European review of social psychology* (Vol. 4, pp. 141–185). London: John Wiley & Sons.

Gollwitzer, P. M. (1996). The volitional benefits of planning. In P. M. Gollwitzer & J. A. Bargh (Eds.), *The psychology of action: Linking cognition and motivation to behavior* (pp. 287–312). New York: Guilford Press.

Gollwitzer, P. M. (1999). Implementation intentions: Strong effects of simple plans. *American Psychologist, 54,* 493–503.

Gollwitzer, P. M., & Kichhof, D. (1999). The willful pursuit of identity. In J. Heckhausen & C. S. Dweck (Eds.), *Motivation and self-regulation across the life span* (pp. 389–423). New York: Cambridge University Press.

Gollwitzer, P. M., & Moskowitz, G. B. (1996). Goal effects on action and cognition. In E. T. Higgins & A. W. Kruglanski (Eds.), *Social psychology: Handbook of basic principles* (pp. 361–399). New York: Guilford Press.

Gray, J. A. (1987). *The psychology of fear and stress* (2nd ed.). Cambridge: Cambridge University Press.

Greenberg, L. S., Elliott, R., & Foerster, F. S. (1991). Experiential process in the psychotherapeutic treatment of depression. In D. McCann & N. Endler (Eds.), *Depression: Development in theory, research and practice* (pp. 157–185). Toronto: Thompson.

Greenberg, J., & Mitchell, S. (1983). *Object relations in psychoanalytic theory.* Cambridge, MA: Harvard University Press.

Greenberg, L. S., Rice, L. N., & Elliott, R. (1993). *Facilitating emotional change: The moment by moment process.* New York: Guilford Press.

Greenspan, S. J. (1997). *The growth of the mind and the endangered origins of intelligence.* Reading, MA: Addison-Wesley.

Gross, J. J. (1998). Antecedent and response-focused emotion regulation: Divergent consequences for experience, expression and physiology. *Journal of Personality and Social Psychology, 74,* 224–237.

Grych, J. H., & Fincham, F. D. (1990). Marital conflict and children's adjustment: A cognitive-contextual framework. *Psychological Bulletin, 108,* 267–290.

Guidano, V. F. (1995). Constructivist psychotherapy: A theoretical framework. In R. A. Neimeyer & M. J. Mahoney (Eds.), *Constructivism in psychotherapy* (pp. 93–110). Washington, DC: American Psychological Association.

Guntrip, H. (1968). *Schizoid phenomena, object relations and the self.* New York: International Universities Press.

Guntrip, H. (1974). Psychoanalytic object relations theory. The Fairbairn-Guntrip approach. In S. Arieti (Ed.), *American handbook of psychiatry* (Vol. 1, pp. 828–842). New York: Basic Books.

Hammer, D. (1996). Misconceptions or p-prisms: How may alternative perspectives of cognitive structure influence instructional perceptions and intentions? *Journal of the Learning Sciences, 5,* 97–127.

Harris, P. L., Olthof, T., & Terwogt, M. M. (1981). Children's knowledge of emotion. *Journal of Child Psychology and Psychiatry and Allied Disciplines, 22,* 247–261.

Harter, S., & Monsour, A. (1992). Developmental analysis of conflict caused by opposing attributes in the adolescent self-portrait. *Developmental Psychology, 28,* 251–260.

Hartman, A. A. (1970). A basic TAT set. *Journal of Projective Techniques and Personality Assessment, 34,* 391–396.

Hatt, C. V. (1985). Review of the Children's Apperception Test. In J. V. Mitchell (Ed.), *The Ninth Mental Measurements Yearbook* (pp. 314–316). Lincoln, NE: Buros Institute of Mental Health.

Haworth, M. R. (1963). A schedule for the analysis of CAT responses. *Journal of Projective Techniques and Personality Assessment, 27,* 181–184.

Haworth, M. R. (1966). *The CAT: Facts about fantasy.* New York: Grune & Stratton.

Haynes, J. P., & Peltier, J. (1985). Patterns of practice with TAT in juvenile forensic settings. *Journal of Personality Assessment, 49,* 26–29.

Henderson, H. A., & Fox, N. A. (1998). Inhibited and uninhibited children: Challenges in school settings. *School Psychology Review, 27,* 492–505.

Henry, W. E. (1956). *The analysis of fantasy: The Thematic Apperception Technique in the study of personality.* New York: John Wiley & Sons.

Hermans, H. J., Kempen, H. J., & Van Loon, R. J. (1992). The dialogical self: Beyond individualism and rationalism. *American Psychologist, 47,* 23–33.

Higgins, E. T. (1987). Self-discrepancy: A theory relating self and affect. *Psychological Review, 94,* 319–340.

Higgins, E. T. (1991). Expanding the law of cognitive structure activation: The role of knowledge applicability. *Psychological Inquiry, 2,* 192–193.

Hoar, M. W., & Faust, W. L. (1973). The Children's Apperception Test: Puzzle and regular form. *Journal of Personality Assessment, 37,* 244–247.

Hoffman, M. L. (1982). Affect and moral development. In D. Cicchetti & P. Hesse (Eds.), *Emotional development* (pp. 83–103). San Francisco: Jossey-Bass.

Hollon, S. D., & Kendall, P. C. (1980). Cognitive self-statements in depression: Development of an automatic thoughts questionnaire. *Cognitive Therapy and Research, 4,* 383–395.

Hollon, S. D., Kendall, P. C., & Lumry, A. (1986). Specificity of depressotypic cognitions in clinical depression. *Journal of Abnormal Psychology, 95,* 52–59.

Holmstrom, R. W., Silber, D. E., & Karp, S. A. (1990). Development of the Apperceptive Personality Test. *Journal of Personality Assessment, 54,* 252–264.

Holt, R. R. (1958). Formal aspects of the TAT: A neglected resource. *Journal of Projective Techniques, 22,* 163–172.

Holt, R. R. (1961). The nature of TAT stories as cognitive products: A psychoanalytic approach. In J. Kagan & G. Lesser (Eds.), *Contemporary issues in thematic apperceptive methods* (pp. 3–40). Springfield, IL: Charles C. Thomas.

Holt, R. R. (1978). *Methods in clinical psychology, Vol. I: Projective assessment.* New York: Plenum Press.

Horney, K. (1950). *Neurosis and human growth; the struggle toward self-realization.* New York: W. W. Norton.

Horowitz, M. J. (1991). States, schemas, and control: General theories for psychotherapy integration. *Journal of Psychotherapy Integration, 1,* 85–102.

Howard, G. S. (1991). A narrative approach to thinking, cross-cultural psychology, and psychotherapy. *American Psychologist, 46,* 187–197.

Hunt, E. B. (1980). Intelligence as an information-processing concept. *British Journal of Psychology, 71,* 449–474.

Hurley, A. D., & Sovner, R. (1985). The use of Thematic Apperception Tests in mentally retarded persons. *Psychiatric Aspects of Mental Retardation Reviews, 4,* 9–12.

Ingram, R. E., & Kendall, P. C. (1986). Cognitive clinical psychology: Implications of an information-processing perspective. In R. E. Ingram (Ed.), *Information processing approaches to clinical psychology* (pp. 3–21). New York: Academic Press.

Isen, A. M. (1993). Positive affect and decision making. In M. Lewis & J. M. Haviland (Eds.), *Handbook of emotions* (pp. 261–278). New York: Guilford Press.

Isen, A. M., & Means, B. (1983). The influence of positive affect on decision-making strategy. *Social Cognition, 2,* 18–31.

James, W. (1890). *The principles of psychology.* New York: Henry Holt.

Johnston, J. L. (1994). The Thematic Apperception Test and Alzheimer's disease. *Journal of Personality Assessment, 62,* 314–319.

Johnston, M. H., & Holzman, P. S. (1979). *Assessing schizophrenic thinking: A clinical and research instrument for measuring thought disorder.* San Francisco: Jossey-Bass.

Karoly, P. (1993). Mechanisms of self-regulation: A systems view. *Annual Review of Psychology, 44,* 23–52.

Karon, B. P. (1981). The Thematic Apperception Test (TAT). In A. J. Rabin (Ed.), *Assessment with projective techniques: A concise introduction* (pp. 85–120). New York: Springer.

Kasser, T., & Ryan, R. M. (1996a). A dark side of the American dream: Correlates of financial success as a central life aspiration. *Journal of Personality and Social Psychology, 65,* 410–422.

Kasser, T., & Ryan, R. M. (1996b). Further examining the American dream: Differential correlates of intrinsic and extrinsic goals. *Personality and Social Psychology Bulletin, 22,* 280–287.

Katz, H. E., Russ, S. W., & Overholser, J. W. (1993). Sex differences, sex roles, and projection on the TAT: Matching stimulus to examinee gender. *Journal of Personality Assessment, 60,* 186–191.

Keiser, R. E., & Prather, E. N. (1990). What is the TAT? A review of ten years of research. *Journal of Personality Assessment, 55,* 800–803.

Kelly, F. D. (1996). *Object relations in younger children: Rorschach and TAT measures.* Springfield, Il: Charles C. Thomas.

Kelly, F. D. (1997). *The assessment of object relations phenomena in adolescents.* Mahwah, NJ: Erlbaum.

Kelly, G. A. (1958). The theory and technique of assessment. In P. R. Farnsworth & Q. McNemar (Eds.), *Annual Review of Psychology, 9,* (pp. 323–352). Palo Alto, CA: Annual Reviews.

Kendall, P. C. (1993). Cognitive-behavioral therapies with youth: Guiding theory, current status, and emerging developments. *Journal of Consulting and Clinical Psychology, 61,* 235–247.

Kenny, D. T., & Bijou, S. W. (1953). Ambiguity of pictures and extent of personality factors in fantasy responses. *Journal of Consulting and Clinical Psychology, 17,* 283–288.

Kernberg, O. (1975a). *Borderline conditions and pathological narcissism.* New York: Jason Aronson.

Kernberg, O. (1975b). *Object relations theory and clinical psychoanalysis.* New York: Jason Aronson.

Kihlstrom, J. F. (1987). The cognitive unconscious. *Science, 237,* 1445–1452.

Kihlstrom, J. F., & Cantor, N. (1984). Mental representation of the self. In L. Berkowitz (Ed.), *Advances in experimental and social psychology* (Vol. 17, pp. 1–47). New York: Academic Press.

Kitron, D. G., & Benzimen, H. (1990). The Children's Apperception test: Possible applications for adults. *Israel Journal of Psychiatry and Related Services, 27,* 29–47.

Klein, M. (1932). *The psychoanalysis of children.* New York: Grove Press.

Klein, M. (1948). *Contributions to psychoanalysis. 1921–1945.* London: Hogarth Press.

Kline, P., & Svaste-Xuto, B. (1981). The responses of Thai and British children to the Children's Apperception Test. *Journal of Social Psychology, 113,* 137–138.

Koestner, R., Weinberger, J., & McClelland, D. C. (1991). Task-intrinsic and social-extrinsic sources of arousal for motives assessed in fantasy and self-report. *Journal of Personality, 59,* 57–82.

Kohut, H. (1977). *The restoration of the self.* New York: International Universities Press.

Kroon, N., Goudena, P. P., & Rispens, J. (1998). Thematic Apperception Tests for child and adolescent assessment: A practitioner's guide. *Journal of Psychoeducational Assessment, 16,* 99–117.

Kuhl, J. (1984). Volitional aspects of achievement motivation and learned helplessness: Toward a comprehensive theory of action-control. In B. A. Maher (Ed.), *Progress in experimental personality research* (Vol. 13, pp. 99–171). New York: Academic Press.

Kuhl, J. (1992). A theory of self-regulation: Action versus state orientation, self-discrimination, and some applications. *Applied Psychology: An International Review, 41,* 97–129.

Kuhl, J. (1996). Who controls whom when "I control myself"? *Psychological Inquiry, 7,* 61–68.

Kuhl, J., & Fuhrmann, A. (1998). Decomposing self-regulation and self-control: The Volitional Components Inventory. In J. Heckhausen & C. S. Dweck (Eds.), *Motivation and self-regulation across the life span* (pp. 15–47). New York: Cambridge University Press.

Lazarus, R. S. (1991a). *Emotion and adaptation.* New York: Oxford University Press.

Lazarus, R. S. (1991b). Progress on a cognitive-motivational-relational theory of emotion. *American Psychologist, 46,* 819–834.

Lazarus, R. S. (1991c). Psychological stress in the workplace. *Journal of Social Behavior and Personality, 6,* 1–13.

Lazarus, R. S. (1994). Meaning and emotional development. In P. Ekman & R. J. Davidson (Eds.), *The nature of emotion: Fundamental questions* (163–171). New York: Oxford University Press.

Lazarus, R. S., & Folkman, S. (1984). *Stress, appraisal, and copying.* New York: Springer Publishing Co.

Lehmann, I. J. (1959). Responses of kindergarten children to the Children's Apperception Test. *Journal of Clinical Psychology, 15,* 60–63.

Leigh, J., Westen, D., Barends, A., & Mendel, M. J. (1992). The assessment of complexity of representations of people using TAT and interview data. *Journal of Personality, 60,* 809–837.

Levine, M. D., Gordon, B. N., & Reed, M. S. (1987). *Developmental variation and learning disorders.* Cambridge, MA: Educators Publishing Service.

Levine, M. (1987). *Developmental variation and learning disorders.* Cambridge, MA: Educators Publishing Service.

Light, B. H. (1954). Comparative study of a series of TAT and CAT cards. *Journal of Clinical Psychology, 17,* 281–297.

Lindzey, G. (1952). Thematic Apperception Test: Interpretive assumptions and related empirical evidence. *Psychological Bulletin, 49,* 1–25.

Linville, P. W. (1987). Self-complexity as a cognitive buffer against stress-related illness and depression. *Journal of Personality and Social Psychology, 52,* 663–676.

Locke, G. P., & Latham, E. A. (1990). Self-regulation through goal setting. *Organizational Behavior and Human Decision Processes, 50,* 212–247.

Locraft, C., & Teglasi, H. (1997). Teacher rated empathic behavior and children's TAT stories. *Journal of School Psychology, 35,* 217–237.

Lundy, A. (1985). The reliability of the Thematic Apperception Test. *Journal of Personality Assessment, 49,* 141–149.

Lutz, C., & White, G. M. (1986). The anthropology of emotions. *Annual Review of Anthropology, 15,* 405–436.

Mahler, M. S. (1966). Some preliminary notes on the development of basic moods, including depression. *Canadian Psychiatric Association Journal, 11* (Suppl.), 250–258.

Mahler, M. S., Pine, F., & Bergman, A. (1975). *The psychological birth of the human infant.* New York: Basic Books.

Mancuso, J. C., & Sarbin, T. R. (1998). The narrative construction of emotional life: Developmental aspects. In M. F. Manscolo & S. Griffin (Eds.), *What develops in emotional development? Emotions, personality, and psychotherapy* (pp. 297–316). New York: Plenum Press.

Mandler, J. M. (1982). Recent research on story grammars. *Language and Communication, 15,* 207–218.

Markus, H., & Nurius, P. (1986). Possible selves. *American Psychologist, 41,* 954–969.

Martin, L. L., & Tesser, A. (1989). Toward a motivational and structural theory of ruminative thought. In J. S. Uleman & J. A. Bargh (Eds.), *Unintended thought* (pp. 306–326). New York: Guilford Press.

Masling, J. M., & Bornstein, R. F. (Eds.). (1994). *Empirical perspectives on object relations theory.* Washington, DC: American Psychological Association.

Mathews, A., & MacLeod, C. (1994). Cognitive approaches to emotion and emotion disorders. *Annual Review of Psychology, 45,* 25–50.

Mayman, M. (1967). Object-representations and object-relationships in Rorschach responses. *Journal of Projective Techniques and Personality Assessment, 31,* 17–24.

McAdams, D. P. (1993). *The stories we live by: Personal myths and the making of the self.* New York: Morrow.

McAdams, D. P., Diamond, A., de St. Aubin, E., & Mansfield, E. (1997). Stories of commitment: The psychosocial construction of generative lives. *Journal of Personality and Social Psychology, 72,* 678–694.

McArthur, D. S., & Roberts, G. E. (1982). *Roberts Apperception Test for Children Manual.* Los Angeles: Western Psychological Services.

McArthur, L. Z., & Baron, R. M. (1983). Toward an ecological theory of social perception. *Psychological Review, 90,* 215–238.

McClelland, D. C. (1987). *Human motivation.* New York: Cambridge University Press.

McClelland, D. C., Atkinson, J. W., Clark, L. A., & Lowell, E. L. (1953). *The achievement motive.* New York: Appleton-Century Crofts.

McClelland, D. C., & Koestner, R. (1992). The achievement motive. In C. P. Smith (Ed.), *Motivation and personality: Handbook of thematic content analysis* (pp. 143–152). New York: Cambridge University Press.

McClelland, D. C., Koestner, R., & Weinberger, J. (1989). How do self-attributed and implicit motives differ? *Psychological Review, 96,* 690–702.

McGrew, M. W., & Teglasi, H. (1990). Formal characteristics of Thematic Apperception Test stories as indices of emotional disturbance in children. *Journal of Personality Assessment, 54,* 639–655.

Meissner, W. W. (1971). Notes on identification. II. Clarification of related concepts. *Psychoanalytic Quarterly, 40,* 277–302.

Meissner, W. W. (1972). Notes on identification. III. The concept of identification. *Psychoanalytic Quarterly, 41,* 224–260.

Meissner, W. W. (1974). Differentiation and integration of learning and identification in the developmental process. *Annual of Psychoanalysis, 2,* 181–196.

Meissner, W. W. (1981). Internalization and psychoanalysis. *Psychological Issues Monograph, 50.* New York: International Universities Press.

Meltzoff, A. (1995). Understanding the intentions of others: Re-enactment of intended acts by 18-month-old children. *Developmental Psychology, 31,* 838–850.

Messick, S. (1989). Validity. In R. L. Linn (Ed.), *Educational measurement* (3rd ed., pp. 13–103). New York: MacMillan.

Mirsky, A. F., Anthony, B. J., Duncan, C. C., Ahearn, M. B., & Kellam, S. G. (1991). Analysis of the elements of attention: A neuropsychological approach. *Neuropsychology Review, 2,* 109–145.

Mischel, W. (1968). *Personality and assessment.* New York: Wiley.

Moore, S., & Gullone, E. (1996). Predicting adolescent risk behavior using a personalized cost-benefit analysis. *Journal of Youth and Adolescence, 25,* 343–359.

Morgan, C. D., & Murray, H. H. (1935). A method for investigating fantasies: The thematic apperception test. *Archives of Neurology and Psychiatry, 34,* 289–306.

Morgan, W. G. (1995). Origin and history of the Thematic Apperception Test images. *Journal of Personality Assessment, 65,* 237–252.

Muraven, M., Tice, D. M., & Baumeister, R. F. (1998). Self-control as limited resource: Regulatory depletion patterns. *Journal of Personality and Social Psychology, 74,* 774–789.

Murray, H. A. (1938). *Explorations in personality.* New York: Oxford University Press.

Murray, H. A. (1943). *Thematic Apperception Test manual.* Cambridge, MA: Harvard University Press.

Murstein, B. I. (1963). *Theories and research in projective techniques: Emphasizing the TAT.* New York: Wiley.

Murstein, B. I. (1965). The stimulus. In B. Murstein (Ed.), *Handbook of projective techniques.* New York: Basic Books.

Murstein, B. I. (1968). The effect of stimulus, background, personality, and scoring system on the manifestation of hostility on the TAT. *Journal of Consulting and Clinical Psychology, 32,* 355–365.

Myler, B., Rosenkrantz, A., & Holmes, G. (1972). A comparison of the TAT, CAT, and CAT-H among second grade girls. *Journal of Personality Assessment, 36,* 440–444.

Nannis, E. D. (1988). Cognitive-developmental differences in emotional understanding. *New Directions for Child Development, 39,* 31–49.

Neuringer, C., & Livesay, R. C. (1970). Projective fantasy on the CAT and CAT-H. *Journal of Projective Techniques and Personality Assessment, 34,* 487–491.

Newmark, C. S., & Flouranzano, R. (1973). Replication of an empirically derived TAT set with hospitalized psychiatric patients, *Journal of Personality Assessment, 37,* 340–341.

Newmark, C. S., Hetzel, W., & Freking, R. A. (1974). The effects of personality tests on state and trait anxiety. *Journal of Personality Assessment, 38,* 17–20.

Newmark, C. S., Wheeler, D., Newmark, L., & Stabler, B. (1975). Test induced anxiety with children. *Journal of Personality Assessment, 39,* 409–413.

Nolen-Hoeksema, S. (1999). Ruminative coping with depression. In J. Heckhausern & C. S. Dweck (Eds.), *Motivation and self-regulation across the life span* (pp. 237–256). New York: Cambridge University Press.

Oatley, K. (1992). Integrative action of narrative. In D. J. Stein & J. E. Young (Eds.), *Cognitive science and clinical disorders* (pp. 151–172). San Diego, CA: Academic Press.

Oppenheim, D., Emde, R. N., & Warren, S. (1997). Children's narrative representations of mothers: Their development and associations with child and mother adaptation. *Child Development, 68,* 127–138.

Parry, A., & Doan, R. E. (1994). *Story re-visions: Narrative therapy in the post-modern world.* New York: Guilford Press.

Pasewark, R. A., Fitzgerald, B. J., Dexter, V., & Cangemi, A. (1976). Responses of adolescents, middle-aged, and aged females on the Gerontological and Thematic Apperception Tests. *Journal of Personality Assessment, 40,* 588–591.

Pennebaker, J. W. (1990). Stream of consciousness and stress: Levels of thinking. In J. S. Uleman & J. A. Bargh (Eds.), *Unintended thought* (pp. 327–350). New York: Guilford Press.

Peterson, C. A. (1990). Administration of the Thematic Apperception Test: Contributions of psychoanalytic psychotherapy. *Journal of Contemporary Psychotherapy, 20,* 191–200.

Peterson, C. A., & Schilling, K. M. (1983). Card pull in projective testing. *Journal of Personality Assessment, 47,* 265–275.

Piaget, J. (1954). *The construction of reality in the child.* New York: Basic Books.

Piaget, J. (1965). *The moral judgment of the child.* New York: Free Press.

Premack, D. (1992). On the origins of domain-specific primitives. In H. L. Pick & P. W. van den Broek (Eds.), *Cognition: Conceptual and methodological issues* (pp. 189–212). Washington, DC: American Psychological Association.

Premack, D., & Woodruff, G. (1978). Does the chimpanzee have a theory of mind? *The Behavioral and Brain Sciences, 1,* 515–526.

Procidano, M. E., & Guinta, D. M. (1989). Object representations and symptomatology: Preliminary findings in young adult psychiatric inpatients. *Journal of Clinical Psychology, 45,* 309–316.

Rabin, A. I., & Haworth, M. R. (1960). *Projective techniques with children.* New York: Grune & Stratton.

Rappaport, D. (1947). The scoring and analysis of the Thematic Apperception Test. *Journal of Psychology, 24,* 319–330.

Rappaport, D., Gill, M., & Schafer, R. (1975). *Diagnostic psychological testing* (Rev. ed.). New York: International Universities Press.

Raynor, J. O., & McFarlin, D. B. (1986). Motivation and the self-system. In R. M. Sorrentino & E. T. Higgins (Eds.), *Handbook of motivation and cognition: Foundations of social behavior* (pp. 315–349). New York: Guilford Press.

Rehm, L. P., & Plakosh, P. (1975). Preference for immediate reinforcement in depression. *Journal of Behavior Therapy and Experimental Psychiatry, 6,* 101–103.

Ritzler, B. A., Sharkey, K. J., & Chudy, J. F. (1980). A comprehensive projective alternative to the TAT. *Journal of Personality Assessment, 44,* 358–362.

Rogers, C. R. (1951). *Client-centered therapy; its current practice, implications, and theory.* Boston: Houghton Mifflin.

Ronan, G. F., Colavito, V. A., & Hammontree, S. R. (1993). Personal problem-solving system for scoring TAT responses: Preliminary validity and reliability data. *Journal of Personality Assessment, 61,* 28–40.

Ronan, G. F., Date, A. L., & Weisbrod, M. (1995). Personal problem-solving scoring of the TAT: Sensitivity to training. *Journal of Personality Assessment, 64,* 119–131.

Rothbart, M. K., & Bates, J. E. (1998). Temperament. In N. Eisenberg (Ed.), *Handbook of Child Development* (pp. 105–176).

Rothbart, M. K., Derryberry, D., & Posner, M. (1994). A psychobiological approach to the development of temperament. In J. E. Bates & T. D. Wachs (Eds.), *Temperament: Individual differences at the interface of biology and behavior* (pp. 83–116). Washington, DC: American Psychological Association.

Rothbart, M. K., & Posner, M. J. (1985). Temperament and the development of self-regulation. In L. C. Hartlage & C. F. Telzrow (Eds.), *The neuropsychology of individual difference: A developmental perspective.* New York: Plenum Press.

Rothbart, M. K., Ziaie, H. & O'Boyle, C. G. (1992). Self-regulation and emotion in infancy. In N. Eisenberg & R. A. Fabes (Eds.), *Emotion and Its Regulation in Early Development: New Directions for Child Development, 55* (pp. 7–24). San Francisco: Jossey-Bass.

Rubin, K. H., Coplan, R. J., Fox, N. A., & Calkins, S. D. (1995). Emotionality, emotion regulation, and pre-schoolers' social adaptation. *Development and Psychopathology, 7,* 49–62.

Rund, B. R. (1986). Communication deviance in parents of schizophrenics. *Family Process, 25,* 133–147.

Russ, S. W. (1998). Teaching child assessment from a developmental-psycho dynamic framework. In L. Handler & M. J. Hilsenroth (Eds.), *Teaching and learning personality assessment* (pp. 453–468). Mahwah, NJ: Erlbaum.

Russell, J. (1984). The subject-object division in language acquisition and ego development. *New Ideas in Psychology, 2,* 57–74.

Russell, R. L., & van den Broek, P. (1988). A cognitive-developmental account of storytelling in child psychotherapy. In S. R. Shirk (Ed.), *Cognitive development and Child Psychotherapy,* (pp. 19–52). New York: Plenum.

Ryan, R. M., & Connell, J. P. (1989). Perceived locus of causality and internalization: Examining reasons for acting in two domains. *Journal of Personality and Social Psychology, 57,* 749–761.

Safran, J. D., & Greenberg, L. S. (1988). Feeling, thinking, and acting: A cognitive framework for psychotherapy integration. *Journal of Cognitive Psychotherapy, 2,* 109–131.

Salz, G., & Epstein, S. (1963). Thematic hostility and guilt responses as related to self-reported hostility, guilt, and conflict. *Journal of Abnormal and Social Psychology, 67,* 469–479.

Sandler, J. (1992). Reflections on developments in the theory of psychoanalytic technique. *International Journal of Psycho-Analysis, 73,* 189–198.

Sandler, J., & Rosenblatt, B. (1962). The concept of the representational world. *The Psychoanalytic Study of the Child, 17,* 128–145.

Santostefano, S. (1991). Coordinating outer space with inner self: Reflections on developmental psychopathology. In D. P. Keating & H. Rosen (Eds.), *Constructivist perspectives on developmental psychopathology and atypical development* (pp. 11–40). Hillsdale, NJ: Erlbaum.

Sappington, A. A., Russell, J. C., Triplett, V., & Goodwin, J. (1981). Self-efficiency expectancies, response-outcome expectancies, emotionally-based expectancies, and their relationship to avoidant behavior. *Journal of Clinical Psychology, 37,* 737–744.

Schafer, R. (1992). *Retelling a life: Narration and dialogue in psychoanalysis.* New York: Basic Books.

Schank, R. C. (1990). *Tell me a story: A new look at real and artificial memory.* New York: Charles Scribner's Sons.

Schank, R. C., & Abelson, R. P. (1977). *Scripts, plans, goals and understanding: An inquiry into human knowledge structures.* Hillsdale, NJ: Erlbaum.

Schneider, M. F. (1989). *Children's Apperceptive Storytelling Test.* Austin, TX: Pro-Ed.

Schroth, M. L. (1977). The use of the Associative Elaboration and Integration Scales for evaluating CAT protocols. *Journal of Psychology, 97,* 29–35.

Schwartz, L., & Eagle, C. J. (1986). *Psychological portraits of children.* Lexington, MA: Lexington Books.

Schwartz, J. C., & Pollack, P. R. (1977). Affect and delay of gratification. *Journal of Research in Personality, 7,* 384–394.

Schwartz, J. C., & Shaver, P. (1987). Emotions and emotion knowledge in interpersonal relations. In W. Jones & D. Perlman (Eds.), *Advances in personal relationships* (pp. 197–241). Greenwich, CT: JAI Press.

Shapiro, T., & Huebner, H. F. (1976). Speech patterns of five psychotic children now in adolescence. *Journal of the American Academy of Child Psychiatry, 15,* 278–293.

Shirk, S. R. (1998). Interpersonal schemata in child psychotherapy. *Journal of Clinical Child Psychology, 27,* 4–16.

Shirk, S. R., Boergers, J., Eason, A., & Van Horn, M. (1998). Dysphoric interpersonal schemata and preadolescents' sensitization to negative events. *Journal of Clinical Child Psychology, 27,* 54–68.

Shirk, S. R., & Russell, R. L. (1996). *Change processes in child psychotherapy: Revitalizing treatment and research.* New York: Guilford Press.

Shneidman, E. S. (1951). *Thematic test analysis.* New York: Grune & Stratton.

Shweder, R. A. (1994). "You're not sick, you're just in love": Emotion as an interpretive system. In P. Ekman and R. J. Davidson (Eds.), *The nature of emotion.* New York: Oxford University Press.

Singer, J. A., & Salovey, P. (1988). Mood and memory: Evaluating the Network Theory of Affect. *Clinical Psychology Review, 8,* 211–251.

Singer, J. A., & Salovey, P. (1991). Organized knowledge structures and personality. In M. J. Horowitz (Ed.), *Personal schemas and maladaptive interpersonal patterns* (pp. 33–80). Chicago: University of Chicago Press.

Singer, J. A., & Salovey, P. (1993). *The remembered self: Emotion and memory in personality.* New York: The Free Press.

Singer, J. L. (1981). Research applications of projective methods. In A. I. Rabin (Ed.), *Assessment with projective techniques* (pp. 297–331). New York: Springer.

Singer, M. T., & Wynne, L. C. (1966). Principles for scoring communication defects and deviances in parents of schizophrenics: Rorschach and TAT scoring manuals. *Psychiatry: Journal for the Study of Interpersonal Processes, 29,* 260–288.

Slemon, A. G., Holzwarth, E. J., Lewis, J., & Sitko, M. (1976). Associative elaboration and integration scales for evaluating TAT protocols. *Journal of Personality Assessment, 40,* 365–369.

Sloman, S. (1994). When explanations compete: The role of explanatory coherence on judgments of likelihood. *Cognition, 52,* 1–21.

Sloman, S. (1996). The empirical case for two systems of reasoning. *Psychological Review, 119,* 3–22.

Smith, C. P. (1992). Reliability issues. In J. W. Atkinson, D. C. McClelland, & J. Veroff (Eds.), *Motivation and personality: Handbook of thematic content analysis* (pp. 126–142). New York: Cambridge University Press.

Smolensky, P. (1988). On the proper treatment of connectionism. *Behavioral and Brain Sciences, 11,* 1–74.

Solomon, I. L., & Starr, B. (1968). *School Apperception Method (SAM).* New York: Springer.

Spangler, W. D. (1992). Validity of questionnaire and TAT measures of need for achievement. *Psychological Bulletin, 112,* 140–154.

Spear, W. E., & Lapidus, L. B. (1981). Qualitative differences in manifest object representations: Implications for a multi-dimensional model of psychological functioning. *Journal of Abnormal Psychology, 90,* 157–187.

Speers, R. W., McFarland, M. B., Arnaud, S. H., & Curry, N. E. (1971). Recapitulation of separation individuation processes when the normal three-year-old enters nursery school. In J. B. McDevitt & C. F. Settlage (Eds.), *Separation individuation: Essays in honor of Margaret Mahler* (pp. 297–321). New York: International Universities Press.

Spitz, H. H. (1988). Mental retardation as a thinking disorder: The rationalist alternative to empiricism. In N. Bray (Ed.), *International review of research in mental retardation* (Vol. 15, pp. 1–32). New York: Academic Press.

Stark, K. D., Rouse, L., & Livingston, R. (1991). Treatment of depression during childhood and adolescence: Cognitive-behavioral procedures for the individual and family. In P. C. Kendall (Ed.), *Child and adolescent therapy: Cognitive and behavioral procedures* (pp. 165–208). New York: Guilford Press.

Stein, D. J., & Young, J. E. (1992). Schema approach to personality disorders. In D. J. Stein, & J. E. Young (Eds.), *Cognitive science and clinical disorders,* San Diego, CA: Academic Press.

Stein, M. J. (1955). *The Thematic Apperception Test* (Rev. ed.). Cambridge, MA: Addison Wesley.

Strelau, J. (1983). A regulative theory of temperament. *Australian Journal of Psychology, 35,* 305–317.

Strelau, J. (1994). The concepts of arousal and arousability as used in temperament studies. In J. E. Bates & T. D. Wachs (Eds.), *Temperament: Individual differences at the interface of biology and behavior* (pp. 117–141). Washington, DC: American Psychological Association.

Streufert, S., & Nogami, G. Y. (1989). Cognitive style and complexity: Implications for I/O psychology. In C. L. Cooper, I. T. Robertson, et al. (Eds.), *International review of industrial and organizational psychology* (pp. 93–143). Chichester, England: John Wiley & Sons.

Streufert, S., & Swezey, R. W. (1986). *Complexity, managers, and organizations.* San Diego, CA: Academic Press.

Stricker, G., & Healy, B. J. (1990). Projective assessment of object relations: A review of the empirical literature. *Psychological Assessment: A Journal of Consulting and Clinical Psychology, 2,* 219–230.

Stuart, J., Westen, D., Lohr, N. E., & Benjamin, J. (1990). Object relations in borderlines, depressives, and normals: An examination of human responses on the Rorschach. *Journal of Personality Assessment, 55,* 296–318.

Suarez-Orozco, M. M. (1989). *Central American refugees and U.S. high schools: A psychosocial study of motivation and achievement.* Stanford, CA: Stanford University Press.

Suedfeld, P., Tetlock, P. E., & Streufert, S. (1992). Conceptual/integrative complexity. In C. P. Smith (Ed.), *Motivation and personality: Handbook of thematic content analysis* (pp. 393–400). New York: Cambridge University Press.

Sullivan, H. S. (1953). *The interpersonal theory of psychiatry.* New York: Norton.

Symonds, P. M. (1939). Criteria for the selection of pictures for the investigation of adolescent phantasies. *Journal of Abnormal and Social Psychology, 34,* 271–274.

Symonds, P. M. (1949). *Adolescent fantasy.* New York: Columbia University Press.

Tannock, R., Purvis, K. L., & Schachar, R. J. (1993). Narrative abilities in children with Attention Deficit Hyperactivity Disorder and normal peers. *Journal of Abnormal Child Psychology, 21,* 103–117.

Taylor, S. E., & Brown, J. D. (1988). Illusion and well-being: A social psychological perspective on mental health. *Psychological Bulletin, 103,* 193–210.

Taylor, S. E., & Crocker, J. (1981). Schematic bases of social information processing. In E. T. Higgins, C. P. Herman, & M. P. Zanna (Eds.), *Social cognition: The Ontario symposium on personality and social psychology.* Hillsdale, NJ: Erlbaum.

Teasdale, J. D., Taylor, M. J., Cooper, Z., Hayhurst, H., & Paykel, E. S. (1995). Depressive thinking: Shifts in construct accessibility or in schematic mental models? *Journal of Abnormal Psychology, 104,* 500–507.

Teglasi, H. (1993). *Clinical use of story telling: Emphasizing the TAT with children and adolescents.* Boston: Allyn & Bacon.

Teglasi, H. (1998). Assessment of schema and problem-solving strategies with projective techniques. In M. Hersen & A. Bellack (Series Eds.) & C. Reynolds (Vol. Ed.), *Comprehensive Clinical Psychology: Vol. 4. Assessment* (pp. 459–499). London, England: Elsevier Science Press.

Teglasi, H., & Epstein, S. (1998). Temperament and personality theory: The perspective of cognitive-experiential self-theory. *School Psychology Review, 27,* 534–550.

Teglasi, H., & Fagin, S. (1984). Social anxiety and self-other biases in causal attribution. *Journal of Research in Personality, 18,* 64–80.

Teglasi, H., & Hoffman, M. A. (1982). Causal attributions of shy subjects. *Journal of Research in Personality, 16,* 376–385.

Teglasi, H., & Rothman, L. (2001). STORIES: A classroom-based program to reduce aggressive behavior. *Journal of School Psychology, 39,* 71–94.

Terwogt, M. M., Kremer, H. H., & Stegge, H. (1991). Effects of children's emotional state on their reactions to emotional expressions: A search for congruency effects. *Cognition and Emotion, 5,* 109–121.

Thompson, A. E. (1986). An object relational theory of affect maturity: Applications to the Thematic Apperception Test. In M. Kissen (Ed.), *Assessing object relations phenomena* (pp. 207–224). Madison, WI: International Universities Press.

Thompson, C. E. (1949). The Thompson modification of the Thematic Apperception Test. *Rorschach Research Exchange and Journal of Projective Techniques, 13,* 469–478.

Thompson, J. M., & Sones, R. A. (1973). *Education Apperception Test.* Los Angeles: Western Psychological Services.

Tomkins, S. S. (1947). *Thematic Apperception Test.* New York: Grune & Stratton.

Tomkins, S. S. (1962). *Affect, imagery, consciousness: Vol. I. The positive affects.* New York: Springer.

Tomkins, S. S. (1987). Script theory. In J. Aronoff, A. J. Rabin, R. A. Zucker (Eds.), *The emergence of personality* (pp. 147–216). New York: Springer.

Torgesen, J. K. (1994). Issues in the assessment of executive function: An information-processing perspective. In G. R. Reid (Ed.), *Frames of reference for the assessment of learning disabilities: New views on measurement issues* (pp. 143–162). Baltimore, MD: Brookes.

Uleman, J. S. (1989). A framework for thinking intentionally about unintended thoughts. In J. S. Uleman & J. A. Bargh (Eds.), *Unintended thought* (pp. 425–449). New York: Guilford Press.

Urist, J. (1977). The Rorschach test and the assessment of object relations. *Journal of Personality Assessment, 41,* 3–9.

Urist, J. (1980) Object relations. In R. H. Woody (Ed.), *Encyclopedia of clinical assessment* (Vol. 2, pp. 821–833). San Francisco: Jossey Bass.

Urist, J., & Shill, M. (1982). Validity of the Rorschach Mutuality of Autonomy Scale: A replication using excerpted responses. *Journal of Personality Assessment, 46,* 450–454.

Vaillant, G. E. (1977). *Adaptation and life.* Boston: Little, Brown.

Vaillant, G. E. (1992). *Ego mechanisms of defense: A guide for clinicians and researchers.* Washington, DC: American Psychiatric Press.

Veroff, J. (1992). Thematic apperceptive methods in survey research. In J. W. Atkinson, D. C. McClelland, & J. Veroff (Eds.), *Motivation and personality: Handbook of thematic content analysis* (pp. 100–109). New York: Cambridge University Press.

Veroff, J., Atkinson, J. W., Feld, S. C., & Gurin, G. (1960). The use of thematic apperception to assess motivation in a nationwide interview study. *Psychological Monographs, 74,* 32.

Vitz, P. C. (1990). The use of stories in moral development: New psychological reasons for an old education method. *American Psychologist, 45,* 709–720.

Watkins, C. E., Campbell, V. L., & McGregor, P. (1988). Counseling psychologists' uses of and opinions about psychological tests: A contemporary perspective. *Counseling Psychologist, 16,* 476–486.

Watkins, C. E., Campbell, V. L., Nieberding, R., & Hallmark, R. (1995). Contemporary practice of psychological assessment by clinical psychologists. *Professional Psychology: Research and Practice, 26,* 54–60.

Watson, D., & Clark, L. A. (1992). Affects separable and inseparable: On the hierarchical arrangement of the negative affects. *Journal of Personality and Social Psychology, 62,* 489–505.

Weiner, I. B. (1966). *Psychodiagnosis in schizophrenia.* New York: John Wiley & Sons.

Weisskopf, E. A. (1950). A transcendence index as a proposed measure in the TAT. *Journal of Psychology, 29,* 379–390.

Weisskopf-Joelson, E. A., & Foster, H. C. (1962). An experimental study of the effect of stimulus variation upon projection. *Journal of Projective Techniques, 26,* 366–370.

Weisskopf-Joelson, E. A., & Lyn, D. B. (1953). The effect of variations in ambiguity on projection in the Children's Apperception Test. *Journal of Consulting Psychology, 17,* 67–70.

Weisskopf-Joelson, E. A., Zimmerman, J., & McDaniel, M. (1970). Similarity between subject and stimulus as an influence on projection. *Journal of Projective Techniques and Personality Assessment, 34,* 328–331.

Wertheim, E. H., & Schwartz, J. C. (1983). Depression, guilt, and self-management of pleasant and unpleasant events. *Journal of Personality and Social Psychology, 45,* 884–889.

Westen, D. (1985). *Self and society: Narcissism, collectivism, and the development of morals.* New York: Cambridge University Press.

Westen, D. (1991). Clinical assessment of object relations using the TAT. *Journal of Personality Assessment, 56,* 56–74.

Westen, D. (1993). Social cognition and social affect in psychoanalysis and cognitive psychology: From regression analysis to analysis of regression. In J. W. Barron, M. N. Eagle, & D. L. Wolitzky (Eds.), *Interface of psychoanalysis and psychology* (pp. 375–388). Washington, DC: American Psychological Association.

Westen, D. (1994). Toward an integrative model of affect regulation: Applications to social-psychological research. *Journal of Personality, 62,* 641–667.

Westen, D., Klepser, J., Ruffins, S. A., Silverman, M., & Boekamp, J. (1991). Object relations in childhood and adolescence: The development of working representations. *Journal of Consulting and Clinical Psychology, 9,* 400–409.

Wilson, A. (1988). Levels of depression and clinical assessment. In H. D. Lerner & P. M. Lerner (Eds.), *Primitive mental states and the Rorschach* (pp. 441–462). Madison, CT: International Universities Press.

Wilson, B. J., & Gottman, J. M. (1996). Attention—the shuttle between emotion and cognition: Risk, resiliency, and physiological bases. In E. M. Hetherington & E. A. Blechman (Eds.), *Stress, coping, and resiliency in children and families* (pp. 189–228). Mahwah, NJ: Erlbaum.

Winnicott, D. W. (1971). *Transitional objects and transitional phenomena.* New York: Basic Books.

Winter, D. A. (1982). Construct relationships, psychological disorder and therapeutic change. *British Journal of Medical Psychology, 55,* 257–270.

Winter, D. G. (1992). Responsibility. In J. W. Atkinson, D. C. McClelland, & J. Veroff (Eds.), *Motivation and personality: Handbook of thematic content analysis* (pp. 500–505). New York: Cambridge University Press.

Woike, B. A. (1995). Most-memorable experiences: Evidence for a link between implicit and explicit motives and social cognitive processes in everyday life. *Journal of Personality and Social Psychology, 68,* 1081–1091.

Woike, B. A., & Aronoff, J. (1992). Antecedents of complex social cognitions. *Journal of Personality and Social Psychology, 63,* 97–104.

Wolk, R. L., & Wolk, R. B. (1971). *The Gerontological Apperception Test.* New York: Behavioral Publications.

Worchel, F. T., Aaron, L. L., & Yates, D. F. (1990). Gender bias on the Thematic Apperception Test. *Journal of Personality Assessment, 55,* 593–602.

Wozniak, R. H. (1985). Notes toward a co-constructive theory of the emotion/cognition relationship. In D. Bearison & H. Zimiles (Eds.), *Thought and emotion: Developmental issues* (pp. 39–64). Hillsdale, NJ: Erlbaum.

Wyer, R. S., Jr., & Srull, T. K. (Eds.). (1994). *Handbook of Social Cognition,* (2nd ed., Vols. 1–2). Hillsdale, NJ: Erlbaum.

Zaleski, Z. (1994). *Psychology of future orientation.* Lublin, Poland: Wydawnictwo Towarzystwa Naukowego Katolickiego Uniwersyteta Lubelskiego.

Zimbardo, P. G., Keough, K. A., & Boyd, J. N. (1997). Present time perspective as a predictor of risky driving. *Personality and Individual Difference, 23,* 1007–1023.

Zubin, J., Eron, L. D., & Schumer, F. (1965). *An experimental approach to projective techniques.* New York: John Wiley & Sons.

Annotated Bibliography

Bellak, L., & Abrams, D. M. (1997). *The Thematic Apperception Test, The Children's Apperception Test, and The Senior Apperception Technique in clinical use.* Boston: Allyn & Bacon.

This book is the latest edition presenting Bellak's psychodynamic interpretive approach, including review of relevant examples and case illustrations.

Cramer, P. (1996). *Storytelling, narrative, and the Thematic Apperception Test (assessment of personality and psychopathology).* New York: Guilford Press.

This book provides a synthesis of the literature on the TAT including clinical case examples and a scholarly review of the technique's reliability and validity.

Gieser, L., & Stein, M. I. (Eds.). (1999). *Evocative images: The Thematic Apperception Test and the art of projection.* Washington, DC: American Psychological Association.

This edited volume features chapters from pioneers in the field who give their impressions about the TAT in clinical practice and research.

Kroon, N., Goudena, P. P., & Rispens, J. (1998). Thematic Apperception Tests for child and adolescent assessment: A practitioner's consumer guide. *Journal of Psychoeducational Assessment, 16,* 99–117.

This review article notes comparative strengths and weaknesses of the 12 (of 23) thematic apperception tests currently available for use with children and adolescents. Authors observe that the well-established methods of the TAT and CAT are supplemented by various tests designed to deal with specific assessment issues.

Kelly, F. D. (1996). *Object relations in younger children: Rorschach and TAT measures.* Springfield, IL: Charles C. Thomas.

Focusing on object relations assessment in younger children, this book provides numerous examples demonstrating the Mutuality of Autonomy Scale (Rorschach) and The Social Cognition Object Relations Scale (TAT).

Kelly, F. D. (1997). *The assessment of object relations phenomena in adolescents.* Mahwah, NJ: Erlbaum.

This book features clinical case examples demonstrating the process of object relations assessment with two measures, the Mutuality of Autonomy Scale (Rorschach) and The Social Cognition Object Relations Scale (TAT).

Smith, C. P. (Ed.). (1992). *Motivation and personality: Handbook of thematic content analysis.* New York: Cambridge University Press.

This edited volume provides the history and coding procedures for the well-known methods for content analysis of the TAT popular in the study of personality but not in clinical use.

Teglasi, H. (1993). *Clinical use of story telling: Emphasizing the TAT with children and adolescents.* Boston: Allyn & Bacon.

Synthesizing interpretive guidelines that combine story content, structure, and narrative process, this book organizes discrete narrative elements into more general cognitive-emotional psychological processes.

Teglasi, H. (1998). Assessment of schema and problem-solving strategies with projective techniques. In M. Hersen & A. Bellack (Series Eds.) & C. Reynolds (Vol. Ed.), *Comprehensive clinical psychology: Vol. 4. Assessment* (pp. 459–499). New York: Elsevier Science Press.

This chapter outlines the relevance of current concepts and research in various subfields of psychology for assessment of schemas and problem solving with projective techniques.

Index

Acknowledgments

In pursuing my work with storytelling, I am indebted to the pioneers of the Thematic Apperception Test who created a compelling and flexible technique for eliciting narratives using pictured scenes. The story form has universal and timeless appeal, and its applicability is limited only by the human imagination.

My appreciation of the value of assessment with storytelling continues to grow through my ongoing involvement with clinical supervision of students and research with the TAT. Many of the protocols included in this volume are from students' cases or participants in research studies. Too many students made important contributions for me to mention names. However, I would be remiss if I did not acknowledge two individuals: Stephanie Rahill, graduate assistant, for the hours spent in the library diligently gathering and checking references, and Tracey Belmont, editor at Wiley, for the guidance that helped bring this project to fruition.

My family deserves credit for incorporating my constant writing into the natural give-and-take of daily interactions without ever letting on that they were indulging me. Additionally, setting up the figures sometimes became a family effort—thank you Saul, Jordan, and Jeremy.

About the Author

Hedwig Teglasi, PhD is a faculty member at the University of Maryland, Department of Counseling and Personnel Services, where she had served as co-director of the School Psychology Program for about a decade. She has supervised students conducting comprehensive psychoeducational evaluations that integrate storytelling methods with other clinical assessment tools. Her research has focused on personality processes including the role of temperament in the interpretation of life experiences and storytelling as a vehicle for assessing how individuals organize their experiences. On the topic of storytelling, she has published journal articles, a book chapter (The Assessment of Schemas and Social Problem Solving with Projective Techniques, *Comprehensive Clinical Assessment,* Elsevier, 1998), and a book (*Clinical Use of Story Telling: Emphasizing the TAT with Children and Adolescents,* Allyn & Bacon, 1993). Dr. Teglasi has served on the Editorial Board of the *School Psychology Review* and guest-edited a special topics issue on the implications of temperament for the practice of school psychology.